# POWER AND SOCIETY

## An Introduction to the Social Sciences

Eighth Edition

## THOMAS R. DYE

McKenzie Professor of Government
Florida State University

**Harcourt Brace College Publishers**

Fort Worth   Philadelphia   San Diego   New York   Orlando   Austin   San Antonio
Toronto   Montreal   London   Sydney   Tokyo

# IN MEMORY OF
# JAMES C. "JEFF" DYE

Publisher        Earl McPeek

Acquisitions Editor        David Tatom

Developmental Editor        Nancy Crochiere

Project Editor        Michael E. Norris

Production Manager        Diane Gray

Art Director        Garry Harman

Cover Design        Mark Hatley

ISBN: 0-15-508080-6

Library of Congress Catalog Card Number: 97-77100

*Address for Editorial Correspondence:* Harcourt Brace College Publishers, 301 Commerce Street, Suite 3700, Fort Worth, TX 76102

*Address for Orders:* Harcourt Brace & Company, 6277 Sea Harbor Drive, Orlando, FL 32887-6777
1-800-782-4479

Website: http://www.hbcollege.com

Portions of this work were published in previous editions.

Printed in the United States of America

9 0 1 2 3 4 5 066 9 8 7 6 5 4

# PREFACE

*Power and Society: An Introduction to the Social Sciences* is designed as a basic text for an introductory, interdisciplinary social science course. It is written specifically for first- and second-year students at community colleges and at four-year colleges and universities that offer a basic studies program.

*Power and Society* introduces students to central concepts in

| | |
|---|---|
| anthropology | psychology |
| sociology | political science |
| economics | history |

But more important, the text focuses these disciplinary perspectives on a central integrative theme—the nature and uses of power in society. In this way, students are made aware of the interdependence of the social sciences. Compartmentalization is avoided, and students are shown how each social science discipline contributes to an understanding of power.

*Power and Society* also introduces students to some of the central challenges facing American society:

| | |
|---|---|
| ideological conflict | crime and violence |
| racism and sexism | urban affairs |
| poverty and powerlessness | international relations |

Each of these challenges is approached from an interdisciplinary viewpoint, with *power* as the integrating concept.

*Power* has been defined as the capacity to modify the conduct of individuals through the real or threatened use of rewards and punishments. Doubtless there are other central concepts or ideas in the social sciences that might be employed to develop an integrated framework for an introduction to social science. But certainly *power* is a universal phenomenon that is reflected in virtually all forms of human interaction. Power is intimately related to many other key concepts and ideas in the social sciences—personality, behavior, aggression, role, class, mobility, wealth, income distribution, markets, culture, ideology, change, authority, oligarchy, the elite. Power is also a universal instrument in approaching the various crises that afflict human beings and their societies—racism, sexism, poverty, violence, crime, urban decay, and ideological and international conflict.

Several special features are designed to arouse student interest in the social sciences as well as to help students understand the meaning of various concepts. The first such feature is the identification of specific *masters of social thought* and the clear, concise presentation of their central contributions to social science. Specific attention is given to the contributions of:

| | | |
|---|---|---|
| Bertrand Russell | Sigmund Freud | John Locke |
| Ruth Benedict | B. F. Skinner | Martin Luther King, Jr. |
| Karl Marx | Adam Smith | |
| C. Wright Mills | John M. Keynes | |

The second special feature is the presentation of timely, relevant *case studies* in each chapter to illustrate important concepts. Topics include:

An Experiment in Crime Fighting
Using the *Statistical Abstract*
Authority and Obedience: The "Shocking" Experiments
Diagnosing Mental Illness
Achieving Economic Stability
Watergate and the Limits of Presidential Power
Vietnam: A Political History
The Rise and Fall of Communism in Russia
Senior Power
The Death Penalty and the Constitution
The Insanity Defense
American Military Power: "Desert Storm"

In addition, illustrative *focuses* throughout the text help maintain student interest. Topics include:

The Vocabulary of Social Science
Explaining Presidential Approval Ratings
Social Science Looks at Sex in America
Women in the Work Force: Changing American Culture
How Men and Women View Their Relations Today
Sociobiology: It's All in Your Genes
Telltale Behavior of Twins
Evolutionary Psychology: The Mating Game
Drug Therapies
The Concentration of Corporate Power
Rating the Presidents
Media Power—The Presidential Debates
Reconstruction and African-American History
How to Tell if You're Liberal or Conservative
A Declaration of Women's Rights, 1848
Who Are the Poor?
Getting High
Urban Stress
It's a Real Crime!

A fourth special feature is the *cross-national perspective* provided on important aspects of life in the United States. As this book introduces students to the social sciences with principal reference to the American experience, discussions in each chapter endeavor to place this experience in a global context. Thus *cross-national perspective* sections include:

> World Populations
> Religious Beliefs
> Beliefs About Equality and Opportunity
> Global Inequalities
> Suicide
> GNP and Standards of Living
> The Multinationals' Worldwide Economic Power
> The Role of Government
> Capitalism and Socialism in the World
> The Earnings Gap
> Income of the Poor in Advanced Democracies
> Worldwide Urbanization
> Murder and Homicide

as well as anthropological observation on power among Polar Eskimos, power among Crow Indians, and power in the Aztec Empire.

A fifth special feature is *controversies in social science,* designed to stimulate student interest in social science, inspire classroom discussion, and warn students that the social sciences deal with many controversial topics that remain largely unresolved:

> Can the Social Sciences Be Scientific?
> Cultural Relativity and Female Circumcision
> *The Bell Curve*
> A Balanced Budget Amendment to the Constitution?
> Direct versus Representative Democracy
> Should We Limit the Terms of Congress Members?
> Charles Beard and the Economic Interests of the Founders
> Affirmative Action and the Constitution
> Do Welfare Programs Cause Poverty?
> Should Drugs Be Legalized?
> Who Really Runs This Town?
> When Should the United States Use Military Force?

Another important special feature is the *running study guide* provided in the wide page margins throughout the text. The study guide defines key vocabulary items and outlines central arguments, keeping pace with the student's progress through the text.

The eighth edition of *Power and Society* strives to make this popular text even more "teachable" by adding a number of stimulative and provocative *focuses* and *case studies,* together with its *masters of social thought* and *cross-national perspectives,* as well as the new feature *controversies in social science*—all of which provide timeliness, relevance, interest, and perspective to each chapter topic. Rather than evade or dilute "hot topics"—for example, genetics versus environmental influences on behavior, power and gender, sexual harassment, mental illness, the neglect of African-American and Native American history, affirmative action, violence in American history, abortion, drug legalization, the death penalty—it focuses on controversy as a means of developing student interest and appreciation for the social sciences. The eighth edition continues to resist the lamentable tendency in introductory texts to "dummy" material for undergraduate students and shows that social science research and scholarship is relevant to our current societal problems. Among the new topics introduced in the eighth edition:

> Cultural Relativity and Female Circumcision
> Power and Political Systems
> *The Bell Curve*
> Nurture and Human Development
> Drug Therapies
> Direct versus Representative Democracy
> Rating the Presidents
> How to Tell If You're Liberal or Conservative
> Immigration to America
> The Insanity Defense
> It's a Real Crime!
> Getting High
> When Should the United States Use Military Force?

This edition continues the book's traditional focus on the condition of women and minorities in American society, with specific discussions of "Power and Gender," "Women in the Work Force: Changing American Culture," "Reconstruction and African-American History," "Martin Luther King, Jr., and the Power of Protest," "Hispanic Power," and "Gender Inequality: Culture or Biology?"

An instructor's manual filled with lecture ideas and test questions is available.

Students may purchase the study guide that provides multiple choice, true-false, completion, and essay questions to lead them through independent study of the text.

Many thanks to those who provided guidance on this and past editions: Charles Cotter, Florida State University; Paul George, Miami Dade Community College; Francis Moran, Jersey City College; Alex Velez, St. Mary's University; Brett Benson, Lewis-Clark State College; Howard Lucky, Prairie State College; and Fred Dauser, Talladega College.

# Contents

## PART TWO

# POWER AND THE SOCIAL SCIENCES ...38

## Chapter 3

# Power and Culture.....41

## Chapter 4

# Power and Social Class.....72

## Chapter 5
# Power and Personality.....99

## Chapter 6
# Power and the Economic Order.....132

## Chapter 7
# Power and Government.....160

## Chapter 8
# Power and History.....196

## PART THREE

# THE USES OF POWER ..........................220

## Chapter 9
# Power and Ideology.....223

## Chapter 10
# Power, Race, and Gender.....245

# Chapter 11
# Poverty and Powerlessness.....276

# Chapter 12
# Power, Crime, and Violence.....293

## Chapter 13
# Power and Community.....323

## Chapter 14
# Power among Nations.....348

# The Nature and Study of Power

PART ONE

The purpose of this book is to introduce you to the social sciences. Because power in society is a theme that pervades each of the social sciences, as well as the problems they study, we have chosen this theme as the focal point for our presentation. Part 1 is designed to familiarize you with the notion of power, with the nature of each of the social sciences, and with the scientific methods they employ. You will find that Chapter 1 reflects the structure of the entire text. Like the book as a whole, its first part focuses on the nature of power, its second part on the individual social sciences and the particular ways in which they contribute to our understanding of power, and its third and final part on the problems with which the social sciences are concerned. Chapter 2 is devoted to a discussion of the methods used in social science research—how social scientists gather data, how they endeavor to employ scientific and experimental methods of research, and the special problems they encounter in doing so.

# Chapter 1

# Power, Society, and Social Science

## The Nature of Power

Ordinary men and women are driven by forces in society that they neither understand nor control. These forces are embodied in governmental authorities, economic organizations and markets, social values and ideologies, accepted ways of life, and learned patterns of behavior. However diverse the nature of these forces, they have in common the ability to modify the conduct of individuals, to control their behavior, to shape their lives. *Power is the capacity to affect the conduct of individuals through the real or threatened use of rewards and punishments.* Power is exercised over individuals and groups by offering them things they value or by threatening to deprive them of those things. These values are the power base, and they can include physical safety, health, and well-being; wealth and material possessions; jobs and means to a livelihood; knowledge and skills; social recognition, status, and prestige; love, affection, and acceptance by others; a satisfactory self-image and self-respect. To exercise power, then, control must be exercised over the things that are valued in society.

**power**
the capacity to affect the conduct of others through the real or threatened use of rewards and punishments

**power**
based on control of valued resources

unequally distributed

exercised in interpersonal relations

exercised through large institutions

*Power is a special form of influence.* Broadly speaking, influence is the production of intended effects. People who can produce intended effects by any means are said to be influential. People who can produce intended effects by the real or threatened use of rewards and punishments are said to be powerful.

*Power can rest on various resources.* The exercise of power assumes many different forms—the giving or withholding of many different values. Yet power bases are usually *interdependent*—individuals who control certain valued resources are likely to control other resources as well. Wealth, economic power, prestige, recognition, political influence, education, respect, and so on, all tend to "go together" in society.

*Power is never equally distributed.* "There is no power where power is equal." For power to be exercised, the "powerholder" must control some base values. By *control* we mean that the powerholder is in a position to offer these values as rewards to others or to threaten to deprive others of these values.

*Power is a relationship* among individuals, groups, and institutions in society. Power is not really a "thing" that someone possesses. Instead, power is a relationship in which some individuals or groups have control over resources valued by others.

## ELITES AND MASSES

**elite and masses**
the few who have power and the many who do not

The *elite* are the few who have power; the *masses* are the many who do not. The elite are the few who control what is valued in society and use that control to shape the lives of all of us. The masses are the many whose lives are shaped by institutions, events, and leaders over which they have little control. Political scientist Harold Lasswell wrote, "The division of society into elites and masses is universal," and even in a democracy, "a few exercise a relatively great weight of power, and the many exercise comparatively little."[1]

## INSTITUTIONAL POWER

*Power is exercised in large institutions*—governments, corporations, schools, the military, churches, newspapers, television networks, law firms, and so on. Power that stems from high positions in the social structures of society is stable and far-reaching. Sociologist C. Wright Mills once observed: "No one can be truly powerful unless he has access to the command of major institutions, for it is over these institutional means of power that the truly powerful are, in the first instance, powerful."[2] Not all power, it is true, is anchored in or exercised through institutions. But institutional positions in society provide a continuous and important base of power. As Mills explained:

> *If we took the one hundred most powerful men in America, the one hundred wealthiest, and the one hundred most celebrated away from the institutional positions they now occupy, away from their resources*

*of men and women and money, away from the media of mass com-
munication that are now focused upon them—then they would be
powerless and poor and uncelebrated. For power is not of a man.
Wealth does not center in the person of the wealthy. . . . To have
power requires access to major institutions, for the institutional positions men occupy determine in large part their chances to have and
to hold these valued experiences.*[3]

# POWER AND THE SOCIAL SCIENCES

*Social science* is the study of human behavior. Actually, there are several social
sciences, each specializing in a particular aspect of human behavior and each
using different concepts, methods, and data in its studies. Anthropology,
sociology, economics, psychology, political science, and history have developed into separate "disciplines," but all share an interest in human behavior.

> **social science**
> the study of human behavior

Power is *not* the central concern of the social sciences, yet all the social
sciences deal with power in one form or another. Each of the social sciences
contributes to an understanding of the forces that modify the conduct of
individuals, control their behavior, and shape their lives. Thus, to fully understand power in society, we must approach this topic in an *interdisciplinary* fashion—using ideas, methods, data, and findings from all the social
sciences.

## ANTHROPOLOGY

*Anthropology* is the study of people and their ways of life. It is the most comprehensive of the social sciences. Some anthropologists are concerned primarily with people's biological and physical characteristics; this field is called
*physical anthropology*. Other anthropologists are interested primarily in the
ways of life of both ancient and modern peoples; this field is called *cultural
anthropology*.

> **anthropology**
> the study of people and their ways of life

*Culture* is all the common patterns and ways of living that characterize a
society. A *society* is a group of people who are dependent on one another for
their well-being and who share in a common culture. Cultural anthropologists describe and compare societies and cultures. They describe and explain
a great many things: child rearing and education, family arrangements, language and communication, technology, ways of making a living, the distribution of work, religious beliefs and values, social life, leadership patterns,
and power structures.

> **culture**
> all the common patterns and ways of living that characterize society

> **society**
> a group of people who are depen-
> dent on one another and share a
> common culture

Power is part of the culture or the way of life of a people. Power is exercised in all societies, because all societies have systems of rewards and sanctions designed to control the behavior of their members. Perhaps the most
enduring structure of power in society is the family: power is exercised
within the family when patterns of dominance and submission are established between male and female and between parents and children. Societies

also develop structures of power outside the family to maintain peace and order among their members, to organize individuals to accomplish large-scale tasks, to defend themselves against attack, and even to wage war and exploit other peoples.

In our study of power and culture, we shall examine how cultural patterns determine power relationships. We shall also examine patterns of authority in traditional and modern families and the changing power role of women in society. We will focus special attention on how social science looks at sex in America in Chapter 3. We will take up a long-standing controversy regarding value judgments about cultural practices in a feature "Cultural Relativity and Female Circumcision." We shall examine the origins and development of power relationships, illustrating them with examples of societies in which power is organized by family and kinship group (polar Eskimos), by tribe (Crow Indians), and by the state (the Aztec Empire). Finally, as a case study, we shall look at the controversy over "sociobiology"—that is, the extent to which genetics or culture determines behaviors.

## SOCIOLOGY

**sociology**
the study of relationships among individuals and groups

*Sociology* is the study of relationships among individuals and groups. Sociologists describe the structure of formal and informal groups, their functions and purposes, and how they change over time. They study social institutions (such as families, schools, churches), social processes (for example, conflict, competition, assimilation, change), and social problems (crime, race relations, poverty, and so forth). Sociologists also study social classes.

**social stratification**
the classification and ranking of members of a society

All societies have some system of classifying and ranking their members— a system of *stratification*. In modern industrial societies, social status is associated with the various roles that individuals play in the economic system. Individuals are ranked according to how they make their living and the power they exercise over others. Stratification into social classes is determined largely on the basis of occupation and control of economic resources.

Power derives from social status, prestige, and respect, as well as from control of economic resources. Thus, the stratification system involves the unequal distribution of power.

In our study of power and social class, we shall describe the stratification system and the extent of inequality in America. We shall discuss the differing lifestyles of upper, middle, and lower classes in America and the extent of class conflict. We will take up a heated controversy over general intelligence—its measurement, distribution and meaning in peoples' lives in a feature, "The Bell Curve." We shall examine the ideas of Karl Marx about the struggle for power among social classes. We shall describe the differential in political power among social classes in America. Finally, we shall explore the ideas of sociologist C. Wright Mills about a "power elite" in America that occupies powerful positions in the governmental, corporate, and military bureaucracies of the nation.

# Psychology

*Psychology* may be defined as the study of the behavior of people and animals. Behavior, we know, is the product of both "nature and nurture"—that is, a product of both our biological makeup and our environmental conditioning. We shall examine the continuing controversy over *how much* of our behavior is a product of our genes versus our environment. There is great richness and diversity in psychological inquiry. *Behavioral psychologists* study the learning process—the way in which people and animals learn to respond to stimuli. Behavioral psychologists frequently study in experimental laboratory situations, with the hope that the knowledge gained can be useful in understanding more complex human behavior outside the laboratory. *Social psychologists,* on the other hand, study interpersonal behavior—the ways in which social interactions shape an individual's beliefs, perceptions, motivations, attitudes, and behavior. Social psychologists generally study the whole person in relation to the total environment. *Psychoanalytic (Freudian) psychologists* study the impact of subconscious feelings and emotions and of early childhood experiences on the behavior of adults. *Humanistic psychologists* are concerned with the human being's innate potential for growth and development. Many other psychologists combine theories and methods in different ways in their attempts to achieve a better understanding of behavior.

*Personality* is all the enduring, organized ways of behavior that characterize an individual. Psychologists differ over how personality characteristics are determined—whether they are learned habits acquired through the process of reinforcement and conditioning (behavioral psychology), products of the individual's interaction with the significant people and groups in his or her life (social psychology), manifestations of the continuous process of positive growth toward "self-actualization" (humanistic psychology), the results of subconscious drives and long-repressed emotions stemming from early childhood experiences (Freudian psychology), or some combination of all these.

In our study of power and personality, we will examine various theories of personality determination in an effort to understand the forces shaping the individual's reaction to power. We will explore the recurring question of "nature versus nurture," biology versus environment, in determining the human condition. Using a Freudian perspective, we shall study the "authoritarian personality"—the individual who is habitually dominant and aggressive toward others over whom he or she exercises power but is submissive and weak toward others who have more power; the individual who is extremely prejudiced, rigid, intolerant, cynical, and power-oriented. We shall explore the power implications of B. F. Skinner's ideas of behavioral conditioning for the control of human behavior. To gain an understanding of humanistic psychology's approach to power relationships, we shall examine Abraham Maslow's theory of a "hierarchy of needs." We will also describe the treatment of mental illness from these various psychological perspectives. Finally, in our case study, we shall describe the startling results of an experiment designed to test the relationship between authority and obedience.

**psychology**
the study of the behavior of people and animals

**behavioral psychology**
the study of human and animal responses to stimuli

**social psychology**
the study of interpersonal behavior

**psychoanalytic (Freudian) psychology**
the study of the effects of subconscious feelings and early childhood experiences on behavior

**humanistic psychology**
the study of the growth and development of the human personality

**personality**
all the enduring, organized ways of behavior that characterize an individual

# ECONOMICS

**economics**
the study of the production and distribution of scarce goods and services

*Economics* is the study of the production and distribution of scarce goods and services. There are never enough goods and services to satisfy everyone's demands, and because of this, choices must be made. Economists study how individuals, firms, and nations make these choices about goods and services.

Economic power is the power to decide what will be produced, how much it will cost, how many people will be employed, what their wages will be, what the price of goods and services will be, what profits will be made, how these profits will be distributed, and how fast the economy will grow.

Capitalist societies rely heavily on the market mechanism to make these decisions. In our study of economic power, we shall explore both the strengths and weaknesses of this market system, as well as the ideas of economic philosophers Adam Smith and John Maynard Keynes. We shall examine America's great wealth—how it is measured, where it comes from, and where it goes. In addition, we shall consider the role of government in the economy, which has vastly increased over the years, with special attention to the growing burdens of government debt. We shall also examine the concentration of corporate power in America, and whether the corporate elite use that power to benefit the stockholders or themselves.

# POLITICAL SCIENCE

**political science**
the study of government and politics

**authority**
the legitimate use of physical force

*Political science* is the study of government and politics. Governments possess *authority*, a particular form of power; that is, the legitimate use of physical force. By *legitimate*, we mean that people generally consent to the government's use of this power. Of course, other individuals and organizations in society—muggers, street gangs, the Mafia, violent revolutionaries—use force. But only government can legitimately threaten people with the loss of freedom and well-being to modify their behavior. Moreover, governments exercise power over all individuals and institutions in society—corporations, families, schools, and so forth. Obviously the power of government in modern society is very great, extending to nearly every aspect of modern life—"from womb to tomb."

Political scientists from Aristotle to the present have been concerned with the dangers of unlimited and unchecked governmental power. We shall examine the American experience with limited, constitutional government and the meaning of democracy in modern society. We shall observe how the U.S. Constitution divides power, first between states and the national government, and second among the legislative, executive, and judicial branches of government. We will review the continuing controversy over whether the people themselves should decide important issues by voting directly on them, or whether elected representatives should do so. We shall examine the growth of power in Washington, D.C., and the struggle for power among the different branches. Finally, in our look at "Media Power: The Presidential Debates," we shall examine the growing power of television in American politics.

# HISTORY

*History* is the recording, narrating, and interpreting of human experience. The historian recreates the past by collecting recorded facts, organizing them into a narrative, and interpreting their meaning. History is concerned with change over time. It provides a perspective on the present by informing us of the way people lived in the past. History helps us understand how society developed into what it is today.

The foundations of power vary from age to age. As power bases shift, new groups and individuals acquire control over them. Thus, power relationships are continuously developing and changing. An understanding of power in society requires an understanding of the historical development of power relationships.

In our consideration of the historical development of power relationships, we shall look at the changing sources of power in American history and the characteristics of the individuals and groups who have acquired power. We shall describe the people of power in the early days of the republic and their shaping of the Constitution and the government it established. We shall discuss Charles Beard's controversial interpretation of the Constitution as a document designed to protect the economic interests of those early powerholders. We shall also discuss how westward expansion and settlement created new bases of power and new powerholders. We shall explore the power struggle between northern commercial and industrial interests and southern planters and slave owners for control of western land, and the Civil War, which resulted from that struggle. In addition, we shall explore the development of an industrial elite in America after the Civil War, the impact of the depression on that elite, and the resulting growth of New Deal liberal reform. In a special feature, "Reconstruction and African-American History," we shall examine how history occasionally overlooks the experiences of powerless minorities and later reinterprets their contributions to society. Finally, we shall undertake a brief historical study, "Vietnam: A Political History," which argues that despite military victory, this war was "lost" through failures of America's political leadership.

**history**
the recording, narrating, and interpreting of human experience

# SOCIAL SCIENCES AND SOCIAL PROBLEMS

Social problems—the major challenges confronting society—include ideological conflict, racism, sexism, poverty, crime, violence, urban decay, and international conflict. These problems do not confine themselves to one or another of the disciplines of social science. They spill over the boundaries of anthropology, economics, sociology, political science, psychology, and history—they are *interdisciplinary* in character. Each of these problems has its *historical* antecedents, its *social* and *psychological* roots, its *cultural* manifestations, its *economic* consequences, and its impact on *government* and public policy. The origins of these social problems, as well as the various solutions proposed, involve complex power relationships.

**interdisciplinary study**
the use of theory, methods, or findings from more than one social science

## IDEOLOGICAL CONFLICT

**ideology**
an integrated system of ideas that rationalize and justify the exercise of power in society

Ideas have power. Indeed, whole societies are shaped by systems of ideas that we call *ideologies*. The study of ideologies—liberalism, conservatism, socialism, communism, fascism, radicalism—is not a separate social science. Rather, the study of ideologies spans all the social sciences, and it is closely related to philosophy. Ideologies are integrated systems of ideas that rationalize a way of life, establish standards of "rightness" and "wrongness," and provide emotional impulses to action. Ideologies usually include economic, political, social, psychological, and cultural ideas, as well as interpretations of history.

Ideologies rationalize and justify power in society. By providing a justification for the exercise of power, the ideology itself becomes a base of power in society. Ideology "legitimizes" power, making the exercise of power acceptable to the masses and thereby adding to the power of the elite. However, ideologies also affect the behavior of the elite, because once an ideology is deeply rooted in society, powerholders themselves are bound by it.

In our study of power and ideology, we shall first explore the ideology of *classical liberalism*—an ideology that attacked the established power of a hereditary aristocracy and asserted the dignity, worth, and freedom of the individual. Classical liberalism and capitalism justify the power of private enterprise and the market system. Whereas classical liberalism limits the powers of government, *modern liberalism* accepts governmental power as a positive force in freeing people from poverty, ignorance, discrimination, and ill health. It justifies the exercise of governmental power over private enterprise and the establishment of the welfare state. In contrast, *modern conservatism* doubts the ability of the governmental planners to solve society's problems; conservatism urges greater reliance on family, church, and individual initiative and effort.

We shall then look at ideologies that have influenced other societies. *Fascism* is a power-oriented ideology that asserts the supremacy of a nation or race over the interests of individuals, groups, and other social institutions. *Marxism* attacks the market system, free enterprise, and individualism; it justifies revolutionary power in overthrowing liberal capitalist systems and the establishment of a "dictatorship of the proletariat." *Socialism* calls for the evolutionary democratic replacement of the private enterprise system with government ownership of industry.

We shall describe the collapse of communism and the reasons for its failure in eastern Europe and the former Soviet Union, as well as its unpopularity among the Chinese people.

## RACIAL AND SEXUAL INEQUALITY

Historically, no social problem has challenged the United States more than racial inequality. It is the only issue over which Americans ever fought a civil war. We shall describe the American experience with racism and the civil rights movement, which brought about significant changes in American life.

## MASTERS OF SOCIAL THOUGHT

Bertrand Russell: Power Is to the Social Sciences What Energy Is to Physics

Bertrand Russell (1872–1970), English philosopher and mathematician, is regarded as one of the twentieth century's greatest thinkers, mainly because of his contributions to mathematics and symbolic logic. However, Russell possessed a great breadth of interest that included history, economics, and political science, as well as education, morals, and social problems. He received the Nobel Prize in literature "in recognition of his many-sided and significant authorship, in which he has constantly figured as a defender of humanity and freedom of thought." He summarized his views about the importance of power in society in a book significantly entitled *Power: A New Social Analysis.*

First of all, power is fundamental to the social sciences:

*The fundamental concept in the social sciences is power, in the same sense in which energy is the fundamental concept in physics.*

Second, the desire for power as well as wealth motivates people:

*When a moderate degree of comfort is assured, both individuals and communities will pursue power rather than wealth: they may seek wealth as a means to power, or they may forgo an increase of wealth in order to secure an increase of power, but in the former case as in the latter their fundamental motive is not economic. . . .*

Third, power takes many forms:

*Like energy, power has many forms, such as wealth, armaments, civil authority, influence on opinion. No one of these can be regarded as subordinate to any other, and there is no one form from which the others are derivative. The attempt to treat*

*one form of power, say wealth, in isolation can only be partially successful. . . . To revert to the analogy of physics: power, like energy, must be regarded as continually passing from any one of its forms into any other, and it should be the business of social science to seek the laws of such transformations.*

Finally, power produces social change:

*Those whose love of power is not strong are unlikely to have much influence on the course of events. The men who cause social changes are, as a rule, men who strongly desire to do so. Love of power, therefore, is a characteristic of the men who are causally important. We should, of course, be mistaken if we regarded it as the sole human motive, but this mistake would not lead us so much astray as might be expected in the search for causal laws in social science, since love of power is the chief motive producing the changes which social science has to study.*

SOURCE: Selection is reprinted from *Power: A New Social Analysis*, by Bertrand Russell, with the permission of W. W. Norton & Company, Inc., p. 11. Copyright 1938 by Bertrand Russell. Copyright renewed 1966 by Bertrand Russell.

We want to understand the philosophy of that movement, particularly the "nonviolent direct action" philosophy of Nobel Peace Prize winner Dr. Martin Luther King, Jr. However, we shall also examine continuing inequalities between blacks and whites in income, employment, and other conditions of life in the United States. We shall also explore the problems confronting Hispanic Americans in our society, and describe the tragic history of Native Americans. In addition, we look at sexism in American life, particularly in the economy. We shall describe the successes and failures of the women's movement over the years, and examine the issue of sexual harassment, and the constitutional status of abortion as a privacy right. We shall explore the controversy over "affirmative action" and "reverse discrimination" and its implication for how America is to achieve real equality.

## POVERTY AND POWERLESSNESS

**powerlessness**
a sociopsychological condition of hopelessness, indifference, distrust, and cynicism

The American economy has produced the highest standard of living in the world, yet a significant number of Americans live in poverty. We shall observe that poverty can be defined as *economic hardship* or as *economic inequality* and that each definition implies a different governmental approach to the problem. Poverty can also be defined as *powerlessness*—a sociopsychological condition of hopelessness, indifference, distrust, and cynicism. We shall then discuss whether or not there is a culture of poverty—a way of life of the poor that is passed on to future generations—and what its implications for government policy are. We shall describe government efforts to cope with poverty and discuss the controversial question of whether or not government welfare policies encourage poverty. We shall focus special attention on homelessness in America. Finally, we shall examine the future of the Social Security program in a look at "Senior Power."

## CRIME AND VIOLENCE

**a problem of democratic government**
to protect its citizens without violating individual liberty

Governmental power must be balanced against *individual freedom*. A democratic society must exercise police powers to protect its citizens, yet it must not unduly restrict individual liberty. We shall explore the problem of crime in society, the constitutional rights of defendants, the role of the courts, and the relationship between drug use and crime. We shall also describe briefly the history of violence in American society and the role that violence has played in American struggles for power. We shall summarize economic, psychological, and social explanations of crime and violence. Finally, we shall examine the arguments for and against the legalization of drugs and for and against the death penalty.

## URBAN LIFE

A variety of social problems affect the quality of life in the United States. The solution to these problems, if there is any solution, depends in great part on how government chooses to exercise its powers. We shall explore the growth of urban and suburban populations in the United States. We shall also explore the social and psychological patterns of urban life—the characteristic forms

*Poverty can also be defined as powerlessness: a homeless woman in New York City searches in a Dumpster for food or rags.*

A. M. Rousseau/The Image Works

of social interaction and organization that typically emerge in a large metropolis—and the socioeconomic conflicts between cities and suburbs. We shall observe how our nation's communities are governed. We shall focus special attention on the social and economic problems of the inner city and how the concentration of social problems can make them worse. Finally, we shall present a social-science controversy, "Who Really Runs This Town?"

## INTERNATIONAL CONFLICT

The struggle for power is global. It involves all the nations and peoples of the world, whatever their goals or ideals. Nearly 200 nations in the world claim *sovereignty:* authority over their internal affairs, freedom from outside intervention, and political and legal recognition by other nations. But sovereignty is a legal fiction; it requires power to make sovereignty a reality. Over the years nations have struggled for power through wars and diplomacy. The struggle has led to attempts to maintain a fragile balance of power among

**sovereignty**
authority over internal affairs, freedom from outside intervention, and recognition by other nations

*Nations struggle for power through wars and diplomacy. Here, U.S.-led coalition forces fight to liberate Kuwait from Iraqi occupation in the Gulf War.*

Georges Merillon/Gamma-Liaison

large and small nations, as well as to attempts to achieve collective security through the United Nations and other alliances. We shall provide a brief history of the long Cold War between the nuclear "superpowers"—the United States and the former Soviet Union. We will describe the especially dangerous issue of nuclear arms and efforts to bring them under control. The United States continues to face challenges around the world; we shall describe various regional minibalances of power, notably in the Middle East. We will take up the highly controversial question "When should the United States use military force?" Finally, we shall observe the continuing need for U.S. military power in our case study, "American Military Power: 'Desert Storm.' "

# NOTES

1. Harold Lasswell and Abraham Kaplan, *Power and Society* (New Haven, Conn.: Yale University Press, 1950), p. 219.
2. C. Wright Mills, *The Power Elite* (New York: Oxford University Press, 1956), p. 9.
3. Ibid., p. 10.

# ABOUT THIS CHAPTER

Power in society is not just an abstract concept or a convenient focus for academic exercise. Nor is power something that is located exclusively in the nation's capitals. Power is very much a real factor that affects the lives of each of us. We experience it in some form in our families, in school, and at work; we feel its effects in the grocery store and on the highway. And we each react to it in characteristic ways. Our aim in this chapter was to understand just what power *is*. We also saw why it provides us with a useful perspective from which to gain a unified view of the social sciences and the social problems that concern us all.

Now that you have read this chapter, you should be able to

- define power in society and describe its characteristics
- define the area of study of each of the social sciences, as well as their common focus, and discuss how each relates to power in society
- identify the major social problems that the social sciences study and explain why they are interdisciplinary in nature and how they relate to power

# DISCUSSION QUESTIONS

1. How would you define power? What characteristics of power deserve to be discussed in any definition of power?
2. Consider the power relationships that directly and indirectly affect your life. On the basis of your experiences and observations, assess the validity of these statements by Bertrand Russell: "The fundamental concept in the social sciences is power, in the same sense in which energy is the fundamental concept in physics. . . . When a moderate degree of comfort is assured, both individuals and communities will pursue power rather than wealth. . . . Love of power is the chief motive producing the changes which social science has to study."
3. Identify and briefly define the area of study of each of the social sciences. Discuss how you would study power from the perspective of each of these disciplines.
4. What is meant by the *interdisciplinary* study of social problems?

**Chapter 2**

# Social Sciences and the Scientific Method

## SCIENCE AND THE SCIENTIFIC METHOD

A *science* may be broadly defined as any organized *body of knowledge,* or it may be more narrowly defined as a discipline that employs the *scientific method.* If we use the broad definition, we can safely say that all the social sciences are indeed sciences. However, if we narrow our definition to only those disciplines that employ the scientific method, then some questions arise about whether the social sciences are really scientific. In other words, if science is defined as a *method of study,* rather than a *body of knowledge,* then not all studies in the social sciences are truly scientific.

**scientific method**
a method of explanation that develops and tests theories about how observable facts or events are related

The *scientific method* is a method of explanation that develops and tests theories about how observable facts or events are related. What does this definition really mean? How is this method of study actually applied in the social sciences? To answer these questions, let us examine each aspect of the scientific method separately.

# EXPLAINING RELATIONSHIPS

*The goal of the scientific method is explanation.* When using this method, we seek to answer *why.* Any scientific inquiry must begin by observing and classifying things. Just as biology begins with the careful observation, description, and classification of thousands upon thousands of different forms of life, the social sciences also must begin with the careful observation, description, and classification of various forms of human behavior. But the goal is explanation, not just description. Just as biology seeks to develop theories of evolution and genetics to explain the various forms of life upon the earth, the social sciences seek to develop theories to explain why human beings behave as they do.

To answer the question of *why,* the scientific method searches for *relationships.* All scientific *hypotheses* assert some relationship between observable facts or events. The social sciences seek to find relationships that explain human behavior. The first question is whether two or more events or behaviors are related in any way—that is, do they occur together consistently? The second question is whether either event or behavior *causes* the other. Social scientists first try to learn whether human events have occurred together merely by chance or accident, or whether they occur together so consistently that their relationship cannot be a mere coincidence. A relationship that is not likely to have occurred by chance is said to be *significant.* After observing a significant relationship, social scientists next ask whether there is a *causal relationship* between the phenomena (that is, whether the facts or events occurred together because one is the cause of the other), or whether both phenomena are being caused by some third factor. The Focus, "The Vocabulary of Social Science," explains some of the terms used in scientific study of data.

**hypothesis**
a tentative statement about a relationship between observable facts or events

**significant**
not likely to have occurred by chance

# DEVELOPING AND TESTING HYPOTHESES

*The scientific method seeks to develop statements (hypotheses) about how events or behaviors might be related and then determine the validity of these statements by careful, systematic, and logical tests.* Scientific tests are really exercises in logic. For example, if we wanted to find out something about the relationship between race and party voting, we might collect and record data from a national sample of African-American and white voters chosen at random.* If our data showed that *all* blacks voted Democratic and *all* whites Republican, it would be obvious that there was a perfect relationship between race and voting. In contrast, if both blacks and whites voted Republican and Democratic in the *same* proportions, then it would be obvious that there was *no* relationship. But in the social sciences we rarely have such obvious, clear-cut results. Generally our data will show a mixed pattern. For example, in

*Throughout this book we use the term *African American* when referring to specific individuals or the racial group, but in text and tables that compare African Americans and whites, we use parallel terms, *black* and *white.*

**FOCUS**
The Vocabulary of
Social Science

Social science researchers use many special terms in their work, some of which have already been defined. It helps in reading social science research reports to understand the specific meanings given to the following terms:

*Theory:* A causal explanation of relationship between observable facts or events. A good theory fits the facts, explains why they occur, and allows us to predict future events.

*Hypothesis:* A tentative statement about a relationship between facts or events. The hypothesis should be derived from the theory and should be testable.

*Variable:* A characteristic that varies among different individuals or groups.

*Independent variable:* Whatever is hypothesized to be the cause of something else.

*Dependent variable:* Whatever is hypothesized to be the effect of something else.

*Significant:* Not likely to have occurred by chance.

*Correlation:* Significant relationships found in the data.

*Spurious:* Describing a relationship among facts or events that is *not* causal, but is a product of the fact that both the independent and dependent variables are being caused by a third factor.

*Case study:* An in-depth investigation of a particular event. A good case study should suggest theories and hypotheses that can then be used to study other cases.

the 1996 presidential election between Democrat Bill Clinton and Republican Bob Dole, polls indicated that 84 percent of African Americans voted Democratic and only 12 percent voted Republican. In that same election, 46 percent of whites voted Republican and only 43 percent voted Democratic. If there had been *no* relationship between race and voting, then blacks and whites would have voted Democratic and Republican in roughly the *same* proportions. But as we have just noted, blacks voted Democratic in far heavier proportions (84 percent) than whites (43 percent). This difference is not likely to have occurred by chance—thus we consider it "significant." The same pattern of heavy Democratic voting among African Americans can be observed in other elections (see Table 2-1). So we can make the *inference* that race is related to voting.

However, the existence of a statistically significant relationship does not prove cause and effect. We must employ additional logic to find out which fact or event caused the other, or whether both were caused by a third fact or event. We can eliminate as illogical the possibility that voting Democratic causes one to become an African American. That leaves us with two

**inference**
a causal statement based on data showing a significant relationship

**TABLE 2-1**

## Voting by Race in Presidential Elections, 1968–1996

Testing the hypothesis: African Americans tend to vote Democratic

| Election year | Candidates | All | Whites | Blacks |
|---|---|---|---|---|
| 1996 | Republican Dole | 41 | 46 | 12 |
| | Democrat Clinton | 49 | 43 | 84 |
| | Independent Perot | 8 | 9 | 4 |
| 1992 | Republican Bush | 38 | 41 | 11 |
| | Democrat Clinton | 43 | 39 | 82 |
| | Independent Perot | 19 | 20 | 7 |
| 1988 | Republican Bush | 54 | 60 | 11 |
| | Democrat Dukakis | 46 | 40 | 89 |
| 1984 | Republican Reagan | 59* | 66 | 9 |
| | Democrat Mondale | 41 | 34 | 90 |
| 1980 | Republican Reagan | 51 | 56 | 10 |
| | Democrat Carter | 41 | 36 | 86 |
| | Independent Anderson | 7 | 7 | 2 |
| 1976 | Republican Ford | 48 | 52 | 15 |
| | Democrat Carter | 50 | 46 | 85 |
| 1972 | Republican Nixon | 62 | 68 | 13 |
| | Democrat McGovern | 38 | 32 | 87 |
| 1968 | Republican Nixon | 44 | 47 | 12 |
| | Democrat Humphrey | 43 | 38 | 85 |
| | Independent Wallace | 13 | 15 | 3 |

*Figures are percentages of the vote won by each candidate. Percentages in each election may not add up to 100 because of voting for minor-party candidates.

SOURCE: Data from the *Gallup Opinion Poll* surveys.

possibilities: being African American may cause Democratic voting, or being an African American and voting Democratic may both be caused by some third condition shared by many African Americans. For example, the real causal relationship may be between low incomes and Democratic voting: low-income groups, which would include a disproportionate number of African Americans, tend to identify with the Democratic party. We can test this new hypothesis by looking at the voting behavior of both black and white low-income groups. It turns out that low-income blacks vote more heavily Democratic than low-income whites, so we can reject the low-income explanation. We may therefore infer that race is independently related to voting behavior. But there may be other possible alternatives to our explanation of the relationship between race and voting behavior. Social scientists must test as many alternative explanations as possible before asserting a causal relationship.

Every time we can reject an alternative explanation for the relationship we have observed, we increase our confidence that the relationship (as between race and voting behavior) is a causal one. Of course, in the areas of interest to social scientists someone can always think of new alternative explanations, so it is generally impossible to establish for certain that a causal relationship exists. Some social scientists react to the difficulties of proving "cause" by refusing to say that the relationships they find are anything more than *correlations*, or simply statistical relationships. The decision whether or not to call a relationship "causal" is difficult. Statistical techniques cannot guarantee that a relationship is causal; social scientists must be prepared to deal with probabilities rather than absolutes.

**correlations**
significant relationships that may or may not be causal

## Dealing with Observable Phenomena

**empirical**
referring to observable facts and events; what is

*The scientific method deals only with observable—empirical—facts and events.* In other words, the scientific method deals with what *is*, rather than what *should be*. It cannot test the validity of values, norms, or feelings, except insofar as it can test for their existence in a society, group, or individual. For example, the scientific method can be employed to determine whether voting behavior is related to race, but it cannot determine whether voting behavior *should be* related to race. The latter question is a *normative* one (dealing with "ought" and "should"), rather than an empirical one (dealing with "is"). The scientific method is *descriptive* and *explanatory*, but not *normative*. The social sciences can explain many aspects of human behavior but cannot tell human beings how they ought to behave. For guidance in values and norms—for prescriptions about how people should live—we must turn to ethics, religion, or philosophy.

**normative**
referring to values or norms; what should be

## Developing Theory

*The scientific method strives to develop a systematic body of theory.* Science is more than crude empiricism—the listing of facts without any statement of relationships among them. Of course, especially in the early stages of a science, research may consist largely of collecting data; but the ultimate goal of the scientific method is to develop verifiable statements about relationships among facts and events. It is the task of social scientists to find patterns and regularities in human behavior, just as it is the task of physicists and chemists to find patterns and regularities in the behavior of matter and energy. The social scientist's use of the scientific method, then, assumes that human behavior is not random, but rather that it is regular and predictable.

**theories**
explanations of facts or events

*Theories* are developed at different *levels of generality*. Theories with low levels of generality explain only a small or narrow range of behaviors. For example, the statement that African Americans tend to vote Democratic is a fairly low-level generality about political behavior. Theories with higher levels of generality explain a greater or wider range of behavior. For example, the statement that racial differences cause political conflict has a higher level of generality. Strictly speaking, *a theory is a set of interrelated concepts at a fairly high level of generality.* Some social scientists concentrate on theory building rather than on empirical research; they try to develop sweeping social theories to explain all, or a large part, of human behavior. Still other social theorists provide insights, hunches, or vague notions that suggest possible explanations of human behavior, thus developing new hypotheses for empirical research.

## MAINTAINING A SCIENTIFIC ATTITUDE

Perhaps more than anything else, *the scientific method is an attitude of doubt or skepticism.* It is an insistence on careful collection of data and systematic testing of ideas; a commitment to keep bias out of one's work, to collect and record all relevant facts, and to interpret them rationally regardless of one's feelings. For the social scientist, it is the determination to test explanations of human behavior by careful observations of real-world experiences. It is a recognition that any explanation is tentative and may be modified or disproved by careful investigation. Even the scientific theories that constitute the core knowledge in any discipline are not regarded as absolutes by the true social scientist; rather, they are regarded as probabilities or generalizations developed from what is known so far.

**scientific attitude**
doubt or skepticism about theories until they have been scientifically tested

## WHAT IS A "FACT"?

In the social sciences very few statements can be made that apply to *every* circumstance. We cannot say, for example, that "all blacks vote Democratic." This is a *universal statement* covering every black person, and universal statements are seldom true in the social sciences. Moreover, it would be difficult to examine the voting behavior of every black person in the past and in the future to prove that the statement is true.

**universal statement**
a statement that applies to every circumstance

A more accurate statement might be: "Most blacks vote Democratic." This is a *probabilistic statement* covering "most" blacks, but it does not exclude the possibility that some blacks vote Republican. An even more accurate statement would be that "82 percent of blacks cast their ballots for Democratic candidate Bill Clinton in the 1992 presidential election." This means there was an 82 percent *probability* of a black voter's casting his or her ballot for Democrat Bill Clinton.

**probabilistic statement**
a statement that applies to some proportion of circumstances

A probabilistic statement is a fact, just like a universal statement. Students in the physical sciences deal with many universal statements—for example, "Water boils at 100°C." Water always does this. But social science students must learn to think in probabilities rather than in absolute terms.

Social scientists must also beware of substituting individual cases for statements of probability. They must be careful about reasoning from one or two observed cases. A statement such as "I know a black family that always votes Republican" may be true, but it would be very dangerous to generalize about the voting habits of all black voters on the basis of this one case. We always build tentative generalizations from our own world of experiences.

However, as social scientists, we must ensure that our own experiences are typical. We should keep in mind that the "facts" of the social sciences are seldom absolute—they rarely cover the complexity of any aspect of human behavior. So we must be prepared to study probabilities.

# THE CLASSIC SCIENTIFIC RESEARCH DESIGN

**experiment**
a scientific test controlled by the researcher to observe effects of a specific program or treatment

An *experiment* is a scientific test that is controlled by the researcher and designed to observe the effect of a specific program or treatment. The *classic scientific research design* involves the comparison of specific changes in two or more carefully selected groups, both of which are identical in every way, except that one has been given the program or treatment under study while the other has not.

This design involves the following:

- Identification of the goals of the study and the selection of specific hypotheses to be tested.

**control group**
a group, identical to the experimental group, that does not undergo treatment; used for comparison

- Selection of the groups to be compared—the *experimental group,* which will participate in the program or undergo the treatment being studied, and the *control group,* which is similar to the experimental group in every way except that it will *not* participate in the program or undergo the treatment being studied.
- Measurement of the characteristics of both the experimental and control groups *before* participation in the experiment.
- Application of the program or treatment to the experimental group, but not to the control group. (Members of the control group may be given a *placebo*—some activity or program known to have no effect—to make them believe they are participating in the experiment. Indeed, the scientific staff administering the experiment may not know which group is the real experimental group and which group is the control group. When neither the staff nor the group members themselves know who is really receiving the treatment, the experiment is called a *double-blind experiment.*)

**null hypothesis**
a statement that the program or treatment has no effect

- Measurement of the condition of both the experimental and control groups *after* the program or treatment. If there are measurable differences between the experimental and control groups, the scientist can begin to infer that the program or treatment has a specific effect. If there are *no* measurable differences, then the scientist must accept the *null hypothesis*—the statement that the program or treatment has no effect.
- Comparison of the preprogram/pretreatment status versus the postprogram/posttreatment status in both groups. This is a check to see if the difference between the experimental and control groups occurred during the experiment. This method, used alone, is sometimes called a "before-after" study.

*A market researcher polls a shopper at a local shopping mall. The wording or phrasing of public opinion questions can often determine their outcome.*

Spencer Grant/Stock Boston

- A search for plausible explanations for differences after treatment between the control and experimental groups that might be due to factors other than the treatment itself.

The classic research design is not without its problems. Social scientists must be aware of the more difficult problems in applying this research design to social science research and must be prepared on occasion to change their procedures accordingly. These problems include the following:

- Members of the experimental group may respond differently to a program if they know it is an experiment. Members of a control group are often told they are participating in an experiment, even though nothing is really being done to the control group.
- If the experimental group is only one part of a larger city, state, or nation, the response to the experiment may be different from what it would have been had all parts of the city, state, or nation

## CASE STUDY
An Experiment in
Crime Fighting

Let us consider an example of applying the classic scientific research design to a specific social problem—neighborhood crime. A local government is considering the installation of street lighting in residential neighborhoods to combat crime. The hypothesis is that increased lighting will reduce crime rates. Before spending large sums of money to light up the entire city without knowing whether the plan will work, the city council decides to put the program to a scientific test. The council selects several neighborhoods that have identical characteristics (crime rate, land use, population density, unemployment, population age, income, racial balance, and so forth). Some of the areas are randomly selected for the installation of new street lighting. Crime rates are carefully measured before the installation of streetlights in those neighborhoods that received new lighting and in those neighborhoods that did not receive streetlights (see figure). After several months of new lighting, crime rates are again carefully measured in the experimental neighborhoods (which received lights) and the control neighborhoods (which did not). The results are compared. If a significant reduction in crime occurred in the neighborhoods with new lights but did not occur in the neighborhoods without lights and no other changes can be identified in the neighborhoods that might account for the differences, then the city can have some confidence that lighting reduces crime. An expansion of lighting to the rest of the city would then seem appropriate.

## A Scientific Research Design for Crime Fighting

been receiving the program. For example, if only one part of a city receives streetlights, criminals may simply operate as usual (even with the lights), and total crime rates will be unaffected.

- If persons are allowed to *volunteer* for the experiment, then experimental and control groups may not be representative of the population as a whole.
- In some situations, political pressures may make it impossible to provide one neighborhood or group with certain services while denying these same services to the rest of the city, state, or nation. If everyone *thinks* the program is beneficial before the experiment begins, no one will want to be in the control group.
- It may be considered morally wrong to provide some groups or persons with services, benefits, or treatment while denying the same to other groups or persons (control groups) who are identical in their needs or problems.
- Careful research is costly and time-consuming. Public officials often need to make immediate decisions. They cannot spend time or money on research even if they understand the long-term benefits of careful investigation. Too often, politicians must operate on "short-run" rather than "long-run" considerations.

# GATHERING SOCIAL SCIENCE DATA

How do social scientists go about observing the behaviors of individuals, groups, and societies? There are a variety of methods for gathering data; some fields rely more heavily on one method than on another. The *controlled experiment,* described earlier, is often used in psychology; the *survey* is frequently employed in political science and sociology; *field research,* or participant observation, is a major source of data in anthropology; and *secondary data analysis* is employed in all social sciences.

## SURVEY RESEARCH

Most surveys ask questions of a representative sample of the population rather than question the entire population. A selected number of people, the *sample,* are chosen in a way that ensures that they are representative of the *universe,* the whole group of people about which information is desired. To ensure that the sample is representative of the universe, most surveys rely on random selection. *Random sampling* means that each person in the universe has an equal chance of being selected for interviewing. Random sampling improves the likelihood that the responses obtained from the sample would be the same as those obtained from the universe if everyone were questioned. Hypothetically, we must obtain a random sample of American voters by throwing every voter's name in a giant box and blindly picking out one thousand names to be interviewed. A more common method is to randomly select telephone area codes and then numbers from across the nation.

**universe**
the whole group about which information is desired

**random sample**
each person in the universe has an equal chance of being selected for interviewing

**sampling error**
the range of responses in which a
95-percent chance exists that the
sample reflects the universe

There is always the chance that the sample selected will *not* be representative of the universe. But survey researchers can estimate this *sampling error* through the mathematics of probability. The sampling error is usually expressed as a range above and below the sample response, within which there is a 95-percent likelihood that the universe response would be found if the entire universe were questioned. For example, if 63 percent of the people questioned (the sample) say they "approve" of the way the president is handling his job, and the sampling error is calculated at plus or minus 3 percent, then we can say that there is a 95-percent likelihood that the president's approval rating among the whole population (the universe) stands somewhere between 60 and 66 percent.

Large samples are not really necessary to narrow the sampling error. Large samples are not much more accurate than small samples. A sample of a few thousand—maybe even one thousand—is capable of reflecting the opinions of one million or 100 million voters fairly accurately. For example, a random sample of one thousand voters across the United States can produce a sampling error (plus or minus) of only 3 percent.

## PROBLEMS IN SURVEY RESEARCH

**survey research problems**
unformed opinions
weakly held opinions
changing opinions

When polls go wrong, it is usually because public opinion is unformed, weakly held, or changing rapidly. If public opinion is really unformed on a topic, as may be the case in early presidential preference polls, people may choose a familiar name or a celebrity who is frequently mentioned in the news. Their thoughts about the presidential race are still largely unformed; as the campaign progresses, candidates who were once unknown and rated only a few percentage points in early polls can emerge as front-runners. Weakly held opinions are more likely to change than strongly held opinions. Political commentators sometimes say a particular candidate's support is "soft," meaning that his or her supporters are not very intense in their commitment, and, therefore, the polls could swing quickly away from the candidate. Finally, widely reported news events may change public opinion very rapidly. A survey can measure opinions only at the time it is taken. A few days later public opinion may change, especially if major events are receiving heavy television coverage. Some political pollsters conduct continuous surveys until election night in order to catch last-minute opinion changes.

A common test of the accuracy of survey research is the comparison of the actual vote in presidential elections to the predictions made by the major polls (see Table 2-2). Discrepancies between the actual and predicted vote percentages are sometimes used as rough measures of the validity of surveys. For example, in the 1980 Carter-Reagan presidential contest opinion was extraordinarily volatile during the campaign. Last-day media coverage of the one-year anniversary of the Iranian seizure of the U.S. embassy and detention of American personnel reminded people of Carter's weaknesses. Polling conducted on Sunday failed to catch persons who switched to Reagan by

**TABLE 2-2**

## FORECASTING ERRORS BY MAJOR POLLS IN PRESIDENTIAL ELECTIONS

| | Predicted vote for winner (%) | Actual vote for winner (%) | Error (%) |
|---|---|---|---|
| 1996 | Clinton | Clinton | |
| *USA Today*/CNN | 52 | | 3 |
| CBS/*N.Y. Times* | 53 | 49 | 4 |
| 1992 | Clinton | Clinton | |
| *USA Today*/CNN | 44 | | 1 |
| Gallup | 44 | 43 | 1 |
| 1988 | Bush | Bush | |
| *USA Today*/CNN | 55 | | 1 |
| CBS/*N.Y. Times* | 53 | 54 | 1 |
| 1984 | Reagan | Reagan | |
| Gallup | 59 | | 0* |
| CBS/*N.Y. Times* | 61 | 59 | 2 |
| ABC/*Washington Post* | 59 | | 0* |
| 1980 | Reagan | Reagan | |
| Gallup | 47 | | 5 |
| CBS/*N.Y. Times* | 49 | 52 | 3 |
| NBC/AP | 48 | | 4 |
| 1976 | Carter | Carter | |
| Gallup | 48 | | 2 |
| Roper | 51 | 50 | 1 |
| NBC | 49 | | 1 |

* less than one-half percentage point

Tuesday (election day). It was not a problem of sample size or accuracy, but rather one of rapidly changing voter opinion.

The wording or phrasing of public opinion questions can often determine the outcome of a poll. Indeed, "loaded" or "leading" questions are often asked by unprofessional pollsters simply to produce results favorable to their side of an argument. Ideally, questions should be clear and precise, easily understood by the respondents, and as neutral and unbiased as possible. But because all questions have a potential bias, it is usually better to examine changes over time in responses to identically worded questions. (The Focus on "Explaining Presidential Approval Ratings" examines responses to the same presidential popularity question asked over a period of over twenty-five years.)

Even the most scientific surveys are not error-free, however. We have already noted that weakly held opinions can change rapidly. Some surveys ask questions about topics that most people had never considered before being interviewed. Then the pollsters report responses as "public opinion," when, in fact, very few people really had any opinion on the topic at all. Many respondents do not like to admit they do not know anything about the topic, so they give a meaningless response. Another problem is the "halo effect"—the tendency of respondents to give "good citizen" responses, whether the responses are truthful or not. For example, people do not like

**halo effect**
the tendency of respondents to give "good citizen" responses to pollsters

**FOCUS**

Explaining
Presidential
Approval Ratings

President watching is a favorite pastime among political scientists. Regular surveys of the American people ask the question: "Do you approve or disapprove of the way _____ is handling his job as president?" By asking this same question over time about presidents, po-

litical scientists can monitor the ups and downs of presidential popularity. Then they can attempt to explain presidential popularity by examining events that correspond to changes in presidential approval ratings.

One hypothesis that helps explain presidential approval ratings centers on the election cycle. The hypothesis is that presidential popularity is usually highest immediately after election or reelection, but it steadily erodes over time. Note that this hypothesis tends to be sup-

ported by the survey data in the figure. This simple graph shows, over time, the percentage of survey respondents who say they approve of the way the president is handling his job. Presidents usually begin their administrations with high approval ratings. Presidents and their advisers generally know about this "honeymoon" period hypothesis and try to use it to their advantage by pushing hard for their policies in Congress early in the term.

Another hypothesis centers

PRESIDENTIAL APPROVAL RATINGS

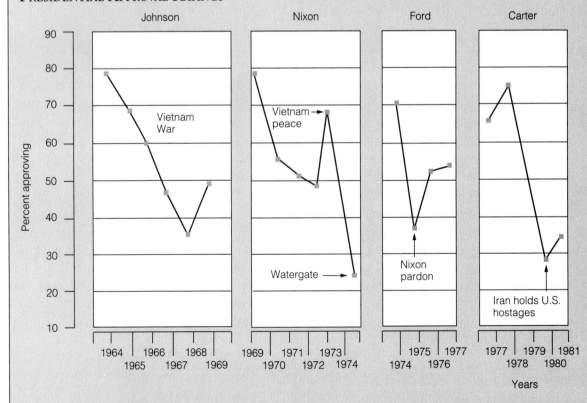

on the effects of international crises. Initially, people "rally 'round the flag" when the nation is confronted with an international threat and the president orders military action. President Bush registered an all-time high in presidential approval ratings during the Persian Gulf War. But prolonged, indecisive warfare erodes popular support for a president. The public approved of President Johnson's handling of his job when he first sent U.S. ground combat troops into Vietnam in 1965; but support for the president waned over time as military operations stalemated and casualties mounted.

Major scandals also hurt presidential popularity and effectiveness. The Watergate scandal produced a low of 22-percent approval for Nixon just prior to his resignation. Reagan's generally high approval ratings were blemished by the Iran-Contra scandal in 1987. Yet Clinton's ratings continued their upward trend despite a White House sex scandal.

Finally, it is widely hypothesized that economic recessions erode presidential popularity. Every president in office during a recession has suffered loss of popular approval, including President Reagan during the 1982 recession. But no president suffered a more precipitous decline in approval ratings than George Bush, whose popularity plummeted from its Gulf War high of 89 percent to a low of 37 percent in only a year, largely as a result of recession.

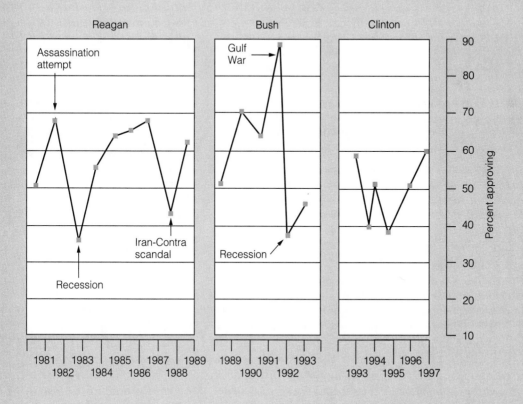

## CROSS-NATIONAL PERSPECTIVE
### World Populations

For thousands of years the world's population grew very slowly—until the Industrial Revolution over one hundred years ago. Improvements in public health and living conditions reduced the death rate, especially for infants and children, and increased life spans. More women survived childbirth and more children grew to adulthood. But all of this good news for the human condition is frequently lamented by some social scientists who believe that the world's population is growing too rapidly and threatens to outrun food supplies and national resources at some future date. (*Demography* is the science of population— size, distribution, change, processes, and characteristics.)

Actually, the *rate* of world population growth has declined since hitting a peak in the 1960s. Currently the world's population is expanding at about 1.7 percent per year. However, inasmuch as the world's population was estimated to be over five billion in 1990, this means that about ninety-three million more people (roughly the population of Mexico) are added to the world's population each year. In 2025, the world's population is projected to be over eight billion. Most of this growth is occurring in the less developed nations of the world. Among the developed nations, fertility rates (the number of children born to women of child-bearing age) have declined to near replacement levels—the number of children born roughly equals the number of deaths. For example, women in the United States are bearing an average of 1.9 children (just below the replacement level); our nation's population is growing primarily because of immigration.

As nations develop economically, they experience a three-stage demographic transition. In the first preindustrial stage, both birthrates and death rates are high. Women must bear six, eight, or ten children just to ensure that two or three survive to adulthood. The population grows very slowly. In the second stage, improved public health, better nutrition and standards of living, and medical advances lower the death rate, especially among women and children, yet birthrates remain high because families have not yet adjusted to changing conditions of life. Old norms of high fertility—once needed to sustain life, to provide agricultural labor, and to care for parents in old age—are not easily changed. The result is rapid population growth in developing nations. The third stage is when birthrates have declined almost to replacement levels. Women increasingly enter the workforce, acquire greater control over their lives, including their reproduction, and plan for smaller families. This full transition has already occurred in most of the developed nations of the world including the United States.

In 1798, Thomas Malthus, an English clergyman, published a famous essay on population, arguing that the human urge to reproduce would outrun the food supply and lead to widespread poverty and disease, which would eventually check population growth. Today's "neo-Malthusians" argue that population growth will outstrip food supplies and national resources as well as degrade the environment so as to make it unlivable. In 1971 biologist Paul Ehrlich called earth a "dying planet" suffering from "overpopulation"; his book *The Population Explosion* inspired Earth Day and generated worldwide publicity. Yet since then, despite the addition of over a billion people, world food prices have *declined* in real terms, as have the prices of most of the world's natural resources including oil. The world's food supply has expanded at a much faster pace than the population. Famine occurs as a product of social disorganization—war, violence, repression—that destroys the infrastructure of a society, denies people access to food, shelter, and medical assistance, and prevents people and governments from dealing effectively with droughts or other adverse conditions.

Only 250 million people, or about 5 percent of the world's population, live in the United States. Well over 1 billion people, or about 21 percent of the world's population, live in China. Shifting population size in developed and developing nations is causing dramatic changes in the ranking of countries by population.

## THE WORLD'S MOST POPULOUS NATIONS RANKED BY POPULATION SIZE, 1950–2050

| 1950 | 1987 | 2025 | 2050 |
|---|---|---|---|
| 1. China | 1. China | 1. China | 1. India |
| 2. India | 2. India | 2. India | 2. China |
| 3. Soviet Union | 3. Soviet Union | 3. Commonwealth* | 3. Nigeria |
| 4. United States | 4. United States | 4. Indonesia | 4. Pakistan |
| 5. Japan | 5. Indonesia | 5. Nigeria | 5. Commonwealth* |
| 6. Indonesia | 6. Brazil | 6. United States | 6. Brazil |
| 7. Brazil | 7. Japan | 7. Brazil | 7. Indonesia |
| 8. United Kingdom | 8. Nigeria | 8. Pakistan | 8. United States |
| 9. Germany | 9. Bangladesh | 9. Bangladesh | 9. Bangladesh |
| 10. Italy | 10. Pakistan | 10. Iran | 10. Iran |
| 11. Bangladesh | 11. Mexico | 11. Ethiopia | 11. Ethiopia |
| 12. France | 12. Vietnam | 12. Mexico | 12. Philippines |
| 13. Nigeria | 13. Philippines | 13. Philippines | 13. Mexico |
| 14. Pakistan | 14. Germany | 14. Vietnam | 14. Vietnam |
| 15. Mexico | 15. Italy | 15. Japan | 15. Kenya |
| 16. Spain | 16. United Kingdom | 16. Egypt | 16. Zaire |
| 17. Vietnam | 17. France | 17. Turkey | 17. Egypt |
| 18. Poland | 18. Thailand | 18. Zaire | 18. Tanzania |
| 19. Egypt | 19. Turkey | 19. Kenya | 19. Turkey |
| 20. Philippines | 20. Egypt | 20. Thailand | 20. Japan |
| 21. Turkey | 21. Iran | 21. Tanzania | 21. Saudi Arabia |
| 22. South Korea | 22. Ethiopia | 22. Burma | 22. Thailand |
| 23. Ethiopia | 23. South Korea | 23. South Africa | 23. Uganda |
| 24. Thailand | 24. Spain | 24. Sudan | 24. Sudan |
| 25. Burma | 25. Burma | 25. South Korea | 25. Burma |
| 26. East Germany | 26. Poland | 26. France | 26. South Africa |
| 27. Argentina | 27. South Africa | 27. United Kingdom | 27. Syria |
| 28. Iran | 28. Zaire | 28. Italy | 28. Morocco |
| 29. Yugoslavia | 29. Argentina | 29. Germany | 29. Algeria |
| 30. Romania | 30. Colombia | 30. Uganda | 30. Iraq |

*Note:* Developing countries are shown in **bold**.
*Commonwealth of Independent States: states of the former Soviet Union including Russia, Ukraine, and Byelorusse, minus Latvia, Lithuania, and Estonia.

SOURCE: U.S. Bureau of the Census, *World Population Profile: 1987* (1987).

to admit that they do not vote or that they do not care about politics. Surveys regularly report higher percentages of people *saying* they voted in an election than the *actual* number of ballots cast would indicate. Many people give socially respectable answers, even to an anonymous interviewer, rather than answers that suggest prejudice, hatred, or ignorance.

## FIELD RESEARCH

**field research**
directly observing social behavior

Fieldwork is the cornerstone of modern anthropology. Many sociologists and political scientists also obtain their information through fieldwork. These social scientists study by direct, personal observation of people, events, and societies. *Field research* is essentially going where the action is, watching closely, and taking notes.

Fieldwork is usually less structured than either experimental or survey research. The scientist is not able to control many variables, as in experimental research. Nor is the scientist able to know whether the peoples or societies being studied are truly representative of all other peoples or societies, as in survey research. However, careful field reports can provide qualitative information that is often missing from experimental and survey research. Researchers can report on emotions, feelings, and beliefs that underlie people's behavioral responses. Researchers can also report on attitudes, myths, symbols, and interpersonal relationships that could not be detected by other research methods. Most important, they can observe individuals, groups, and societies as they live in their subjects' environment.

**participant-observation**
researchers both observe and participate in the behavior being studied

Field research often involves *participant-observation,* where the researcher both observes and participates in the society being studied. Direct participation (moving to Appalachia and getting a job as a coal miner) can provide insights that would otherwise escape a researcher. However, personal participation can also interfere with the detachment required for scientific inquiry. There is also the question of whether the scientist should identify himself or herself as a researcher, which could change the behavior of the people being studied, or conceal his or her identity, which could encourage people to act naturally but raises ethical questions. Some behavior simply cannot be observed if social scientists are identified as researchers. Consider the dilemma of the sociologist who wanted to study homosexual behavior in public toilets. It was not really feasible for him to go on field trips to public toilets identifying himself as a sociologist, asking people if they were homosexuals seeking contacts, and, if so, could he watch. So instead he began visiting public toilets where he suspected homosexual activity was taking place and volunteering to act as a "lookout" for those engaging in the action. He discovered that a lookout was an acceptable, even important, position, and he took advantage of it to study homosexual behavior. Later, after the publication of his study, he came under attack by homosexuals and others for deceiving his subjects.[1]

Anthropology relies heavily on field research. To describe cultures accurately, many anthropologists choose to live among the people they are studying, directly observing and participating in their lives. Many early anthropological studies were intuitive: they produced in-depth, firsthand, long-term observations of societies, but these observations were not very systematic. Some would focus on child rearing or religion or art or language or particularly strange or bizarre practices. Later, anthropological fieldwork became more disciplined, and anthropologists began systematic comparisons of cultures.

*Ethnography* is the systematic description of a society's customary behaviors, beliefs, and attitudes. Ethnographic studies are usually produced by anthropologists who have spent some time living with, interviewing, and observing the people. Anthropologists in the field can test hypotheses by directly asking and observing the people and learning about the context of their behavior and beliefs. For example, an anthropologist in the field may think that the society he or she is studying practices polygamy (one man marries more than one woman simultaneously) because it has more women than men. But as ethnographic studies are gradually acquired for a larger number of different cultures, anthropologists can begin to test hypotheses by cross-cultural comparisons. They may find reports of some societies that practice polygamy even though the number of men and women is equal. This finding would cast doubt on the hypothesis that polygamy is caused by gender-ratio imbalances.

**ethnography**
systematic description of a society's customary behaviors, beliefs, and attitudes

A *case study* is an in-depth investigation of a particular event in order to understand it as fully as possible. A case study may involve an examination of a single governmental decision, or a single business firm, or a single town, or a single society. A hypothesis may be tested in a case study, but researchers know that a single case is not sufficient to make generalizations about other cases. A single case study is more useful for generating hypotheses to be explored later in comparative studies involving larger numbers of cases. However, some case studies involve limited comparisons, as when two, three, or four cases are studied simultaneously.

**case study**
in-depth investigation of a particular event in order to understand it as fully as possible

## SECONDARY SOURCE DATA

Social scientists do not always collect their own data, that is, primary source data. Often, social scientists rely on data collected by government agencies, other organizations, or other researchers (see the Cross-National Perspective, "World Populations," for international sources on p. 30); these data are known as secondary source data. One of the most important sources of data for social scientists is the U.S. Census Bureau, which not only provides the decennial census data on the population of the United States, but also regularly collects and publishes data on governments, housing, manufacturing, and so on. Each year, the Census Bureau also publishes the *Statistical Abstract of the United States*, which summarizes facts about birthrates and death rates, education, income, health, welfare, housing, election outcomes, government taxing and spending, crime, national defense, employment, prices, business, transportation, agriculture, trade, and manufacturing. Footnotes to the data summarized in the *Statistical Abstract* tell where additional data can be found on each topic. (See the Case Study, "Using the *Statistical Abstract*.")

**secondary source data**
data used by social scientists that have been collected by other organizations or governments or researchers

## CASE STUDY
Using the
*Statistical Abstract*

The *Statistical Abstract of the United States* is published annually by the U.S. Census Bureau. Statistics in each edition are for the most recent year or period available by October of the preceding year. Each new edition contains nearly nine hundred tables. Most of the tables are updated versions of tables that appeared in previous editions. The original source of the data is provided in footnotes to each table, and headnote references indicate where historical data on the same topic can be found.

For example, the table shown below is a reproduction of *Table 310* in the *Statistical Abstract of the United States 1996*, which summarizes U.S. crime rates from 1984 to 1994. The headings along the top of the table are column headings, and the headings at the left are row headings. In this table the column headings indicate the total and type of crime, while the row headings indicate the number of crimes, the percentage of change, and the rate (number of crimes per 100,000

### No. 310. Crimes and Crime Rates, by Type: 1984 to 1994

[Data refer to offenses known to the police. Rates are based on Bureau of the Census estimated resident population as of **July 1, 1990, enumerated as of April 1.** See source for details. Minus sign (-) indicates decrease. For definitions of crimes, see text, section 5. See *Historical Statistics, Colonial Times to 1970*, series H 952-961 for related data]

| ITEM AND YEAR | Total | VIOLENT CRIME | | | | | PROPERTY CRIME | | | |
|---|---|---|---|---|---|---|---|---|---|---|
| | | Total | Murder[1] | Forcible rape | Robbery | Aggra-vated assault | Total | Burglary | Larceny—theft | Motor vehicle theft |
| **Number of offenses (1,000):** | | | | | | | | | | |
| 1984 | 11,882 | 1,273 | 18.7 | 84.2 | 485 | 685 | 10,609 | 2,984 | 6,592 | 1,032 |
| 1985 | 12,431 | 1,329 | 19.0 | 88.7 | 498 | 723 | 11,103 | 3,073 | 6,926 | 1,103 |
| 1986 | 13,212 | 1,489 | 20.6 | 91.5 | 543 | 834 | 11,723 | 3,241 | 7,257 | 1,224 |
| 1987 | 13,509 | 1,484 | 20.1 | 91.1 | 518 | 855 | 12,025 | 3,236 | 7,500 | 1,289 |
| 1988 | 13,923 | 1,566 | 20.7 | 92.5 | 543 | 910 | 12,357 | 3,218 | 7,706 | 1,433 |
| 1989 | 14,251 | 1,646 | 21.5 | 94.5 | 578 | 952 | 12,605 | 3,168 | 7,872 | 1,565 |
| 1990 | 14,476 | 1,820 | 23.4 | 102.6 | 639 | 1,055 | 12,656 | 3,074 | 7,946 | 1,636 |
| 1991 | 14,873 | 1,912 | 24.7 | 106.6 | 688 | 1,093 | 12,961 | 3,157 | 8,142 | 1,662 |
| 1992 | 14,438 | 1,932 | 23.8 | 109.1 | 672 | 1,127 | 12,506 | 2,980 | 7,915 | 1,611 |
| 1993 | 14,145 | 1,926 | 24.5 | 106.0 | 660 | 1,136 | 12,219 | 2,835 | 7,821 | 1,563 |
| 1994 | 13,992 | 1,864 | 23.3 | 102.1 | 619 | 1,120 | 12,128 | 2,712 | 7,876 | 1,539 |
| **Percent change, number of offenses:** | | | | | | | | | | |
| 1984 to 1994 | 17.8 | 46.4 | 24.6 | 21.3 | 27.6 | 63.5 | 14.3 | -9.1 | 19.5 | 49.1 |
| 1991 to 1992 | -3.0 | 1.0 | -3.8 | 2.3 | -2.4 | 3.0 | -3.6 | -5.9 | -2.9 | -3.2 |
| 1992 to 1993 | -2.1 | -0.3 | 2.9 | -2.9 | -1.8 | 0.8 | -2.3 | -5.1 | -1.2 | -3.1 |
| 1993 to 1994 | -1.1 | -3.3 | -5.2 | -3.8 | -6.6 | -1.4 | -0.8 | -4.5 | 0.7 | -1.6 |
| **Rate per 100,000 population:** | | | | | | | | | | |
| 1984 | 5,031 | 539 | 7.9 | 35.7 | 205 | 290 | 4,492 | 1,264 | 2,791 | 437 |
| 1985 | 5,207 | 557 | 7.9 | 37.1 | 209 | 303 | 4,651 | 1,287 | 2,901 | 462 |
| 1986 | 5,480 | 618 | 8.6 | 37.9 | 225 | 346 | 4,863 | 1,345 | 3,010 | 508 |
| 1987 | 5,550 | 610 | 8.3 | 37.4 | 213 | 351 | 4,940 | 1,330 | 3,081 | 529 |
| 1988 | 5,664 | 637 | 8.4 | 37.6 | 221 | 370 | 5,027 | 1,309 | 3,135 | 583 |
| 1989 | 5,741 | 663 | 8.7 | 38.1 | 233 | 383 | 5,078 | 1,276 | 3,171 | 630 |
| 1990 | 5,820 | 732 | 9.4 | 41.2 | 257 | 424 | 5,089 | 1,236 | 3,195 | 658 |
| 1991 | 5,898 | 758 | 9.8 | 42.3 | 273 | 433 | 5,140 | 1,252 | 3,229 | 659 |
| 1992 | 5,660 | 758 | 9.3 | 42.8 | 264 | 442 | 4,903 | 1,168 | 3,103 | 631 |
| 1993 | 5,484 | 747 | 9.5 | 41.1 | 256 | 440 | 4,738 | 1,099 | 3,032 | 606 |
| 1994 | 5,374 | 716 | 9.0 | 39.2 | 238 | 430 | 4,658 | 1,042 | 3,025 | 591 |
| **Percent change, rate per 100,000 population:** | | | | | | | | | | |
| 1984 to 1994 | 6.8 | 32.8 | 13.9 | | 16.1 | 48.3 | 3.7 | -17.6 | 8.4 | 35.2 |
| 1991 to 1992 | -4.2 | - | | -5.4 | 9.8 | 2.0 | -4.8 | -7.2 | -4.1 | -4.4 |
| 1992 to 1993 | -3.2 | -1.5 | 2.1 | 1.2 | -3.3 | -0.5 | -3.5 | -6.3 | -2.3 | -4.1 |
| 1993 to 1994 | -2.0 | -4.3 | -5.6 | -4.1 | -3.1 | -7.6 | -1.7 | -5.5 | -0.2 | -2.5 |

- Represents zero.    [1] Includes nonnegligent manslaughter.

Source: U.S. Federal Bureau of Investigation, *Crime in the United States*, annual.

inhabitants) for the years 1984 through 1994. So, for example, we can see there were 23,300 murders in the United States in 1994 (note that the number of offenses is given in thousands), and we can see that there were 18,700 murders in 1984. We can also observe that the murder rate per 100,000 inhabitants rose from 7.9 in 1984 to 9.0 in 1994. And we can see that since its high in 1991 (9.8), the murder rate has fallen in recent years.

It is possible to construct charts of the changes in crime rates from 1980 through 1994. For example, the Census Bureau constructed the two charts in the figure; one chart depicts the violent crime rate (violent crimes are defined as murder, forcible rape, robbery, and aggravated assault) and one chart shows the rate for nonviolent crime (larceny, burglary, and motor vehicle theft).

The original source of these data is indicated in the footnote—annual publication by the Federal Bureau of Investigation, *Crime in the United States*. For more detailed data, social scientists would go to a library to find this publication or write to the U.S. Government Printing Office in Washington, D.C., and request a copy.

### VIOLENT AND PROPERTY CRIME RATES: 1980 TO 1994

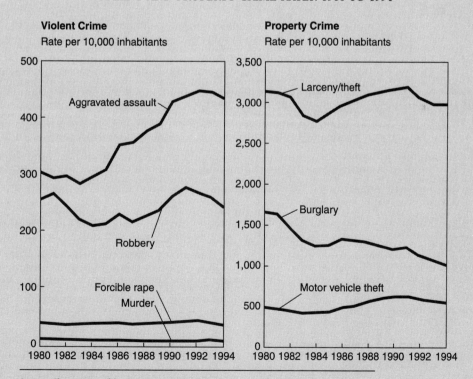

Source: Chart prepared by U.S. Bureau of the Census. For data, see table 310.

## CONTROVERSIES IN SOCIAL SCIENCE
### Can Social Science Be Scientific?

The scientific method was devised in the physical and biological sciences. There are many difficulties in applying this method to the study of individuals, groups, economies, classes, governments, nations, or whole societies. Let us examine some of the obstacles to the development of truly *scientific* social sciences.

### Personal Bias

*Social science deals with subjective topics and must rely on interpretation of results.* Social scientists are part of what they investigate—they belong to a family, class, race, gender, political party, interest group, profession, nation. If the topic is an emotional one, the social scientist may find it much harder to suppress personal bias than does the investigator in the physical sciences: it is easier to conduct an unbiased study of migratory birds than of migrant workers.

Even the selection of a topic reveals the values of the researcher. Researchers study what they think is important in society, and what they think is important is affected by their personal values. Moreover, researchers' values are also frequently reflected in their perceptions of the data, in their statement of the hypotheses, in their design of the test for the hypotheses, and in their interpretation of the findings. An extreme version of this criticism of the social sciences (sometimes referred to as "post-structuralism") argues that no knowledge is free of the race, gender, and class bias of the researcher. Indeed, it is even argued that the scientific method itself is a "white male way of thinking."

### Public Attitudes

*Another problem in the scientific study of human behavior centers on public attitudes toward social science.* Few people would consider arguing with atomic physicists or biochemists about their respective fields, but most people believe they know something about social problems. Many people think they know exactly what should be

## NOTES

1. Laud Humphreys, *Tearoom Trade: Impersonal Sex in Public Places* (Chicago: Aldine, 1970), cited in *Sociology: An Introduction,* 2nd ed., ed. Earl R. Babbie (Belmont, Calif.: Wadsworth, 1980).

## ABOUT THIS CHAPTER

What is a science, and what is the scientific method? How can the subject matter of the social sciences be studied scientifically? What are the obstacles to the scientific study of human behavior and social relations? How can theories and hypotheses be tested in social science research? How can data be collected? Social scientists are often accused of not being truly scientific. Are they guilty as charged, and if so, why? What are the problems, the promise, and the sometimes paradoxical effects of social science research?

These are the questions that Chapter 2 addressed. Now that you have read it, you should be able to

- define science and describe the scientific method
- illustrate how social scientists develop and test hypotheses

done about juvenile delinquency, welfare dependency, and race relations. Very often their information is limited, and their view of the problem is simplistic. When a social scientist suggests that a problem is very complex, that it has many causes, and that information on the problem is incomplete, people may believe that the social scientist is simply obscuring matters that seem obvious.

Social science sometimes develops explanations of human behavior that contradict established ideas. Of course, the physical and biological sciences have long faced this same problem: Galileo faced the opposition of the established church when he argued that the earth revolved around the sun, and Darwin's theory of evolution continues to be a public issue. But social science generates even more intense feelings when it deals with poverty, crime, sexual behavior, race relations, and other sensitive topics.

### Limitations and Design of Social Science Research

*Another set of problems in social science centers on the limitations and design of social science research.* It is not really possible to conduct some forms of controlled experiments on human beings. For example, we cannot deliberately subject people to poverty and deprivation just to see if it makes them violent. Instead, social researchers must find situations of poverty and deprivation in order to make the necessary observations about causes of violence. In a laboratory, we can control all or most of the factors that go into the experimental situation. But in real-world observations, we cannot control many factors; this makes it difficult to pinpoint what it is that causes the behavior we are studying. Moreover, even where some experimentation is permitted, human beings frequently modify their behavior simply because they know they are being observed in a social science experiment. This phenomenon (known as the "Hawthorne effect") makes it difficult to determine whether the observed behavior is a product of the stimulus being introduced or merely a product of the experimental situation itself.

■ describe the classic research design and discuss some of the problems that social scientists have in applying this design and the scientific method to their research

## DISCUSSION QUESTIONS

1. You are about to begin a social science research project, and you want it to be scientific rather than normative. Describe the method you would choose, explaining how it works and what its goals are. Using this method, will you be able to prove cause and effect? Why or why not?

2. Discuss some of the difficulties the social scientist has in applying the scientific method to the study of social problems.

3. Suppose you are a school psychologist who wishes to determine if students learn more when television is used in the classroom than when only conventional teaching methods are used. Construct a classic research design for this purpose. Describe some of the problems you might encounter in applying the design.

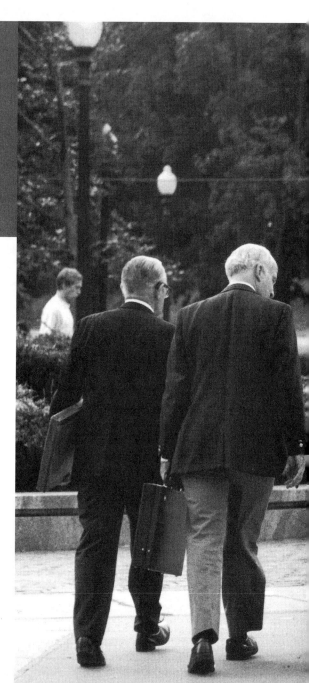

# Power and the Social Sciences

## PART TWO

I n Part 2 we shall take a close look at the ways in which each of the social sciences contributes to our understanding of power in society. In so doing, we hope to gain some feel not only for the different topics, theories, methods, and data of each of the social sciences but also for the goal they share—that is, an improved understanding of human behavior.

In Chapter 3 we shall focus on what *anthropology*, with its concern for culture, has to tell us about the growth of power relationships in societies. In Chapter 4 we shall examine the *sociology* of relationships between power and social class, particularly as evidenced by stratification in American society. In Chapter 5 we shall attempt to determine how and why individuals react in characteristic and different ways to power and authority. Here we shall turn to the theories of personality determination offered by various schools of *psychology*. Control of economic resources is an important base of power in any society, and in Chapter 6 we shall turn our attention to *economics*. In Chapter 7 we shall examine government and power from the point of view of *political science*. Finally, in Chapter 8 we shall look at how the perspective of *history* can increase our understanding of power in society.

# Chapter 3

# Power and Culture

## The Origins of Power

Power is exercised in all societies. Every society has a system of sanctions, whether formal or informal, designed to control the behavior of its members. Informal sanctions may include expressions of disapproval, ridicule, or fear of supernatural punishments. Formal sanctions involve recognized ways of censuring behavior—for example, ostracism or exile from the group, loss of freedom, physical punishment, mutilation or death, or retribution visited upon the offender by a member of the family or group that has been wronged.

*Power in society* is exercised for four broad purposes:

- to maintain peace within the society
- to organize and direct community enterprises
- to conduct warfare, both defensive and aggressive, against other societies
- to rule and exploit subject peoples

**functions of power in society**
maintain internal peace

organize and direct community enterprises

conduct warfare

rule and exploit

Even in the most primitive societies, power relationships emerge for the purposes of maintaining order, organizing economic enterprise, conducting offensive and defensive warfare, and ruling over subject peoples.

At the base of power relationships in society is the family or kinship group. Power is exercised, first of all, within the family, when work is divided between male and female and parents and children, and when patterns of dominance and submission are established between male and female parents and children. In the simplest societies, power relationships are found partially or wholly *within* family and kinship groups. True political (power) organizations begin with the *development* of power relationships *among* family and kinship groups. As long as kinship units are relatively self-sufficient economically and require no aid in defending themselves against hostile outsiders, political organization has little opportunity to develop. But the habitual association of human beings in communities or local groups generally leads to the introduction of some form of political (power) organization. The basic power structures are voluntary alliances of families and clans who acknowledge the same leaders, habitually work together in economic enterprises, agree to certain ways of conduct for the maintenance of peace among themselves, and cooperate in the conduct of offensive and defensive warfare. Thus, power structures begin with the development of cooperation among families and kinship groups.

Warfare frequently leads to another purpose for power structures: ruling and exploiting peoples who have been conquered in war. Frequently, primitive societies that have been successful in war learn that they can do more than simply kill or drive off enemy groups. Well-organized and militarily successful tribes learn to subjugate other peoples for purposes of political and economic exploitation, retaining them as subjects. The power structure of the conquering tribe takes on another function—that of maintaining control over and exploiting conquered peoples.[1]

# CULTURE: WAYS OF LIFE

**culture**
ways of life common to a society

The ways of life that are common to a society make up its *culture*. The culture of any society represents *generalizations* about the behavior of many members of that society; culture does not describe the personal habits of any one individual. Common ways of behaving in different societies vary enormously. For example, some societies view dog meat as a delicacy, whereas others find the idea of dog meat nauseating. Some people paint their entire bodies with intricate designs, while others paint only the faces of the females.

**anthropology**
the study of cultures

The concept of culture is basic to what *anthropology* is all about. One could say that anthropology is the study of culture. Anthropologist Clyde Kluckhohn has defined culture as all the "historically created designs for living, explicit and implicit, rational, irrational, and nonrational which may exist at any given time as potential guides for the behavior of man."[2] In contrast with psychologists, who are interested primarily in describing and explaining individual behavior, anthropologists tend to make *generalizations about behavior in a whole society.* Of course, generalizations about behavior in a whole society do not describe the personal habits of any one individual. Some of them apply only to a portion of that society's membership. In other words, there may be *variations* in ways of life among different groups within one society, variations frequently referred to as *subcultures.*

Anthropologists believe culture is learned. They believe that culture is transferred from one generation to another, but it is *not* genetically transmitted. Culture is passed down through the generations because people in different societies are brought up differently. Individuals learn from other people how to speak, how to think, and how to act in certain ways.

**subcultures**
variations in ways of life within a society

# The Components of Culture

Anthropologists often subdivide a culture into various components in order to simplify thinking about it. These components of culture—symbols, beliefs, values, norms, sanctions, and artifacts—are closely related in any society.[3]

## Symbols

*Symbols* play a key role in culture. The creation and use of symbols—including words, pictures, and writing—distinguish human beings from other animals. A symbol is anything that has meaning bestowed on it by those who use it. Words are symbols, and language is symbolic communication. Objects or artifacts can also be used as symbols: a cross may be a symbol of Christianity. The color red may stand for danger, or it may be a symbol of revolution. The creation and use of such symbols enable human beings to transmit their learned ways of behaving to each new generation. Children are not limited to knowledge acquired through their own experiences and observations; they can learn about the ways of behaving in society through symbolic communication, receiving, in a relatively short time, the result of centuries of experience and observation. Human beings therefore can learn more rapidly than other animals, and they can employ symbols to solve increasingly complex problems. Because of symbolic communication, human beings can transmit a body of learned ways of life accumulated by many people over many generations.

**symbols**
anything that communicates meaning, including language, art, music

## Beliefs

*Beliefs* are generally shared ideas about what is true. Every culture includes a system of beliefs that are widely shared, even though there may be some disagreement with these beliefs. Culture includes beliefs about marriage

**beliefs**
shared ideas about what is true

## MASTERS OF SOCIAL THOUGHT
Ruth Benedict and Patterns of Culture

The concept of culture helps us to understand ourselves by allowing us to see ourselves in relation to individuals in other societies and other cultures. Through the study of diverse cultures we realize that there are many different ways of living—many different ways in which people can satisfy their social and psychological needs as well as their biological requirements; that our own culture is not the only possible way of life.

Perhaps this perception of the diversity of human existence was the most important contribution of cultural anthropologist Ruth Benedict in her widely read *Patterns of Culture*. As professor of anthropology at Columbia University, Ruth Benedict (1887–1947) popularized the notion that different cultures can be organized around characteristic purposes or themes. According to Benedict, each culture has its own patterns of thought, action, and expression dominated by a certain theme that is expressed in

social relations, art, and religion.

For example, Benedict identified the characteristic themes of life among Zuñi Pueblo Indians as moderation, sobriety, and cooperation. There was little competition, contention, or violence among tribal members. In contrast, the Kwakiutls of the northwestern United States engaged in fierce and violent competition for prestige and self-glorification. Kwakiutls were distrustful of one another, emotionally volatile, and paranoid. Members of the Dobu tribe of New Guinea, too, were suspicious, aggressive, and paranoid:

*Life in Dobu fosters extreme forms of animosity and malignancy which most societies have minimized by their institutions. Dobuan institutions, on the other hand, exalt them to the highest degree. The Dobuan lives out without repression man's worst nightmares of the ill-will of the universe, and according to his view of life virtue consists in selecting a victim upon whom he can vent the malignancy he attributes alike to human society and to the powers of nature. All existence appears to him as a cutthroat struggle in which deadly antagonists are pitted against one another in a contest for each one of the goods of life. Suspicion and cruelty are his trusted weapons in the strife and he gives no mercy, as he asks for none.[a]*

Yet Benedict was convinced that *abnormality* and *normality* were relative terms. What is "normal" in Dobuan society would be regarded as "abnormal" in Zuñi society, and vice versa. She believed that there is hardly a form of abnormal behavior in any society that would not be regarded as normal in some other society. Hence, Benedict helped social scientists realize the great variability in the patterns of human existence. People can live in competitive as well as cooperative societies, in peaceful as well as aggressive societies, in trusting as well as suspicious societies.

Today many anthropologists have reservations about Benedict's idea that the culture of a society reflects a single dominant theme. There is probably a multiplicity of themes in any society, and some societies may be poorly integrated. Moreover, even within a single culture wide variations of individual behavior exist.

[a]Ruth Benedict, *Patterns of Culture* (Boston: Houghton Mifflin, 1934), p. 172.

and family, religion and the purpose of life, and economic and political organization. (In Chapter 9, "Power and Ideology," we shall discuss the importance of belief systems in organizing the economic and political systems of societies.)

# RELIGION

*Religion* is evident in all known cultures (see the Cross-National Perspective, "Religious Beliefs"). Although there are differences between societies in the nature of their religious beliefs, all cultures include some beliefs about supernatural powers (powers not human and not subject to the laws of nature) and about the origins of life and the universe. Various theories have arisen about why religious beliefs are universal. Some theories contend that religious beliefs arise out of human anxieties about death and the unknown or out of human curiosity about the meaning, origins, and purpose of life. Other theories stress the social functions of religion, providing goals, purposes, rituals, and norms of behavior for people.

# VALUES

*Values* are shared ideas about what is good and desirable. Values tell us that some things are better than others; values provide us with standards for judging ways of life. Values may be related to beliefs. For example, if we believe that human beings were endowed by God with rights of life, liberty, and property, then we will value the protection of these rights. Thus, belief can justify our values. But values can conflict with each other (that is, the value of individual freedom conflicts with the need to prevent crime), and not everyone in society shares the same values. Yet most anthropologists believe that every society has some widely shared values.

**values**
shared ideas about what is good and desirable

# NORMS

*Norms* are shared rules and expectations about behavior. Norms are related to values in that values justify norms. If, for example, we value freedom of speech, we allow people to speak their minds even if we do not agree with them. The norm of tolerance derives from the value we place on individual freedom. Fairly trivial norms, like lining up at ticket windows instead of pushing to the front, are called *folkways.* Folkways may determine our style of clothing, our diet, or our manners. *Mores* (pronounced "morays") are more important norms. These are rules of conduct that carry moral authority; violating these rules directly challenges society's values. Yet, like values and beliefs, some norms within a given culture conflict with each other, and not everyone shares a belief in all of society's norms.

**norms**
shared rules and expectations about behavior

# SANCTIONS

*Sanctions* are the rewards and punishments for conforming to or violating cultural norms. Rewards—praise, affection, status, wealth, reputation—reinforce cultural norms. Punishments—criticism, ridicule, ostracism, penalties, fines, jail, executions—discourage violations of cultural norms. But conformity to

**sanctions**
rewards and punishments for conforming to or violating norms

## CROSS-NATIONAL PERSPECTIVE
### Religious Beliefs

Social science cannot assist us in determining the truth or falsity of any religious belief. Social science cannot investigate the supernatural, determine the meaning or purpose of life, or evaluate competing religious beliefs. We must rely on faith, scripture, or revelation for our religious beliefs. However, social science *can* try to assess the prevalence of religious belief in a society and even theorize about the relationships between characteristics of societies and the nature of religious beliefs.

The United States is one of the most religious societies in the world in terms of the proportion of people who say they believe in God (89%), identify with an organized religion (70%), and regularly attend church (43%). These beliefs and practices are wholly voluntary in the United States; the First Amendment to the Constitution prohibits the official "establishment of religion" and guarantees the "free exercise" of religion.

The professed importance of religion and church attendance has declined only slightly over recent decades in the United States. The figures that follow summarize national poll results to questions that attempt to track religious beliefs and practices over time:

*Question:* How important would you say religion is in your life?

| | 1952 | 1965 | 1989 | 1994 | 1996 |
|---|---|---|---|---|---|
| Very important | 75% | 70% | 55% | 59% | 58% |

*Question:* Did you yourself happen to attend church or synagogue in the last seven days?

| | 1958 | 1967 | 1977 | 1987 | 1991 | 1996 |
|---|---|---|---|---|---|---|
| Yes | 49% | 43% | 41% | 40% | 43% | 43% |

Americans pray and attend church more often than other peoples living in advanced industrial societies (see table). Surveys comparing religious beliefs in the United States with those in European nations indicate that Americans are also more likely to believe in life after death and in heaven and hell than Europeans. Note that among Germans, those who live in the former East Germany, where religion was suppressed by a communist government for over forty years, are less religious than those who live in West Germany, where religious freedom prevailed.

### RELIGIOUS BELIEFS OF INDUSTRIAL SOCIETIES

| | Attend religious services once a week | Pray once a day or more | Believe in life after death: definitely/probably | Believe in heaven: definitely/probably | Believe in hell: definitely/probably |
|---|---|---|---|---|---|
| United States | 43 | 42 | 78 | 86 | 71 |
| United Kingdom | 14 | 18 | 54 | 54 | 28 |
| West Germany | 21 | 21 | 54 | 43 | 25 |
| East Germany | 7 | 7 | 14 | 20 | 7 |

SOURCES: Various national polls. Reported in *The American Enterprise* (May/June 1990): 100; (November/December 1992): 93–97; (September/October 1994): 90–91; and *Gallup Poll Monthly* (January 1996): 21–23.

cultural norms does not depend exclusively on sanctions. Most of us conform to our society's norms of behavior even when no sanctions are pending, even when we are alone. We do so because we have been taught to do so, because we do not envision any alternatives, because we share the values on which the norms are based, and because we view ourselves as part of society.

## ARTIFACT

An *artifact* is a physical product of a culture. An artifact can be anything from a piece of pottery or a religious object from an ancient culture to a musical composition, a high-rise condominium, or a beer can from a modern culture. But usually we think of an artifact as a physical trace of an earlier culture about which we have little written record. Anthropologists and archaeologists try to understand what these early cultures were like from the study of the artifacts they left behind.

**artifact**
physical product of a culture

## POWER, AUTHORITY, AND LEGITIMACY

*Legitimacy* is the belief that the exercise of power is "right" or "proper," that people are morally obligated to submit to it. Legitimacy depends on people believing that the exercise of power is necessary and valuable to society. As long as people believe in the legitimacy of the institutions in which power is lodged and believe that power is being used rightfully and properly, then force will seldom be required. People feel obliged to obey laws, follow rules, and abide by decisions that they believe to be legitimate. But if people begin to question the legitimacy of institutions (that is, governments, corporations, churches, the military, and so on), and if people come to believe that laws, rules, and decisions are no longer rightful or proper, then they will no longer feel morally obligated to abide by them. Institutional power will then rest on sheer force alone, as, for example, when unpopular, "illegitimate" governments rely on repression by police or military forces to exercise power over their populations.

**legitimacy**
the belief that the exercise of power is right and proper

## AUTHORITY

*Authority* refers to power that is exercised legitimately. Not all power is legitimate: a thief who forces us to turn over money at gunpoint is exercising power, not authority. A tax collector from the Internal Revenue Service who forces us to turn over money under threat of a fine or jail sentence is exercising authority—power that is perceived as legitimate. Authority, then, is a special type of power that is believed to be rightful and proper.

**authority**
power that is exercised legitimately

Authority and legitimacy depend on beliefs, attitudes, and values of the masses. Authority, like beauty, is in the eye of the beholder. The elite know this, so they try to influence mass beliefs and values in order to maintain the legitimacy of institutions they control and to reinforce their own authority. The elite do not like to rely on force alone.

*Political leaders in all societies surround themselves with elaborate symbols of office in order to help legitimize their authority.*

United Nations

## SOURCES OF LEGITIMACY

**sources of legitimacy**

tradition

charisma

legality

What are the sources of legitimacy? Years ago a German sociologist, Max Weber (pronounced "Vayber"), suggested three general sources of legitimacy:

1. *Tradition:* Legitimacy rests on established beliefs in the sanctity of authority and the moral need to obey leaders.
2. *Charisma:* Legitimacy rests on the personal heroic qualities of a particular leader.
3. *Legality:* Legitimacy is based on a commitment to rules that bind both leaders and the people.

Historically, most elites have depended on tradition for their authority. The rule of tribal chieftains, pharaohs and kings, and feudal lords and ladies has been accepted as right because "it has always been that way." Some have relied on charismatic leadership—from Napoleon to Hitler to Gandhi to Mao Zedong. The authority of these leaders was based on the faith of their followers. Still other elites depend on legitimacy conferred by rules agreed on by both leaders and followers. Weber referred to this as rational-legal authority. The elite exercise their authority not because of tradition or personal charisma but because of the office or position they occupy.

# THE FUNCTIONS OF CULTURE

Culture assists people in adapting to the conditions in which they live. Even ways of life that at first glance appear quaint or curious may play an important role in helping individuals or societies cope with problems. Many anthropologists approach the study of culture by asking what function a particular institution or practice performs for a society. How does the institution or practice serve individual or societal needs? Does it work? How does it work? Why does it work? This approach is known as *functionalism.*[4]

## FUNCTIONALISM

Functionalism assumes that there are certain minimum *biological needs,* as well as *social and psychological needs,* that must be satisfied if individuals and society are to survive. The biological needs are fairly well defined: food, shelter, bodily comfort, reproduction, health maintenance, physical movement, and defense. Despite great variety in the way these needs are met in different cultures, we can still ask how a culture goes about fulfilling them and how well it does so. Social and psychological needs are less well defined, but they probably include affection, communication, education in the ways of the culture, material satisfaction, leadership, social control, security, and a sense of unity and belonging. Functionalists tend to examine every custom, material object, idea, belief, and institution in terms of the task or function it performs.

> **functionalism**
> the assumption that cultural institutions and practices serve individual or societal needs

To understand a culture functionally, we have to find out how a particular institution or practice relates to biological, social, or psychological needs and how it relates to other cultural institutions and practices. For example, a society that fulfills its biological needs by hunting may fulfill its psychological needs by worshiping animals. Similarly, we find an agricultural society worshiping a sun-god or a rain-god. The function of magic is to give human beings courage to face the unknown; myth preserves social traditions; religion fosters individual security and social solidarity; and so forth.

Anthropology helps us appreciate other cultures. It requires impartial observation and testing of explanations of customs, practices, and institutions. Anthropologists cannot judge other cultures by the same standards that we use to judge our own. *Ethnocentrism,* or judging other cultures solely in terms of one's own culture, is an obstacle to good anthropological work.

> **ethnocentrism**
> judging other cultures solely in terms of one's own culture

## CULTURAL RELATIVITY

**cultural relativity**
uncritical acceptance of customs, practices, and institutions of other cultures

But *cultural relativity*—uncritical acceptance of customs, practices, and institutions of other cultures—leads to moral dilemmas for scholars and students. While it is important to assess the elements of a culture in terms of how well they work for their own people in their own environment, an uncritical or romantic view of other cultures is demoralizing. Consider, for example, the practice of female infanticide, a common practice in many cultures, including India (before infanticide was declared illegal by British rulers in 1870). Anthropologists might explain the preference for sons in terms of economic production based on hard manual labor in the fields. But understanding the functional relationship between female infanticide and economic conditions must not be viewed as a moral justification of the practice.

Some elements of a culture not only differ from those of another culture, but are *better*. The fact that all peoples—Asians, Europeans, Africans, Native Americans, and others—have often abandoned features of their own culture in order to replace them with elements from other cultures implies that the replacements served peoples' purposes more effectively.[5] Arabic numerals are not simply different from Roman numerals, they are *better*. This is why the European nations, whose own culture derived from Rome, replaced Roman numerals with numerals derived from Arab culture (which had learned them from the Hindus of India). It is inconceivable today that we would express large numbers in Roman numerals; for example, the year of American independence—MDCCLXXVI—requires more than twice as many Roman numerals as Arabic numerals and requires subtracting as well as adding numbers, depending on their place in the sequence. So it is important for scholars and students to avoid the assumption of cultural relativity—that all cultures serve their people equally well.

## AUTHORITY IN THE FAMILY

The family is the principal agent of socialization into society. It is the most intimate and important of all social groups. Of course, the family can assume different shapes in different cultures, and it can perform a variety of functions and meet a variety of needs. But in *all* societies, the family relationship centers on sexual and child-rearing functions. A cross-cultural comparison reveals that in all societies the family possesses these common characteristics:[6]

**characteristics of the family**

- sexual mating
- childbearing and child rearing
- a system of names and a method of determining kinship
- a common habitation
- socialization and education of the young
- a system of roles and expectations based on family membership

These common characteristics indicate why the family is so important in human societies. It replenishes the population and rears each new generation. Within the family, the individual personality is formed. The family

Anthropologists frequently battle against ethnocentrism and the tendency of western Europeans and Americans to view some cultures as "savage." They argue that as anthropologists they must suspend judgment on other peoples' cultural practices, asking only how a people's culture satisfies their particular needs and expectations. But this cultural relativism often conflicts with the idea of universal human rights.

Female circumcision is common in parts of Africa, Malaysia, and Indonesia. Worldwide, between 100 million and 200 million females have been circumcised. In some cultures only the girl's clitoris is cut off, in others the clitoris and both the labia majora and the labia minora are excised. In most cultures the surgery takes place between the ages of four and eight. It is often done without anesthesia; the pain is so excruciating that adults must hold the young girl down. Some of the risks are shock, extensive bleeding, infection, infertility, and death. Ongoing results include vaginal spasms, painful intercourse, and lack of orgasms.

What is the cultural explanation for this custom? Cultures that practice female circumcision believe that it reduces female sexual desire, thus making it more likely that a woman will be a virgin until marriage, and, afterward, remain faithful to her husband. Female circumcision is also a form of ritual torture to control female sexuality; the societies that practice it are male dominated. Mothers cooperate with the circumcision because in these societies an unmarried woman has virtually no rights, and an uncircumcised woman is considered impure and is not allowed to marry.

Immigrants from Africa have brought the custom with them to the United States. Although the practice is specifically banned only in a few states, U.S. physicians will not perform it because they could be charged with child abuse. Some immigrant families take their daughters to their homeland for the operation. Should Western nations try to make African nations and others stop this custom? Or would this be ethnocentric, the imposition of Western values on other cultures?

transmits and carries forward the culture of the society. It establishes the primary system of roles with differential rights, duties, and behaviors. And it is within the family that the child first encounters *authority*.

## MARRIAGE

To an anthropologist, marriage does not necessarily connote a wedding ceremony and legal certificate. Rather, *marriage* means a socially approved sexual and economic union between a man and a woman, intended to be more or less permanent and implying social roles between the spouses and their children. Marriage is found in all cultures, and anthropologists have offered a variety of explanations for its universality. One theory explaining marriage

**marriage**
a socially approved sexual and economic union between a man and a woman, intended to be lasting, and implying social roles between the spouses and their children

focuses on the prolonged infant dependency of humans. In most cultures infants are breast-fed for up to two years. This results in a division of roles between the female nurturer and the male protector that requires some lasting agreement between the partners. Another theory focuses on sexual competition among males. Marriage minimizes males' rivalry for female sexuality and thus reduces destructive conflict (see the Focus, "Social Science Looks at Sex in America"). Still another theory focuses on the economic division of labor between the sexes. Males and females in every culture perform somewhat different economic activities; marriage is a means of sharing the products of their divided labor.

## Monogamy

**monogamy**
marriage union of one husband and one wife

Family arrangements vary. First of all, the marriage relationship may take on such institutional forms as monogamy, polygyny, and polyandry. *Monogamy* is the union of one husband and one wife; *polygyny,* the union of one husband and two or more wives; *polyandry,* the union of one wife and two or more husbands. Throughout the world, monogamy is the most widespread marriage form, probably because the *gender ratio* (number of males per one hundred females) is near one hundred in all societies, meaning there is about an equal number of men and women.

## The Family in Agricultural Societies

**the patriarchal family**
the male is the dominant authority and kinship is determined through the male line

In most agricultural societies the family is *patriarchal* and *patrilineal:* the male is the dominant authority and kinship is determined through the male line. The family is an economic institution, as well as a sexual and child-rearing one; it owns land, produces many artifacts, and cares for its old as well as its young. Male family heads exercise power in the wider community; patriarchs may govern the village or tribe. Male authority frequently means the subjugation of both women and children. This family arrangement is buttressed by traditional moral values and religious teachings that emphasize discipline, self-sacrifice, and the sanctity of the family unit.

Women face a lifetime of childbearing, child rearing, and household work. Families of ten or fifteen children are not uncommon. The property rights of a woman are vested in her husband. Women are taught to serve and obey their husbands and are not considered as mentally competent as men. The husband owns and manages the family's economic enterprise. Tasks are divided: men raise crops, tend animals, and perform heavy work; women make clothes, prepare food, tend the sick, and perform endless household services.

## The Family in Industrialized Societies

**effects of industrialization on the family**

Industrialization alters the economic functions of the family and brings about changes in the traditional patterns of authority. In industrialized societies the household is no longer an important unit of production, even though it

## FOCUS
Social Science
Looks at Sex in
America

The popular media—advertising, films, television, magazines, novels—portrays sex in American culture as pervasive and relentless. The highly publicized "sexual revolution" of the 1960s, presumably fostered by birth control pills and women's renewed quest for equality, was widely believed to have inspired more, better, and livelier sex. Indeed, TV talk shows, *Cosmopolitan* and *Playboy* magazine polls, music videos, and a host of R-rated movies depict America as a nation preoccupied with sex.

But the best social science evidence indicates that most Americans enjoy faithful, monogamous, conventional sex lives. The most comprehensive national survey of sex practices, conducted by the National Opinion Research Center of the University of Chicago, interviewed 3,432 Americans aged eighteen to fifty-nine. Unlike earlier magazine-reader polls, respondents were randomly selected to constitute a cross section of Americans. (The study was originally planned by the U.S. National

Institutes of Health, but opposition in Congress to government-funded "sex research" obliged social scientists to seek financial support from private foundations.) Trained interviewers were sent to households throughout the nation; respondents were interviewed in person and were also given a confidential form to fill out and return. The results destroy many popular myths about sex in America. Among the key findings:

- The vast majority of Americans (83%) have only one (or zero) sex partner in a year. Over a lifetime, 31% of women have had only one partner and an additional 36% have had only two partners; the median number of partners for women is two, for men, six.
- The vast majority of married Americans (75% of men and 85% of women) have never been unfaithful to their spouses.
- Only one-third of Americans have sex twice a week or more; an additional one-third have sex a few times a month, and one-third only a few times a year or not at all.
- Married people have more sex, and experience orgasm

more often, than single people.
- Over 75% of men, but just 29% of women, almost always have an orgasm during sex.
- Among sexual practices, vaginal sex is the most popular practice (90% men, 86% women), followed by masturbation (63% men, 42% women), with oral sex a distant third (27% men, 19% women).
- Homosexuality is rare. Only 2.7% of men and 1.3% of women report having had a homosexual experience in the past year. Only 9% of men and 4% of women have ever had a homosexual experience in their lifetime.
- Fifty-four percent of men and 19% of women report that they think about sex daily.

The sociologists who conducted the study argue that our sex lives, in large part, follow social "scripts," that is, cultural norms that influence sexual behavior. They note that most Americans choose sexual partners who are close in age and educational and ethnic background. The result is greater sexual compatibility and more stable relationships.

SOURCE: Edward Laumann, Robert Michael, Stuart Michaels, and John Gaynon, *The Social Organization of Sexuality* (Chicago: University of Chicago Press, 1994). The popular bookstore version is *Sex in America: A Definitive Study* (New York: Little, Brown, 1994).

*Combining paid work with child-rearing creates multiple burdens for women.*

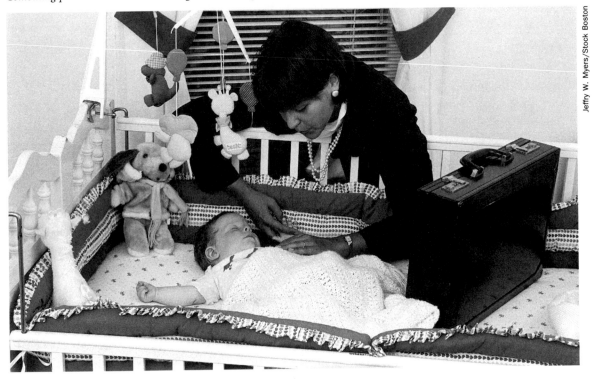

Jeffry W. Myers/Stock Boston

retains an economic role as a consumer unit. Work is to be found outside the home, and industrial technology provides gainful employment for women as well as for men. This means an increase in opportunities for women outside the family unit and the possibility of economic independence. The number of women in the labor force increases; today in the United States about 65 percent of adult women are employed outside the home.

**role of women**

The patriarchal authority structure that typifies the family in an agricultural economy is altered by the new opportunities for women in an advanced industrial nation. Not only do women acquire employment alternatives (see the Focus, "Women in the Workforce: Changing American Culture"), but their opportunities for education also expand. Independence allows them to modify many of the more oppressive features of patriarchy. Women in an advanced industrialized society have fewer children. Divorce becomes a realistic alternative to an unhappy marriage.

**role of government**

At the same time, governments in industrialized societies assume many of the traditional functions of the family, further increasing opportunities for women. The government steps into the field of formal education—not just in the instruction of reading, writing, and arithmetic, but in support of home economics, driver training, health care, and perhaps even sex education, all areas that were once the province of the family. Governmental welfare programs provide assistance to dependent children when a family bread-winner is absent, unemployed, or unable to provide for the children. The government undertakes to care for the aged, the sick, and others incapable of supporting themselves, thus relieving families of still another traditional function.

Despite these characteristics of industrial society, however, *the family remains the fundamental social unit.* The family is not disappearing; marriage and family life are as popular as ever. But the father-dominated authority structure, with its traditional duties and rigid gender roles, is changing. The family is becoming an institution in which both husband and wife seek individual happiness rather than the perpetuation of the species and economic efficiency. Many women still choose to seek fulfillment in marriage and child rearing rather than in outside employment. The important point is that now this is a *choice* and not a cultural requirement.

**family as fundamental social unit**

## THE AMERICAN FAMILY

The American family endures. Its nature may change, but the family unit nonetheless continues to be the fundamental unit of society.

Today there are more than 70 million families in America, and 225 million of the nation's 262 million people live in these family units.[7] Only about 14 percent of the population lives outside family units.

However, the nature of the family unit has indeed been changing. Husband-wife families compose 69 percent of all families with children, whereas 31 percent of all families consist of a single adult and children. Female-headed families with no spouse present have risen from 10 percent of all families in 1970 to 26 percent of all families in 1995. (See Figure 3-1.) The

**FIGURE 3-1**

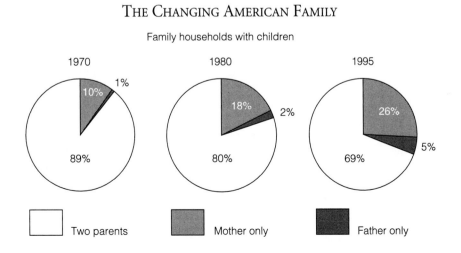

### THE CHANGING AMERICAN FAMILY

Family households with children

1970 | 1980 | 1995

1% / 10% / 89% (1970)

2% / 18% / 80% (1980)

5% / 26% / 69% (1995)

☐ Two parents    ▨ Mother only    ■ Father only

Women in the Work-
force: Changing
American Culture

The number of American
women who work has been rising steadily since 1947. Responding both to changing
views of their role in society and
to economic pressures on family
budgets, women have entered
the U.S. labor force at an unprecedented rate. Not even in
World War II, in the days of
Rosie the Riveter, did so many
women work outside the home.
About 65 percent of American
women aged sixteen to sixty-
four held jobs or were actively
looking for work in 1992. About
70 percent of married women
with children work outside of
the home (see the table,
"Women in the Workforce").

Like all complex social
changes, the back-to-work
movement has been shaped by
many economic and cultural
forces. These factors include (1)
more effective means of birth
control and the trend toward
fewer children, (2) the increased
life expectancy of women, (3)
the greater number of college-
educated women, and (4) the

widespread use of labor-saving
devices in the home. Other factors are (5) the expansion of the
white-collar job market in which
most women are employed, (6)
the increase in opportunities for
part-time employment, and (7)
legal action prohibiting job discrimination based on gender.

Women's pay has increased
significantly in recent years, but

### WOMEN IN THE WORKFORCE

| Year | Number (millions) | Percentage of adult female population* | Percentage of married female population with children |
|------|-------------------|----------------------------------------|-------------------------------------------------------|
| 1940 | 13.8 | 27.4 | 16.7 |
| 1950 | 17.9 | 31.4 | 24.8 |
| 1960 | 22.5 | 37.7 | 27.6 |
| 1970 | 31.2 | 43.3 | 39.7 |
| 1980 | 44.9 | 51.5 | 54.1 |
| 1990 | 56.8 | 57.5 | 66.3 |
| 1995 | 60.9 | 65.5 | 70.2 |

*Age 16 and over

SOURCE: U.S. Bureau of the Census, *Statistical Abstract of the United States 1996*
(Washington, D.C.: U.S. Government Printing Office, 1996), p. 399.

birthrate has declined from 3.7 births per woman of childbearing age in the
1950s to 2.4 in the 1970s and to only 1.8 in 1990. This last figure is *below*
the projected zero population growth rate (2.1 children per female of childbearing age). In addition, there are about four abortions for every ten live
births in the United States.

It is not really clear what factors are contributing to these changes in
the American family. Certainly new opportunities for women in the occupational world have increased the number of women in the workforce
and altered the "traditional" patterns of family life. Economic concerns
may be an even more important factor: families must increasingly depend
on the incomes of both husband and wife to maintain a middle-class
lifestyle.

it is still well below the pay of men. Currently, the average weekly earnings of women are 72 percent of that of men.[a]

This wage gap reflects the continued concentration of women in relatively low-skilled, low-paying jobs. More than two-fifths of all female workers were employed in just ten job categories: secretary, retail sales worker, bookkeeper, private household worker, elementary school teacher, waitress, typist, cashier, sewer and stitcher, and registered nurse.

Occupational segregation stems from many sources—discrimination, cultural conditioning, and the personal choices of women themselves. The jobs women have traditionally held are frequently related to the work they perform in the home—teaching children and young adults, nursing the sick, preparing food, and assisting their husbands and other men. Some employers still hold to the traditional view that women are only temporary entries in the labor force; some employers tend to shuttle women into jobs in which the skills can be quickly learned and that hold little opportunity for advancement.

However, growing numbers of women are gaining access to such traditionally male-dominated professions as law, medicine, architecture, business, and engineering. Consider, for example, the changes over thirty years in various traditionally male occupations (see the table).

## WOMEN IN TRADITIONALLY MALE OCCUPATIONS

|  | Percentage of women | | |
|---|---|---|---|
|  | 1960 | 1983 | 1995 |
| Physicians | 10 | 16 | 24 |
| Lawyers | 4 | 15 | 26 |
| Engineers | 1 | 6 | 8 |
| College professors | 28 | 36 | 45 |
| Chemists | 10 | 23 | 27 |
| Architects | 3 | 13 | 20 |
| Computer analysts | 11 | 28 | 32 |

SOURCE: *Statistical Abstract of the United States 1996* (Washington, D.C.: U.S. Government Printing Office, 1996), p. 408.
[a]*Statistical Abstract of the United States 1996*, p. 426.

## DIVORCE

Almost all societies allow for the separation of husband and wife. Many primitive societies have much higher divorce rates than the United States and other advanced industrialized societies. In 1995 in the United States, there were 4.6 divorces per 1,000 population, compared with 9.1 marriages. At this rate, we would expect nearly half of all marriages to end in divorce. The U.S. divorce rate has moderated somewhat in recent years; it was slightly higher at 5.2 divorces per 1,000 population in 1970. The median duration of marriages that end in divorce is seven years.

Women are more burdened by divorce than men. Most mothers retain custody of children. Although both spouses confront reduced family income from the separation, the burden falls more heavily on the mother who must both support herself and rear the children. Divorced fathers are generally required by courts to provide child support payments; however, these payments rarely amount to full household support, and significant numbers of absent fathers fail to make full payments.

Most divorced persons eventually find new spouses, but these remarriages are even more likely to end in divorce than first marriages.

# POWER AND GENDER

**gender role differences in most cultures**

Although some societies have reduced sexual inequalities, no society has entirely eliminated male dominance.[8] *Gender role differentiation* in work differs among cultures (see Table 3-1), but the most common pattern is for women to work close to home. (See the Focus, "How Men and Women View Their Relations Today.") Moreover, comparisons of numbers of different cultures studied by anthropologists reveal that men rather than women are usually dominant in *political leadership and warfare*. A cross-cultural survey reports that in 85 percent of the societies studied, *only* men were political leaders.[9] In the other 15 percent of societies studied, female leaders were either outnumbered by male leaders or were less powerful than the males. In 88 percent of the world's societies women never participate in war.

*Why have men dominated in politics and war in most cultures?* There are many theories on this topic.

**theories to explain male dominance**

physical strength

hunting

child care

aggression

A theory of *physical strength* suggests that men prevail in warfare, particularly in primitive warfare, which relies mainly on physical strength of the combatants. Because men did the fighting, they also had to make the decisions about whether or not to engage in war. Decisions about whether to fight or not were vital to the survival of the culture; therefore, decisions about war were the most important political decisions in a society. Dominance in those decisions assisted men in other aspects of societal decision making and led to their general political dominance.

A related *hunting* theory suggests that in most societies men do the hunting, wandering far from home and using great strength and endurance. The skills of hunting are closely related to the skills of war; people can be hunted and killed in the same fashion as animals. Because men dominated in hunting, they also dominated in war.

A *child care* theory argues that women's biological function of bearing and nursing children prevents women from going far from home. Infants cannot be taken into potential danger. (As we stated earlier in this chapter, in most cultures women breast-feed their children for up to two years.) This circumstance explains why women in most cultures perform functions that allow them to remain at home—for example, cooking, harvesting, and planting—and why men in most cultures undertake tasks that require them to leave home—hunting, herding, fishing. Warfare, of course, requires long stays away from home.

Still another theory, an *aggression* theory, proposes that males on the average possess more aggressive personalities than females. Some anthro-

**TABLE 3-1**

## DIVISION OF LABOR BY GENDER: A CROSS-CULTURAL COMPARISON

Numbers of cultures dominated by

|  | Men always | Men usually | Either gender equally | Women usually | Women always |
|---|---|---|---|---|---|
| Hunting | 166 | 13 | 0 | 0 | 0 |
| Herding | 38 | 4 | 4 | 0 | 5 |
| Fishing | 98 | 34 | 19 | 3 | 4 |
| Planting | 31 | 23 | 33 | 20 | 37 |
| Harvesting | 10 | 15 | 35 | 39 | 44 |
| Cooking | 5 | 1 | 9 | 28 | 158 |
| Carrying water | 7 | 0 | 5 | 7 | 119 |

SOURCE: Adapted from George P. Murdock, "Comparative Data on the Division of Labor by Sex," *Social Forces* 15 (May 1985): 551–553.

pologists contend that male aggression is biologically determined and occurs in all societies. (See the Focus, "Sociobiology: It's All in Your Genes.") Even at very young ages, boys try to hurt others and establish dominance more frequently than girls; these behaviors seem to occur without being taught and even when efforts are made to teach boys just the opposite.[10]

All these theories are arguable, of course. Some theories may be thinly disguised attempts to justify an inferior status for women—for keeping women at home and allowing them less power than men. Moreover, these theories do not go very far in explaining why the status of women varies so much from one society to another.

Although these theories help explain male dominance, we still need to explain: *why do women participate in politics in some societies more than in others?* Generally, women exercise more political power in societies where they make substantial contributions to economic subsistence. Thus, women have less power in societies that depend on hunting or herding and appear to have less power in societies that frequently engage in warfare. Finally, some evidence exists that women have more power in societies that rear children with greater affection and nurturance.[11]

# POWER AND POLITICAL SYSTEMS

The *political system* is the way that power is organized and distributed in a society, whether it is organizing a hunt and designating its leader, or raising and commanding an army of millions. Some form of political system exists in all societies.

**political system**
the organization and distribution of power in society

Anthropologists have identified various types of political systems. These systems can be arranged according to the extent to which power is organized and centralized, from family and kinship group to band, tribe, chiefdom, state, and nation.

**FOCUS**

How Men and
Women View Their
Relations Today

When a majority of women entered the workforce in the 1970s, expectations were high that soon equality of the sexes in both home and the workplace would become an accepted norm in our culture. But we have already observed continued gender differentiation in the workforce—the persistence of predominantly male and female occupations—as well as a continuing earnings gap. Moreover, the expectation that men would undertake to shoulder an equal burden in household and child-rearing duties has also failed to materialize. Survey evidence suggests that American women continue to perceive male advantages in the marketplace and male reluctance to undertake household chores.

A majority of women believe that men "still run almost everything," and a substantial number of women believe that "there are more advantages to being a man" in American society today (see the table). Marriage is still very popular, with nine out of ten saying they would marry the same person again. But women are still burdened with most of the household chores, whether they work outside of the home or not.

## MARRIAGE ROLES FOR MEN AND WOMEN

|  | Responses by | |
|---|---|---|
|  | Men | Women |
| Men still run almost everything and usually do not include women when important decisions are made. | 41% | 57% |
| In our society today, | | |
| there are more advantages to being a man. | 30% | 43% |
| there are more advantages to being a woman. | 16% | 8% |
| Would marry the same person again. | 93% | 88% |
| Do you or your husband/wife share household chores equally? | | |
| woman does more | 45% | 59% |
| share equally | 46% | 35% |
| man does more | 8% | 6% |
| Percent saying they | | |
| never cook meals | 12% | 2% |
| never put out garbage | 17% | 22% |
| never clean bathroom | 60% | 10% |
| never iron clothes | 82% | 47% |
| never do laundering | 51% | 5% |
| never vacuum | 51% | 16% |
| never do household repairs | 31% | 64% |
| never wash dishes | 40% | 9% |

SOURCES: Various national polls reported in *The American Enterprise* (September/October 1993): 88–95.

## FAMILY AND KINSHIP GROUPS

In some societies no separate power organization exists outside the *family or kinship group*. In these societies there is no continuous or well-defined system of leaders over or above those who head the individual families. These societies do not have any clear-cut division of labor or economic organization outside the family, and there is no structured method for resolving differences and maintaining peace among members of the group. Further, these societies

*While American men have begun to take a more active role in child-care and household duties, surveys indicate that American women continue to perceive male reluctance to undertake household chores.*

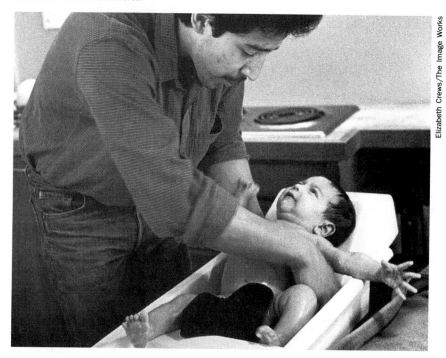

Elizabeth Crews/The Image Works

do not usually engage in organized offensive or defensive warfare. They tend to be small and widely dispersed, to have economies that yield only a bare subsistence, and to lack any form of organized fighting force. Power relationships are present, but they are closely tied to family and kinship.

## BANDS

*Bands* are small groups of related families who occupy a common territory and come together periodically to hunt, trade, and make marriage arrangements. Bands are often found among nomadic societies, where groups of families move about the land in search of food, water, game, and subsistence. Anthropologists believe that bands were the oldest form of political organization outside of the family, that all humans were once food foragers who moved about the land in small bands numbering at most a hundred people.

Authority in the band is usually exercised by a few senior heads of families; their authority most often derives from achievements in hunting or fighting. The senior headmen must decide when and where to move and choose a site for a new settlement. People follow the headmen's leadership primarily because they consider it in their own best interest to do so. Sanctions may range from scorn and ridicule, to ostracism or exile from the band.

**band**
a small group of related families who occupy the same territory and interact with each other

## Sociobiology: It's All in Your Genes

A highly controversial topic in the social sciences is *sociobiology*. Sociobiology may be defined as the branch of biology that deals with the biological basis of social behavior in all kinds of organisms, including human beings. In general, sociobiologists argue that at least some aspects of human behavior are based on *genetics;* that is, these behaviors are the result of millions of years of heredity and evolution. Some sociobiologists, whose ranks include biologists and zoologists as well as social scientists, believe that genetics largely determines culture—from educational and child-rearing practices to sexual behavior.

Sociobiologists claim that their research builds on our scientific knowledge of genetics and applies this knowledge to animal and human behavior. They maintain that many of the behavioral patterns of humans, as well as of other animals, are not "learned" but are instead the results of genetic coding. Songbirds that have been raised in complete isolation from any other members of their own species can sing the exact melody that their species sings, even though the isolated birds never had any opportunity to "learn" the melody. The melody is built into the DNA sequences in their genes. Many similar animal experiments reveal that behaviors occur in a species even though the animal has never had the opportunity to "learn" the behaviors.

### Sociobiology, Natural Selection, and the Selfish Gene

Sociobiology is related to Darwin's theory of evolution, which holds that all animals (including humans) evolve by *natural selection*—those that are better adapted to their environment survive and reproduce; the rest tend to become extinct. Darwin, however, in attempting to explain natural selection, focused on the animal itself rather than its particular genetic code. Sociobiologists, on the other hand, focus on the genetic coding, for they believe that it is within this coding that natural selection takes place. The genes struggle *within* the animal to protect themselves. Darwin was never really able to explain why some animals (including humans) acted altruistically—giving up their own lives to save others. Such behavior—birds risking their own lives to cry out to warn the flock of danger, dolphins swimming beside an injured companion to keep it from drowning, ants giving up their lives fighting for the colony— seems to contradict the theory of natural selection.

Sociobiologists explain this altruism by claiming that the genetic coding of each animal in these particular species includes directions to save the others in order to protect the same genes. In other words, altruism is really *genetic selfishness.* Moreover, most sociobiologists argue that animals will act more altruistically to save relatives (who share more of their own genes) than nonrelatives. Altruism extended to general charitable acts (even by

## TRIBES

**tribe**
a group of separate bands or villages sharing a common language and culture who come together for greater security

Anthropologists describe *tribes* as groups of bands or villages that share a common language and culture who unite for greater security against enemies or starvation (*Tribe* also has a distinct legal definition in the United States, referring to recognized political organizations of Native Americans.)

human beings) may simply be a genetic code that urges individuals to risk their lives to save their genes. Many true heroes who feel they acted on impulse in risking their lives to save others may really have been obeying genetically coded directions.

### Sociobiological Explanations of Various Behavior

Sociobiologists do *not* necessarily agree that humans are always instinctively aggressive. The optimal genetic coding for survival will include just enough aggression not to be beaten out by others, but not too much to waste energy and risk death by pointless fighting. In other words, genetic coding includes a rough cost-benefit analysis for aggression.

Is it possible that upper social classes acquire power because they have acquired superior genes? Responsible sociobiologists reject this notion. It requires millions of years for any significant change to occur in the genetic coding of a group. Culture moves too fast for genes to be able to create any permanent class system. Even the two-thousand-year-old castes of India are not genetically different, despite their prohibitions on intermarriage and rigid separation between castes (restrictions that have been lifted since India's independence). On the other hand, sociobiologists may attribute an individual's success in such areas as sports, business, war, or science to the individual's genetic makeup.

Sociobiologists also offer genetic explanations for sexual behavior. They contend that the object of sexual behavior in animals and humans is to pass on as many of their own genes to succeeding generations as possible, at the lowest possible cost in energy and time. Because a male can start thousands of pregnancies, thus ensuring that some of his offspring will survive, he can ignore the nurturing of his offspring. But a female can give birth only a limited number of times during her lifetime and therefore must invest more time in nurturing her young in order to ensure their survival. Thus, promiscuity among males of many species is common, as is the nesting urge of females. Females of many species stay near the nest, while males roam far in search of opportunities to breed. Moreover, males often engage in openly aggressive behavior against other males, not only to beat out the competition for available females, but also to impress females with the strength of their genes. Over millions of years of evolution, the result, say the sociobiologists, is a different and stronger male physique. Of course, these views have irritated many women, who fear that sociobiologists are telling them to stay home and mind the babies.

It is difficult to estimate how much human behavior is genetically directed (as the sociobiologists contend) and how much is learned from parents and others (as cultural anthropologists contend). It is impossible to say, for example, that 20 or 30 percent of human behavior is genetically based and the rest is culturally based. All we know now is that both genetics and culture affect human behavior.

Typically tribes are engaged in hunting, herding, or farming and they live in areas of greater population density than bands. Tribal authorities must settle differences between bands, villages, and kinship groups. They must organize defenses as well as plan and carry out raids on other tribes. They must pool resources when needed as well as decide upon the distribution of common resources—the product of an organized hunt, for example. Authority may rest in the hands of one or more leaders respected for age, integrity, wisdom, or skills in hunting and warfare.

## CHIEFDOMS

**chiefdom**
a centralized society in which power is concentrated in a single chief who heads a ranked hierarchy of people

Anthropologists also identify *chiefdoms*—highly centralized, regional societies in which power is concentrated in a single chief who is at the head of a ranked hierarchy of people. The position of chief is usually hereditary. People's status in the chiefdom is decided by their kinship to the chief; those closest to him are ranked socially superior and receive deferential treatment from those in lower ranks. The chief's responsibilities extend to the distribution of land and resources, the recruitment and command of warriors, and control over the goods and labor of the community. The chief may amass considerable personal wealth and other evidence of his high status.

## STATES

**state**
a permanent centralized organization with a defined territory and recognized authority to make and enforce rules

A *state* is a permanent, centralized organization with a well-defined territory and the recognized authority to make and enforce rules of conduct. The power of the state is legitimate, that is, considered rightful by its members. In state societies, populations are large and highly concentrated; the economy produces a surplus; and there are recognized rules of conduct for the members of the society, with positive and negative sanctions. These societies have an organized military establishment for offensive and defensive wars. In war, conquered people are not usually destroyed but instead are held as tributaries or incorporated as inferior classes into the state. In the vast majority of these societies, power is centered in a small, hereditary elite.

## NATIONS

**nation**
a society that sees itself as one people with common culture, history, institutions, ideology, language, and territory

A nation differs from a state in important ways. A *nation* is a society that sees itself as "one people" with a common culture, history, institutions, ideology, language, territory, and (often) religion. By this definition, there are probably five thousand or more nations in the world today. (The United Nations has only 181 member states; see Chapter 14.) Only rarely do nation and state coincide, as in Japan. Many states are multinational, that is, they include within their territorial boundaries more than one nation. When a state and nation do coincide, it is usually referred to as a nation-state.

The United States declares itself to be "one nation, indivisible, under God." Yet it encompasses multiple nationalities, languages, and cultures. The claim to nationhood by the United States rests primarily on a common allegiance to the institutions of democracy. Most other nation-states base their claim to nationhood on common ethnicity and ancestry as well as language and territory.

These types of power relationships in societies certainly do not exhaust the variety of current and past power arrangements. They represent only broad divisions, each of which can be subdivided. (For example, a state can be classified in Aristotelian fashion as a *monarchy, aristocracy,* or *democracy*—rule by the one, the few, or the many.) Sharp lines cannot be drawn among these three states; each stage shades into the next, and there are many transitional forms.

Let us consider three examples of societies in which power is organized by these broad divisions: (1) family and kinship group (polar Eskimos), (2) tribe (Crow Indians), and (3) state (the Aztec Empire).

## POWER AMONG THE POLAR ESKIMOS

Societies lacking formal power organizations are found today only in the very marginal areas of the world. These societies, with no formal power structures beyond family and kinship groups, exist only in the most difficult environments, where physical hardship and a lack of adequate food resources keep the human population small and thinly scattered.

environment

Anthropologists who have observed the polar Eskimo culture of northern Greenland note that it has just two social units: the primary family, a small but autonomous kinship group; and the winter village, an unstable association of primary families who are not necessarily linked by kinship ties. The winter village is only partially a power grouping. Its member families do not stay together long enough or undertake the common enterprises necessary for the development of a stable leadership system. Ordinarily the families in a winter village, though temporarily united by common residence, act independently of one another. Their technology, whether in food gathering or house building, requires no high degree of cooperative labor. In times of stress, when a storm or lack of game reduces food stores to the danger point, a *shaman,* respected for his supernatural powers, may call the families together to participate in a ceremony intended to restore the food supply. But the shaman's authority is limited to such occasions; at other times he has no right to direct or command.

economy

A strong and aggressive hunter may gain the esteem and respect of his fellows, but there are few occasions when he may capitalize on this prestige to assume a position of leadership. In short, the winter village has little need for leadership outside the family. There is not even the occasion of warfare to call for the organization of families for offensive or defensive action. Leadership resides only within the primary family, where it is shared by husband and wife, each in his or her sphere of activity. The family maintains itself largely through its own efforts. It is linked to other families through intermarriage, remote kinship, or ties of mutual affection and regard. Conflicts are often resolved by song sessions in which the disputants lampoon each other in songs, which they sing before an audience of their neighbors. More aggressive behavior is inhibited by fear of retaliation by kinsmen of the victims. Protracted disputes may be resolved

leadership

among some Eskimos by one party's moving to another winter village, although an overbearing and abusive individual may be speared while on a hunt.

**organization**

Among these Eskimos, then, there is no structure of power outside the family group. Leadership outside the family is seldom evidenced, usually only during a crisis, when some particularly able member of the community takes charge. Ecological circumstances prohibit large permanent groupings of people, and the technology of the society is so simple that it utilizes individual rather than group effort. Variations on this fundamental type of power system that exists solely within the family group are also found among other primitive peoples living in harsh environments.

## POWER AMONG THE CROW INDIANS

Anthropological research on the American Crow Indians in the early nineteenth century provides an example of the development of power relationships at the tribal level. The Crow were more or less continually hostile to their neighbors. Any non-Crow was automatically an enemy. Warfare, however, was largely a matter of small-scale raiding, either to steal horses or to avenge the death of a tribesman. Horse-stealing parties tried to take as many horses as they could without disturbing the enemy camp; they fought only when necessary to defend themselves. When revenge was the object of a war party, however, they tried to surprise the enemy and kill as many as possible without losing any of their own men. A war leader, whether he set out to capture horses or to get revenge, was not considered successful unless he brought his own party home intact.

Success in warfare was very important. Crow men achieved reputation and prestige through the slow accumulation of war honors. War honors were clearly defined. They were awarded for (1) leading a successful war party, (2) capturing an enemy's weapon in actual combat, (3) being first to strike an enemy in the course of a fight, and (4) driving off a horse tethered in an enemy encampment. A man who performed all these deeds became, in Crow terms, a "good and valiant man," and his status increased as the number of his earned war honors increased.

**economy**

The warriors formed a kind of military aristocracy that made up the band council. One of their number, usually an older man with many war honors, was recognized as chief. He decided when the band was to move or settle down in its yearly wanderings in search of food and when war parties were to be sent out. He directed the annual buffalo hunt, a cooperative endeavor in which the whole band united to secure a store of winter food.

**authority**

However, the chief's authority was by no means absolute; he was "neither a ruler nor a judge." In effect, the chief was a leader rather than a ruler; it was his function to persuade and influence rather than to command. On some occasions, mainly the annual buffalo hunts, the chief and other council warriors had the authority to resort to force rather than persuasion to maintain order. In such instances the senior warriors "severely whipped anyone who prematurely attacked the herd, broke his weapons, and confiscated the game he had illegally killed."[12] The need for a winter's supply of food, and the fact that this need could not be adequately served without the closest coordination of effort, clearly justified, in Crow eyes, the chief's authority over his tribesmen. However, apart from such special occasions as the community buffalo hunt, members of the band were allowed to act pretty much as they pleased, subject only to the discipline of public opinion. The threat of ridicule and the obligations imposed by kinship were normally sufficient deterrents to antisocial behavior.

## POWER AND THE AZTEC EMPIRE

The most fully developed system of power relationships is the state. Power in the state is employed to maintain order among peoples and to carry on large-scale community enterprises, just as in the band or tribe. But power in the state is also closely linked to defense, aggression, and the exploitation of conquered peoples. Frequently states emerge in response to attacks by others. Where there is a fairly high density of population, frequent and continuing contact among bands, and some commonality of language and culture, there is the potential for "national" unity in the form of a state. But a state may not emerge if there is no compelling motivation for large-scale cooperation. Motivation is very often provided initially by the need for defense against outside invasion.

States differ from bands or tribes to the extent that there is a *centralized authority* with recognized power, backed by force, to carry out its decrees. This *legitimate use of force* distinguishes the state as a form of power structure from the band or tribe, in which power depends largely on persuasion or the personal achievements of individuals. Power in the state is a more impersonal kind of authority. **authority**

The Aztec Empire, which was conquered by the Spaniards under Hernando Cortés in 1521, is an excellent example of an early state. The rich agricultural economy developed by the Aztecs produced far in excess of their immediate needs. With the exchangeable surplus, there soon evolved a complex specialization of labor and an extensive trade that brought the Aztecs into frequent and profitable contact with neighboring groups. **economy**

Early in the fifteenth century, the Aztecs embarked on a series of military conquests that led ultimately to their economic and political control over most of central and southern Mexico. The Aztecs did not destroy the cities and states they had conquered. On the contrary, the commercially minded Aztecs permitted those cities and states to retain local autonomy, demanding only political allegiance and a yearly tribute in goods and services to the Aztec emperor. It was this economic empire, politically a loose aggregate of city-states controlled from the Aztec capital city of Tenochtitlán, that Cortés took over in 1521. **warfare and exploitation**

*The Great Temple of Mexico, Tenochtitlán, as reconstructed by the twentieth-century pre-Conquest architectural historian Ignacio Marquina, according to the plans of Bernardino de Sahagún and Diego Durán.*

American Museum of Natural History, Neg. #326597

The early Aztec power structure, although more complicated than that of primitive tribes, still retained a measure of democratic procedure. The core of the Aztec Empire was ruled by its citizens, the members of the *calpulli*, small groups composed of nuclear families that farmed their own land. Although the positions of chief and king were in part hereditary (they were customarily chosen from particular families), the choice of a leader also depended on reputation and ability. The king had great power as a military leader in a state more or less continuously at war, but his power was modified by councils of family heads.

**upper class**

As the Aztecs grew wealthier from their numerous conquests and ever-widening control of trade, the power structure underwent a gradual change. Most important, a class division developed in Aztec society along socioeconomic lines. An upper class appeared, composed of honorary lords known as *tecutin*. These were men, *calpulli* members, who were given titles for outstanding services to the state as warriors, merchants, public officials, or priests. They were universally esteemed; had many privileges, including certain exemptions from taxation; were preferred for high governmental and military positions; and were given large estates and shares of tribute by the king, to be held as private property during their lifetime. These rewards clearly made the *tecutin* economically independent of their *calpulli* and, moreover, allied them with the king, who, while he gave the *tecutin* their honors, also had the power to withdraw them.

**middle class**

A middle class also emerged, made up of *calpulli* members who were not *tecutin*. These formed the bulk of the population of the capital city. They were self-supporting through their membership in the *calpulli* and had a voice in the government through their representatives in the state and great councils. Often they rented their *calpulli* lands, and some acquired great wealth.

Finally, a lower class was divided into propertyless freemen and slaves. Slaves were attached to the lands of the nobility. The propertyless were men exiled from the *calpulli* for various crimes and who thus had no way of making a living except by hiring themselves out as agricultural laborers or as porters in the caravans of the merchants. Slaves were similarly dependent for a living on their own labor. Neither slaves nor propertyless freemen had a voice in the government. Though initially small, the lower class grew as conquests increased.

*slaves*

As class lines became more sharply drawn, Aztec government moved inevitably in the direction of an absolute *hereditary monarchy. Tecutin* clearly supported this tendency to their advantage and increasingly, by various devices, managed to pass on their titles and private property to their heirs. Slowly a *hereditary nobility* arose. At the time of the conquest, the Aztec Empire was essentially an emerging feudal order, with political power centered increasingly in the king and his *tecutin* rather than in the elected representatives of the *calpulli*.

*hereditary monarchy and nobility*

## POWER AND SOCIETY: SOME ANTHROPOLOGICAL OBSERVATIONS

Let us summarize the contributions that anthropological studies can make to our understanding of the growth of power relationships in societies. First, it is clear that the *physical environment* plays an important role in the development of power systems. Where the physical environment is harsh and the human population must of necessity be spread thinly, power relationships are restricted to the family and kinship groupings. Larger political groupings are essentially impossible. The elite emerge only after there is some concentration of population, where food resources permit groupings of people larger than one or two families.

*power and the physical environment*

Second, power relationships are linked to the *economic patterns* of a culture. In subsistence economies, power relationships are limited to the band or tribal level. Only in surplus-producing economies do we find states or statelike power systems. Developed power systems are associated with *patterns of settled life,* a certain degree of *technological advance,* and *economic surplus.*

*power and the economy*

Third, *patterns of warfare* are linked to the development of power relationships. Warfare is rare or lacking among people such as the Eskimos who have no real power system outside the family. Where power relationships emerge at the band or tribal level, as in the culture of the Crow, warfare appears to be continuous, in the form of periodic raiding for small economic gains or the achievement of personal glory and status; victory assumes the

*power and warfare*

form of killing or driving off enemy groups. Only at the state level is warfare well organized and pursued for the purpose of conquest and economic exploitation. This does not mean necessarily that statelike power systems *cause* war, but rather, that some common factor underlies both the rise of state power systems and organized warfare. Warfare and conquest are not essential to the maintenance of the state; in fact, in the modern world, warfare between major states may slowly give way to other forms of competition, if only because of the increasing threat of total destruction.

**power in advanced societies**    Fourth, anthropological research makes it clear that power relationships exist in simple forms in primitive societies and that *no society is void of a power structure.* Power structures become more complex and hierarchical, and more impersonal and based on physical force, as societies move from the subsistence level with simple technology to a surplus-producing level with advanced technology and large cooperative enterprises. The simpler power systems are frequently headed by chiefs and councils selected for their age, wisdom, or demonstrated capacity as hunters or warriors. These leaders tend to rule more by example and persuasion than by formal decree or force. As more complex state systems emerge, leaders are endowed with the exclusive right to coerce. Characteristically, political and economic power in the state is concentrated in a small hereditary elite. Modern representative government, in the form of European and American democracies, is relatively rare in the history of human societies.

# NOTES

1. See Marvin Harris, *Cannibals and Kings: The Origins of Cultures* (New York: Random House, 1977).
2. Clyde Kluckhohn and William Kelly, "The Concept of Culture," in *The Science of Man in the World Crisis,* ed., Ralph Linton (New York: Columbia University Press, 1945), p. 97.
3. See Serena Nanda, *Cultural Anthropology,* 5th ed. (Belmont, Calif.: Wadsworth, 1994).
4. This approach was developed by Bronislaw Malinowski in *A Scientific Theory of Culture and Other Essays* (Chapel Hill: University of North Carolina Press, 1944).
5. See the argument presented by Thomas Sowell in "Cultural Diversity: A World View," *The American Enterprise* 2 (May/June 1991): 44−55.
6. William W. Stephens, *The Family in Cross-Cultural Perspective* (New York: Holt, Rinehart & Winston, 1963).
7. U.S. Bureau of the Census, *Statistical Abstract of the United States 1996* (Washington, D.C.: U.S. Government Printing Office, 1996), p. 59.
8. Carol R. Ember and Melvin Ember, *Cultural Anthropology,* 6th ed. (Englewood Cliffs, N.J.: Prentice-Hall, 1990), ch. 9; George P. Murdock and Caterina Post,

"Factors in the Division of Labor by Sex: A Cross-Cultural Analysis," *Ethnology* 12 (1973): 203−225.
9. Martin K. Whyte, "Cross-Cultural Codes Dealing with the Relative Status of Women," *Ethnology* 17 (1978): 217.
10. Beatrice B. Whiting and Carolyn P. Edwards, "A Cross-Cultural Analysis of Sex Differences in the Behavior of Children Aged Three Through Eleven," *Journal of Social Psychology* 91 (1973): 171−188; Eleanor E. Maccoby and Carol N. Jacklin, *The Psychology of Sex Differences* (Stanford, Calif.: Stanford University Press, 1974).
11. Marc H. Ross, "Female Political Participation: A Cross-Cultural Explanation," *American Anthropologist* 88 (1986): 841−858.
12. Robert H. Lowie, *The Crow Indians* (New York: Rinehart, 1935), p. 5.

# ABOUT THIS CHAPTER

Anthropologists, in their study of human culture, have been able to document that the exercise of power and the division of labor within the family constitute the most basic power relationship, the one from which true political power structures develop. What causes these structures to develop? Why should we need to control each other's behavior, and how do we manage to do it? How do anthropologists document the growth of power relationships? How, in fact, do they approach the study of something as diverse as human culture?

These questions were the focus of Chapter 3. Now that you have read it, you should be able to

- describe how power in society is exercised and for what purposes
- discuss how and why the family is the fundamental social unit in which power relationships originate
- discuss the changing roles of women in American society
- discuss the stages of development of power relationships and the factors that influence this development
- discuss anthropological approaches to the study of culture

## DISCUSSION QUESTIONS

1. Describe how societies attempt to control the behavior of their members. Discuss the four broad purposes for which societies exercise power.
2. Describe how power and relationships begin within the family and how they develop into political organizations. What effect can warfare have on the power structure?

3. Choose a "subculture" that is familiar to you. If you were asked to explain in anthropological terms what sets this subculture apart from the society at large, what cultural categories would you examine? Identify the variations in lifestyle that make this a subculture.
4. Describe how an anthropologist of the functionalist school would approach the study of culture.
5. Discuss Ruth Benedict's contributions to anthropology.
6. Identify the characteristics of marriage that are found in all societies. Explain why the family is the most important social group.
7. Discuss changes in the American family. Comment on the continuing strength of family life, the number of families with a single adult, and the declining birthrate.
8. Discuss the changing roles of women in American society, particularly their changing role in the workforce.
9. Describe the broad stages of development of power relationships and the power groups associated with them. Compare these groups in terms of leadership, economic systems, patterns of warfare, population density, and patterns of settlement. How have anthropological studies contributed to our understanding of these power relationships?
10. "Culture is learned. . . . Culture is transferred from one generation to another, but . . . it is *not* genetically transmitted." What arguments do sociobiologists advance against this contention? Why does sociobiology arouse so much controversy? Identify the areas of human social behavior that sociobiologists believe may be genetically directed. Discuss your opinions about the relative effects on human behavior of genetics and culture.

## Chapter 4

# Power and Social Class

## POWER PYRAMIDS AND PECKING ORDERS

All known societies have some system of ranking their members along a superiority-inferiority scale. Although many societies claim to grant "equality" to their members, in no society have people in fact been considered equal. The *stratification* of society involves the *classification* of individuals and the *ranking* of classifications on a superiority-inferiority scale. This system of classification and ranking is itself a source of prestige, wealth, income, authority, and power.

Individuals can be classified on a wide variety of characteristics—physical strength, fighting prowess, family lineage, ethnicity or race, age, gender, religion, birth order, and so on. But *the most important bases of stratification in a modern industrial society are the various roles that individuals play in the economic system.*

Individuals are ranked according to how they make their living and how much control they exercise over the livelihood of others. Ranking by occupation and control of economic resources occurs not only in the United States but in most other modern nations as well.[1]

The evaluation of individuals along a superiority-inferiority scale means, of course, a differential distribution of prestige. Thus, the elite strata will receive the *deference* of individuals who are ranked below them. Deference may take many forms: acquiescence in the material advantages or privileges of the elite (the use of titles and symbols of rank, distinctive clothing, housing, and automobiles); accordance of influence and respect; acceptance of leadership in decision making; and so on. The stratification system also involves *different styles of life:* foods eaten, magazines and books read, places of residence, favorite sports, schools attended, pronunciation and accent, recreational activities, and so forth. In addition, of course, the stratification system is associated with the *uneven distribution of wealth and income:* in every society higher-ranking persons enjoy better housing, clothing, food, automobiles, and other material goods and services than persons ranked lower on the scale.

**stratification results in inequality**
deference
styles of life
wealth and income
power

Finally, the stratification system involves the *unequal distribution of power*—the ability to control the acts of others. Sociologists agree that power and stratification are closely related, but they disagree on the specific value of this relationship. Some theorize that power is a *product* of economic well-being, prestige, or status. Others believe that power *determines* the distribution of wealth, prestige, and status.[2]

The stratification system creates social classes. The term *social class* simply refers to all individuals who occupy a broadly similar category and ranking in the stratification system. Members of the same social class may or may not interact or even realize that they have much in common. Because all societies have stratification systems, all societies have social classes.

**social class**
a category and ranking in the stratification system

# STRATIFICATION IN AMERICAN SOCIETY

Social classes are of interest to sociologists, with their concern for the relationships among individuals and groups. Sociologists have devised several methods of identifying and measuring social stratification. These include: (1) the *subjective method*, in which individuals are asked how they see themselves in the class system; (2) the *reputational method*, in which individuals are asked to rank positions in the class system; and (3) the *objective method*, in which social scientists observe characteristics that discriminate among patterns of life they associate with social class.

**methods of identifying and measuring stratification**

## SUBJECTIVE SELF-CLASSIFICATION

The American ideology encompasses the notion that status should be based on personal qualities and achievements. Individuals in a free society should have the opportunity to achieve the social rankings they can earn by ability, effort, and moral worth. These individuals are supposed to rise or fall according to their merits. In view of this ideology, it is not surprising that

**subjective identification**
individuals identify their own social class

most Americans think of themselves as middle class. Nearly nine out of ten will describe themselves as middle class when they are forced to choose between this term and either upper or lower class. It is apparent that to characterize oneself as upper class is regarded as "snobbish," and to view oneself as lower class is to admit that one is a loser in the great game of life. Even people who admit to being poor consider it an insult to be called "lower class."[3]

However, the fact that most Americans label themselves as middle class does not mean that American society is one big middle-class society. In fact, when *working class* is added to the list of choices, and individuals are asked for subjective evaluations of their own class membership, a different picture emerges. When given the option, about 45 percent of Americans identify themselves as "working class," and only slightly more identify themselves as "middle class." About 5 percent say they are "lower class," and even fewer, 2 to 3 percent, say they are "upper class." Over time "middle class" appears to be gaining in popularity as a label people apply to themselves.[4] (See Table 4-1.)

## REPUTATIONAL PRESTIGE

**reputational identification**
individuals ranking the prestige of occupations

Social scientists have spent a great deal of time studying the prestige ranking of occupations as a measure of the stratification system of modern society. Individuals are asked in national surveys to make a superiority-inferiority ranking of specific occupations. The resulting prestige scores for various occupations are shown in Table 4-2. Note that prestige is not the equivalent of income. Apparently prestige is awarded on the basis of ability, education, and training required for an occupation. Generally "white-collar" occupations that involve mental activity are awarded greater prestige than "blue-collar" occupations that require physical labor. These rankings have remained stable for several decades.

**TABLE 4-1**

### CLASS-IFYING OURSELVES

*Question:* If you were asked to use one of these four names for your social class, which would you say you belong to?

|  | 1949 | 1975–1988 | 1988–1991 |
|---|---|---|---|
| Upper class | 2 | 3 | 3 |
| Middle class | 32 | 45 | 48 |
| Working class | 60 | 48 | 44 |
| Lower class | 6 | 4 | 5 |

SOURCE: Data derived from various surveys by the National Opinion Research Center as reported in *The American Enterprise* (May/June 1993): 82–83.

**TABLE 4-2**

## OCCUPATIONAL PRESTIGE IN THE UNITED STATES

| White-collar occupations | Prestige score | Blue-collar occupations |
|---|---|---|
| Physician | 82 | |
| College/university professor | 78 | |
| Lawyer | 76 | |
| Dentist | 74 | |
| Physicist/astronomer | 74 | |
| Bank officer | 72 | |
| Architect | 71 | |
| Aeronautical/astronautical engineer | 71 | |
| Airplane pilot | 70 | |
| Clergy | 69 | |
| Secondary school teacher | 63 | |
| Registered nurse | 62 | |
| Pharmacist | 61 | |
| Elementary school teacher | 60 | |
| Veterinarian | 60 | |
| | 49 | Electrician |
| | 48 | Aircraft mechanic |
| | 48 | Machinist |
| | 48 | Police officer |
| Bookkeeper | 48 | |
| Insurance agent | 47 | |
| | 46 | Secretary |
| | 44 | Firefighter |
| Air traffic controller | 43 | |
| | 42 | Mail carrier |
| | 41 | Farmer |
| | 40 | Welder |
| Restaurant manager | 39 | |
| Building superintendent | 38 | |
| | 37 | Auto body repairperson |
| | 36 | Brick/stone mason |
| | 35 | TV repairperson |
| | 34 | Baker |
| | 33 | Hairdresser |
| | 33 | Bulldozer operator |
| | 32 | Bus driver |
| | 32 | Truck driver |
| Cashier | 31 | |
| File clerk | 30 | |
| | 22 | Gas station attendant |
| | 22 | Taxi driver |
| | 20 | Bartender |
| | 20 | Waiter/waitress |
| | 18 | Farm laborer |
| | 17 | Car washer |

SOURCE: Adapted from *General Social Surveys, 1972–1989: Cumulative Codebook* (Chicago: National Opinion Research Center, 1989), pp. 685–698.

# OBJECTIVE CLASSIFICATIONS

**objective identification**
ranking by occupation, income, or education

The principal *objective criteria* of social class are income, occupation, and education. If sociologists are correct in the assumption that occupation and control of economic resources are the source of stratification in society, then these indexes are the best available measures of class. Certainly income, jobs, and education are unequally distributed in American society, as they are in all other societies.

College graduates comprise about 21 percent of the adults in the United States (see Figure 4-1). About 80 percent are high school graduates, about 20 percent having dropped out of formal education without a high school degree. This is a dramatic increase in formal education over previous generations.

Income is closely related to education. Generally individuals who have acquired higher educations tend to enjoy higher annual incomes. However, Table 4-3 also shows that there are two separate scales by which income is distributed—one male and one female. Women with equivalent educations tend to earn less than men.

Ethnic and racial stratification is visible on virtually all measures of social class—income, education, occupation. For example, in Figure 4-1, showing adult educational attainment levels since 1960, while all groups have gained in education, African-American and especially Hispanic high school and college completion percentages remain below those of whites. The educational

## FIGURE 4-1

## EDUCATIONAL ATTAINMENT

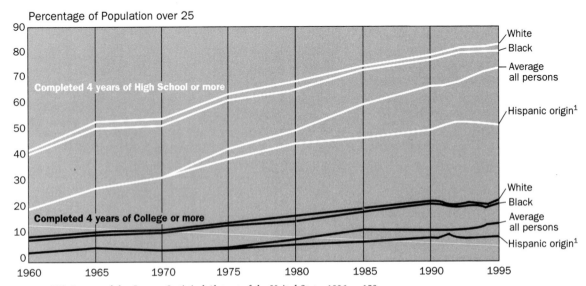

SOURCE: U.S. Bureau of the Census, *Statistical Abstract of the United States 1996*, p. 159.

**TABLE 4-3**

## DISTRIBUTION OF FAMILY INCOME IN THE UNITED STATES

| Family income | Percentage of families |
|---|---|
| Less than $10,000 | 9.6 |
| $10,000–$24,999 | 22.7 |
| $25,000–$49,999 | 32.7 |
| $50,000–$74,999 | 19.4 |
| Over $75,000 | 15.5 |
| Median family income in 1993 = $36,959 | |

| | Average earnings | |
|---|---|---|
| Education | Male | Female |
| Less than 9th grade | $20,461 | $13,349 |
| 9th to 12th | 24,377 | 16,188 |
| High school graduate | 31,081 | 21,383 |
| Some college | 35,639 | 24,787 |
| Associate degree | 38,944 | 26,903 |
| B.A. or more | 61,008 | 39,271 |

SOURCE: U.S. Bureau of the Census, *Statistical Abstract of the United States 1996*, p. 471.

gap between blacks and whites has narrowed somewhat over the years, but not the gap between Hispanics and whites. We will examine "Power, Race, and Gender" in greater detail in Chapter 10.

# WHY DO WE HAVE SOCIAL CLASSES?

Sociologists disagree on why societies distribute wealth, power, and prestige unequally. On one side are the *functional theorists,* who argue that stratification is necessary and perhaps inevitable for maintaining society. On the other side are the *conflict theorists,* who argue that stratification results from the selfish interests of groups trying to preserve their advantages over others.

## FUNCTIONAL THEORY

The functional argument might be summarized as follows:

- Certain positions are more important to a society's survival than other positions and require special skills. For example, in most societies, occupations such as governor, physician, teacher, and priest are considered vital.
- Only a few persons in society have the ability (intelligence, energy, personality) to perform well in these positions.

**functional theory**
inequality is necessary to get people to work harder in more demanding jobs that require longer training and greater skills

- These positions require persons who do have ability to undergo extensive training and education before they occupy these positions.
- In order to motivate able people to endure the training and to sacrifice their time and energy for education, society must provide them with additional rewards.
- The result is social inequality, with some classes of people receiving more rewards than others. Inequality is inevitable and essential in order to "insure that the most important positions are conscientiously filled by the most qualified persons."[5]

In other words, an expectation of inequality is essential in getting people to work harder in more difficult jobs that require longer training and greater skill.

## CONFLICT THEORY

**conflict theory**
inequality is imposed on society by those who want to retain their wealth and power

In contrast, *conflict theory* focuses on the struggle among competing groups in society over scarce resources. Conflict theorists have argued as follows:

- People who possess property, income, power, or prestige—the upper classes—simply wish to protect their position in society. Thus, the stratification system is perpetuated.
- There are many "functionally important" positions in society that are not highly rewarded. It might be argued that an electrician, an auto mechanic, or a plumber is just as important to the survival of society as is a doctor or a lawyer.
- Many persons in the lower classes have the ability to perform in high-status occupations, but because of unequal educational opportunities they never get the chance to do so.
- Wealth is not the only way of motivating people. Conceivably, societies might reward people merely by recognizing their services. Cooperation could then replace competition as a motivating force.
- Stratification negatively affects the thinking of members of the lower class. Stratification may even be "dysfunctional" to society if it fosters feelings of suspicion, hostility, and disloyalty to society among those in the lower classes.

In short, the stratification system is imposed on society by those at the top. It allows them to use their power and prestige to keep what they have. Later in this chapter we will examine the ideas of Karl Marx, who argued that the struggle between classes was the driving force in history and politics.

## INEQUALITY IN AMERICA

Income is a key component of stratification, and income is unequally distributed in all societies. As long as societies reward skills, talents, knowledge, hard work, innovation, initiative, and risk taking, there will be inequalities of income. But the question remains how much inequality is required to provide adequate rewards and incentives for education, training, work, enterprise, and risk.

## Income Distributions

Let us try to systematically examine income inequality in America. Table 4-4 divides all American families into five groups—from the lowest one-fifth in personal income to the highest one-fifth—and shows the percentage of total family personal income received by each group over the years. (If perfect income equality existed, each fifth would receive 20 percent of all family personal income, and it would not even be possible to rank fifths from highest to lowest.) The poorest one-fifth received 3.5 percent of all family personal income in 1929; in 1995, this group received 4.2 percent of all family personal income. (Most of the increase occurred during World War II.) The highest one-fifth received 54.4 percent of all family personal income in 1929; in 1995 this percentage was 46.9.

**measuring inequality**
percentage of total national income received by each fifth of income earners

## Rising Income Inequality

Note, however, an *increase* in inequality in the United States since 1970. Social scientists and policy makers have voiced concern over this reversal of the historical trend toward greater income equality. This recent increase in inequality appears to be a product of several social and economic trends: (1) the relative decline of the manufacturing sector of the economy, with its middle-income blue-collar jobs, and the ascendancy of the information and service sectors, with a combination of high-paying and low-paying jobs; (2) an increase in the number of two-wage families, making single-wage households

### TABLE 4-4

Percentage Distribution of Family Personal Income, by Quintiles, and Top 5 Percent of Consumer Units in Selected Years, 1929–1995

| Quintiles | 1929 | 1950 | 1960 | 1970 | 1980 | 1990 | 1995 |
|---|---|---|---|---|---|---|---|
| Lowest | 3.5 | 4.5 | 4.8 | 5.4 | 5.2 | 4.5 | 4.2 |
| Second | 9.0 | 12.0 | 12.2 | 12.2 | 11.6 | 10.7 | 10.0 |
| Third | 13.8 | 17.4 | 17.8 | 17.6 | 17.5 | 16.6 | 15.7 |
| Fourth | 19.3 | 23.4 | 24.0 | 23.9 | 24.1 | 24.1 | 23.3 |
| Highest | 54.4 | 42.7 | 41.2 | 40.9 | 41.5 | 44.2 | 46.9 |
| Top 5 percent ratio | 30.0 | 17.3 | 15.9 | 15.6 | 15.6 | 17.1 | 20.1 |

SOURCE: U.S. Bureau of the Census, *Statistical Abstract of the United States 1996*, p. 467.

**FIGURE 4-2**

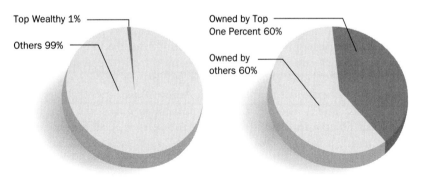

DISTRIBUTION OF FAMILY WEALTH

**Total Family Wealth**

Top Wealthy 1%

Others 99%

Owned by Top
One Percent 60%

Owned by
others 60%

SOURCE: U.S. Bureau of the Census, *Statistical Abstract of the United States 1996*, p. 478.

relatively less affluent; and (3) demographic trends that include larger proportions of aged and larger proportions of female-headed families; and (4) global competition, which lowers wages in unskilled and semiskilled jobs while rewarding people in high-technology, high-productivity occupations.

## INEQUALITY OF WEALTH

Inequalities of wealth in the United States are even greater than inequalities of income. *Wealth* is the total value of a family's assets—bank accounts, stocks, bonds, mutual funds, business equity, houses, cars, and major appliances—minus outstanding debts, such as credit card balances, mortgages, and other loans. Americans enjoy about $23 *trillion* in net worth.[6] About $6 trillion of this wealth is in land, homes, and durable goods; about $17 trillion is in financial assets. The top 1 percent of families in the United States own almost 40 percent of all family wealth (see Figure 4-2). Inequality of wealth appeared to be diminishing until the mid-1970s, but in recent years it has surged sharply. Not surprisingly, age is the key determinant of family wealth; persons age fifty to sixty-five are by far the wealthiest, with persons over sixty-five close behind; young families generally have less than one-third of the assets of older retirees.

## EQUALITY OF OPPORTUNITY

**equality of opportunity**
equal chances for success based on ability, work, initiative, and luck

But most Americans are concerned more with equality of opportunity than with equality of results. (See the Cross-National Perspective, "Beliefs About Equality and Opportunity.") *Equality of opportunity* refers to the ability to

American social culture emphasizes equality of opportunity over equality of results. The western European democracies also foster a belief in equality of opportunity but are much more inclined toward *equality of results*—reducing income differences between people—than Americans. Americans generally believe that government should provide a *floor*, or safety net, to protect people against true hardship; but they are generally unwilling to place a *ceiling* on incomes, or to give government the power to equalize income differences among people. Europeans are more likely than Americans to perceive obstacles to equality of opportunity in their countries. Thus, for example, Europeans are more likely than Americans to think that "coming from a wealthy family" or "having political connections" is very important for getting ahead in life. The following three questions demonstrate the various cross-national beliefs about equality and opportunity:

1. "It is the government's responsibility to reduce income differences between people."

| | Percent agree |
|---|---|
| Italy | 81 |
| Hungary | 77 |
| Netherlands | 64 |
| Great Britain | 62 |
| Germany | 56 |
| Australia | 42 |
| United States | 29 |

2. "Differences in income in my country are too large."

| | Percent strongly agree |
|---|---|
| Austria | 47 |
| Italy | 44 |
| Hungary | 41 |
| Great Britain | 27 |
| Germany | 25 |
| Netherlands | 19 |
| Switzerland | 19 |
| Australia | 14 |
| United States | 12 |

**CROSS-NATIONAL PERSPECTIVE**
Beliefs About Equality and Opportunity

3. "For getting ahead in life, how important is . . ."

| | "coming from a wealthy family?" Percent very important | "having political connections?" Percent very important |
|---|---|---|
| Italy | 40 | 55 |
| Hungary | 34 | 30 |
| Austria | 30 | 43 |
| Germany | 25 | 23 |
| Great Britain | 22 | 7 |
| Australia | 18 | 15 |
| Switzerland | 15 | 25 |
| United States | 14 | 9 |
| Netherlands | 11 | 7 |

SOURCES: Question 1: Gallup International Research Institute as reported in *U.S. News & World Report*, August 7, 1989, p. 25. Questions 2 and 3: International Social Survey Program, 1987, as reported in Rodney Stark, *Sociology*, 5th ed. (Belmont, Calif.: Wadsworth, 1994), p. 273.

make of oneself what one can, to develop talents and abilities, and to be rewarded for work, initiative, and achievement. Equality of opportunity means that everyone comes to the same starting line in life with the same chance of success, that whatever differences develop over time do so as a result of abilities, talents, initiative, hard work, and perhaps good luck. Americans do not generally resent the fact that physicians, engineers, airline pilots, or others who have spent time and energy acquiring particular skills make more money than those whose jobs require fewer skills and less training. Nor do most Americans resent the fact that people who risk their own time and money to build a business, bring new or better products to market, and create jobs for others make more money than their employees. Nor do many Americans begrudge multimillion-dollar incomes to sports figures, rock singers, or movie stars, whose talents entertain the public. Indeed, few Americans object when someone wins a million-dollar lottery, as long as everyone had an equal chance at winning.

## EQUALITY OF RESULTS

**equality of results**
equal incomes regardless of ability, work, or initiative

*Equality of results* refers to the equal sharing of income and material rewards regardless of one's condition in life. Equality of results means that everyone starts *and finishes* the race together, regardless of ability, talent, initiative, or work. Most Americans support a "floor" on income and material well-being—a level below which no one, regardless of their condition, should be permitted to fall. But very few Americans want to place a "ceiling" on income or wealth. This unwillingness to limit top income extends to nearly all groups in America, the poor as well as the rich.[7] Generally Americans want people who cannot provide for themselves to be well cared for, especially children, the elderly, the ill, and the disabled. However, most Americans believe that a "fair" economic system rewards people for ability and hard work.

# SOCIAL MOBILITY: THE UPS AND DOWNS

**social mobility**
the movement of people upward or downward in social class

Although all societies are stratified, societies differ greatly in social mobility—that is, in the opportunity people have to move from one class to another. The *social mobility* of individuals may be *upward,* when they achieve a status higher than that of their parents, or *downward,* when their status is lower. In the United States, there is a great deal of social mobility, both upward and downward.

The United States describes itself as the land of opportunity. The really important political question may be how much real opportunity exists for individual Americans to improve their conditions in life relative to others. The impression given by Table 4-5 is one of a static distribution system, with families permanently placed in upper or lower fifths of income earners. But there is considerable evidence of both upward and downward movement by people among income groups. Children do not always end up in the same

**TABLE 4-5**

### INCOME MOBILITY IN AMERICA

| Parents' family income quintile | Young adults' income quintile | | | | | |
|---|---|---|---|---|---|---|
| | Highest | Second | Third | Fourth | Lowest | Total |
| Highest | 36 | 23 | 19 | 13 | 9 | 100% |
| Second | 25 | 26 | 22 | 17 | 10 | 100% |
| Third | 17 | 26 | 23 | 23 | 11 | 100% |
| Fourth | 15 | 19 | 19 | 24 | 23 | 100% |
| Lowest | 2 | 9 | 18 | 27 | 44 | 100% |

NOTE: The table shows the percentage of young adults, whose parents' income was in various quintiles, who ended up in various income quintiles themselves. Thus, for example, only 36 percent of the children of highest income parents ended up in the highest income quintile themselves. A few (9 percent) ended up in the lowest quintile. Among offspring of lowest-income quintile families, 44 percent ended up in the lowest quintile themselves, but over half moved up to higher income quintiles, including a few (2 percent) who rose to the highest quintile.

SOURCE: Data derived from the Panel Study on Income Dynamics. See Martha S. Hill et al., "Final Report of the Project: Motivation and Economic Mobility of the Poor" (Ann Arbor: Survey Research Center, 1983).

income category as their parents. Indeed, one study reports that only about 36 percent of the offspring of highest-income category families end up in that same category themselves (see Table 4-5). Others fall to lower categories. Among the offspring of lowest-income category families, only 44 percent end up in the lowest category themselves. Over half climb to higher categories.

Overall, there has been more upward mobility than downward mobility over the years. This upward movement is made possible by economic growth. However, the rate of upward mobility appears to be slowing down. This trend may reflect slower rates of economic growth in the 1990s and loss of jobs in industry and technology to foreign competition.

## CLASS AS A DETERMINANT OF LIFESTYLE

Life in each social class is different. Differences in ways of life mean differences in culture, or rather (because the style of life in each class is really a variant of one common culture in American society) a division of the culture into *subcultures*. Class subcultures have been described by many sociologists. Class differences exist in almost every aspect of life: health, hygiene, vocabulary, table manners, standards of right and wrong, recreation and entertainment, religion, sexual activity, family and child-rearing practices, political beliefs and attitudes, club memberships, dress, birthrates, attitudes toward education, toilet training, reading habits, and so on (see Table 4-6). It is impossible to provide a complete description of all the class differences that have been reported by sociologists. Moreover, class lifestyles overlap, and

## CONTROVERSIES IN SOCIAL SCIENCE
### *The Bell Curve*

Two social scientists generated intense controversy following publication of their book *The Bell Curve: Intelligence and Class Structure in American Life* in 1994. Richard Herrnstein and Charles Murray set forth the argument that general intelligence largely determines success in life. General intelligence, they contend, is distributed among the population in a bell-shaped curve, with most people clustered around the median, a smaller "cognitive elite" with higher intelligence occupying one end, and an unfortunate few trailing behind (see Figure 4-3). Over time intelligence is becoming even more necessary for the performance of key jobs in the "information society." The result will be the continuing enhancement of the power and wealth of the cognitive elite and the further erosion of the lifestyle of the less intelligent.

Even more controversial is Herrnstein and Murray's contention that general intelligence is mostly (60 percent) genetic. And since intelligence is mostly inherited, they argue that programs to assist the underprivileged have few practical effects.

The cognitive elite, they predict, will continue to distance themselves from the masses in knowledge, skills, technical

| Cognitive Class | High School Dropout % | Women on Welfare Assistance % | Mean Age at First Childbearing | Criminal Convictions % (Young white males) |
|---|---|---|---|---|
| I    Very Bright | 0 | 0 | 27.2 | 3 |
| II   Bright | 0 | 2 | 25.5 | 7 |
| III  Normal | 6 | 8 | 23.4 | 15 |
| IV   Dull | 35 | 17 | 21.0 | 21 |
| V    Very Dull | 55 | 31 | 19.8 | 14 |

SOURCE: Adapted from various chapters in Herrnstein and Murray, *The Bell Curve* (New York: Free Press, 1994).

in America there are no rigid boundaries between classes. Class subcultures should be thought of as being on a *continuous scale* with styles of life that blend; thus there are many "in-between" positions. And finally, it should be remembered that any generalizations about broad classes in the United States do not necessarily describe the lifestyle of any particular individuals; the following paragraphs are merely a general summary of the subcultures.

## THE UPPER CLASS

The typical upper-class individual is future-oriented and cosmopolitan. Persons of this class expect a long life, look forward to their future and the future of their children and grandchildren, and are concerned about competence, income, and power, while social problems will be concentrated among the "dullest." Indeed, the authors amass statistics showing that educational deficiencies, emotional problems, welfare reliance, early childbirth, and even criminal behavior are disproportionately concentrated in low-intelligence groups.

But critics of *The Bell Curve* point out that there is no consensus on the role of genetics in intelligence. Indeed, recent research on infant development indicates that brain activity and the interconnections among brain cells are greatly impacted by early human interaction. Infants who are frequently coddled, spoken to,

sung to, etc., exhibit more brain activity on PET scans than those with little environmental stimuli (see Chapter 5). Moreover, the implication of *The Bell Curve* thesis is that social classes and elitism are both natural and evitable, and that most efforts to ensure equality of opportunity are useless. This thesis might be seen as a justification for widening inequality in society. Finally, *The Bell Curve's* authors' add a racial dimension to their discussion that is unnecessary to their thesis. They contend that African Americans on average score fifteen IQ points below whites and that Asians on average score three points above. While they claim that these average racial scores should not matter if every individual were judged separately on IQ, clearly their argument reinforces racial stereotypes.

**FIGURE 4-3**

POPULATION DISTRIBUTION OF IQ SCORES

what lies ahead for the community, the nation, and humanity. They are self-confident, believing that within limits they can shape their own destiny and that of the community. They are willing to invest in the future—that is, to sacrifice some present satisfaction in the expectation of enjoying greater satisfaction in time to come. They are self-respecting; they place great value on independence and creativity and on developing their potential to the fullest. In rearing their children, they teach them to be guided by abstract standards of social justice rather than by conformity to a given code. Women enjoy nearly equal status with men in family relationships. The goals of life include individuality, self-expression, and personal happiness. Wealth permits a wide variety of entertainment and recreation: theater, concerts, art, yachting, tennis, skiing, travel abroad, and so on.

**TABLE 4-6**

## SOCIAL CLASS LIFESTYLES

| | Approximate Percentage of Population | Representative Occupations | Likely Education | Leisure Activities | News Sources |
|---|---|---|---|---|---|
| Upper Class | 7 | Banker<br>Corporate executive<br>Physician<br>Architect | Advanced degree (M.B.A., M.D.)<br>Elite schools | Theater, travel, tennis, yachting, sailing, charity celebrity events | *Wall Street Journal, New York Times, New Yorker Magazine*, PBS |
| Middle Class | 38 | Small business owner<br>Lawyer<br>Professor<br>Teacher<br>Accountant<br>Corporation middle manager | B.A. degree and some professional degrees (M.A., Ph.D., L.L.B.)<br>State universities | Golfing, travel, parties, watching TV, sports, church events | *Time, Newsweek, U.S. News & World Report*, Local paper, TV |
| Working Class | 40 | Electrician<br>Machinist<br>Police officer<br>Secretary<br>Cashier<br>Bartender | High school, some college including A.A. degree<br>Community college, vo-tech schools | Bowling, movies, visiting friends, watching TV, sports, church | *National Enquirer*, Local paper, TV |
| Lower Class | 15 | Unskilled, minimum-wage workers, or unemployed and welfare | High school dropout | Watching television | TV or none |

Upper-class individuals take a tolerant attitude toward unconventional behavior in sex, the arts, fashions, lifestyles, and so forth. They deplore bigotry and abhor violence. They feel they have a responsibility to "serve" the community and to "do good." They are active in "public service" and contribute time, money, and effort to worthy causes. They have an attachment to the community, the nation, and the world, and they believe they can help shape the future. This "public-regardingness" inclines them toward "liberal" politics; the upper classes provide the leadership for the liberal wings of both the Republican and Democratic parties.

## THE MIDDLE CLASS

Middle-class individuals are also future-oriented; they plan ahead for themselves and their children. But they are not likely to be as cosmopolitan as the upper-class person, because they are more concerned with their immediate families than with "humanity" in the abstract. They are confident about their ability to influence their own futures and those of their children, but they do not really expect to have an effect on community, state, or national events.

*Wealth permits a wide variety of entertainment and recreation, including theater, concerts, and opera.*

Wayne Eastep/Tony Stone Images

The middle-class individual is perhaps even more self-disciplined and willing to sacrifice present gratification for future advantage than the upper-class individual. Investing time, energy, and effort in self-improvement and getting ahead are principal themes of life. Middle-class people strongly want their children to go to college and acquire the kind of formal training that will help them get ahead.

Middle-class women enjoy greater equality in the family than working-class women, and they have fewer children (though home activities are frequently child-centered). Recreation and entertainment include golf, swimming, movies, sports events, and travel in the United States. In general, the middle-class person is less able than the upper-class one to afford an interest in theater, art, symphonies, or travel abroad.

Middle-class individuals tend to be middle-of-the-road or conservative in politics, and to vote Republican. They have regard for the rights of others and generally oppose bigotry and violence. However, they do not hold those attitudes as strongly as do members of the upper class, nor do they feel as much responsibility to the community as the upper-class individual does. Though they join voluntary organizations, many of which are formally committed to community service, they are less willing to give their money and effort to public causes.

## THE WORKING CLASS

Working-class individuals do not invest heavily in the future; they are much more oriented toward the present. They expect their children to make their own way in life. They have less confidence than the middle class in their ability to shape the future and a stronger sense of being at the mercy of fate and other uncontrollable forces. They are self-respecting and self-confident, but these feelings extend over a narrower range of matters than they do in middle-class individuals. The horizon of the working class is limited by job, family, immediate friends, and neighborhood.

Working-class individuals work to maintain themselves and their families; they do not look at their jobs as a means of getting ahead and certainly not as a means of self-expression. In rearing their children, they emphasize the virtues of neatness, cleanliness, honesty, obedience, and respect for authority. They would like their children to go to college, but if they do not, it is no great matter. The working-class woman is often relegated to a subordinate role in family affairs.

The working-class individual's deepest attachment is to family. Most visiting is done with relatives rather than friends. Working-class persons usually do not belong to many organizations other than union and church. Whether Protestant or Catholic, their religious beliefs are fundamentalist in character; they believe in the literal meaning of the scriptures and respect the authority of the church. In their views toward others in the community, they are very "private-regarding"; they believe they work hard for a living and feel others should do the same. They are not interested in public service or "do-goodism"; they look down on people who accept welfare or charity unless those people are forced to do so by circumstances over which they have no control. When they vote, they generally vote Democratic, but they are often apathetic about politics. The working-class position in politics is motivated not by political ideology but by ethnic and party loyalties, by the appeal of personalities, or by occasional favors. For recreation the working-class individual turns to bowling, stock-car racing, circuses, fairs, and carnivals.

## THE LOWER CLASS

Lower-class individuals live from day to day, rather than plan for the future. They have no confidence in their ability to influence what happens to them. Things happen *to* them; they do not *make* them happen. They do not discipline themselves to sacrifice for the future because they have no sense of future. When they work, it is often from payday to payday, and they frequently drift from one unskilled job to another, taking scant interest in the work. Their self-confidence is low, and occasionally they even suffer from feelings of self-contempt. In relations with others, they are suspicious, hostile, and aggressive. They feel little attachment to community, neighbors, and friends and resent all authority (for example, that of policemen, social workers, teachers, landlords, and employers). Lower-class individuals are nonparticipants—they belong to no voluntary organizations, attend church infrequently, have no political interests, and seldom vote. (For a look at the lower class in other countries, see Cross-National Perspective, "Global Inequalities.")

The lower-class family is frequently headed by a woman. For the male offspring of a lower-class matriarchal family, the future is often depressing, with defeat and frustration repeating themselves throughout his life. He may drop

*The working class generally finds entertainment of a different nature, such as this carnival.*

Alan Carey, The Image Works

out of school in the eighth or ninth grade because of lack of success. Without parental supervision, and having little to do, he may get into trouble with the police. The police record will further hurt his chances of getting a job. With limited job skills, little self-discipline, and low aspiration levels, the lower-class male is not likely to find a steady job that will pay enough to support a family. Yet he yearns for the material standard of living of higher classes—a car, a television set, and other conveniences. Frequently, to compensate for defeat and frustration, the lower-class male will resort to risk taking, conquest, and fighting to assert his masculinity. Entertainment may be limited to drinking and gambling. Many aspects of lower-class culture are unattractive to women. Sociologist Herbert Gans wrote: "The woman tries to develop a stable routine in the midst of poverty and deprivation; the action-seeking man upsets it."[8]

## SOCIAL CLASSES: CONFLICT AND CONCILIATION

An awareness of class membership is not the same as class consciousness. *Class consciousness* is the belief that all members of one's social class have similar economic and political interests that are adverse to the interests of other classes and ought to be promoted through common action. As we have already seen, Americans are *aware* of class membership, but members of the same class do not always share political interests, feel that collective class action is necessary, or see themselves as locked in a struggle against

**class consciousness**
believing that all members of one's class have similar political and economic interests, adverse to those of other classes

## CROSS-NATIONAL PERSPECTIVE
### Global Inequalities

Three of every four persons in the world today live in a Third World culture. The term *Third World* refers to poor, agrarian societies. *First World* refers to industrial societies with free-market economics, democratic governments, and high standards of living. These societies include the United States, western Europe, and Japan. *Second World* refers to industrial societies with government-directed socialist economies, one-party authoritarian governments, and generally lower standards of living. Until recently these societies included the states of the former Soviet Union and all of eastern Europe. (See Chapter 9 for an understanding of socialism as well as of changes taking place in Russia.) Traditionally, the Third World encompassed most of the globe: South and Central America; Africa; the Middle East, with the exception of Israel; and Asia, with the exception of Japan and the rapidly developing "Four Dragons"— Hong Kong, South Korea, Taiwan, and Singapore.

While these broad categories of "worlds" are commonly used by social scientists and others, it is important to remember that each category encompasses societies with different languages, diverse people, and distinct cultures. Nonetheless, there are common characteristics of Third World societies that can be observed by visitors as well as by social scientists. Americans can better appreciate their own society by knowing how the majority of the world's population lives.

### Poverty

Poverty in the Third World is widespread and severe. The vast majority of the world's population lives well below the standard of living of America's poorest families. Hunger and ill health are common. It is estimated that one out of every five persons in the world today does not eat enough to enable him or her to work; one child in four dies before reaching the age of five. Life expectancy is short (see table).

### Inequality

The limited resources of Third World societies are unequally distributed, with small elites controlling large proportions of land and wealth. In some societies a caste system determines one's social position at birth with no opportunity for upward social mobility. The subordination of women in Third World societies is very pronounced; women are commonly denied education, land ownership, and a voice in public affairs.

### Traditionalism

Third World cultures generally place great value on traditional ways of life passed down, virtually unchanged, from generation to generation. Traditionalism also means the

opposing classes. Few Americans believe in the militant ideology of class struggle. Americans do not have a strong sense of class consciousness.

Nonetheless, there is some evidence of awareness of class interest in voting behavior. Although Democratic and Republican candidates draw their support from all social classes in America, social-class bases of the Democratic and Republican parties are slightly different (see Chapter 7). Professional and managerial groups and other white-collar employees give greater acceptance of one's life and one's fate, however poor. It also means resisting innovation and change.

### High Fertility

Birthrates are generally very high in the Third World. Family reliance on human labor, high infant mortality rates, the low status of women, and the absence of birth control information or technology all contribute to high birthrates. China has attempted to force families to have only one child; sterilization and abortion are common, but so also are abortion of female fetuses only and female infanticide.

### Primitive Technology

Most energy in Third World societies is directly supplied by human and animal muscle power. A lifetime of hard manual labor, just to meet minimum needs, confronts most of the people of the world. Animal labor is more common than farm machinery.

### LIFE IN THE THIRD WORLD

| | GNP per capita (U.S. $) | Birthrate* | Life expectancy (years) | Infant mortality rate† |
|---|---|---|---|---|
| United States | 25,810 | 14.8 | 76.0 | 6.7 |
| Mexico | 3,940 | 26.2 | 73.7 | 25.0 |
| Colombia | 1,753 | 21.3 | 72.8 | 25.8 |
| Venezuela | 2,807 | 24.4 | 72.1 | 29.5 |
| Egypt | 689 | 28.2 | 61.4 | 72.8 |
| Nigeria | 421 | 42.9 | 54.3 | 72.4 |
| Zaire | 133 | 48.1 | 46.7 | 108.0 |
| Kenya | 232 | 33.4 | 55.6 | 55.3 |
| Ghana | 309 | 35.0 | 56.2 | 80.3 |
| China | 1,860 | 17.0 | 69.6 | 39.6 |
| India | 312 | 25.9 | 59.7 | 71.1 |
| Pakistan | 399 | 36.2 | 58.5 | 96.8 |
| Bangladesh | 206 | 30.5 | 55.9 | 102.3 |

*Live births per 1,000 population per year.
†Number of deaths of children under one year of age per 1,000 live births per year.

SOURCE: U.S. Bureau of the Census, *Statistical Abstract of the United States 1996* (Washington, D.C.: U.S. Government Printing Office, 1996), pp. 831–832, 835.

support to the Republican party than do skilled, semiskilled, and unskilled workers. Likewise, people with some college education tend to vote Republican more often than persons with a high school or grade school education do. Of course, not all the upper-class vote goes to the Republican party, and not all the lower-class vote goes to the Democratic party. In fact, the differences in voter support are not very great. But there is some indication that class has an impact on voting behavior.

## MASTERS OF SOCIAL THOUGHT

### Karl Marx and the Class Struggle

Conflict between social classes is a central feature of communist ideology. In the opening of his famous *Communist Manifesto*, Karl Marx wrote:

*The history of all hitherto existing society is the history of class struggles. Freeman and slave, patrician and plebeian, lord and serf, guild-master and journeyman, in a word, oppressor and oppressed, . . .* [a]

Karl Marx was born in Prussia in 1818. His parents were Jews who converted to Christianity when Marx was a child. He studied history, law, and philosophy at Bonn, Berlin, and Jena and received his doctor of philosophy degree in 1841.

Soon after, he entered revolutionary socialist politics as a journalist and pamphleteer; he was expelled from Prussia and engaged in conspiratorial activities in France and Belgium from 1843 to 1849. *The Communist Manifesto*, written with Friedrich Engels, appeared in 1848 as a revolutionary pamphlet. In 1849 Marx fled to London, where he spent the remainder of his life writing occasional pamphlets on socialism, advising socialist leaders, and setting forth his views in a lengthy work, *Das Kapital*. He lived largely on the money given him by Friedrich Engels, who was the son of a wealthy textile manufacturer.

According to Marx, social classes develop on the basis of the different positions that individuals fulfill in the prevailing "mode of production"—that is, the economy. In

an agricultural economy, the principal classes are landowner and tenant, serf, or slave; and in an industrial economy, the capitalist or "bourgeois" (owner of the factory) and the non-property-owning worker or "proletarian." The bourgeoisie have an interest in maximizing profit and seek to keep for themselves the surplus of profit that has been created by the worker. Workers are exploited in that they produce more than they receive in wages; this "surplus value" is stolen from the workers by the capitalists. In the long run bourgeois society is doomed to destruction because gradually the workers will realize they are being exploited, will become aware of their historic role, and ultimately will take over the ownership of the instruments of production in violent revolution. In Marx's opinion it

## ABSENCE OF CLASS CONFLICT

**class conflict**
conflict between upper and lower social classes over wealth and power

**factors in American life reducing class conflict**
high standard of living
upward mobility
large middle class
widespread belief in the system
many cross-cutting allegiances

Why is there no militant class consciousness or *class conflict* in America? This is a difficult question to answer precisely, but we can summarize some of the factors that appear to help stabilize the existing class system in America and reduce class conflict:

■ a relatively high standard of living of Americans of all social classes
■ a great deal of upward mobility in the American system, which diverts lower-class attention away from collective class action and focuses it toward individual efforts at "getting ahead"
■ the existence of a large middle-income, middle-prestige class
■ widespread belief in the legitimacy of the class structure and the resulting acceptance of it

was inevitable that the development of capitalism would lead eventually to the proletarian revolution.

Marx viewed class consciousness as an important prerequisite to successful proletarian revolution. Class consciousness would increase as the proletariat grew in numbers, as workers communicated among themselves and achieved solidarity in unions and political organizations, and as conflict between workers and owners intensified. The bourgeoisie would not relinquish their control over the means of production without a fight, and therefore violent revolution was necessary and inevitable. Marx said little about the details of revolution; this aspect of communist ideology was developed later by Lenin (see Chapter 9). But after the successful proletarian revolution, Marx envisioned a society without social classes. This *classless society* would be a "dictatorship of the proletariat" with all other social classes eliminated. The state would control the means of production, and everyone would be in the same relationship to the state as everyone else. Eventually, the state, which functions in bourgeois society to help the bourgeoisie oppress the masses, would gradually "wither away" in a communist society.

The truth is, of course, that neither capitalist societies nor communist societies conformed to Marx's analysis. Workers in capitalist societies did not become poorer over time but rather greatly improved their standards of living. Indeed, the masses in capitalist societies came to enjoy more material comforts than masses in communist societies. More importantly, people in capitalist societies retained individual freedom and political democracy.

In communist societies, even though the bourgeois class was eliminated at great cost in human lives, communist party rulers emerged who were more oppressive than the former bourgeoisie. Communist party officials, government bureaucrats, and military officers monopolized power, prestige, and wealth. The state did not wither away at all, but instead became all-encompassing and all-powerful.

ªKarl Marx, *The Communist Manifesto,* ed. A. J. P. Taylor (New York: Penguin, 1967), p. 79.

- many cross-cutting allegiances of individuals to churches, communities, races, unions, professional associations, voluntary organizations, and so forth, which interfere with class solidarity

In stabilizing the class system, these factors also stabilize the existing distribution of power in America.

The American system has produced a high level of material comfort for the great majority of the population. The real possibilities of acquiring greater income and prestige have reinforced efforts to strive within the system rather than to challenge it. Even individuals who realize that their own social mobility is limited can transfer their hope and ambition to their children. A large middle class, diverse in occupation and ambiguous in political orientation, helps to blur potential lines of class identification and conflict. This class stands as a symbol and an embodiment of the reality of opportunity. A widely accepted set of ideologies, beliefs, and attitudes supports the existing system. Finally, cleavages caused by religious affiliations, ethnic backgrounds, and racial categories, as well as by other types of diversity (region, skill level, occupational group), have all worked against the development of a unified class movement.

# SOCIAL CLASS AND POLITICAL POWER

**social class and legislative power**

Government leadership is recruited mainly from the upper and upper-middle social classes. Most government officials, particularly at the national level (cabinet officers, presidential advisers, congressional representatives, Supreme Court judges, and so on), are members of the well-educated, prestigiously employed, successful, and affluent classes. With few exceptions, they are the children of professionals, business owners and managers, or successful farmers and landowners. Only a small minority are the children of wage earners or salaried workers. The occupational characteristics of representatives also show that they are generally of higher social standing than their constituents; professional and business occupations dominate the halls of Congress. One reason is, of course, that congressional candidates are more likely to win the election if their occupations are socially "respectable" and provide opportunities for extensive public contacts. The lawyer, insurance agent, and real estate agent establish in their businesses the wide circle of friends necessary for political success. Another, subtler reason is that candidates and elected legislators must come from occupational groups with flexible work responsibilities. Lawyers, landowners, and business owners can adjust their work to the campaign and legislative schedules, whereas office managers cannot.

## LAWYERS IN POLITICS

The overrepresentation of lawyers as an occupational group in Congress and other public offices is particularly marked. (Lawyers constitute no more than two-tenths of 1 percent of the labor force.) Lawyers have always played a prominent role in the American political system. Twenty-five of the fifty-two signers of the Declaration of Independence and thirty-one of the fifty-five members of the Continental Congress were lawyers. The legal profession has also provided 70 percent of the presidents, vice-presidents, and cabinet officers of the United States and one-third to one-half of all U.S. senators and members of the House of Representatives (see Table 4-7). Lawyers are in a reasonably high-prestige occupation, but so are physicians, businesspeople, and scientists. Why, then, do lawyers, rather than members of those other high-prestige groups, dominate the halls of Congress?

It is sometimes argued that lawyers bring a special kind of skill to Congress. Since their occupation is the representation of clients, they make no great change in occupation when they move from representing clients in private practice to representing constituents in Congress. Also, they are trained to deal with public policy as it is reflected in the statute books, so they may

**TABLE 4-7**

OCCUPATIONS OF MEMBERS OF CONGRESS

|  | 1955 | 1965 | 1975 | 1985 | 1997 |
|---|---|---|---|---|---|
| Farm owners | 53 | 44 | 31 | 29 | 30 |
| Businessmen & Bankers | 127 | 156 | 140 | 147 | 214 |
| Educators | 47 | 68 | 64 | 37 | 87 |
| Journalists | 33 | 43 | 24 | 20 | 21 |
| Lawyers | 245 | 247 | 221 | 190 | 225 |
| Engineers | 5 | 9 | 3 | 6 | 8 |
| Physicians | 5 | 3 | 5 | 5 | 14 |

SOURCE: *Congressional Quarterly Almanac*, various years.

be reasonably familiar with public policy before entering Congress. But professional skills alone cannot explain the dominance of lawyers in public office. Another answer is that of all those in high-prestige occupations, only lawyers can really afford to neglect their careers for political activities. For the physician, the corporate businessperson, and the scientist, such slighting of their vocations is very costly. However, for the lawyer, political activity can be a positive advantage in terms of occupational advancement; free public advertising and opportunities to make contacts with potential clients are two important benefits. Yet another answer is that lawyers naturally have a monopoly on public offices in the legal and judicial system, and the office of judge or prosecuting attorney often provides a stepping-stone to higher public office, including Congress. Finally, inasmuch as the tradition of lawyers in public office is well known, many politically ambitious young people enter law school, not so much with the expectation of practicing law in the future, but rather with the notion of using their law school experience as a springboard to a career in politics.

## SOCIAL CLASS AND EXECUTIVE POWER

Power in the *executive branch,* which most analysts now see as more important than Congress in policy formulation, is also exercised by individuals from the upper and upper-middle classes. Cabinet secretaries, under-secretaries, and top civil servants tend to come from eastern Ivy League schools; most are lawyers or businesspeople at the time of their appointment; many accept lower salaries out of a sense of obligation to perform "public service"[9] (see Table 4-8).

## UPPER-CLASS RULE?

We know that political power is largely in the hands of individuals from upper social classes, but what does this really mean for the great majority of Americans? We might *infer* that people drawn from upper social classes share

**upper-class power**
modified by competition
public-regarding values
electoral accountability

## MASTERS OF SOCIAL THOUGHT
## C. Wright Mills and the Power Elite

The most popular and controversial analysis of power in the United States is *The Power Elite*, by sociologist C. Wright Mills. Since its appearance in 1956, most writers have been unable to discuss national power without reference to this important study.

According to Mills, power in the United States is concentrated at the top of the nation's corporate, governmental, and military organizations, which closely interlock to form a single structure of power: *a power elite*. Power rests in these three domains: "the corporation chieftains, the political directorate, and the warlords." Occasionally there is tension among them, but they share a broad consensus about the general direction of public policy. Other institutions (the family, churches, schools, and so forth) are subordinate to the three major institutions of power.

The power elite holds power because of its position at the top of the institutional structures of society. These people are powerful *not* because of any individual qualities—wealth, prestige, skill, or cunning—but

because of the *institutional positions* they occupy. As society has concentrated more and more power in a few giant institutions, the people in command of these institutions have acquired enormous power over all of us. As Mills put it:

*The history of modern society may readily be understood as the story of the enlargement and the centralization of the means of power—in economic, in political, and in military institutions.*[a]

Mills is aware that his description of power in the United States conflicts with the "pluralist" interpretation. But he believes that notions of powerholders who balance and compromise interests or who engage in competition between parties and groups apply to middle-level powerholders in America and not to the top power elite.

The *unity* of the top elite rests on several factors. First of all, these people are recruited from the same upper social classes; they have similar education, wealth, and upbringing. Moreover, they continue to associate with each other, reinforcing their common feelings. They belong to the same clubs, attend the same parties, meet at the same resorts, and serve on the same civic, cultural, and

philanthropic committees. Factions exist and individual ambitions clash, but their community of interest is far greater than any divisions among them. Perhaps what accounts for their consensus more than anything else is their experience in command positions in giant institutions. "As the requirements of the top places in each of the major hierarchies become similar, the types of men occupying these roles at the top—by selection and by training in the jobs—become similar."

Mills and his work are frequently cited by radical critics of American society. According to Mills, the power elite is guilty of "a higher immorality," that is, not necessarily personal corruption or even mistaken policies and deeds, but rather the moral insensitivity of institutional bureaucracy. More important, it is the failure of the power elite to be responsive and responsible to "knowledgeable publics." Mills implies that true democracy is possible only where persons in power are truly responsible to "men of Knowledge." He is not very specific about who the "men of Knowledge" are, but the reader is left with the impression that he means intellectuals like himself.

[a]C. Wright Mills, "The Structure of Power in American Society," in *Power, Politics and People: The Collected Writings of C. Wright Mills*, ed. Irving L. Horowitz (New York: Oxford University Press, 1963), p. 24.

**TABLE 4-8**

## SOCIAL BACKGROUNDS OF CABINET-LEVEL APPOINTEES IN PRESIDENTIAL ADMINISTRATIONS

|  | Truman through Carter | Reagan | Bush | Clinton |
|---|---|---|---|---|
| Education |  |  |  |  |
| Advanced degree | 69% | 68% | 80% | 89% |
| Law degree | 40 | 26 | 40 | 67 |
| Ivy League degree | 48 | 58 | 50 | 50 |
| Ph.D. | 19 | 16 | 25 | 22 |
| No college degree | 0 | 0 | 0 | 0 |
| Women | 4% | 5% | 10% | 17% |
| African Americans | 4% | 5% | 5% | 17% |

SOURCES: For Reagan, Bush, and Clinton administrations, see Thomas R. Dye, *Who's Running America? The Clinton Years*, 6th ed. (Englewood Cliffs, N.J.: Prentice-Hall, 1994); for Truman through Carter see Phillip H. Burch, Jr., *Elites in American History*, vol. 3 (New York: Holmes and Meier, 1980).

values and interests different from those of the majority of people. On the other hand, several factors may modify the impact of upper social classes in politics. First, there may be considerable conflict among members of upper social classes about the basic directions of public policy—that is, despite similarity in social backgrounds, individuals may *not* share a consensus about public affairs. Competition rather than consensus may characterize their relationships. Second, the elite may be very "public-regarding" in their exercise of power; they may take the welfare of the masses into account as an aspect of their own sense of well-being. Indeed, there is a great deal of evidence that America's upper classes are liberal and reformist and that "do-goodism" is a widespread impulse. Many public leaders from very wealthy families of the highest social status (for instance, Franklin D. Roosevelt, Adlai Stevenson, and John F. Kennedy) have championed the interests of the poor and the downtrodden. Thus, upper-class values may foster public service rather than political exploitation. Third, upper-class leaders, whatever their values, can be held accountable for their exercise of power by the majority in elections. Our system of parties and elections forces public officials to compete for mass support to acquire public office and the political power that goes with it. This competition requires them to modify their public statements and actions to fit popular preferences. Hence, in a democracy the fact that the upper social classes tend to hold public office does not necessarily mean that the masses are oppressed, exploited, or powerless.

## NOTES

1. Melvin M. Tumin, *Social Stratification: The Forms and Functions of Social Inequality* (Englewood Cliffs, N.J.: Prentice-Hall, 1985).
2. Gerhard Lenski, *Power and Privilege* (New York: Mc-Graw-Hill, 1966); Jack Roach, Llewellyn Gross, and Orville R. Gursslin, *Social Stratification in the United States* (Englewood Cliffs, N.J.: Prentice-Hall, 1969).
3. Richard Centers, *The Psychology of Social Classes* (Princeton, N.J.: Princeton University Press, 1949).
4. *The American Enterprise* (May/June 1993): 82.
5. Kingsley Davis and Wilbert Moore, "Some Principles of Stratification," *American Sociological Review* 10 (April 1945): 243.
6. U.S. Bureau of the Census, *Statistical Abstract of the United States 1996* (Washington, D.C.: U.S. Government Printing Office, 1996), p. 478.
7. See Sidney Verba and Gary R. Orren, *Equality in America* (Cambridge, Mass.: Harvard University Press, 1985).
8. Herbert Gans, *The Urban Villagers* (New York: Free Press, 1962), p. 246. See also Edward C. Banfield, *The Unheavenly City* (Boston: Little, Brown, 1968), ch. 3.
9. Thomas R. Dye, *Who's Running America? The Clinton Years* (Englewood Cliffs, N.J.: Prentice-Hall, 1994).

## ABOUT THIS CHAPTER

After traveling to the new American nation in 1835, the French social commentator Alexis de Tocqueville wrote: "When it is birth alone, independent of wealth, which classes men in society, every one knows exactly what his own position is upon the social scale; he does not seek to rise, he does not fear to sink. . . . [But in America] as the social importance of men is no longer ostensibly and permanently fixed by blood, and is infinitely varied by wealth, ranks still exist, but it is not easy clearly to distinguish at a glance those who respectively belong to them."* Thus, Tocqueville acknowledged that there were social classes in America, but unlike Europe at the time, class membership was based on wealth and achievement, not birth, and individuals could rise or fall in social position.

In this chapter we looked at how Americans "stratify" themselves into social classes, how sociologists measure

*Alexis de Tocqueville, *Democracy in America* (New York: New American Library, 1956), p. 40.

this stratification, and the relationship between social class and lifestyle and power. Now that you have read Chapter 4, you should be able to

- describe the stratification system and the methods that sociologists use to identify and measure stratification
- describe functional and conflict explanations of social classes
- define class consciousness and identify the factors that help to stabilize the existing class system in America
- discuss the basic notions set forth by Karl Marx about social classes and describe what some of the problems are in Marxist analysis
- discuss the relationships between social class and lifestyle and between social class and political power

## DISCUSSION QUESTIONS

1. Discuss the social stratification system. Include in your discussion a description of the bases used for stratification, as well as the characteristics associated with the stratification system.
2. Describe the functional and conflict theories of social class.
3. If you were studying social class, what methods might you use to identify and measure social stratification? If in the course of your study you were to ask average Americans how they see themselves in the class system, what class would they choose, and why? How might the respondents' subjective evaluations differ from the results you as a social scientist obtained? What are the objective criteria you would use to identify social class?
4. Choose two of the American social classes and contrast them according to orientation toward life, individual self-confidence, women's roles, activities and interests, and political participation and party identification.
5. Contrast class consciousness with class awareness. Discuss the factors that appear to stabilize the existing class system in the United States and reduce class conflict.
6. Distinguish between inequality and social mobility. How is inequality usually measured? How can we measure mobility?
7. Discuss Karl Marx's views of economic roles and class consciousness in the struggle for power among social classes.
8. Define the *power elite* that was identified by C. Wright Mills and describe the factors that contribute to the emergence of such an elite. What is its actual base of power, and on what factors does its unity rest? How does Mills's interpretation of power in the United States conflict with the "pluralist" interpretation?

Chapter 5

# Power
# and Personality

## PERSONALITY AND INDIVIDUAL
## RESPONSES TO POWER

Individuals react toward power and authority in characteristic ways. In many different situations their responses to power and authority are fairly predictable. Some individuals regularly seek power and authority, whereas others avoid seeking them. Some individuals are submissive to authority, whereas others are habitually rebellious. Some individuals try to conform to the expectations of other people, and others are guided by internalized standards. Some individuals feel powerless, helpless, and isolated; they believe they have little control over their own lives. Other individuals are self-assured and aggressive; they speak out at meetings, organize groups, and take over leadership positions. Some individuals are habitually suspicious of others, unwilling to compromise; they prefer simple, final, and forceful solutions to complex problems. Some individuals are assertive, strong-willed, and self-confident; others are timid, submissive, and self-conscious. There are as many different ways of responding to power as there are types of personalities.

**personality**
characteristic ways of behaving; the enduring and organized responses that individuals habitually make to particular stimuli

*Personality is all the characteristic ways of behaving that an individual exhibits; it is the enduring and organized sets of responses an individual habitually makes when subjected to particular stimuli.* By *characteristic* and *habitual* we mean that individuals tend to respond in a similar fashion to many separate situations. For example, their attitudes toward authority in general may affect their response to any number of different leaders, supervisors, directors, or other authority figures in different situations. By *enduring* we mean that these characteristic ways of behaving may operate over a long time, perhaps through youth, young adulthood, and maturity. Attitudes toward authority in the home may carry over to school, university, job, church, government, and so forth. By *organized* we mean that there are relationships between various elements of an individual's personality. A change in one element (let us say, a growing need for social approval) would bring about a change in another element (let us say, an increased willingness to conform to group norms). Thus, personality is not just a bundle of traits but an *integrated pattern of responses.*

## NATURE VERSUS NURTURE

Children often have the same personality characteristics as their parents. Is the similarity a result of what they learned in the home? Or do children inherit personality characteristics from their parents? Actually, this is not an "either-or" question: psychologists generally acknowledge that personality is shaped by *both* heredity and environment. The only question is what is the relative influence of these factors on personality.

The question of the relative influence of heredity versus environment on personality is part of a larger controversy about the influence of genetics on behavior. (We encountered this same controversy in our discussion of sociobiology in Chapter 3.) Some psychologists attribute greater influence to heredity in determining many personality characteristics by chemical and hormonal balances, the functioning of the senses (sight, hearing, smell, taste, touch), and physique. Other psychologists attribute greater influence to environment. The influence of the environment may begin even before birth, depending, for example, on whether the mother has a good diet, avoids smoking, alcohol, and drugs, is active or inactive, and is in good emotional health. Infants respond to their earliest environment and acquire characteristic ways of responding—that is, personality—very early in life.

It is very difficult to determine whether a specific personality characteristic shared by a parent and child has been genetically inherited or transferred through social interaction in the home. However, some studies of twins have suggested that heredity plays an important role in personality. Identical twins (who have the same genetic composition) score more alike on standard personality tests than fraternal twins (whose genetic composition is different).[1] Identical twins reared in separate families tend to share more personality and behavior characteristics than fraternal twins raised in the same household.

*Research on the behavior of identical twins suggests the importance of genetic influences.*

Thomas Wanstall/The Image Works

According to one study, separated identical twins shared the same smoking and eating habits and scored similarly on tests of intelligence, extroversion, and neuroticism.[2] (For more information on research in genetics, see Focus: DNA: Blueprint to Life.)

## Nurture and Human Development

The mother is the single most important influence in anyone's early environment. We cannot deprive human babies of contact with their mothers for the sake of experimentation, but psychologists have placed newborn monkeys in isolation and observed their development. The results showed abnormal and irreversible behavior: extreme fear, anxiety, avoidance of all social contact with other monkeys, and emotional and intellectual retardation.

### Newborn Instincts

Some psychologists argue that early mother-child relationships are instinctual. Newborn babies possess five instinctual responses: sucking, crying, smiling, clinging, and following. Together these responses bind the child to the mother and the mother to the child. Some psychologists contend that these inherited responses were acquired over millions of years by natural selection. There is also evidence that clinging and following are inherited responses.

## FOCUS
## DNA:
## Blueprint to Life

In recent years, scientific advances in genetics have influenced all of the social sciences. Genes are hereditary units of life. They contain DNA (deoxyribonucleic acid)—a complex code of instructions to cells of plants, animals, and humans that determines the cells' structure, appearance, and function. Each gene has a DNA of slightly different chemical components that determine the inheritance of specific tracts. (In 1953 geneticists James Watson and Francis Crick discovered the double helix structure of DNA that resembles a spiral staircase. See Figure 5-1.) Every living organism has different kinds and numbers of genes, ranging from a small number for simple forms of life, to a very large number for complex organisms such as humans. Genes with their DNA codes determine everything from the color of eyes, hair, and skin, to the number of arms and legs and whether the organism will have a tail or not.

The *Human Genome Project,* begun in 1973, is attempting to identify all of the fifty thousand to one hundred thousand human genes, to develop a complete genetic map of human beings—a "genome." The task is a staggering one: deciphering requires the sequencing of over three billion letters of the human genetic code. So far researchers have identified several thousand genes, including some which predispose people to such diseases as breast cancer and colon cancer.

Every human has a unique DNA code. Indeed, DNA evidence, derived from hair, skin, or bodily fluids, can be used to identify or exclude suspects in criminal cases. Genes are arranged in units called chromosomes. Humans normally have forty-six chromosomes arranged in matching pairs—twenty-three are inherited from the mother and twenty-three from the father. Human offspring appear somewhat different from either parent because of the reshuffling of inherited genes.

Normally DNA is very stable, that is, not subject to change. But occasionally a change does occur and a slightly different code of instructions is transmitted to later generations. Such permanent genetic change is known as mutation. Geneticists do not really know all of the causes of mutation but suspect that radiation, certain chemicals, and heat may contribute to its occurrence.

### Genetic Research

Genetic research has led to genetic engineering, deliberately rearranging genetic material to create new or different forms of life. Initially food grains were altered to make them grow faster and resist disease better. Some fruits have been genetically altered to keep them fresh and unspoiled long after they have been picked. Mice are often genetically altered—making them stronger, larger, more or less aggressive, and even longer lived—to observe the function of specific genes. In 1997 sheep were "cloned"—that is, offspring

Infant monkeys reared in isolation from their mothers were supplied with two surrogate mother figures. One was made of wire mesh, while the other was made of soft "cuddly" cloth. The baby monkeys chose to be near the soft surrogate, even when the wire mesh surrogate had a bottle attached to it for feeding.

were produced with the exact same genetic structure.

#### Genetic Engineering

Genetic engineering has led to speculation and debate about its future uses. Controversies have arisen regarding the ethics of engineering specific characteristics of humans. "Cloning" of humans or creating a "superrace" is well beyond the capabilities of geneticists today. But "gene splicing" to assist humans in fighting disease is a real possibility. And so is the identification of genes likely to create medical conditions. Should insurance companies be allowed to discriminate against people whose DNA indicates the likely occurrence of cancer, diabetes, anemia, or immune deficiencies?

**FIGURE 5-1**

A REPRESENTATION OF THE DOUBLE HELIX STRUCTURE OF THE DNA MOLECULE AND ITS CODE

## NURTURE AND BRAIN ACTIVITY

But newer technology, notably PET (positron-emission tomography) scanning of brain activity in infants, has provided convincing evidence of the significance of very early learning. Simple activities, like cuddling and rocking,

**DNA**
code of instructions to cells determining their structure, appearance, and function

and singing and talking to babies, stimulate electrical activity in a baby's brain and actually build neuron connections. In the first few months of life the number of these connections (synapses) increase over twentyfold from 100 billion to more than 1 trillion. An infant's earliest experiences exert a dramatic impact on the brain's growth, physically determining the number and strength of neural connections. These connections govern everything from language and music to mathematics and emotions. The brain of a baby not only grows bigger, but its actual wiring is set in place. Infants who are deprived of human interaction fail to develop as many active areas of the brain and as many neural connection as infants who experience more stimulation.

Early traumas elevate stress hormones in an infant's brain. These hormones actually reduce electrical activity. Abused children have smaller brains than normal children and fewer neural connections (see Figure 5-2). These conditions are associated with later language, cognitive, learning, and emotional problems.

**FIGURE 5-2**

## PET Scans of Healthy and Abused Brains

*Courtesy of Children's Hospital of Michigan/Detroit Medical Center*

a. *PET scan of the healthy brain of a normal child shows regions of high and low activity. Circles show temporal lobes.*

b. *This PET scan of the brain of a Romanian orphan institutionalized shortly after birth shows the effects of extreme deprivation; areas of high activity are few. Circles show temporal lobes.*

Photos courtesy of Children's Hospital of Michigan in *Newsweek*, special issue, April 1997, 30–31.

**FOCUS**
Inside the Brain

**FOCUS**
Inside the Brain

A newborn infant's brain is already wired for rudimentary behaviors—breathing, heartbeat, reflexes, crying, sucking, etc. But in higher regions of the brain, neural connections are still being created (see Figure 5-3). These connections are stimulated and reinforced by an infant's exposure to language, images, sounds, and even facial expressions. Because no two babies have the exact same experience, no two brains are wired exactly the same.

As we examine personality in this chapter, we should remember that both heredity and environment, "nature" and "nurture," play important roles in shaping human beings. We will examine some theories of personality that emphasize instincts and heredity, others that emphasize early childhood experiences, and still others that emphasize continuing growth and development over a lifetime. There is no single "right" theory of personality.

**FIGURE 5-3**

BRAIN FUNCTION IN NEWBORNS

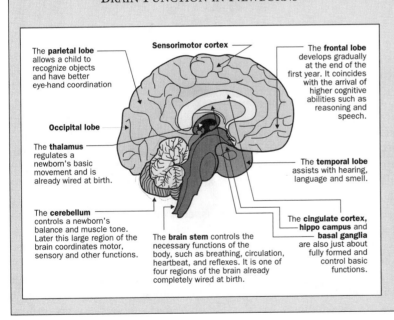

The **parietal lobe** allows a child to recognize objects and have better eye-hand coordination

**Sensorimotor cortex**

The **frontal lobe** develops gradually at the end of the first year. It coincides with the arrival of higher cognitive abilities such as reasoning and speech.

**Occipital lobe**

The **thalamus** regulates a newborn's basic movement and is already wired at birth.

The **temporal lobe** assists with hearing, language and smell.

The **cerebellum** controls a newborn's balance and muscle tone. Later this large region of the brain coordinates motor, sensory and other functions.

The **brain stem** controls the necessary functions of the body, such as breathing, circulation, heartbeat, and reflexes. It is one of four regions of the brain already completely wired at birth.

The **cingulate cortex, hippo campus** and **basal ganglia** are also just about fully formed and control basic functions.

# APPROACHES TO PSYCHOLOGY AND PERSONALITY

Psychologists differ over the precise meaning of *personality*. Definitions tend to be linked to major approaches to individual behavior and to the major approaches within psychology itself. These approaches are not necessarily exclusive; many psychologists employ more than one approach in their efforts to understand behavior (see Figure 5-4).

**FIGURE 5-4**

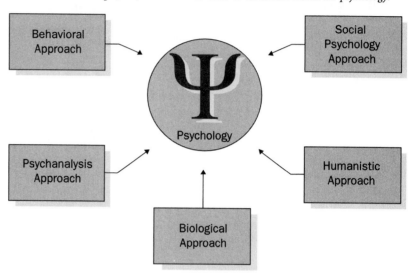

APPROACHES TO PSYCHOLOGY

The Greek letter *psi,* Ψ, is sometimes used as an abbreviation for *psychology.*

## BIOLOGICAL PSYCHOLOGY

**biological psychology**
the study of electrical and chemical events in the brain and nervous system

**neurotransmitters**
Electrical and chemical connections between brain cells

**evolutionary psychology**
the study of relationships between biological needs, genetic coding, and psychological traits of humans

*Biological psychology* attempts to relate specific behaviors to electrical and chemical events taking place within the brain and nervous system. The human brain contains well over ten *billion* nerve cells and an almost infinite number of connections between them. Electrical and chemical processes, known as *neurotransmitters,* make connections between these cells. Electrical stimulation and chemical therapies are known to change mental processes and behaviors.

Personality traits as varied as shyness, curiosity, risk-taking, and aggressiveness have been identified in genetic research. And there appear to be genetic predispositions to alcoholism, schizophrenia, depression, and other mental disorders.

A related field of *evolutionary psychology* describes relationships between biological needs, genetic coding, and psychological traits of humans. It assumes that psychological traits have evolved over millions of years through the process of natural selection, that is, the development of genetic traits that improve survival and are passed on to future generations. (See Focus: "Evolutionary Psychology: The Mating Game.")

But genes provide only a probability for a specific personality trait. A neurotransmitter must be "turned on" before genes can do their job. The effect of early childhood experiences can be profound. Genetics may increase the probability of personality traits—and even predict the likelihood of various

**FOCUS**
Evolutionary
Psychology: The
Mating Game

Understanding sexual behavior has long posed a challenge to psychologists as well as the rest of us. Why do men ogle women's breasts and evaluate women so much on their physical attractiveness? Why do women judge men more on their power, resources, and earnings potential? Why are men more likely to engage in short-term and extramarital affairs than women?

Evolutionary psychologists are proposing answers to these and similar questions about sexual behavior by reference to the mating concerns of our prehistoric ancestors. They argue that human sexual behavior, and human behavior generally, has been shaped by biological challenges confronting men and women and the evolutionary development of mental devices for coping with these challenges.

Evolutionary psychologists contend that men and women are as different psychologically as they are physically. In every culture, men consistently value youth and physical attractiveness in a mate more than women do. Women are consistently more concerned with a man's power, status, and resources. These preferences evolved from the different biological challenges facing men and women. Women invest far more time and energy in child rearing than men; human infants require years of nurturing. Over millions of years women evolved a psychology that preferred men who appeared to have the power and resources to offer protection and assistance in the tasks of child rearing. In contrast, men's reproductive success depends on the fertility of their mates. So men have developed a mindset that searches for signs of fertility—youth, large breasts, good looks. (Cultures where food is less plentiful may prefer heavier women, while more affluent cultures may prefer slimness. But in all cultures the hips should be roughly one-third larger than the waist, a ratio that suggests high fertility and good health.) Women also appreciate men's physical attractiveness because it promises good genes for their offspring. Thus men as well as women in most cultures, modern as well as ancient, "beautify" themselves. However, women must balance good looks against men's willingness and ability to provide continuing subsistence for the nest. Women must be concerned with men's commitment to a relationship long enough to nurture children.

While men have a stake in maintaining a long-term relationship with women in order to help ensure the survival of offspring, yet another strategy available to men is to impregnate as many women as possible to increase the likelihood that their genes will be continued. Thus, men, even those with long-term mates, are psychologically more disposed toward short-term anonymous affairs. Women in long-term relationships may also engage in affairs, but it is likely to be part of a search for a new, more attractive, more resourceful, or more committed mate.

Male-oriented erotica, as in pornographic videos, feature lust-driven females willing to engage in sex acts with multiple partners with no emotional attachment. Female-oriented erotica, as in romance novels, feature handsome, powerful males with fiercely passionate commitments to the heroines.

Evolutionary psychology does not offer any solution to the battle between the sexes. But it suggests that a better understanding of the contrasting psychologies of men and women might lessen the damages arising from the war.

mental illnesses. But experiences largely determine whether the wiring for these genes will be developed or not. It is very difficult to estimate what proportion of an adult's personality is determined by genes versus developed by interaction with his or her environment.

## BEHAVIORAL PSYCHOLOGY

**behavioral psychology**
the study of how people and animals learn to respond to different stimuli

*Behavioral psychology,* another major approach to psychology, is concerned with the scientific study of the behavioral responses of human beings to various stimuli. Behavioral psychology focuses on observed behavior; frequently its setting is the academic laboratory, and rats and pigeons are often subjects of experimentation. There is an emphasis on careful observation, quantitative data, and statistical methods. Behavioral psychology relies heavily on *learning theory* (stimulus-response theory), which views all behavior as a product of learning or conditioning. Behavioral patterns are learned through a process whereby a stimulus evokes a response that is either rewarded or punished, and habits are formed. The behavioral approach to personality views personality as a *pattern of learned, reinforced responses.*

## PSYCHOANALYTIC OR FREUDIAN PSYCHOLOGY

*Psychoanalytic or Freudian psychology* views behavior as a product of the interaction between biologically based instincts (for example, hunger, sex, survival, aggression) and our efforts to satisfy these instincts in socially acceptable fashions. Early childhood experiences that forbid immediate gratification of instinctual drives tend to force them into the unconscious, where they remain to affect dreams, speech, mannerisms, and to create anxieties, some of which may develop into emotional problems or mental illness.

**psychoanalysis**
insight-oriented therapy

*Psychoanalysis* is a type of insight-oriented therapy that encourages patients to think about themselves—their problems, dreams, memories—so they can gain insight into the causes of their own difficulties. Psychoanalysis encourages patients to talk about early childhood experiences and thus to reveal unconscious motivations, emotions, and conflicts. The psychoanalytic approach to personality emphasizes *childhood experiences* and *unconscious feelings* as determining factors in personality development. Although traditionally the practice of psychoanalysis has been the domain of the Freudian-trained psychiatrist, many clinical psychologists do use psychoanalytic psychology in their approach to therapy.

## SOCIAL PSYCHOLOGY

**social psychology**
the study of the individual's relationships with other individuals and groups

*Social psychology* is concerned with the individual's relationship with other individuals and groups. The social psychologist studies the whole person and the impact of the social world on the person—the world of social interaction and group life, which constantly shapes and modifies the individual's goals, perceptions, attitudes, and behavior. The social-psychological approach to personality emphasizes the individual's *socialization*—the development of individual identity through *interpersonal experiences* and the *internalizing of the expectations of significant others.*

## HUMANISTIC PSYCHOLOGY

*Humanistic psychology* focuses on human experience and human fulfillment; it emphasizes the individual's innate potential to grow and develop. According to the humanists, human beings are unique among animals because they alone have psychological as well as biological needs. The individual is internally motivated to fulfill those needs, to grow and develop and to expand the capacity for creativity. Humanistic psychology views personality development as a *continuous process of positive growth* in which the individual, having fulfilled a lower need, pursues the fulfillment of a higher one.

**humanistic psychology**
the study of human experience and human fulfillment

In the following pages we will see how each of these approaches can contribute to our understanding of personality and individual reactions to power and authority.

## THE AUTHORITARIAN PERSONALITY

*The Freudian approach to power relationships* focuses on early childhood determinations of habitual responses to power and authority. Power motives—for example, a need to dominate others or, the opposite, comfort in accepting direction—are organized into the personality early in life.

**the Freudian approach to power relationships**

An early influential study of power, authority, and personality, one that was conducted mainly within the framework of Freudian theory, was the landmark study *The Authoritarian Personality.*[3] This study was undertaken after World War II by a group of psychologists who sought to identify potentially antidemocratic individuals—those whose personality structures render them particularly susceptible to authoritarian appeals. One of the tools developed in the course of the study was the F (fascism) Scale, now widely used by social scientists to identify authoritarianism. Part of the original F Scale is reproduced in Table 5-1. Persons who agree with all or most of the items in the F Scale are said to be authoritarian.

The central attitudes of authoritarianism are *dominance* and *submission*—dominance over subordinates in any power hierarchy and submissiveness toward superiors. Authoritarians are highly ambivalent in their attitudes toward authority. They are outwardly servile toward those they perceive as their superiors, but in fact they also harbor strong negative feelings toward them. Their repressed rage toward their superiors is redirected into hostility toward the weak and inferior.

**characteristics of the authoritarian personality**
dominance and submission
orientation toward power
rigidity
exaggerated concern with strength
cynicism
ethnocentrism

Authoritarians are *oriented toward power.* They tend to think in power terms, to be acutely sensitive in any situation to questions of who dominates

### MASTERS OF SOCIAL THOUGHT
## Sigmund Freud and Psychoanalytic Theory

Viennese psychiatrist Sigmund Freud (1856–1939) was principally responsible for the development of psychoanalytic theory. He first studied hypnosis because he learned that neurotic symptoms could be removed during hypnotic trance. But he soon found that patients did not really need to be in a full hypnotic trance so long as they felt relaxed and uninhibited. He encouraged them to engage in *free association*—that is, to say anything that came into their minds without regard to organization, logic, or embarrassment over socially unacceptable ideas. He wanted to make the patient's *unconscious* motives, drives, feelings, and anxieties *conscious* ones. The goal of psychoanalysis, as it was called, was to help patients attain *insight*, or self-knowledge. Once that was achieved, the neurotic symptoms tended to disappear.

According to Freud, the personality is composed of three major systems: the *id*, the *ego*, and the *superego*. The *id* is the basic system of life instincts, or drives—hunger, thirst, sex, rest, pain avoidance, and so on. The id is in close touch with the body's needs; these needs produce psychic energy, which is experienced as uncomfortable states of tension. A newborn baby's personality is almost pure id. It seeks immediate gratification of bodily urges and has no knowledge of reality or morals. The *ego* is the part of the personality that is in contact with objective reality. It directs the energies of the id toward real-world objects that are appropriate for the satisfaction of the urge and the reduction of tension. The *superego*, the last part of the personality to develop, is the internal representative of the values, standards, and morals that the child is taught.

*Anxiety* is a state of tension that results from an apprehension of impending pain or danger, whether physical or psychological. Anxiety reduction is a drive like hunger or thirst, the difference being that it results from psychological, rather than bodily, discomfort.

whom. They are very uncomfortable when they do not know what the chain of command is. They need to know whom they should obey and who should obey them.

Authoritarians are *rigid*. They are "intolerant of ambiguity." They like order and are uncomfortable in the presence of disorder. When matters are complex, they impose their own rigid categories on them. Their thinking, therefore, is largely in stereotypes.

Authoritarians show *exaggerated concern with strength*. Feelings of personal weakness are covered with a facade of toughness. They are unusually preoccupied with masculine virtues, and they stereotype women as feminine and soft.

Authoritarians are *cynical*. They distrust the motives of others and are generally pessimistic about human nature. They are disposed to believe that the world is a jungle and that various conspiracies exist to threaten them and their ways of life.

Authoritarians are *ethnocentric*. They view members of social groups other than their own as outsiders who are different, strange, unwholesome, and

When its intensity and nature are appropriate to the real situation, the anxiety is *normal.* When there does not seem to be adequate cause for it in the real world, when it is caused by unconscious or irrational fears, and when it interferes with the person's functioning, the anxiety is *neurotic.*

The most important of the *defense mechanisms* that the body uses, often unconsciously, to reduce anxiety and tension is *repression:* the ego protects the individual from unbearable impulses by forcing them out of consciousness. This defensive maneuver may occur when an impulse would endanger life, risk punishment, or risk feelings of guilt. But there are costs to repression. A severely repressed individual who has denied many strong impulses may suffer fatigue, nervousness, or depression. Freud's seeming emphasis on sex was a product not of his belief that this drive was any more powerful than others, but of his view that it was the most repressed and therefore the source of many personality disorders.

Perhaps no other social science theory has been subjected to such searching and bitter criticism as Freudian theory. The criticism ranges from charges that Freud was a "sex maniac" (Freud was a dedicated father and husband whose marriage lasted a lifetime; Freud's daughter, Anna, became a distinguished psychoanalyst herself) to more serious scientific reservations. One criticism centers on psychoanalytic therapy: it can be long and costly, and it is not always successful. Drugs and behavioral therapy frequently produce more complete results in less time and at less expense. Another criticism is that Freud's observations were based on abnormal, clinical cases rather than on normal adults; most of his patients were middle-class Europeans; and he worked in a cultural period when sexual repression in society was much greater than it is today. Another problem with Freudian theory is that it is difficult to test scientifically. Freudian explanations proceed from observed behavior *back* to unconscious feelings and childhood experiences; but they do not permit exact predictions of future behavior from these factors.

threatening. They hold an exalted opinion of their own groups. They reject outsiders and project many of their own aggressive impulses on them. They place stereotyped labels on outsiders.

A great deal of research followed *The Authoritarian Personality* study, much of it using the F Scale to identify authoritarians and then observing related attitudes, environments, and behaviors. Some of the subsequent research on authoritarianism raised serious criticisms and reservations about the original work. First, it was observed that poorly educated persons tend to agree with F Scale statements more frequently than do well-educated persons. This finding does not necessarily mean that a lack of education causes authoritarianism, but it does suggest that differences in F Scale scores may be a product of education and *not* of personality development. Well-educated persons, whether they are authoritarian or not, simply know enough not to agree with the obviously biased statements on the F Scale.

Another problem is that the F Scale tests only for *right-wing* (fascist) authoritarianism and fails to identify *left-wing* authoritarianism. Yet there is

**criticisms of *The Authoritarian Personality***

educated persons recognize bias in the F Scale

fails to identify left-wing authoritarians

not really a complete and separate syndrome

## TABLE 5-1

### COMPONENTS OF THE F (FASCISM) SCALE WITH SAMPLE ITEMS

**Conventionalism** Rigid adherence to conventional middle-class values.
- Obedience and respect for authority are the most important virtues children should learn.
- A person who has bad manners, habits, and breeding can hardly expect to get along with decent people.

**Authoritarian submission** Submissive, uncritical attitude toward idealized moral authorities of the in-group.
- What this country needs most, more than laws and political programs, is a few courageous, tireless, devoted leaders in whom the people can put their faith.

**Authoritarian aggression** Tendency to be on the lookout for and to condemn, reject, and punish people who violate conventional values.
- What the youth needs most is strict discipline, rugged determination, and the will to work and fight for family and country.
- An insult to our honor should always be punished.

**Anti-introception** Opposition to the subjective, the imaginative, the tender-minded.
- When people have problems or worries, it is best for them not to think about it, but to keep busy with more cheerful things.
- Nowadays more and more people are prying into matters that should remain personal and private.
- If people would talk less and work more, everybody would be better off.

**Power and "toughness"** Preoccupation with the dominance–submission, strong–weak, leader–follower dimension; identification with power figures; overemphasis upon the conventionalized attributes of the ego; exaggerated assertion of strength and toughness.
- No weakness or difficulty can hold us back if we have enough willpower.
- What the youth needs most is strict discipline, rugged determination, and the will to work and fight for family and country.
- People can be divided into two distinct classes: the weak and the strong.

**Destructiveness and cynicism** Generalized hostility, vilification of the human.
- Human nature being what it is, there will always be war and conflict.
- Familiarity breeds contempt.

SOURCE: Abridgement of Table 7 (pp. 255–257), "The F (Fascism) Scale," from T. W. Adorno et al., *The Authoritarian Personality*. Copyright 1950 by The American Jewish Committee. Reprinted by permission of HarperCollins, Inc.

ample evidence of exaggerated submission to authority in revolutionary and communist movements; aggression and sadism practiced by left-wing authoritarians against the hated out-group, the "bourgeoisie"; rigidity, toughness, and an orientation toward power among revolutionaries; extreme cynicism toward society among leftists as well as conspiratorial views about politics; and rigid conformity to stereotyped Marxist ideas. Unfortunately, the F Scale equates authoritarianism with only fascist ideas. (For an interesting look at authority, see the Case Study, "Authority and Obedience: The 'Shocking' Experiments.")

Despite these reservations, *The Authoritarian Personality* provides us with valuable insights into the psychological mechanisms by which some individuals adjust themselves to power and authority.

# BEHAVIORISM AND LEARNING THEORY

Behavioral psychology is heavily indebted to learning theory or, more precisely, stimulus-response (SR) theory. It is not an overstatement to say that rats have had more to do with shaping this theory than human beings; SR theory grew out of experimental laboratory studies with animals. Academic psychology is based largely on SR theory; many college courses in psychology are oriented toward this approach. Behavioral psychology asserts that the goal of psychologists should be to study *behavior* by employing the same *scientific* tests as the natural sciences. Behavioral psychologists discount Freudian notions about the mind or the personality, which cannot be directly observed. For the behaviorists, one is what one does; personality *is* behavior, a pattern of learned, reinforced responses.

**behaviorism**
an approach to psychology that asserts that only observable behavior can be studied

## CONDITIONED RESPONSES

The founder of modern stimulus-response theory was the Russian physiologist Ivan Petrovich Pavlov (1849–1936), who had already won a Nobel Prize for his studies of digestive glands before he undertook his landmark experiments with salivating dogs. Pavlov's early experiments established the notion of *conditioning*. Saliva flows when meat is placed in a dog's mouth. If a bell is consistently sounded just a moment before the meat is placed in its mouth, the dog will soon begin to salivate merely upon hearing a bell even if the meat is not given. Dogs do not normally salivate at the sound of a bell, so such a response is a *conditioned response*. The bell and the meat have become associated in the dog's mind by their occurring together.

**Pavlov's dogs**

**conditioned response**
a behavior that is elicited by a previously neutral stimulus

The learning process is a bit more complex than it first appears. *To establish a linkage between a conditioned stimulus and response*, there must be a *drive*, a *cue*, a *response*, and *reinforcement*. Learning depends on the establishment of this SR linkage. In simple terms, in order to learn, one must want something as a result of one's action (*drive*). For example, for a rat that is placed in a box and given electric shocks through a wire grid floor, reinforcement is the relief of pain. Pain provides the *drive*, which is the first factor that must be present if learning is to occur. Hunger, thirst, or curiosity may also provide the drive to learn. In our example, the electric shocks that the rat receives are accompanied by a buzzer. The buzzer provides the *cue*, the stimulus associated with the response. The stimulus may be visual (objects, colors, lights, designs, printed words), auditory (bells, whistles, spoken words), or related to any of the other senses. Of course, for a response to be linked to a cue, a response must first occur. A critical stage in the learning process is the production of the *appropriate response*. The rat experiencing an electric shock and hearing the buzzer will make a variety of responses; eventually it may pull on the lever that turns off the current. The particular response that satisfies the drive is likely to recur the next time the same situation is encountered. Learning takes place not so much through

**conditioned SR linkage requires**
drive
cue
response
reinforcement

## CASE STUDY
Authority and
Obedience: The
"Shocking"
Experiments

A significant theme in the
study of human behavior has
been the reaction of individuals who were commanded to
inflict pain, injury, or death
upon others. An estimated six
million Jews—men, women,
and children—were murdered
in Nazi death camps in World
War II by individuals who frequently claimed they were
"only carrying out orders."

*Authority*, as we have noted,
is a form of power that is perceived as legitimate by society.
Doubtless, throughout the ages
more pain, injury, and death
have been inflicted on humanity by "authorities" than by recognized "criminals." The
criminal's claim to power is
sanctioned only by guns,
knives, fists, or fraud, not by

"legitimacy." But what are the
psychological mechanisms that
provide legitimacy to the exercise of power, and how far will
ordinary Americans go in inflicting pain, injury, or even
death if they believe they are
acting legitimately?

These are some of the questions explored by psychologist
Stanley Milgram in a series of
classic experiments in which ex-
perimenters told subjects to administer electric shocks to other
people.[a] The subjects in these
experiments were all adult
males of various ages and represented a cross section of occupations. Each subject was told
that he was participating in a
"learning experiment"; the
"learner" (actually an associate
of the experimenter) was
strapped into an "electric chair"
and given a list of questions and
answers to memorize. The subject was told by the experimenter to administer an
ever-increasing electric shock
every time the "learner" made a
mistake. Thirty separate voltage

levers were used, with signs
reading from 15 to 450 volts.
Signs also announced that the
shocks ranged from "Slight
Shock" to "Danger: Severe
Shock." Actually the "learner"
did not receive any shocks at all,
but the subject did not know
this. Moreover, the subject could
watch the "learner" through a
window and hear any sounds
the "learner" made. Starting
with 75 volts the "learner" began to twitch, grunt, and groan
with each shock. At 150 volts
the "learner" demanded that he
be let out of the experiment. At
180 volts the "learner" screamed
that he could no longer stand
the pain. At 300 volts the
"learner" slumped over, refused
to provide any more answers to
questions, and appeared in dire
distress. In response to each of
the acts by the "learner," the experimenter told the subject,
who was administering the
shocks: "You have no choice,
you must go on!"

The shocking results of Milgram's "shocking" experiments

"trial and error" as through "trial and success." The rat's first success in
pulling the lever will be an accident. After several shocking experiences, however, the rat will learn to pull the lever immediately to stop the current.

## REINFORCEMENT

**reinforcement**
repeating conditioned stimulus
and response

The key to the learning process is the *reinforcement* of the appropriate behavior. Reinforcement occurs each time the behavior is accompanied by reduction in the drive. The cue itself will eventually elicit the same response as the

| | |
|---|---|
| 150 volts | "You want me to keep going?" |
| 165 volts | "That guy is hollering in there. He's liable to have a heart attack. You want me to go on?" |
| 180 volts | "He can't stand it. I'm not going to kill that man in there! You hear him hollering. He's hollering. He can't stand it. What if something happens to him? . . . I mean who is going to take the responsibility if something happens to that gentleman?" (The experimenter says he will accept responsibility.) |
| 195 volts | "You see he's hollering. Hear that? Gee, I don't know." (The experimenter says, "The experiment requires that you go on.") |
| 210 volts | |
| 225 volts | |
| 240 volts | "Aw, no. You mean I've got to keep going up the scale? No, sir. I'm not going to kill that man! I'm not going to give him 450 volts!" (The experimenter repeats, "The experiment requires that you go on.") |
| | The subject proceeds to the highest shock level, 450 volts.[b] |

were that 62 percent of the subjects obeyed the experimenter's commands completely and proceeded to administer the highest shock level on the board (450 volts). Only 38 percent of the subjects broke off the experiment when the "learner" groaned, screamed, demanded to be released, and finally pretended to be near death.

Many subjects expressed concern about their "learner" victims and about their part in the experiments but continued the experiment anyway.

One point made in these experiments is that the subjects were not simply sadistic. They were average men selected from all walks of life. Most objected verbally to what they were doing at some point in the experiment. But in the context of *authority* (an experimenter who told them to continue no matter what happened) and *legitimacy* (the idea that they were participating in a scientific experiment at a prestigious university), these individuals performed acts of brutality that they would not otherwise consider doing.

It is not clear how far we can generalize from these experiments. But it is certainly not far-fetched to suspect that under the right conditions otherwise normal people can become unusually cruel. If those who are invested with authority and legitimacy encourage sadistic behavior toward others, we can reasonably expect that a substantial proportion of the population will engage in such behavior. Another holocaust is not impossible.

[a]Stanley Milgram, "Some Conditions of Obedience and Disobedience to Authority," *Human Relations* 18 (February 1965): 57–76.
[b]Excerpt from *Obedience to Authority*, by Stanley Milgram. Copyright © 1974 by Stanley Milgram. Reprinted by permission of HarperCollins, Inc.

original drive. Thus, the rat will pull the lever when it hears the sound of the buzzer whether it is shocked or not. In this way a previously neutral stimulus (the buzzer) becomes a *conditioned stimulus,* the rat having learned to respond to it in a particular way.

The *strength* of the SR linkage depends on (1) the strength of the original drive, (2) the closeness of the drive reduction to the response, and (3) the number of consistently reinforced trials. Thus the combination of a strong shock, the quick elimination of the shock after the rat pulls the lever, and a large number of trials makes a well-trained rat.

**strength of SR linkage depends on**
strength of drive
immediate drive reduction
number of trials

This rat's stimulus-response behavior is reinforced with food pellets.

## BEHAVIORAL THERAPY

In recent years behavioral psychologists have come out of the laboratory to engage in some types of treatment for mental disorders. Behaviorists define disorders in terms of the undesirable behaviors that are exhibited. Behavioral psychologists seldom talk about anxiety or repression; they talk in terms of *functional* (desirable) and *dysfunctional* (undesirable) behaviors. They believe neurotic behavior has been learned—generally by inconsistent use of rewards and punishment. (Hungry rats that are shocked when they pull a lever that previously produced food develop symptoms similar to nervous breakdowns!) Undesirable behaviors can be extinguished by withholding rewards or by administering punishment. Neurotic behavior can be unlearned by the same combination of principles by which it was taught. *Behavioral psychotherapy* establishes a set of conditions by which neurotic habits are unlearned and nonneurotic habits learned. The behavioral therapist is regarded as a kind of teacher and the

**behavioral therapy**
treatment based on learning or unlearning behavior

## MASTERS OF SOCIAL THOUGHT
### B. F. Skinner and the Control of Human Behavior

Power is the capacity to control human behavior. Behavioral psychologist B. F. Skinner (1904–1990) believed that society could no longer afford individual freedom and self-determination. He argued that human behavior must be controlled to ensure the survival of humanity and that *behavioral conditioning* must be employed on a massive scale to remold human beings and human culture. In the Skinnerian world, people would be conditioned to be humanitarian rather than selfish and to refrain from polluting, overpopulating, rioting, and making war. Outmoded ideas of individual freedom and self-determination would be discarded in favor of a scientifically designed culture that would condition people to be "good."

Skinner believed that the freedom and dignity of an autonomous human being are "illusions" anyhow. All behavior is determined by prior conditioning. The apparent freedom of human beings is merely inconspicuous control: a permissive government is simply relying on other sources of control—family, church, schools, values, ideologies. There is, however, ample evidence—war, crime, poverty, racism—that existing control mechanisms are inadequate for survival. Behavioral conditioning replaces imperfect and haphazard control methods with a more effective technology of behavioral control. *Brainwashing* is attacked by scholars who otherwise support changing people's minds by less obvious control mechanisms. Yet, according to Skinner, brainwashing is an effective means of accomplishing *behavioral modification*.

*A common technique is to build up a strong aversive condition, such as hunger or lack of sleep, and, by alleviating it, to reinforce any behavior which "shows a positive attitude" toward a political or religious system. A favorable "opinion" is built up simply by reinforcing favorable statements.*[a]

Skinner developed his ideas through a lifetime of laboratory research on behavioral conditioning. He was the inventor of the famous "Skinner box," a soundproof enclosure with a food dispenser that can be operated by a rat pressing a lever or a pigeon pecking at a bar. He pioneered in the development of teaching machines and programmed instruction, which employ conditioning principles by reinforcing correct answers with a printed statement that the student's response is correct.

Serious dilemmas of power are raised by Skinner's proposals. Who is to determine what is "good" and "bad" behavior? In Skinner's utopia immense power would be placed in the hands of the behavioral scientist who designs the culture. Skinner's utopia, although benevolent, is totalitarian. Can the behavioral scientist always be trusted to be "good"? How can the power entrusted in the scientist be checked if the scientist has full capacity to manipulate human behavior? Moreover, what kind of human beings would be produced under a system that manipulates behavior, choices, tastes, and desires? If we believe individual freedom and dignity are essential components of humanity, then behavioral conditioning on a massive scale is dehumanizing. Giving up freedom and dignity to achieve a secure, comfortable, unpolluted, egalitarian world may be too high a price to pay.

[a]B. F. Skinner, *Beyond Freedom and Dignity* (New York: Knopf, 1971), p. 5.

patient as a learner. Thus, the behavioral therapist may reward patients in mental hospitals for good behavior with tokens to be used to buy small luxuries. A therapist of this school believes that smokers can learn avoidance reaction by having thick, obnoxious cigarette smoke blown in their faces; or that bed wetters can unlearn their habit by sleeping on a wire blanket that produces a mild shock when it becomes wet. Even repression (viewed by the behaviorists as "learned nonthinking") can be overcome by forcing individuals to confront situations, events, or experiences they have repressed.

# SOCIAL PSYCHOLOGY—THE SELF IN RELATION TO OTHERS

**Gestalt psychology**
the study of the whole individual

Social psychology is concerned primarily with interpersonal interactions—how the individual interacts with others. The social psychologist studies the individual as a whole person interacting with the environment, rather than studying particular responses, behaviors, or reflexes. Many social psychologists are critical of the "reductionism" of behavioral psychology—the tendency to reduce individual behavior to a series of stimulus-response linkages. Social psychology is strongly influenced by early *Gestalt psychologists,* who argued that the whole person is an entity that cannot be understood by breaking it into sensory elements. (The German word *Gestalt* means "whole," "pattern," or "configuration.")

## SELF-AWARENESS

**self**
the individual's awareness of himself or herself derived from interpersonal interaction

Social psychologists view *interpersonal interaction* as the critical determinant of personality development. Indeed, an individual develops an awareness of *self* only by interaction with the environment. The newborn infant cannot distinguish its own body from the outer world. It acquires an identity—a sense of self—only by moving out into the world and relating to other people. As the infant observes and responds to its mother, the mother becomes a meaningful object, bringing pleasure, frustration, pain, and so on. The infant becomes aware of itself only in relation to others. An infant who is totally ignored withdraws to a corner of its crib, does not talk or develop in any way, and withers away physiologically and psychologically. The emergence of self-identity requires interpersonal interaction; without others there is no self.

## SOCIALIZATION

**socialization**
assuming the roles expected of us by others

The process by which an individual internalizes the values, attitudes, and judgments of others is called *socialization.* By *interacting* with others, people come to understand what is expected of them and *internalize* these expectations as

*Self-awareness develops through early interpersonal interactions.*

Elizabeth Crews/The Image Works

part of their personalities. George Herbert Mead conceived the notion of *roles* to explain how the individual internalizes the expectations of others and acquires the values of society. The essential process in the development of self is the individual's taking on the roles of others.

Through interaction with its parents, the child learns that certain sounds, such as "Mama" and "Daddy," gain favorable attention. The child begins to repeat these sounds because of the response they evoke in others and in this way begins to learn language. Children also learn that the things they do are meaningful to those around them, and thus they develop a sense of *self*. Infants who are ignored fail to develop either language or self-identity. Later the small child at play tries on a variety of *roles*—"mother," "father," "firefighter," "soldier"—and increases self-realization in the process. Even such basic social roles as male and female may be viewed as products of socialization rather than biology. Masculine and feminine traits develop through the child's internalization of the expectations of others and through role playing. Schools, games, and group activities provide more and more role-playing opportunities. Of course, not all the "others" in one's life are equally influential in shaping self-identity; each person has some *significant others* whose judgments carry more weight than the judgments of others. As socialization continues, knowledge of roles and attitudes of others becomes more generalized, and we gradually unify and consolidate the many roles we have played into a generalized self-conception. At this point the mature personality emerges.

**role playing**
developing a sense of self by trying on a variety of roles

## Personality as Interpersonal Response Traits

**interpersonal response traits**
the sum of all of an individual's socializing experience, or personality

Over time an individual acquires a distinctive pattern of *interpersonal response traits,* relatively consistent and stable dispositions to respond in a distinctive way toward others. These interpersonal response traits constitute the *personality.* They represent the sum of one's socialization, one's role experiences, and one's history of successes and failures with various interpersonal responses. Table 5-2 presents twelve interpersonal response traits.

**causes of personality disorder**
conflicting role expectations

abrupt changes in roles

inadequate socialization

desocialization: consistent defeat, frustration, and withdrawal

Many social psychologists believe that interpersonal-interaction theory provides a basis for the treatment of *personality disorders.* They define an *integrated personality* as one in which the individual plays fairly well-defined and stable roles that are not incompatible or conflicting and that are consistent with the values of the groups and culture in which the individual lives. *Personality disorganization* occurs when people find themselves in highly conflicting roles. Most people can handle mildly conflicting roles, such as being mother and office worker simultaneously; but serious role conflicts, such as an inability to assume fully either a male or a female identification,

**TABLE 5-2**

### Some Interpersonal Response Traits

**Role dispositions**

- Ascendance (*social timidity*): defends one's rights; does not mind being conspicuous; is not self-reticent; is self-assured; forcefully puts self forward
- Dominance (*submissiveness*): assertive; self-confident; power-oriented; tough; strong-willed; order-giving or directive leader
- Social initiative (*social passivity*): organizes groups; does not stay in background; makes suggestions at meetings; takes over leadership
- Independence (*dependence*): prefers to do own planning, to work things out in own way; does not seek support or advice; emotionally self-sufficient

**Sociometric dispositions**

- Acceptance of others (*rejection of others*): nonjudgmental in attitude toward others; permissive; believing and trustful; overlooks weaknesses and sees best in others
- Sociability (*unsociability*): participates in social affairs; likes to be with people; outgoing
- Friendliness (*unfriendliness*): genial, warm; open and approachable; approaches other people easily; forms many social relationships
- Sympathy (*lack of sympathy*): concerned with the feelings and wants of others; displays kindly, generous behavior; defends underdog

**Expressive dispositions**

- Competitiveness (*noncompetitiveness*): sees every relationship as a contest in which other people are rivals to be defeated; self-aggrandizing; noncooperative
- Aggressiveness (*nonaggressiveness*): attacks others directly or indirectly; shows defiant resentment of authority; quarrelsome; negativistic
- Self-consciousness (*social poise*): embarrassed when entering a room after others are seated; suffers excessively from stage fright; hesitates to volunteer in group discussions; bothered at work when people watch; feels uncomfortable if different from others
- Exhibitionism (*self-effacement*): is given to excess and ostentation in behavior and dress; seeks recognition and applause; shows off and behaves in odd ways to attract attention

*NOTE:* Opposite trait appears in parentheses.

may create deeper problems. Another source of personality disorganization may be an abrupt change in roles—caused, for example, by the loss of a job by a breadwinner, the loss of a wife or husband by a devoted spouse, even war and natural disaster. Failure to be adequately "socialized" in the first place is another recognized source of personality disorder—for example, the adult who exhibits childlike behavior, or adolescents who cannot "find themselves," that is, find mature responsible roles for themselves in society. *Desocialization* occurs when an individual, encountering consistent defeat and frustration in interpersonal situations, withdraws from contacts with others. Thus, social psychologists tend to view mental disorders in terms of people's relationships to their social environment—whether they are well adjusted and capable of functioning in a socially acceptable fashion. (See the Cross-National Perspective, "Suicide.")

# HUMANISTIC PSYCHOLOGY— THE INNATE HUMAN POTENTIAL

*Humanistic psychology,* like social psychology, focuses on the *whole* person, rather than on particular defensive structures or behavioral responses. However, while social psychology focuses on the process of socialization as the key factor in determining personality, humanistic psychology emphasizes the individual's innate potential for development, the human need for self-fulfillment.

**humanistic psychology**
a focus on individual development and self-fulfillment

Humanistic psychology represents a reaction against behaviorism and psychoanalytic theory, the two forces that dominated psychology for many years. Humanistic psychology rejects behaviorism's insistence on using the strictly scientific, objective, value-free methods of the natural sciences. It views behaviorism, with its narrow focus on behavior itself and its disregard of the subjective human experience, as unable to explain the totality of the person. Humanistic psychology also rejects the Freudian emphasis on the biological needs, or drives, of the body and on the defensive structure of the personality. For the humanists, the basic "self" is not a negative force that must be repressed or controlled; the self is good and has the innate and unique capacity to grow and to develop and expand its creativity.

**humanistic psychology as an alternative to psychoanalysis and behaviorism**

## SELF-ACTUALIZATION

According to the humanists, our needs include the need for safety and security, for friendships and intimacies, for self-esteem and self-expression. The highest psychological need is the need for *"self-actualization."* Human beings are internally motivated to fulfill these needs, to realize their potential; they have an innate propensity toward self-actualization. Personality development is the continuous process of positive growth in search of fulfilling ever-higher needs, the ultimate goal being self-actualization.

**the need to "self-actualize"**

## CROSS-NATIONAL PERSPECTIVE
### Suicide

Suicide is an individual act. At first glance, it would appear to be solely a product of internal conflicts within the individual. But the pioneering sociologist Emile Durkheim, writing a century ago, argued convincingly that social relations played a major role in the incidence of suicide. Durkheim studied records of suicide in various regions of Europe and observed that some categories of people were much more likely than others to commit suicide. Durkheim found that males, Protestants, wealthy people, and unmarried people all had higher suicide rates than females, Catholics and Jews, poor people, and married people. Durkheim theorized that differences in social integration—the strength of social attachments—explained differences in suicide rates. Lower rates were found among people who forged stronger bonds with others, and higher rates were found among people whose lifestyles were typically individualistic and autonomous. Durkheim reasoned

that because men have more autonomy in most societies than women, they are more likely to kill themselves. Because Catholic life fosters family, church, and community ties, Catholics are less likely to commit suicide than Protestants, whose doctrine emphasizes individual and autonomous life. The wealthy have more independence than the poor, who are frequently dependent on others, but the result of this independence is a higher suicide rate. Finally, Durkheim reasoned that single people's suicide rates were higher because they usually had fewer and weaker social attachments than married people.

A century later, Durkheim's general observations still hold true. In the United States, the suicide rate for white males (21.4 per 100,000 persons) is much higher than black males (12.5), and the rates for both white and black males are higher than those for white females (5.0) and black females (2.1).

Cross-national comparisons also tend to confirm Durkheim's original theory. Suicide rates are higher for men than for women in all the nations for which we have reliable data (see table). Suicide rates are generally higher in richer and predominantly Protestant nations.

### SUICIDE RATES (RATE PER 100,000 POPULATION)

|                | Male | Female |
|----------------|------|--------|
| United States  | 19.9 | 4.6    |
| Australia      | 21.0 | 5.6    |
| Austria        | 34.8 | 13.4   |
| Canada         | 20.4 | 5.3    |
| Denmark        | 32.2 | 16.3   |
| France         | 30.5 | 11.7   |
| Italy          | 11.1 | 4.4    |
| Japan          | 20.4 | 12.4   |
| Netherlands    | 13.0 | 7.5    |
| Poland         | 22.0 | 4.5    |
| Sweden         | 26.4 | 11.5   |
| United Kingdom | 12.1 | 3.7    |
| Germany        | 23.5 | 10.0   |

SOURCE: U.S. Bureau of the Census, *Statistical Abstract of the United States 1996* (Washington, D.C.: U.S. Government Printing Office, 1996), 102, 832.

**factors in personality development**

Self-actualization requires first of all that individuals be aware of their own feelings; without such self-awareness, they can never know themselves, let alone realize their innate potential. In addition, self-actualization is affected by social, or environmental, factors. Like the social psychologists, humanistic psychologists believe that an individual's concept of "self" is in large measure socially determined, that others in one's world have an important impact on the way one feels about oneself. If one is fully and unconditionally accepted as a person, then one develops positive feelings about oneself; if, on the other hand, acceptance is contingent on certain types of behavior, then one may experience anxiety and the need to function defensively, to close oneself off from feelings and a subjective experience of the world. This type of functioning interferes with the process of self-actualization.

## HIERARCHY OF NEEDS

From the point of view of humanistic psychology, the ultimate power of the individual might be regarded as the ability to achieve self-actualization. Abraham Maslow, one of the foremost spokespersons of the humanistic movement, devised a *hierarchy of needs* that distinguishes between the "higher" and "lower" needs inherent in each individual. The highest need is, of course, self-actualization. However, before one can fulfill the higher needs, one must first satisfy the lower needs. Individual behavior at any time is determined by the individual's strongest need at that time. The higher needs reflect later stages of personality development. Figure 5-5 shows Maslow's formulation of the hierarchy of needs. (Note that the peak of an earlier main class of needs must be passed before the next "higher" need can begin to assume a dominant role. Note also that as psychological development takes place, the number and variety of needs increase.)

**hierarchy of needs**
the arrangement of needs from lowest to highest in potency

**FIGURE 5-5**

MASLOW'S HIERARCHY, SHOWING PROGRESSIVE CHANGES IN NEEDS

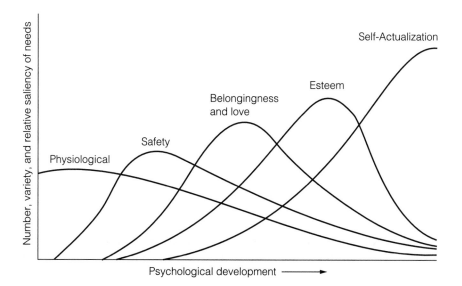

**physiological needs**
the most basic cluster of needs, including water, food, oxygen, sleep, elimination, and sex

**safety needs**
include order, security, and predictability

**belongingness and love needs**
include affiliation with others and the feeling of being loved

**esteem needs**
include status, prestige, competence, and confidence

**self-actualization**
the highest level in the hierarchy, reached only if the preceding need levels have been adequately satisfied; the self-actualizing individual operates at full capacity

At the base of Maslow's hierarchy are *physiological needs* (food, clothing, shelter). These basic needs must be satisfied first. Once they have been satisfied, other levels of needs become important and begin to motivate individual behavior. Above physiological needs are the needs for safety and security. These needs may not always be apparent to the individual; they may be subconscious and not easily identified. A need for *safety* or *security* may become highly motivating, depending on early childhood experiences. The insecure child may later prefer occupations that offer insurance, retirement, protection from layoffs, and a predictable life. In contrast, the adult who had a secure childhood may prefer occupations that offer continuing challenges to imagination and ingenuity and that penalize failure.

Once physiological and safety needs are fairly well satisfied, *social needs* become dominant. The individual, according to Maslow, now seeks group acceptance, friendships, and intimacies. Indeed, studies of group dynamics suggest that group approval may occasionally become so important that it tends to override realistic appraisal of other sources of action. The individual may actually become a victim of group pressures in his or her search to satisfy social needs and find acceptance in life.

Assuming that an individual's social needs are reasonably well satisfied, a fourth need comes into prominence: *esteem*. Failure to understand this need may lead parents to complain, "We've given our child everything—a good home, stable family, all the things he ever asked for, even our own time and assistance—yet he is still dissatisfied." However, it may be that it is precisely because such children have had the three basic needs sufficiently satisfied that a fourth need emerges—recognition of worth as an individual. Like the need for security or social needs, the need for personal esteem appears in a variety of forms; a search for *recognition* is one manifestation of the need for personal esteem. Evidence from studies of large corporate and governmental organizations suggests that recognition or symbols of prestige are often more important in motivating management employees than money. Salary carries some prestige value, but often an impressive-sounding title (for example, "vice-president for operations," "director of planning," or "deputy secretary") is even more important. Many individuals will sacrifice salary to achieve these symbols of esteem.

When the first four needs are more or less satisfied, we can expect to witness the emergence of Maslow's fifth and final need: the need for *self-actualization*. It is not always clear what self-actualization really is. According to Maslow, "Self-actualizing people are, without one single exception, involved in a cause outside of their own skin, in something outside of themselves."[4] Despite problems in defining self-actualization, it does seem true that at some point in life, frequently in the late thirties or early forties, many individuals feel a vague sense of dissatisfaction. This "mid-life crisis" may be related to the need for self-actualization. Individuals who have provided well for themselves and their families; who face no serious threats to their security; who are well accepted by their family, friends, and neighbors; and who have won recognition in their field of work may nonetheless feel that something is missing. These individuals may have been content while striving to achieve their position in life, but once they have achieved this position, they ask, "Is that all there is?" According to Maslow, these individuals have reached a point at which they must turn to their fifth and final need, self-actualization.

# Treating Mental Illness

It is not always easy to distinguish mental health from mental illness. Generally people are said to have a mental disorder when they feel distressed by their condition *and* it impairs their ability to pursue their normal functions in life. (See the Case Study, "Diagnosing Mental Illness.") Brief stresses and strains of daily living usually do not require treatment, while severe, lasting, and incapacitating mental suffering clearly does so. But most symptoms of mental illness are less than completely incapacitating. How much sadness indicates depression? How much suspicion indicates paranoia? How much self-confidence indicates mania? Most of us bear some mental stress without seeking professional help. But some people do not recognize their need for treatment even in the midst of acute mental illness.

## Clinical Psychology

*Clinical psychology* focuses on the treatment of psychological disorder. It is closely related to *psychiatry* in that both clinical psychologists and psychiatrists deal with the diagnosis and treatment of psychological disorders. (The psychiatrist, however, is also a medical doctor.) Clinicians deal with real people with real psychological problems. They enter the patient's world and concern themselves with the subjective human experience, including wishes, fears, anxieties, ambitions. Clinical psychology stresses therapy, ranging from chemical therapy and shock treatment to various behavior therapies and insight therapies.

**clinical psychology**
treatment of psychological disorder

## Professional Care

Professional assistance can be rendered by a *psychiatrist*—a medical doctor (M.D.) who specializes in the diagnosis and treatment of mental disorders; or a *clinical psychologist*—a therapist with graduate training, usually a Ph.D., in psychological testing and treatment; or a *psychological counselor*—often a person with graduate training in psychology, marriage and family life, alcohol and drug abuse treatment, social work, or related fields.

Diagnosing mental illness requires psychiatrists and psychologists to recognize a pattern of symptoms that correspond to an illness. This is often done by asking questions or giving written tests about a person's mental state. The American Psychiatric Association publishes *The Diagnostic and Statistical Manual (DSM)* that defines various mental disorders,

**psychiatrist**
an M.D. who specializes in the treatment of mental disorders

**clinical psychologist**
a therapist with a Ph.D. in psychological treatment and testing

**psychological counselor**
a therapist with graduate training in psychology or related fields

## CASE STUDY
### Diagnosing Mental Illness

The American Psychiatric Association has tried to increase public awareness of the symptoms of mental illness as well as to remove the social stigma that surrounded mental illness in the past. Mental illness is not a character weakness but a treatable illness.

### Schizophrenia

Schizophrenia is one of the most debilitating mental illnesses. Often characterized by distorted thinking, hallucinations, delusions, and a dulling of normal emotions, schizophrenia is considered a brain disease. An estimated 1.5 million Americans suffer from this mental illness.

The following symptoms are sometimes associated with schizophrenia:

- hearing nonexistent sounds
- seeing nonexistent images
- thoughts that dart uncontrollably from subject to subject
- unfounded fears that one is being plotted against or watched
- loss of self-esteem
- withdrawal from friends and family
- inappropriate reactions to situations
- deteriorating work and school performance
- neglect of social relationships and personal appearance

### Depression

The most common and treatable mental illness, depression affects eight million to fourteen million Americans each year. Characterized by feelings of sadness, helplessness, hopelessness, and irritability, depression affects one in four women and one in ten men at some point during their lifetime.

If four or more of the following symptoms persist for more than two weeks, you should seek professional help:

- change in appetite (significant weight loss or gain)
- change in sleeping patterns
- loss of interest in pleasurable activities
- loss of energy; fatigue
- feelings of worthlessness
- feelings of inappropriate guilt
- inability to concentrate; indecisiveness
- recurring thoughts of death or suicide
- melancholia (overwhelming feelings of sadness and grief)
- disturbed thinking (out of touch with reality)
- physical symptoms (headaches or stomach aches)

### Manic Depression

Manic depression (bipolar illness) is a more severe form of depression. An estimated two to three million people will

---

describing typical observable behavior and responses to examiners' questions. While the *DSM* can be very helpful, seldom do patients' symptoms and responses fit perfectly with a recognized disorder. Indeed, sometimes fully qualified professionals render very different diagnoses of the same patients.

Treatment may come in the form of psychotherapy or drug therapy or some combination of the two. *Psychotherapy,* or "talk" therapy, involves communication between patient and therapist designed to help the patient better understand and deal effectively with troubling feelings and behavior. Psychotherapy includes a wide variety of techniques—some that depend on

**psychotherapy**
"talk" therapy, involving communication between patient and therapist; includes a wide variety of techniques

suffer from this disorder at some time in their lives. People with manic depression experience mood swings from euphoria to depression.

All symptoms of depression can also be symptoms of manic depression. These are some of the typical symptoms of the manic (euphoric) phase of the disorder:

- an "on top of the world" mood that appears overly euphoric
- expressions of unwarranted optimism
- lack of judgment
- grandiose delusions of connections with God, celebrities, or political leaders
- hyperactivity and excessive participation in numerous activities
- racing, uncontrollable thoughts
- decreased need for sleep
- attention easily diverted to inconsequential or unimportant details

- sudden irritability, rage, or paranoia

### Anxiety Disorders

There are several types of anxiety disorders, each with somewhat different symptoms. Anxiety disorders are very common, affecting an estimated 10 to 15 percent of the population.

- *social phobia:* an intense fear of being scrutinized or evaluated by others
- *simple phobia:* an intense fear of a particular object or situation
- *posttraumatic stress disorder:* undesired recollections or reexperiences of a prior intense experience, often accompanied by chronic anxiety, angry outbursts, sleep disturbances, and emotional distress
- *panic disorder:* repeated bouts of intense anxiety, often causing shortness of breath, dizziness, sweating, fainting, vomiting, racing and pounding heart; not necessarily related to any particular situation
- *obsessive/compulsive disorder:* obsessions are recurrent and persistent ideas, thoughts, or images that cannot be ignored or suppressed or stopped; compulsions are repetitive and persistent behaviors usually performed in a ritualistic manner that are not connected in any reasonable fashion with subjective circumstances
- *generalized anxiety disorder:* generalized anxiety experienced for six months or longer that is not associated with life circumstances or a particular stimulus; symptoms include shakiness, restlessness, fatigue, shortness of breath, heart palpitations, sweating, dizziness, hot flashes, difficulty concentrating, irritability

SOURCE: The American Psychiatric Association.

developing the patient's understanding of deeply ingrained motives and conflicts, and others that help patients cope with their problems without necessarily exploring their underlying causes.

## PSYCHOANALYSIS

Traditional psychoanalysis is a therapy based on the Freudian notion that mental illness is most often a product of unconscious conflicts. If patients can acquire an insight into their own motives and needs, presumably they can develop more effective ways of handling their problems. When patients can freely express previously repressed emotions or relive intense emotional experiences, they are believed to be better equipped to face their current problems effectively. Sometimes insights are found in spontaneous talk or "free association," or in the interpretation of dreams, or in hypnosis. But psychoanalysis is very time-consuming and expensive. It may require weekly sessions over several years.

## BEHAVIORAL THERAPIES

Behavioral therapy assumes that disturbed behavior has been learned and that it can be unlearned or modified by new conditioning techniques. Behavioral therapists are more concerned with changing specific behavioral patterns than with understanding or analyzing a patient's personality. For example, in relaxation training, people learn to relax various muscles and eventually learn to relax their entire body. After learning to relax, they may be asked to confront a previously anxiety-producing stimulus. "Desensitization" occurs when people are able to maintain their relaxed condition while gradually encountering fears and phobias. "Assertiveness training" is another form of behavioral therapy in which people are taught to "speak up" or "say no" when others try to take advantage of them. Positive reinforcement is sometimes employed in mental hospitals when patients are rewarded for socially acceptable behavior. Negative reinforcement, or adverse conditioning, is occasionally employed in modifying alcohol and substance abuse.

## HUMANISTIC THERAPIES

Humanistic therapies tend to emphasize "client-centered" solutions to individual problems. The humanistic therapist does not try to interpret patients' behavior (as would a psychoanalyst) or modify it (as would a behavioral therapist), but rather allows patients to develop their own self-actualizing solution to their problems. The therapist does not render judgments or opinions but rather tries to create an open and tolerant atmosphere for the patient's self-expression. The goal is to enable patients to clarify their feelings.

Group therapy is a means of encouraging people to express their feelings in the presence of others with similar problems. Group therapy saves time and money because one therapist can work with six to twelve patients at once. People may derive some comfort and support from observing others with similar or perhaps even worse problems. And people may learn vicariously—by watching how others deal with their problems.

## DRUG THERAPIES

Drug therapy has had a revolutionary impact on mental health care. Beginning in the late 1950s, psychiatric drugs dramatically improved the effectiveness of treatment for a vast array of disorders. Prior to the advent of drug therapies, mental hospitals were very dismal places; physicians were able to offer little more than custodial care. Hallucinating patients talked to "voices"; catatonic patients sat in stupors; and manic patients paced the floors. The most agitated patients were sedated or placed in restraints. There were few "cures." But drug therapies changed these scenes. Currently, hospital stays are relatively brief; patients are medically and psychologically evaluated; drug therapies are initiated and are closely supervised. Patients who pose no danger to themselves or others are released.

The impact of the drug revolution is apparent in the depopulation of mental hospitals. During the first half of the century, the number of mental hospital patients rose steadily. But the introduction of drug therapies reversed this trend, and mental hospitals were emptied of all but temporary patients and a few very severe cases.

Indeed, the drug revolution was exploited as a means of reducing public spending for mental health care. Many patients are being released into the community with instructions for drug therapies and outpatient care. But they often have been unable to follow their instructions, and community care frequently has been lacking. It is estimated that one-quarter to one-third of the nation's street-wandering "homeless" population suffers from serious mental illness.

Schizophrenia, mania, and depression are the categories of mental illness that are frequently and successfully treated with drugs.[5] Four classes of drugs are commonly urged in psychiatry today: antianxiety drugs, antipsychotics, antidepressants, and mood stabilizers. These drugs frequently provide immediate and effective relief for symptoms of mental illness. Patients are medically monitored for potential unwanted side effects. But the newer drugs have proven very effective with only minimal side effects.

## POWERLESSNESS AND MENTAL HEALTH

There is a common adage that "power tends to corrupt, and absolute power corrupts absolutely." It reflects our negative view of power and our association of power with abuse. But the distinguished psychologist Rollo May, whose contributions to the humanistic movement are highly significant, contends that power is a fundamental aspect of the life process. Indeed, he believes that *powerlessness* corrupts the human personality by robbing the individual of a sense of meaning and significance.

Rollo May's argument is that power occurs in an individual's life in five functional forms.[6] The first is the *power to be*. The word *power* comes from the Latin root meaning "to be able." The newborn infant must have the power to make others respond to its needs—it cries and waves its arms violently as signs of its discomfort. An infant who cannot elicit a response from others fails to develop as a separate personality. *Power as self-affirmation* is the recognition of one's own worth and significance in life. Some power is essential for self-esteem and self-belief. *Power as self-assertion* makes it

**power is functional**

power to be

power as self-affirmation

power as self-assertion

power as aggression

power as violence

clear who we are and what we believe. It gives us the potential to react to attack and protect ourselves from becoming victims. Power also occurs in everyone's life as *aggression*—thrusting out against a person or thing seen as an adversary. The constructive aspects of aggression include cutting through barriers to initiate relationships; confronting another person, not with the intent to hurt, but in order to penetrate that individual's consciousness; and actualizing one's own self in a hostile environment. The destructive side of aggression, of course, includes thrusting out to inflict injury and taking power simply to increase one's own range of control. Finally, power occurs as *violence*. May believes that violence is an attempt to exercise power. Violence may result from a failure at self-affirmation or self-assertion, or it may accompany aggression. Nonetheless, it can be regarded as functional to the individual if there is no other way for that person to gain significance in life.

It is May's belief that modern mass society impairs the individual's self-esteem and self-worth. The feeling of personal powerlessness is widespread.

> To admit our own individual feelings of powerlessness—that we cannot influence many people; that we count for little; that the values to which our parents devoted their lives are to us insubstantial and worthless; that we feel ourselves to be "faceless others," insignificant to other people and therefore not worth much to ourselves—that is, indeed, difficult to admit.[7]

He believes that much irrational violence—riots, assassinations, senseless murders—is a product of feelings of powerlessness.

# NOTES

1. I. J. Gottesman, "Heritability of Personality," *Psychological Monographs* 77 (1963): 1–21.
2. J. Shields, *Monozygotic Twins Brought Up Apart and Brought Up Together* (London: Oxford University Press, 1962).
3. T. W. Adorno et al., *The Authoritarian Personality* (New York: Harper, 1950).
4. A. H. Maslow, *The Farther Reaches of Human Nature* (New York: Viking Press, 1971), p. 43.
5. Marvin E. Lickey and Barbara Gordon, *Medicine and Mental Illness* (New York: W. H. Freeman, 1991).
6. Rollo May, *Power and Innocence* (New York: Norton, 1972).
7. Ibid., p. 21.

# ABOUT THIS CHAPTER

An understanding of personality, of individual behavioral responses and their determinants, is essential to a full understanding of power in society. In this chapter we have explored the meaning of personality and various psychological theories regarding the determinants of personality. We also saw what various schools of psychology have to say about the relationship between personality and power. Now that you have read Chapter 5, you should be able to

- describe the "nature versus nurture" controversy in the shaping of personality
- discuss how psychoanalytic (Freudian) theory views personality and its development and how this theory interprets individual responses to power and authority

- discuss behavioral psychology's use of learning theory in its approach to the study of personality, and B. F. Skinner's ideas for the control of human behavior
- describe humanistic psychology's view of the "self," Abraham Maslow's construction of a "hierarchy of needs," and Rollo May's concept of powerlessness
- discuss how power in the form of authority and legitimacy can command obedience, and the implications of such obedience

# DISCUSSION QUESTIONS

1. Describe the "nature versus nurture" controversy over the determination of personality. How does research on the personality characteristics of identical twins help us learn more about the relative effects of heredity versus environment on human behavior?

2. Discuss the psychoanalytic (Freudian) view of the determinants of behavior. Identify the three major systems that Freudians believe compose the personality and describe the roles played by each of these systems. Differentiate between normal and neurotic anxiety and describe the functions of identification.

3. Describe the authoritarian personality. What are some psychoanalytic explanations of the authoritarian personality? Discuss the criticisms of the *Authoritarian Personality* study.

4. How would a behavioral psychologist define personality and the goal of psychology? Describe how a linkage between a conditioned stimulus and response is established.

5. Describe how a social psychologist would approach the study of personality. Identify the processes that social psychologists believe are critical determinants of personality development.

6. Discuss humanistic psychology's view of the individual, Rollo May's formulation of the functions of power, and Abraham Maslow's "hierarchy of needs."

7. Discuss the results of the experiments that psychologist Stanley Milgram carried out at Yale University. What do these results tell us about the power of authority and legitimacy to command obedience? What are the implications of such obedience?

8. If you were interested in becoming a clinical psychologist, which type of therapy do you think you would want to practice—psychoanalytic therapy, behavioral therapy, a therapy based on the principles of interpersonal-interaction theory, or one that uses the approach of humanistic psychology? Describe how the theory you would choose views "personality disorder."

9. Which of the theories studied do you think provides the most cogent view of personality and the relationship between personality and power? Discuss your reasoning, including any criticisms you may have about any of these theories.

## Chapter 6

# Power
# and the Economic Order

### POWER AND ECONOMIC ORGANIZATION

A great deal of power in the United States is centered in large economic organizations—corporations, banks, utilities, investment firms, and government agencies charged with the responsibility of overseeing the economy. Not all power, it is true, is anchored in or exercised through these institutions; power is also embodied in class, cultural, political, and ideological institutions and processes, as discussed elsewhere in this volume. *But control of economic resources provides a continuous and important base of power in any society.*

*Economics* is the study of the production and distribution of scarce goods and services. Economics decides the following questions:

**economics**
the study of the production and distribution of scarce resources

**economic decisions**
what to produce
how to produce it
for whom it will be produced

- *What should be produced?* What goods and services should be produced and in what quantities? Should we produce more automobiles or more trains and subways, more food and fertilizer or more clean air and water, more police protection or higher Social Security benefits? Should we produce more for immediate consumption, or should we save and invest more now in order to be able to enjoy even more later? Every economic system must answer questions like these.

■ *How will goods and services be produced?* The decision to produce particular goods and services does not accomplish the task. Resources must be organized and allocated, and people must be motivated to work. Various combinations of resources—land, labor, capital (factories, machinery, supplies), and technology—might be used to produce a particular item. All these resources must be organized for production, either by providing economic incentives (wages and profits) or by threats of force.

■ *For whom will goods and services be produced?* Who will consume these products and services? Economists refer to this question as the question of *distribution.* Should people be paid according to their skills, or knowledge, or contribution to the production of goods and services? Or should everyone be paid equally regardless of their skills, knowledge, or contribution to production? Should people be allowed to bid for goods and services, with the most going to the highest bidders? Or should goods and services be distributed by government, with the most going to those who are best able to influence government decisions?

In general, there are two ways of making these economic decisions: (1) individually, through the market system; or (2) collectively, through governments.

The *market* system allows individuals and firms to make their own decisions about who gets what and how. Markets implement decisions through voluntary exchange. Markets work through unregulated prices and decentralized decisions of many separate individuals and businesses.

Governments also decide who gets what and how by *collective decision making.* Governments implement decisions through coercion (fines, penalties, imprisonment) and threats of coercion. In democracies, collective decisions are influenced by individual voters, interest groups, and parties; in nondemocratic governments, the decisions are influenced primarily by ideology and the interests of government leaders themselves.

In most economies, including that of the United States, economic decisions are made by *both* the market system and the government.

**economic decision making**
markets: individually through voluntary exchange

governments: collectively through coercion

# THE MARKET SYSTEM, HARD-BOILED AND IMPERSONAL

The economic system consists of the *institutions and processes by which a society produces and distributes scarce resources.* There is not enough of everything for all of us to have all we want. If nature provided everything that everyone wanted without work, there would be no need for an economic system. But resources are "scarce," and some scheme must be created to decide who gets

**economic system**
institutions and processes by which society produces and distributes scarce resources

*Markets can be small sidewalk enterprises. Here, a fruit vendor sells grapes in Chinatown, New York City.*

J. Kramer/The Image Works

what. Scarcity, together with the problem of choice it raises, is the fundamental question of economics.

The American economic system is a market, or free enterprise, system. It is largely "unplanned"; no government bureau tells all 115 million workers in the United States where to work, what to do, or how to do it. On the whole, the private enterprise economy organizes itself, with a minimum of centralized planning or direction. The American system relies chiefly on private individuals, in search of wages and profits, to get the job done. No government agency directs that shirts be produced: if people want shirts, then there is profit to be made in producing them, and businesspeople who recognize the potential profit will begin turning them out. No government agency directs how many shirts will be produced: as shirt output increases, a point is reached at which there are so many shirts that the price that people are willing to pay falls below the cost of producing them, and businesspeople then begin curtailing their production of shirts. This same production-in-search-of-profits goes on for thousands of other products simultaneously.

**private enterprise economy**
private individuals in search of wages and profit, acting on their own, without government direction

## MARKETS

A private enterprise economy decides what is to be produced, how it is to be produced, and how it is to be distributed, all in a fashion that is for the most part impersonal. Everyone, by following self-interest, decides who gets what. The absence of planning and control does not mean chaos. Rather, it means a complex system of production and distribution that no single mind, and probably no government planning agency, could organize or control in all its infinite detail.

A *market* is any place or arrangement that enables people to exchange money for goods, services, or labor. The exchange rate is called the *price*. Under the private enterprise system, the *market determines what is to be produced, how much it will cost, and who will be able to buy it.* Consumers decide what should be produced by expressing their preferences in terms of the amount of money they spend on various goods and services (*consumer demand*). When consumers *are willing and able to pay* for something, they will bid up the *price* of that item. The price is an indication of how much of the item consumers want produced.

**market**
arrangement that enables people to exchange money for goods, services, and labor

**consumer demand**
preferences for goods and services, expressed by willingness to pay

## PROFITS

Businesses are out to make *profits*. Profits motivate producers to satisfy consumer demands. Profits drive the free enterprise system. Profits occur when selling prices are higher than the costs of production. Businesspeople move into industries in which consumers bid up prices. Where consumer demand bids up prices, businesspeople can afford to pay higher wages; and workers tend to move toward those industries with higher pay and better working conditions. Thus, consumer demand shifts both business and labor into industries in which prices are high. Businesspeople play a key role in a private enterprise system because they channel production toward industries having the strongest consumer demand and organize productive activity in the most efficient (lowest-cost) way possible. Profits are the mainspring of the market system. In seeking profits, businesspeople perform a vital economic function.

**profits**
motivate producers to satisfy consumer demand and to produce goods and services in the most efficient way possible

## PRICES

Who gets the goods that are produced? The price system allocates goods to those who have both the *willingness to pay* and the *ability to pay*. The willingness to pay determines the desirability of producing a certain item. No government agency determines whether we "need" goods and services; the market reveals whether individuals are willing to pay for them. Consumers, however, must also have the ability to pay: they must earn incomes by working to produce goods and services that consumers want. The *labor market* largely determines where people will work and how much they will be paid. The income received for their labor depends primarily on their worth to the businesses that employ them. They are worth more when they contribute more to production and profit. Where production and profits are low, wages will be low and individuals will be frequently unemployed.

The market is hard-boiled and impersonal. If a business produces too much of a particular item—more than consumers are willing to buy at a particular price—the price will have to be lowered or production (supply) will have to be cut back. Competition among businesses also checks prices, for a business that sets a price higher than that set by competitors will lose sales. Thus *consumer demand, product supply, and competition determine prices.* In the absence of interfering factors, the *price* depends on a relationship of supply

**prices**
allocate goods and services by willingness and ability to pay

determined by consumer demand, product supply, and competition and demand at any given time. If demand increases, prices tend to rise; if demand decreases, prices tend to fall. If supply increases, prices tend to fall; if supply decreases, prices tend to rise.

## THE IDEAL MARKET

The market reconciles the interests of buyers and sellers, labor and business, in the process of getting people to agree on prices. The market in a free enterprise system undertakes this reconciliation automatically, without assistance from outside individuals or forces. The ideal conditions for a market operation are these:

*ideal conditions for a market operation*

*competition among many buyers and sellers*

*ability of buyer to exclude others from benefits of purchase*

*mobility of resources and labor*

- *Competition:* The existence of a perfect competition, in which the market has so many buyers and sellers that no single trader has any control over the price of the good or service being exchanged, and the price is made by the market through the impersonal forces of supply and demand. (If one or a few sellers have control over supply, the market is said to be *monopolistic;* if one or a few buyers have control over demand, the market is said to be *monopsonistic.*)
- *Exclusion:* The ability of a buyer of the good to exclude others from the satisfactions that good provides so no one can enjoy the benefits of someone else's purchase. (When people benefit from the purchases of others, there are said to be *spillover effects,* as, for example, in the case of national defense products, which cannot be sold on the open market.)
- *Mobility:* The complete mobility of resources and labor so they can move in response to changes in prices. (In a completely mobile economy, each individual [or business] is prepared to alter the pattern of spending and working in response to changes in prices of goods and labor.)

In other words, in an ideal market there is a great deal of competition, and prices are determined solely by supply and demand. All must pay for the goods and benefits they receive, and resources and labor shift easily in response to changes in prices and wages.

## SUPPLY, DEMAND, AND THE MARKET PRICE

*an example of market pricing*

Let us illustrate what happens in a true market economy, where price is governed by supply and demand.

Along with many other commodities, millions of bushels of wheat are bought and sold every day at the Chicago Board of Trade. Let us suppose that the first buyer of the day offers $2 per bushel for wheat. Let us also suppose that there are buyers for 20 million bushels of wheat at this low price (demand). However, few owners are willing to sell at this price, and therefore there are only 10 million bushels of wheat offered at $2 per bushel (supply).

*The New York Stock Exchange is a market on a larger scale.*

Peter Menzel/Stock Boston

The result is an imbalance in supply and demand, a 10-million-bushel short-fall in supply at the low $2 price. Those still wishing to buy must therefore raise their price to attract more wheat to the market. Let us suppose that the price then shoots up to $4 per bushel. At this price there are fewer buyers (let us say only an 8-million-bushel demand) and many more sellers (let us say an 18-million-bushel supply). The result is an excess supply of 10 million bushels at the high price; this excess will eventually push prices back down.

Thus, the price tends to stabilize at a point low enough to attract suffi-cient demand for wheat but high enough to attract an equivalent supply of wheat. In our example, this price is $3 per bushel, where 14 million bushels are demanded and 14 million bushels are offered.

Figure 6-1 shows our example of supply and demand in graphic form. The supply curve is low at a low price, but it increases as the price increases. Demand is high at a low price, but it declines as the price increases. The two lines for supply and demand intersect at a price where the amount demanded just matches the amount supplied. This will tend to be the market price. In our example, it is set at $3 per bushel. Any other price will produce either an excess supply (at a higher price) or an excess demand (at a lower price).

**FIGURE 6-1**

## AN EXAMPLE OF SUPPLY AND DEMAND

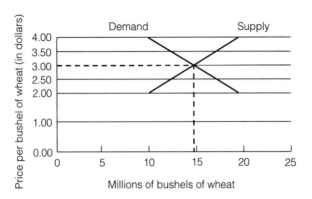

# MEASURING AMERICA'S WEALTH: NATIONAL INCOME ACCOUNTING

Underlying the power of nations is the strength of their economy—their total productive capacity. The United States can produce over $7 trillion worth of goods and services in a single year for its 250 million people. To understand America's vast wealth, we must learn how to measure it. We need to know where the wealth comes from and where it goes. The system of *national income accounts* provides these measures.

**GNP (gross national product)** total value of nation's production of goods and services for a year

Let us begin with the gross national product. *The GNP is the nation's total production of goods and services for a single year valued in terms of market prices.\** It is the sum of all the goods and services that people have been willing to pay for, from wheat production to bake sales, from machine tools to maid service, from aircraft manufacturing to bus service, from automobiles to chewing gum, from wages and salaries to interest on bank deposits.

## COMPUTING THE GNP

To compute the GNP, economists sum up all the expenditures on goods and services, plus government purchases. Care is taken to count *only the final product* sold to consumers so that raw materials will not be counted twice, that is, in the original sale to a manufacturer and in the final price of the product. Business investment includes *only new investment goods* (buildings, machinery, and so on) and does not include financial transfers such as the purchase of stocks and bonds. Government purchases for goods and services

*Increasingly economists are using a slightly different measure of national output: the gross domestic product; the GDP measures total output attributable to production located in the United States, while the GNP measures output attributable to U.S. residents.

## MASTERS OF SOCIAL THOUGHT

Adam Smith and
Laissez Faire
Economics

In the same year the Declaration of Independence was signed, Adam Smith, a Scottish professor of philosophy, published his *The Wealth of Nations* and thereby secured recognition as the founder of free enterprise economics. Today the economic model set forth by Adam Smith is frequently referred to as *classical economics* or *laissez faire economics* (from the French phrase meaning "allow to do as one pleases"). Smith wrote *The Wealth of Nations* as an attack on the *mercantilism* of nations in his day, that is, the attempt of governments to intervene in the economy with special tariffs, regulations, subsidies, and exclusive charters to businesses, all designed to maximize the accretion of gold and silver in government treasuries. Smith argued against mercantilism and for *free competition* in the marketplace. He believed that a worldwide market, *unfettered by government restrictions or subsidies,* would result in lower prices and high standards of living for all. A free market would allow the businesses and nations most capable of producing particular goods cheaply and efficiently to do so. The outcome of the specialization and efficiency created by free competition would be a high standard of living for everyone. Thus, pursuit of private profit was actually in the public interest.

Laissez faire economics is based on the idea that people are rational, that they will pursue their own economic self-interest, and that they are mobile and able to shift their resources and labor as the market demands. According to this economic system, there should be no artificial blocks to the most efficient use of people and materials. The market has a large number of competitors buying and selling products, services, and labor; and no one alone has control over supply, demand, or price. Buyers buy from producers who make the best goods at the lowest price. Thus, efficiency is rewarded and inefficiency driven out of the economy. As competition increases supply and lowers prices, some producers shift to more lucrative lines. The market continuously corrects unproductive use of resources. The system is *self-adjusting* and *self-regulating.*

Smith objected to government interference in the natural operations of the marketplace. Government should do only two things: (1) create an environment for an orderly marketplace, that is, maintain law and order, protect private property, enforce contracts, and provide a monetary system; and (2) supply those services the marketplace cannot provide, such as defense, public works, and care of widows, orphans, and other helpless people.

Today many "classical" economists echo Adam Smith's ideas. Although it is now widely recognized that government must play an important role in stabilizing the economy (avoiding both inflation and depression), protecting consumers, regulating business and labor practices, and assisting individuals who cannot care for themselves, classical economists nonetheless argue that economic planning by government is incompatible with *personal freedom.* They contend that bureaucratic intervention in the economy not only is inefficient and wasteful but also gradually erodes individual freedom and initiative.

Thus, the appeal of laissez faire economics is based not only on the efficiency of the marketplace in channeling labor and resources into their most productive uses, but also on the personal freedom this system guarantees.

include the money spent on *goods* (weapons, roads, buildings, parks, and so on), as well as the *wages* paid for the *services* of government employees. "Transfer payments" such as welfare payments, unemployment insurance, and Social Security payments are *not* part of the GNP because they are not payments for currently produced goods or services. Thus, the GNP becomes a measure of the nation's production of goods and services. It can be thought of as the total national economic pie for a given year.

## GNP AS CIRCULAR FLOW

National income accounting helps us understand the circular flow that makes up the *income* and *expenditure* sides of the GNP. Figure 6-2 shows the circular flow of goods and services. Note that the GNP is composed of consumer outlays, plus business investment, plus government purchases of goods and services.

## CURRENT DOLLARS VERSUS CONSTANT DOLLARS

Because prices have increased over time through inflation, to get a meaningful measure of actual growth and output we must view the gross national product in *constant* dollars. Doubling the GNP merely by doubling prices signifies no real gain in production, so in order to separate *real increases* in the GNP from mere *dollar increases,* we must adjust for changes in the value of the dollar over the years. Economists account for changes in the value of a dollar by establishing the value of a dollar in a particular time base (for example, 1992) and then using *constant dollars* to measure the value of goods over time. Figure 6-3 shows that the GNP has grown both in current dollars *and* in constant dollars. Thus, America's economic growth is not just a product of inflation. (See the Cross-National Perspective for a look at GNP in other countries.)

## GOVERNMENT IN A FREE MARKET ECONOMY

**reasons for government intervention**

protect property

enforce contracts

provide money

assure fair competition

set minimum wages

regulate public industries

protect consumers

provide public services

care for persons not in the marketplace

stabilize the market

The free enterprise system we have just described is subject to major modifications by the activities of government. In fact, government is now so involved in the economy that we might call the American economic system a *mixed* economy rather than a *private enterprise* economy. Government intervenes in the free market for many reasons:

- To protect private property and enforce contracts
- To provide a stable money supply
- To assure competition among businesses by breaking up monopolies and prohibiting unfair competitive practices
- To set minimum standards for wages and working conditions
- To regulate industries (like banking, communications, broadcasting, and transportation) in which there is a strong public interest

**FIGURE 6-2**

## Circular Flow of GNP

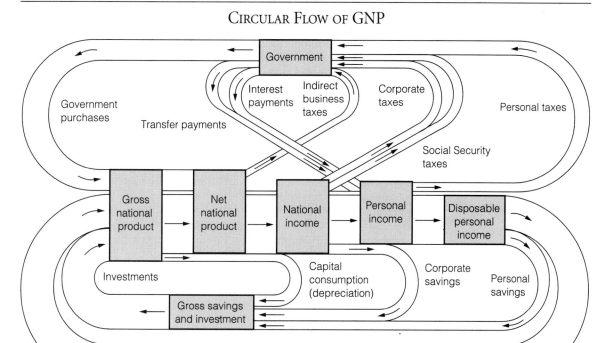

Consumer outlays

*Gross national product*
*Less* capital consumption (depreciation of capital goods that
  must be replaced) equals:
*Net national product*
*Less* indirect business taxes (sales, excise, property taxes) equals:
*National income*
*Less* corporate profit taxes,
Net interest, and
Social Security taxes,
*Plus* government transfer payments (Social Security, welfare),
Personal interest income,
Dividends, and
Business transfer payments equals:
*Personal income*
*Less* personal taxes, equals:
*Disposable personal income*
*Less personal savings* equals:
*Consumer outlays*

- To protect the consumer from phony goods and services and
  false or misleading advertising
- To provide a wide range of public services (defense, education,
  highways, police protection) that cannot be reasonably provided
  on a private-profit basis

- To provide support and care (welfare, Social Security, unemployment compensation, health care, and so forth) to individuals who cannot supply these things for themselves through the market system
- To ensure that the economic system functions properly and avoids depression, inflation, or unemployment

## CUSHIONING THE UPS AND DOWNS

Today the government of the United States is fully committed to preserving economic prosperity and using fiscal and monetary policies to try to offset the effects of inflation and recession (see the Case Study, "Achieving

**FIGURE 6-3**

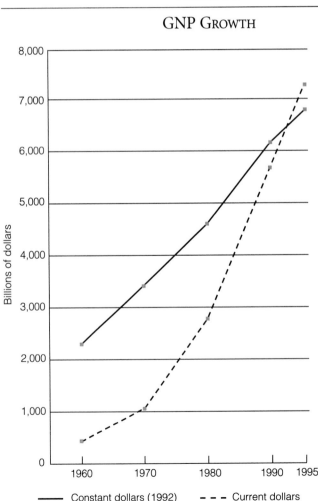

GNP GROWTH

SOURCE: Drawn from data in *Statistical Abstract of the United States 1996.*

## CROSS-NATIONAL PERSPECTIVE
GNP and Standards of Living

A nation's GNP is the most common measure of its total production of goods and services. National income accounting is highly refined in the western industrialized nations. But figures for Third World nations are often estimates by agencies of the United Nations or the United States. We can compare the relative size of national economies, as well as the distribution of some key consumer items, by observing the table.

The United States is the world's largest national economy. However, the European Economic Community, which promises to eliminate national trade barriers between the western European nations and to create a single united economy, may eventually create a larger market than the United States. Third World nations, despite accounting for three-fourths of the world's population, have very modest GNPs.

Productivity, or economic output per person, is frequently measured by GNP per person. Note that although the United States has the largest economy, productivity in several nations equals or exceeds productivity in the United States. Japan, for example, has an economy slightly over half the size of the United States; but Japan has a population of only 125 million, compared to 250 million in the United States. This means that productivity in Japan, measured by GNP per capita, is greater than in the United States.

The United States is the most consumer-oriented society in the world. Americans enjoy more consumer items—automobiles, television sets, and many other goods—than any other people. Note that the Japanese, despite their high per capita aggregate output, do not generally enjoy the same high standard of living as the average American. Many consumer items that Americans consider necessities are rarities in Third World countries. For example, although there is one automobile for every 1.8 Americans, there is only one automobile for every 1,075 Chinese.

## GNP AND STANDARDS OF LIVING IN SELECTED NATIONS

| | GNP (billions $1994) | GNP (per capita 1994) | Automobiles (persons per car) | Televisions (per 1,000 people) |
|---|---|---|---|---|
| United States | 6,727 | 25,810 | 1.8 | 816 |
| Brazil | 559 | 3,655 | 16.0 | 209 |
| Canada | 523 | 18,600 | 2.2 | 618 |
| China | 2,214 | 1,860 | 1,075.0 | 38 |
| France | 1,316 | 22,760 | 2.5 | 412 |
| Germany | 2,045 | 25,220 | 2.1 | 559 |
| India | 286 | 312 | 566.0 | 40 |
| Italy | 1,008 | 17,330 | 2.5 | 429 |
| Japan | 4,630 | 37,000 | 4.2 | 618 |
| Mexico | 363 | 3,940 | 16.0 | 150 |
| Pakistan | 51 | 399 | 404.0 | 18 |
| Philippines | 66 | 926 | 173.7 | 47 |
| Poland | 206 | 5,336 | 9.6 | 298 |
| North Korea | 21 | 906 | N.A. | N.A. |
| South Korea | 356 | 7,896 | 54.0 | 215 |
| Spain | 478 | 12,150 | 3.9 | 400 |
| United Kingdom | 1,027 | 17,670 | 2.8 | 435 |

SOURCE: *Statistical Abstract of the United States 1996*, pp. 835, 838.

**Employment Act of 1946**
pledges the federal government to use all practicable means to promote maximum employment, production, and purchasing power

**Council of Economic Advisers**
advises the president on national economic policies

Economic Stability"). The *Employment Act of 1946* specifically pledges the federal government "to promote maximum employment, production, and purchasing power."

The act created the *Council of Economic Advisers* (CEA) to "develop and recommend to the president national economic policies." The CEA is composed of three economists, appointed by the president, and a staff of analysts who collect data on the economy and advise the president on what to do to offset cycles of inflation or recession. The act also requires the president to submit to Congress an annual economic report assessing the state of the economy and recommending economic legislation.

## FISCAL POLICY

**fiscal policy**
effects of government taxing, spending, and deficits on the economy

*Fiscal policy* refers to the effects of government taxing, spending, and deficits on the economic condition of the nation. In Keynesian theory (see Masters of Social Thought, "John M. Keynes and the Mixed Economy"), during recessions when consumer demand must be increased, Congress should increase government spending, thereby adding to the total demand, or it should cut taxes, thereby putting more money into the pockets of consumers. Conversely, during inflation, when strong consumer demands are pushing prices up, Congress should cut its own spending, thereby reducing total demand, or it should raise taxes, thereby restricting the spending power of consumers. During recessions the government must run a deficit (debt) in order to pour money into the economy. During inflations the government must cut its spending or raise taxes and create a surplus in its budget: that is, it must take money out of the economy and reduce its debt in order to lower consumer demand and stabilize prices.

## AUTOMATIC STABILIZERS

**automatic stabilizers**
government programs that act to counter economic cycles

*Automatic stabilizers* are government programs that act automatically to counter the effects of economic cycles. For example, since income taxes increase in proportion to one's earnings, the income tax automatically restricts spending habits in times of prosperity by taking larger bites of income. In times of adversity and low earnings, taxes drop automatically. Welfare programs also act automatically to counter economic cycles: in recessions, more people apply for welfare and unemployment payments, and those payments help offset declines in income.

## MONETARY POLICY

**monetary policy**
government's influence over the supply of money and credit and interest rates

*Monetary policy* refers to the government's influence over the supply of money and credit and over interest rates. Because banks are the major source of money and credit, the government can influence investment spending by making it easy or difficult to borrow money from banks. The

## CASE STUDY
Achieving
Economic Stability

Socialist critics of free market economies have long argued that the "internal contradictions of capitalism" would eventually bring about the downfall of free markets. They contended that economic cycles of inflation and depression would undermine public support for free markets and pave the way for socialism. And indeed, before 1950, economic cycles in the United States produced extreme ups and downs, with double-digit swings in real gross national product (GNP). In recent decades, however, economic fluctuations have been more moderate. We still experience economic cycles, but many economists believe that countercyclical government fiscal and monetary policy has succeeded in achieving greater stability (see figure).

### ECONOMIC CYCLES SINCE 1910

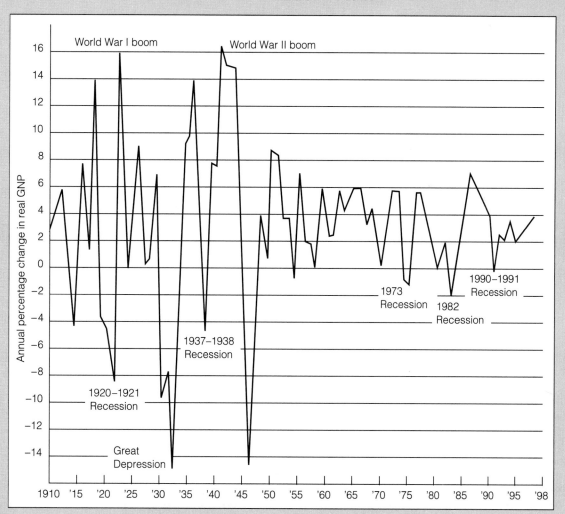

## MASTERS OF SOCIAL THOUGHT
John M. Keynes and the Mixed Economy

The Great Depression of the 1930s significantly altered American thinking about laissez faire economics. It is difficult to realize today what a tremendous economic disaster befell the nation in those days. Following the stock market crash of October 1929 the American economy virtually collapsed. Businesses failed, factories shut down, new construction practically ceased, banks closed, and millions of dollars in savings were wiped out. One out of four American workers was unemployed, and one out of six was receiving welfare relief. Many lost faith in the free enterprise system and urged the abandonment of the market economy. The "solutions" of fascism in Italy and Germany and communism in the Soviet Union were looked to as alternatives to a "doomed" capitalist system.

In 1936 John M. Keynes, a British economist, wrote a landmark book called *The General Theory of Employment, Interest and Money.* Keynes attacked the basic notion of classical economics—that the free enterprise system was a self-adapting mechanism that tended to produce full employment and maximum use of resources. He believed that not all savings went into investment. When there was little prospect of profit, savings were likely to be hoarded and not used. This removal of money from the economy brought depression. Moreover, he argued, low interest rates would not necessarily stir businesses to reinvest; the expectation of *profit*, not the availability of money, motivated investment. Keynes believed that as confidence in the future diminishes, investment will decline, regardless of interest rates.

In Keynes's view only *government* can reverse a downward economic cycle. Private businesses cannot be expected to invest when consumer demand is low and there is no prospect of profit. And consumers cannot be expected to increase their purchases when their incomes are falling. So the responsibility rests on the government to take *countercyclical* action to increase income and consumption. In recessions government can *increase its own expenditures or lower taxes or do both* in order to raise total demand and private income. Of course, increasing expenditures or lowering taxes or both means an *increase in government debt,* but only in this fashion can government pump money into the economy.

Keynes also argued that governments should pursue countercyclical fiscal policies to offset inflation as well as depression. *Inflation* means a general rise in the price level of goods and services. Inflation occurs when total demand exceeds or nears the productive capacity of the economy. An excess of demand over supply forces prices up. Keynes believed that when inflation threatens, government should gear its fiscal policy toward *reducing its own expenditures or increasing taxes or both.*

Keynes was no revolutionary. On the contrary, he wished to preserve the private enterprise system by developing effective governmental measures to overcome disastrous economic cycles.

**Federal Reserve Board** controls the supply of money and credit and interest rates (sets monetary policy)

*Federal Reserve Board* (the Fed) was created in 1913 to regulate the nation's supply of money through its *power to control the amount of money that commercial banks can lend.* The Fed is headed by a seven-person board of governors, appointed by the president, for overlapping terms of fourteen years.

In periods of *recession,* the Fed can *loosen controls* on lending and encourage banks to lend more money to businesspeople at lower interest rates. During *inflation,* the Fed can pursue *tight money policies,* policies that make it more difficult for banks to lend money, and thus reduce inflationary pressures.

## GOVERNMENT USE OF COUNTERCYCLICAL TOOLS

In practice there have been many difficulties in government use of fiscal and monetary policy.

**problems with countercyclical policy**

economic predictions not exact

politicians reluctant to counter inflation

conflicts between fighting inflation and fighting recession

occasional lack of coordination between Congress (fiscal policy) and Federal Reserve Board (monetary policy)

deficit spending appeals to politicians

- *Economic prediction is not an exact science;* honest economists will admit to a lot of uncertainty about just what policy should be adopted and when. Actions taken by the government may not have an impact on the economy until many months later, when conditions have changed from those that existed at the time the policy was adopted. There is a "lag" between government action and its effect.
- Presidents and members of Congress are afraid of being blamed for a depression. Inflation frequently goes unchecked because *public officials fear that "tight money," reduced spending, or higher taxes might set off a recession.* Besides, these counterinflationary actions are politically unpopular.
- *Inflation and recession can occur at the same time* if prices are pushed up because business anticipates that inflation is a permanent way of life. Thus, even with high unemployment, prices can continue to climb. In such a situation, the government is forced into the difficult choice of fighting inflation at the cost of continued high unemployment or reducing unemployment at the cost of runaway inflation.
- Fiscal and monetary policy must be *effectively coordinated* for optimal results. Unless they are, one may offset the other. But the president and Congress largely determine fiscal policy, while the independent Federal Reserve Board determines monetary policy. Occasionally, the Fed has disagreed with politicians about what policy should be applied at what time. The Fed is frequently more concerned with inflation than are the president and Congress (who are usually more concerned with unemployment).
- *Deficit spending appeals to politicians,* whether the economy is expanding or contracting. It allows them to provide benefits to their constituents while avoiding the onerous task of taxing them for their full costs. To be sure, the burden of paying the interest on current deficits is shifted to future generations. But politicians focus their attention on the next election rather than the long-term effects of their deficit spending.

# SUPPLY-SIDE ECONOMICS

**supply-side economics**
government policies designed to increase the supply of goods and services through incentives to work, save, and produce

Keynesian economics emphasizes the *demand side* of the economy—increasing government spending and expanding the money supply in periods of recession and doing the opposite in periods of inflation. In other words Keynesian economics calls for government manipulation of aggregate (total) demand for goods and services. However, other economists call for increased attention to the *supply side* of the economy—to government activities that affect the aggregate supply of goods and services. High government tax rates and costly regulations reduce incentives for Americans to work, save, invest, and produce. Supply-side economists believe that government should act to increase incentives to produce. Increased production will keep prices down (reduce inflation) and open up new employment opportunities (avoid recession).

## REDUCING TAX RATES

**marginal tax rates**
tax rates applied to additional income

**results of high marginal tax rates**
less work

less investment risk

more unproductive "tax shelters"

a large "underground economy" hiding income

Central to supply-side economics is the idea of reducing *marginal rates of taxation*. (The marginal rate of taxation is the rate at which *additional* income is taxed.) Before 1981, the marginal rates of the federal personal income tax ranged from 14 to 70 percent. Supply-side economists argued that these high marginal rates of taxation (especially the 50- to 70-percent brackets) reduced economic output and productivity. People prefer leisure time over extra work if, for example, 50 percent of the additional money they make from the extra work is "snatched away" by income taxes. Individuals avoid risking their money in new business investments if, for example, 70 percent of the income from the investment will be taken away by income taxes. High marginal tax rates also encourage people to seek out "tax shelters," unproductive investments that are favored by special provisions in the tax laws that reduce personal income taxes. In addition, a large "underground economy" flourishes when tax rates are high; in the underground economy people hide their real incomes and/or trade goods and services rather than conduct transactions out in the open where they will be subject to taxation.

## REAGAN TAX CUTS

**tax cut results**
economic growth

more jobs

huge government deficits

When the Reagan administration arrived in Washington in 1981, its first priority was to reduce high marginal rates of income taxation in the hope of stimulating economic growth. In two tax cut acts (1981 and 1986) pushed through Congress by President Ronald Reagan, the top marginal tax rate came down from 70 to 28 percent. These tax rate reductions succeeded in stimulating the economy. The United States experienced a nine-year period of continuous GNP growth. Runaway inflation was halted, unemployment was reduced from double-digit levels, and the number and proportion of Americans with jobs reached all-time highs. However, the incentive effects of the tax cuts did not produce enough new tax revenues to make up for lower rates. Tax revenues lagged far behind federal expenditures. Neither President Reagan, President Bush, nor Congress was willing to cut expenditures enough to reduce the gap between lower taxes and continued high spending levels. This resulted in the largest deficits in the nation's history.

## BUSH AND CLINTON TAX INCREASES

Neither President George Bush nor President Bill Clinton was fully convinced by the arguments of supply-side economics. At the Republican National Convention in 1988 George Bush made a firm pledge to the American people that he would veto any tax increase passed by the Democratic-controlled Congress. "Read my lips. No new taxes." But the pressure of continuing high deficits, and the unwillingness to cut spending, caused President Bush to reverse course in a 1990 economic "summit" meeting with congressional Democrats. Bush agreed to an increase in the top marginal income tax rate to 31 percent, thereby abandoning the supply-side economic policies of his predecessor Ronald Reagan. By breaking his solemn pledge on taxes, Bush contributed heavily to his own defeat in the 1992 presidential election. Moreover, the tax increase failed to reduce the continuing government deficits. On the contrary, economic recession in 1991 led to the highest deficits in history (see Figure 6-4).

**FIGURE 6-4**

ANNUAL FEDERAL DEFICITS

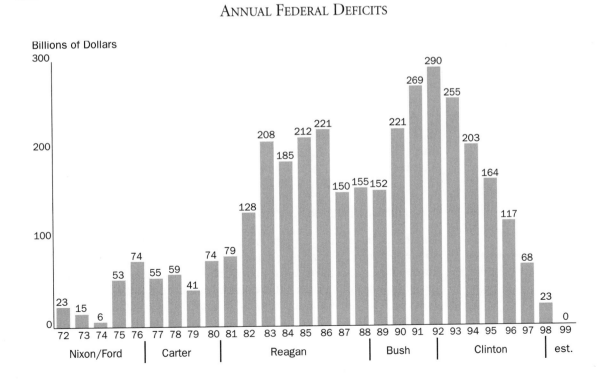

Bill Clinton won the presidency largely on his pledge to revive the economy. (At his campaign headquarters aides reportedly posted a large sign, "It's the economy, stupid" to help maintain the focus of the campaign.) Clinton repeatedly referred to the supply-side economics of the Reagan years as "failed, trickle-down" economics. Soon after taking office he presented Congress with a new economic plan calling for a large tax increase, cuts in defense spending, increases in spending for health, education, communications, and transportation, and a schedule for gradually lowering annual federal deficits. Clinton succeeded in getting the Democratic-controlled Congress to raise top marginal income tax rates to 36 and 39.6 percent on high income earners.

# THE BURDENS OF GOVERNMENT DEBT

**national debt**
the accumulated debt of the U.S. government of over $5 trillion owed to purchasers of U.S. bonds

**federal deficits**
the annual negative imbalances between revenues and expenditures of the U.S. government that add to the national debt

Decades of deficits—thirty years in which the federal government spent more than it received in revenues—have driven up the accumulated debt of the U.S. government to well over $5 *trillion*. The *national debt* now exceeds $18,000 for every man, woman, and child in the nation, or about $68,000 for every one of America's 66 million families!

The U.S. government debt is owed mostly to American banks and financial institutions and private citizens who buy Treasury bonds. Only about 20 percent of this debt is owed to foreign banks, firms, and individuals. As old debt comes due, the Treasury Department sells new bonds to pay off the old, that is, it continues to "roll over" or "float" the debt. The debt today is smaller as a percentage of the gross national product than at some periods in U.S. history. Indeed, in order to pay the costs of fighting World War II, the U.S. government ran up a debt of 110 percent of GNP; the current debt is the highest in history in dollar terms but only about 68 percent of the GNP. This suggests that the debt is still manageable, because of the size and strength of the U.S. economy.

The ability to float such a huge debt depends on public confidence in the U.S. government—confidence that it will continue to pay interest on its debt, that it will pay off the principal of bond issues when they come due, and that the value of the bonds will not decline over time because of inflation.

## BURDENING FUTURE GENERATIONS

**burden of government debt**
interest payments by future generations

slower economic growth

limits on policy initiatives

Interest payments on the national debt come from current taxes and divert money from *all* other government programs. Even if the federal government manages to balance its current annual budgets, these payments will remain obligations of the children and grandchildren of the current generation of policymakers and taxpayers. In short, today's high spending and low taxing shifts the burden of debt from the current generation to future generations.

## SLOWING ECONOMIC GROWTH

The huge federal debt, and the need to sell even more government bonds each year to cover annual increases in the debt (owing to new deficits), requires the U.S. Treasury Department to borrow large amounts of money each year. This money is diverted from the private sector, where it would otherwise be available as loans for new and expanding businesses, for modernizing industrial plants and equipment, and for financing the purchase of homes, cars, appliances, and other credit items for consumers. In other words, the federal government's borrowing "crowds out" capital markets. The less capital available in the private sector, the slower the growth rate of the economy.

## LIMITING POLICY INITIATIVES

Continuing government deficits and the increasing costs of interest payments limit the president and Congress's ability to deal with other problems confronting the nation. Any new spending initiatives for health, schools, research, or infrastructure add to federal deficits, and by so doing, slow economic growth. Thus, if the federal government tries to stimulate the economy by increasing its spending, it simultaneously increases already burdensome deficits, takes more money away from the private sector, and thereby threatens to undo whatever stimulative effect was intended.

## THE POLITICS OF DEFICITS

Over the years, all of the pious rhetoric in Washington about the need to "balance the budget," neither presidents nor Congresses, Democrats nor Republicans have been willing to reduce expenditures or raise taxes enough to produce a balanced budget. Congressional leaders consistently sidetracked proposed amendments to the U.S. Constitution that would require a balanced budget. It was politically more expedient to shift the burden of current government spending to future generations by incurring deficits than it was to cut favorite programs or raise taxes. Politicians were (and still are) especially reluctant to challenge the politically powerful older citizens who receive the largest proportions of federal spending through the Social Security and Medicare programs (see Figure 6-5).

The nation's booming economy in the 1990s added more revenues to the federal treasury and gradually reduced annual deficits. In 1998 President Clinton was able to present the first balanced federal budget in thirty years to the Congress, and to project surpluses for future years. The political question became: what to do with the surplus? (Of course, the question assumes that the economy continues its rapid growth and surpluses actually result.) The president and both Republicans and Democrats in Congress pledged to "save Social Security first" before adding new spending programs or cutting taxes.

**FIGURE 6-5**

FEDERAL SPENDING BY FUNCTION

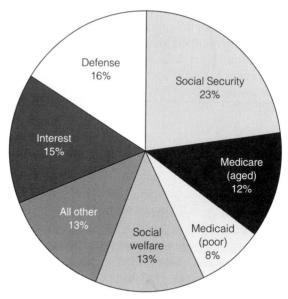

SOURCE: *Budget of the United States Government, 1998.*

## POWER IN THE CORPORATION

**governing the corporation**
"inside" and "outside" directors

The modern corporation is governed by its board of directors. The directors include the chairman of the board, the president or CEO (chief executive officer), selected senior vice-presidents, and some "outside" members who are not managers of the corporation. The "inside" directors, who are also full-time presidents or vice-presidents of the corporation, tend to dominate board proceedings because they know more about the day-to-day operations of the corporation than do the outside directors. Outside directors may sit on the corporate board as representatives for families who still own large blocks of stock or as representatives for banks that have lent money to the corporation. Occasionally, outside directors are prominent citizens, members of minority groups, or representatives of civic associations. Outside directors are usually chosen by the CEO and the inside directors. All directors are officially elected by the corporation's stockholders. However, the CEO and inside directors draw up the "management slate," which almost always wins, because top management casts many proxy votes, which they solicit in advance from stockholders. Corporate power does *not* rest in the hands of masses of corporate employees or even in the hands of millions of middle- and upper-middle-class Americans who own corporate stock. (See the Focus, "The Concentration of Corporate Power.") When confronted with mismanagement, these stockholders simply sell their stock, rather than try to challenge the power of the directors.

# MANAGERIAL POWER

Following the Industrial Revolution in America in the late nineteenth century and well into the twentieth century, the nation's largest corporations were controlled by the tycoons who created them—Andrew Carnegie (Carnegie Steel, later United States Steel, and today USX), Andrew Mellon (Alcoa and Mellon banks), Henry Ford (Ford Motor), J. P. Morgan (J. P. Morgan), and John D. Rockefeller (Standard Oil Company, later broken into Exxon, Mobil, Chevron, Atlantic Richfield, and other large oil companies). But by the 1930s control of most large corporations had passed from owners to professional managers. The theory of *managerialism* became the conventional wisdom about corporate governance.[1]

**managerialism**
control of the corporation by professional managers rather than stockholders

It was recognized early on that corporate managers might run their firms to best serve their own interests rather than those of the owners—for example, paying themselves multimillion-dollar annual salaries and providing themselves with lavish corporate-paid lifestyles. But for decades, individual and institutional stockholders largely ignored this potential principal-agent problem. Stockholders' power was fragmented and dispersed; there was not much the stockholders could do, other than sell their stock, even if they knew that managers were taking personal advantage of their position. But perhaps a more important reason that managers were largely unchallenged was that the American economy prospered from the 1940s through the 1970s. Governance of the U.S. corporation seemed to be working well, rewarding both managers and owners.

**principal-agent problem**
ensuring that managers (agents) operate firms in the best interest of the owners (principals) rather than themselves

# CORPORATE COUNTERREVOLUTION

Traditionally, the top managers of large corporations were considered impregnable; nothing short of bankruptcy could dislodge them. Corporate managers ran the American economy, perpetuating themselves in office; they ruled without much interference from outside directors, stockholders, employees, or consumers. But beginning in the 1980s, new challenges to the imperial position of top management arose, most notably from: (1) a new activism by outside directors and large stockholders, checking the power of corporate chief executives and occasionally forcing their retirement; and (2) a rise in "hostile takeovers" led by corporate raiders, who acquire corporate stock and voting power in order to force the ouster and replacement of existing management.

**managerial challenges**
new activism by outside directors representing financial institutions

hostile takeovers by corporate raiders

The new activism by outside directors and large stockholders, particularly those representing large financial institutions—pension funds, mutual funds, insurance companies, and banks—is largely attributable to slower economic growth in recent years and the failure of some American corporations to remain competitive in global markets. Mutual and pension funds, as well as banks and insurance companies, are more likely than small individual investors to take action against the managers of poorly performing corporations in which they have invested funds.[2]

**hostile takeover**
the purchase of stock in a corporation by an outsider and the subsequent ousting of the prior management

## CONTROVERSIES IN SOCIAL SCIENCE

### A Balanced Budget Amendment to the Constitution?

Government expenditures have exceeded revenues for every one of the last thirty years. Democrats and Republicans, liberals and conservatives all contributed to government deficits; they differed only in where they placed the blame. Conservatives blamed "runaway" government entitlement programs, such as Social Security and Medicare, as well as large-scale spending programs for welfare, education, job training, and agriculture. Liberals claimed that the nation's high deficits resulted largely from cutting the taxes of the wealthy during the Reagan administration. Democrats pointed out that the nation's largest annual deficits occurred in the Reagan and Bush administrations. Republicans argued

that Democrats in the Congress were responsible for these deficits because they failed to cut domestic spending as Republican presidents wished.

Regardless of who is to blame, the implications of the debt are serious. The painful legacy of these annual deficits will linger for generations. Interest payments on the debt consume about $1 out of every $6 of federal expenditures. This means that taxpayers can receive at most only $5 of public goods and services for every $6 paid to the federal government.

The simplest solution to federal deficits is to have the president and Congress prepare and pass only balanced budgets. But that solution eluded policy makers for three decades. Neither presidents nor Congresses, Democrats nor Republicans were willing to reduce expenditures or raise taxes enough to balance budgets. Indeed, deficit spending allowed elected politicians to spend heavily on their constituents while shifting the full costs to younger generations; politicians know that

young people vote less often than older people.

Public opinion has long favored an amendment to the U.S. Constitution requiring the federal government to balance its budget each year unless a supermajority (three-fifths or perhaps two-thirds) of both the House and Senate vote to allow a deficit. In 1995, the House of Representatives by a vote of 300 to 132 passed an amendment to the Constitution requiring a balanced budget by 2002 (or the second year after ratification, whichever is later). But the amendment failed by a single vote in the Senate to get the necessary two-thirds majority that would have sent it to the states for ratification. (See figure.)

Opponents of a balanced budget amendment have demanded to know what the effect will be on Social Security, Medicare, and welfare spending, whether taxes will have to be raised, and whether costs will be shifted to state and local governments. One of the strongest lobbying groups opposing the amendment was the National

## CORPORATE RAIDERS

**corporate raiders**
investors who arrange to purchase stock in a hostile takeover effort

A hostile takeover involves the purchase of enough stock in a publicly held corporation to force the ouster and replacement of existing corporate management. Usually a hostile takeover begins with a "corporate raider" buying the stock of a corporation on the open market, often with money borrowed for this purpose. After establishing a stock ownership position in the

Association of Retired Persons, which feared that a balanced budget might mean less generous Social Security payment.

A balanced budget amendment would place great pressure on Congress to "cut" federal spending. (Actually, federal spending would continue to rise. But in Washington jargon, a "cut" means a reduction in what the government would spend in the absence of new, restraining legislation, that is to say, if spending were allowed to continue to increase at current rates.) Balancing the budget requires very difficult political decisions.

Proponents argue that the constitutional amendment should be put in place first, in order to force politicians to make these difficult decisions. Otherwise, federal spending will continue unrestrained and future generations will suffer even larger debt burdens. They acknowledge that future Congresses and presidents may find loopholes in such an amendment that will allow continuing deficits. And they acknowledge that enforcement of such an amendment would be difficult, perhaps involving the Supreme Court in budget decisions. But they contend, nonetheless, that only the moral pressure of a clear constitutional mandate is likely to force politicians to cut spending or raise taxes—decisions politicians otherwise are loath to make.

The pressure to pass a balanced budget amendment evaporated when economic growth resulting in increases in federal revenues allowed the president to present the nation with a balanced budget in 1998.

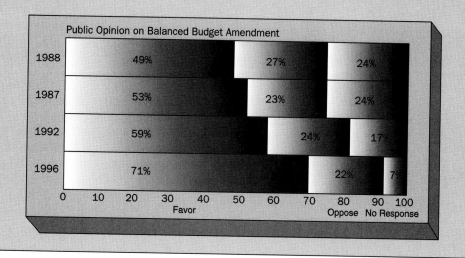

Public Opinion on Balanced Budget Amendment

| Year | Favor | Oppose | No Response |
|------|-------|--------|-------------|
| 1988 | 49% | 27% | 24% |
| 1987 | 53% | 23% | 24% |
| 1992 | 59% | 24% | 17% |
| 1996 | 71% | 22% | 7% |

corporation, the raider may then offer a takeover bid to existing management. Management may reject the bid outright or try to buy back the stock purchased by the raider at a higher price, that is, to offer the raider "greenmail." If the raider and management cannot reach agreement, the hostile takeover proceeds. The raider arranges to borrow additional money—perhaps several billion dollars—to make a purchase offer to the target corporation's stockholders, usually at a price higher than the current stock

**FOCUS**
The Concentration
of Corporate Power

Control over the nation's economic resources is becoming increasingly concentrated in the hands of very few people, largely because of the *consolidation of economic enterprise* into a small number of giant corporations. The following statistics can only suggest the scale and concentration of modern corporate enterprise in the United States: there are over 200,000 industrial corporations in the United States, but the 100 largest corporations hold over two-thirds of the nation's industrial assets. Indeed, just ten industrial corporations hold one-third of the nation's industrial assets (see table). Banking is also highly concentrated. There are nearly 15,000 banks in the United States, but the 10 largest banks hold one-third of all banking assets. The rate of corporate and banking mergers in recent years suggests that this concentration of economic resources is increasing.

| The largest U.S. industrial corporations (ranked by revenues) | The largest U.S. commercial banks (ranked by assets) |
|---|---|
| 1. General Motors | 1. Chase Manhattan |
| 2. Ford Motor | 2. Citicorp |
| 3. Exxon | 3. BankAmerica |
| 4. Wal-Mart Stores | 4. NationsBank |
| 5. General Electric | 5. J. P. Morgan |
| 6. IBM | 6. First Union |
| 7. AT&T | 7. Bank One |
| 8. Mobil | 8. First Chicago |
| 9. Chrysler | 9. Bankers Trust New York |
| 10. Phillip Morris | 10. Norwest |

SOURCE: Derived from data in *Fortune*, April 28, 1997.

exchange price. If the raider wins control of the corporation, the old managers are replaced.

Following a successful takeover, the corporation is heavily laden with new debt. The raider may have borrowed billions to buy out shareholders. The investment firms that provided the loans to finance the corporation's purchase may issue "junk bonds" with high interest rates to attract investors to these risky ventures. The corporation must pay off these bonds with its own revenues. Additionally, there may be many millions of dollars in bond-sale commissions and attorneys' fees to pay out. The raider may be forced to sell off parts of the corporation or some of its valuable assets in order to help pay off part of the debt. Thus, the target corporation itself must eventually bear the burden of the takeover battle.

Are corporate takeovers good or bad for America? The raiders claim that their activities force improvements in efficiency and productivity. Even the potential threat of a takeover forces corporate managers to streamline their operations, eliminate waste, increase revenues, raise profits, and distribute profits to their shareholders rather than spend them on the management comforts. The raiders argue that American management has grown soft, lazy, and self-satisfied—that, as a result, the American corporation has lost its competitive edge in the world marketplace. (See the Cross-National Perspective, "The Multinationals' Worldwide Economic Power.")

Opponents of the corporate takeover movement argue that fear of the raider forces management to focus on short-range profits at the expense of long-range research and development. Management must keep the current price of its stock high in order to deter a takeover attempt. Even worse, management often resorts to "poison pills" to deliberately weaken its own corporation to make it unattractive to raiders: it may increase its debt, buy other poorly performing corporations, devalue stockholders' voting powers, or provide itself with "golden parachutes" (rich severance benefits) in the event of ouster. While the original stockholders are paid handsomely by the raider, the corporation must labor intensively to pay off the debt incurred. The corporation may be broken apart and its separate pieces sold, which may disrupt and demoralize employees. If the corporation cannot meet the high interest payments, bankruptcy threatens. And the diversion of American capital from productive investments to takeovers threatens to weaken national productivity.

## CROSS-NATIONAL PERSPECTIVE

### The Multinationals' Worldwide Economic Power

The concentration of economic power in relatively few large institutions is not an exclusively American phenomenon. On the contrary, the trend toward corporate concentration of resources is worldwide. It is not only large American corporations that have expanded their markets throughout the world, invested in overseas plants and banks, and merged with foreign corporations; large European and Japanese firms compete very effectively for world business. Just as American companies have greatly expanded investments abroad, so too have foreign companies sharply increased their business in the United States. The result is the emergence of truly "multinational" corporations, which not only trade worldwide but also build and operate plants in many nations.

The world's largest corporations are listed in the table. General Motors and Ford are the world's largest automobile companies, followed by Mitsubishi and Toyota. Germany's Daimler-Benz and Volkswagen follow these Japanese carmakers. Royal Dutch Shell (Netherlands) is the largest oil company in the world, larger than its American competitor, Exxon. America's Mobil oil company ranks just ahead of Great Britain's British Petroleum (whose symbol in the U.S. is "BP").

In brief, the central feature of the American and world economy is the concentration of resources in relatively few large corporations.

### WORLD'S LARGEST CORPORATIONS

| Rank | Corporation | Country |
|------|-------------|---------|
| 1. | General Motors | USA |
| 2. | Ford Motor | USA |
| 3. | Mitsui | Japan |
| 4. | Mitsubishi | Japan |
| 5. | Itochu | Japan |
| 6. | Royal Dutch Shell | Netherlands |
| 7. | Marubeni | Japan |
| 8. | Exxon | USA |
| 9. | Sumitomo | Japan |
| 10. | Toyota | Japan |
| 11. | Wal-Mart Stores | USA |
| 12. | General Electric | USA |
| 13. | Nissho Iwai | Japan |
| 14. | Nippon Telephone | Japan |
| 15. | IBM | USA |
| 16. | Hitachi | Japan |
| 17. | AT&T | USA |
| 18. | Nippon Life Insurance | Japan |
| 19. | Mobil | USA |
| 20. | Daimler-Benz | Germany |
| 21. | British Petroleum | Great Britain |
| 22. | Matsushita Electric | Japan |
| 23. | Volkswagen | Germany |
| 24. | Daewoo | South Korea |
| 25. | Siemens | Germany |

SOURCE: Derived from *Fortune*, July 15, 1997.

# NOTES

1. A. A. Berle, Jr., *Power Without Property* (New York: Harcourt Brace Jovanovich, 1959).
2. Margaret M. Blair, "Who's in Charge Here?" *Brookings Review* (Fall 1991): 8–13.

# ABOUT THIS CHAPTER

In this chapter we have examined power in the economy. Economic power is deciding about the production and distribution of goods and services—what will be produced, how it will be produced, and to whom it will be distributed. After reading Chapter 6, you should be able to

- describe the operation of a free market
- identify the ideal conditions for market operations
- show how prices reflect supply and demand
- define the gross national product (GNP), and describe the difference between constant and current dollars
- describe the reasons for government intervention in the economy and the major tools of government intervention
- compare the ideas of Keynesian economics with modern "supply-side" economic ideas
- describe how power is exercised in the corporation, contrasting the positions of managers, outside directors, large stockholders, and "corporate raiders"

# DISCUSSION QUESTIONS

1. Discuss how the market in a private enterprise economy determines what is to be produced, how much it will cost, and who will be able to buy it. Comment on the roles that the following factors play in a market operation: consumer demands, profits, prices, willingness to pay and ability to pay, labor market, competition, product supply.

2. Describe the ideal conditions for a market operation in a free enterprise system. What are the reasons for government interference in such a system?

3. Discuss the similarities between laissez faire (classical) economics and a traditional democratic political system. Describe the conflict between laissez faire economics and Keynesian economics over the self-adaptability of the free enterprise system.

4. Describe the kinds of fiscal and monetary policies that a Keynesian economist would recommend during a recessionary period and an inflationary period. How do the automatic stabilizers work during each of these periods?

5. Define supply-side economics. What government policies are proposed by supply-side economists?

6. Explain how economists compute the gross national product (GNP). Differentiate between actual increases in the GNP and "dollar" increases in GNP.

7. What proportion of the GNP is produced by all governments—federal, state, and local—in the United States? What are the major sources of revenue of the *federal* government, and what are its major spending categories?

8. Describe the power of managers, directors, and large institutional stockholders in corporate governance. What challenges have arisen to the power of managers? Why is the corporate raider feared by management? Are corporate takeovers good or bad for the economy as a whole?

9. Distinguish between annual federal government deficits and the national debt. What are the major burdens created by a large national debt?

## Chapter 7

# Power and Government

## POLITICS, POLITICAL SCIENCE, AND GOVERNMENTAL POWER

**politics**
the study of power

A distinguished American political scientist, Harold Lasswell, defined *politics* as "who gets what, when, and how." "The study of politics," he said, "is the study of influence and the influential. The influential are those who get the most of what there is to get. . . . Those who get the most are the *elite;* the rest are *mass.*"[1] He went on to define *political science* as the study of "the shaping and sharing of power." Admittedly, Lasswell's definition of political science is very broad. Indeed, if we accept Lasswell's definition of political science as the *study of power,* then political science includes cultural, economic, social, and personal power relationships—topics we have already discussed in chapters on anthropology, economics, sociology, and psychology.

Although some political scientists have accepted Lasswell's challenge to study power in all its forms in society, most limit the definition of political science to *the study of government.*

**distinguishing governmental power**
the legitimate use of force; coverage of the whole society

What distinguishes *governmental power* from the power of other institutions, groups, and individuals? The power of government, unlike that of other institutions in society, is distinguished by (1) *the legitimate use of physical force* and (2) *coverage of the whole society* rather than only segments of it. Because governmental decisions extend to the whole of society and because only government can legitimately use physical force, government has the primary responsibility for maintaining order and for resolving differences that arise *between* segments of society. Thus, government must regulate conflict by establishing and enforcing general rules by which conflict is to be carried on in society, by arranging compromises and balancing interests, and by imposing settlements that the parties in the dispute must accept. In other words, government lays down the "rules of the game" in conflict and competition between individuals, organizations, and institutions within society.

## THE MEANING OF DEMOCRACY

Ideally, *democracy* means *individual participation* in the decisions that affect one's life. In traditional democratic theory, popular participation has been valued as an opportunity for individual self-development. Responsibility for governing one's own conduct develops character, self-reliance, intelligence, and moral judgment—in short, dignity. Even if a benevolent king could govern in the public interest, the true democrat would reject him.

Procedurally, popular participation was to be achieved through *majority rule* and *respect for the rights of minorities.* Self-development means *self-government,*

**democracy's meaning:**

popular participation in government

majority rule, with minority rights

the value of individual dignity

equality of opportunity

*Democracy means individual participation in government.*

Bob Daemmrich/Stock Boston

and self-government can be accomplished only by encouraging each individual to contribute to the creation of public policy and by resolving conflicts over public policy through majority rule. Minorities who had had the opportunity to influence policy but whose views had not succeeded in winning majority support would accept the decisions of majorities. In return, majorities would permit minorities to attempt openly to win majority support for their views. Freedom of speech and press, freedom to dissent, and freedom to form opposition parties and organizations are essential to ensure meaningful individual participation.

The underlying value of democracy is *individual dignity.* Human beings, by virtue of their existence, are entitled to life, liberty, and the pursuit of happiness. Governmental control over the individual should be kept to a minimum; this means the removal of as many external restrictions, controls, and regulations on the individual as possible without infringing on the freedom of other citizens.

Another vital aspect of classic democracy is a belief in the *equality* of all people. The Declaration of Independence expresses the conviction that "all men are created equal." The Founders believed in equality *before the law,* notwithstanding the circumstances of the accused. A person was not to be judged by social position, economic class, creed, or race. Many early democrats also believed in *political equality,* that is, equal opportunity to influence public policy. Political equality is expressed in the concept of "one person, one vote."

Over time, the notion of equality has also come to include *equality of opportunity* in all aspects of American life—social, educational, and economic, as well as political—and to encompass employment, housing, recreation, and public accommodations. All people are to have equal opportunity to develop their individual capacities to their natural limits.

In summary, democratic thinking involves the following ideas:

- Popular participation in the decisions that shape the lives of individuals in a society
- Government by majority rule, with recognition of the rights of minorities to try to become majorities; these rights include the freedoms of speech, press, assembly, and petition, and the freedom to dissent, to form opposition parties, and to run for public office
- A commitment to individual dignity and the preservation of the liberal values of liberty and property
- A commitment to equal opportunity for all to develop their individual capacities

# POWER IN THE AMERICAN CONSTITUTION

**Bill of Rights**
first ten amendments to the U.S. Constitution listing individual freedoms and restrictions on governmental power

The Constitution also contains many specific restrictions on governmental power. The original text of the Constitution that emerged from the Philadelphia convention in 1787 did *not* contain a "Bill of Rights"—a listing of indi-

## MASTERS OF SOCIAL THOUGHT
### John Locke and Constitutionalism

The potential power of governments has worried people for a long time.

*Constitutionalism* is the belief that governmental power should be *limited*. A fundamental ideal of constitutionalism—"a government of laws and not of men"—suggests that those who exercise governmental authority are restricted in their use of it by a higher law. A *constitution* governs government.

A famous exponent of the idea of constitutional government was the English political philosopher John Locke (1632–1704). Perhaps more than anyone else, Locke inspired the political thought of our nation's Founders in that critical period of American history in which the new nation won its independence and established its constitution. Locke's ideas are written into both the Declaration of Independence and the Constitution of the United States.

According to Locke, all people possess natural rights. These rights are not granted by government but derive from human nature itself. Governments cannot deprive people of their "inalienable rights to life, liberty, and property." People are rational beings, capable of self-government and able to participate in political decision making. Locke believed that human beings formed a contract among themselves to establish a government in order to better protect their natural rights, maintain peace, and protect themselves from foreign invasion. The *social contract* that established government made for safe and peaceful living and for the secure enjoyment of one's life, liberty, and property. Thus, the ultimate *legitimacy* of government derived from a contract among the people themselves and not from gods or kings. It was based on the *consent* of the governed. To safeguard their individual rights, the people agreed to be governed.

Because government was instituted as a contract to secure the rights of citizens, government itself could not violate individual rights. If government did so, it would dissolve the contract establishing it. Revolution, then, was justified if government was not serving the purpose for which it had been set up. However, according to Locke, revolution was justified only after a long period of abuses by government, not over any minor mismanagement.

Thomas Jefferson eloquently expressed Lockean ideals in the Declaration of Independence:

*We hold these truths to be self-evident, that all men are created equal, that they are endowed by their Creator with certain inalienable rights, that among these are life, liberty, and the pursuit of happiness. That to secure these rights, governments are instituted among men, deriving their just powers from the consent of the governed.*

vidual freedoms and restrictions on governmental power. The nation's Founders argued that a specific listing of individual freedoms was unnecessary because the national government possessed only enumerated powers; the power to restrict free speech or press or religion was not an enumerated power, so the national government could not do these things. But anti-Federalists in the state ratifying conventions were suspicious of the power of the new national government. They were not satisfied with the mere inference

## CROSS-NATIONAL PERSPECTIVE
The Role of Government

The idea of *limited* government, found in the writings of John Locke and echoed by the Founders of the American nation, continues to influence American politics. Indeed, public opinion in the United States about the role of government in society differs significantly from public opinion in other nations, even in other advanced Western industrial nations.

Americans generally believe they are individually responsible for their own well-being, while Europeans tend to look toward government as their protector and benefactor. For example, Americans are much less likely than Europeans to believe that government "should provide everyone with a guaranteed basic income," or that government "should provide a job for everyone who wants one." Americans are more likely than Europeans to believe their taxes are "too high," even though taxes in the United States are generally lower than those in European nations. Americans are also generally less supportive of governmental regulation, even for purposes of public safety and health. Americans seem to prefer that individuals, rather than governments, make the decisions that shape their lives (see table).

RESULTS OF SURVEYS RELATED TO THE ROLE OF GOVERNMENT (PERCENTAGE WHO "STRONGLY AGREE" OR "AGREE" WITH EACH STATEMENT)

| | Government should provide everyone with a guaranteed basic income | Government should provide a job for everyone who wants one | Taxes are much too high/too high |
|---|---|---|---|
| Switzerland | 43 | 50 | 51 |
| Great Britain | 61 | 59 | 41 |
| Netherlands | 50 | 75 | 60 |
| West Germany | 56 | 77 | 52 |
| Austria | 57 | 80 | 47 |
| Italy | 67 | 82 | 62 |
| Hungary | 77 | 92 | 39 |
| United States | 21 | 45 | 70 |

SOURCE: Derived from international surveys reported in *The American Enterprise* (March/April 1990): 113–115.

that the national government could not interfere with personal liberty; they wanted specific written guarantees of fundamental freedoms. The Federalist supporters of the new Constitution agreed to add a "Bill of Rights" as the first ten amendments to the Constitution in order to win ratification in the state conventions. This is why our fundamental freedoms—speech, press, religion, assembly, petition, and due process of law—appear in the Constitution as *amendments*.

The Constitution that emerged from the Philadelphia convention on September 17, 1787, founded a new government with a unique structure. That structure was designed to implement the Founders' belief that government rested on the consent of the people, that government power must be limited, and that the purpose of government was the protection of individual liberty and property. But the Founders were political realists; they did not have any romantic notions about the wisdom and virtue of "the people." James Madison wrote: "A dependence on the people is, no doubt, the primary control on the government; but experience has taught mankind the necessity of auxiliary precautions." The *key structural arrangements* in the Constitution—national supremacy, federalism, republicanism, separation of powers, checks and balances, and judicial review—all reflect the Founders' desire to create a strong national government while at the same time ensuring that it would not become a threat to liberty or property.

**key structural arrangements in American Constitution**
national supremacy
federalism
republicanism
separation of powers
checks and balances
judicial review

## NATIONAL SUPREMACY

The heart of the Constitution is the National Supremacy Clause of Article VI:

> *This Constitution, and the Laws of the United States which shall be made in Pursuance thereof; and all Treaties made, or which shall be made, under the Authority of the United States, shall be the supreme Law of the Land; and the Judges in every State shall be bound thereby, any Thing in the Constitution or Laws of any State to the Contrary notwithstanding.*

This sentence ensures that the Constitution itself is the supreme law of the land. Laws made by Congress must not conflict with the Constitution. The Constitution and the laws of Congress supersede state laws.

## FEDERALISM

The Constitution *divides power* between the nation and the states. It recognizes that both the national government and the state governments have independent legal authority over their own citizens: both can pass their own laws, levy their own taxes, and maintain their own courts. The states have an important role in the selection of national officeholders—in the apportionment of congressional seats and in the allocation of electoral votes for president. Most important, perhaps, both the Congress and three-quarters of the states must consent to changes in the Constitution itself.

**federalism**
the division of power between states and nations

## REPUBLICANISM

To the Founders, a *republican* government meant the delegation of powers by the people to a small number of representatives "whose wisdom may best discern the true interest of their country, and whose patriotism and love of justice, will be least likely to sacrifice it to temporary or partial considerations." The Founders believed that government rests ultimately on "the consent of the governed." But their notion of republicanism envisioned decision

**republicanism**
government by elected representatives of the people

# CONTROVERSIES IN SOCIAL SCIENCE
Direct versus Representative Democracy

"Democracy" means popular participation in government. (The Greek roots of the word mean "rule by the many.") But "popular participation" can have different meanings. To our nation's Founders, who were quite ambivalent about the wisdom of democracy, it meant that the voice of the people would be *represented* in government. "Representational democracy" means the selection of government officials by vote of the people in periodic elections open to competition in which candidates and voters can freely express themselves.

"Direct democracy" means that the people themselves can initiate and decide policy questions by popular vote. The Founders were profoundly skeptical of this form of democracy. *The U.S. Constitution has no provision for direct voting by the people on national policy questions.* It was not until over 100 years after the U.S. Constitution was written that widespread support developed in the American states for direct voter participation in policy making. Direct democracy developed in states and communities, and it is to be found today *only* in state and local government.

## Initiative and Referendum

The *initiative* is a form of direct democracy whereby a specific number or percent of voters, through the use of petition, may have a proposed state constitutional amendment or state law placed on the ballot for adoption or rejection by the electorate of a state. This process bypasses the legislature and allows citizens to both propose and adopt laws and constitutional amendments. The *referendum* is a device by which the electorate must approve citizen initiatives or decisions of the legislature before these become law or become part of the state constitution. Most states require a favorable referendum vote for a state constitutional amendment. Referenda on state laws may be submitted by the legislature (when legislators want to shift decision-making responsibility to the people), or referenda may be demanded by popular petition (when the people wish to change laws passed by the legislature).

## Arguments for Direct Democracy

Proponents of direct democracy make several strong arguments on behalf of the initiative and referendum devices.

■ Direct democracy enhances government responsiveness and accountability. The threat of a successful initiative and referendum drive—indeed sometimes

making by *representatives* of the people, not the people themselves. The U.S. Constitution does not provide for *direct* voting by the people on national questions; that is, unlike many state constitutions today it does not provide for national *referenda*. (See Controversies in Social Science, "Direct versus Representative Democracy.") Moreover, in the original Constitution of 1787 only the House of Representatives (sometimes referred to even today as "the people's house") was to be elected directly by voters in the states. Members of the Senate were to be elected by state legislatures; not until the ratificathe mere circulation of a petition—encourages officials to take the popular actions.

■ Direct democracy allows citizen groups to bring their concern directly to the public. Taxpayer groups, for example, who are not especially well represented in state capitols, have been able through the initiative and referendum devices to place their concerns on the public agenda.

■ Direct democracy stimulates debate about policy issues. In elections with important referendum issues on the ballot, campaigns tend to be more issue-oriented.

■ Direct democracy stimulates voters' interest and improves election-day turnout. Controversial issues on the ballot—the death penalty, abortion, gun control, taxes, gay rights, a ban on racial preferences, and so on—bring out additional voters.

### Arguments for Representative Democracy

Opponents of direct democracy, from our nation's Founders to the present, argue that representative democracy offers far better protection for individual liberty and the rights of minorities than direct democracy. The Founders constructed a system of checks and balances not so much to protect against the oppression of a ruler, but to protect against the tyranny of the majority. Opponents of direct democracy echo many of the Founders' arguments:

■ Direct democracy encourages majorities to sacrifice the rights of individuals and minorities. This argument supposes that voters are generally less tolerant than elected officials.

■ Voters are not sufficiently informed to cast intelligent ballots on many issues. Many voters cast their vote in a referendum without ever having considered the

issue before going into the polling booth.

■ A referendum does not allow consideration of alternative policies or modifications or amendments to the proposition set forth on the ballot. In contrast, legislators devote a great deal of attention to writing, rewriting, and amending bills, and seeking out compromises among interests.

■ Direct democracy enables special interests to mount expensive initiative and referendum campaigns. Although proponents of direct democracy argue that these devices allow citizens to bypass legislatures dominated by special-interest groups, in fact only a fairly well-financed group can mount a statewide campaign on behalf of a referendum issue.

---

tion of the Seventeenth Amendment in 1913 would voters directly elect their U.S. senators. The president was to be elected by "electors" (chosen in a way prescribed by state legislatures) and the Supreme Court and other federal judges were appointed by the president with the consent of the Senate.

These republican arrangements may appear undemocratic from our perspective today, but in 1787 this Constitution was more democratic than any other governing system in the world. Most other nations of that time were governed by monarchs, emperors, chieftains, and hereditary aristocracies.

Later democratic impulses in America greatly altered the original Constitution and reshaped it into an even more democratic document.

## THE SEPARATION OF POWERS

**separation of powers**
the principle of dividing governmental powers among the executive, legislative, and judicial branches

The *separation of powers* in the national government—separate legislative, executive, and judicial branches—was intended by the nation's Founders as an additional safeguard for liberty. *The Federalist* paper No. 51 expresses the logic behind creating separate branches of government and giving them checks over each other:

> Ambition must be made to counteract ambition. . . . It may be a reflection on human nature, that such devices should be necessary to control the abuses of government. But what is government itself, but the greatest of all reflections on human nature? If men were angels, no government would be necessary. If angels were to govern men, neither external nor internal controls on government would be necessary. In framing a government which is to be administered by men over men, the great difficulty lies in this: you must first enable the government to control the governed; and in the next place oblige it to control itself.[2]

## CHECKS AND BALANCES

**checks and balances**
the principle whereby each branch of the government exercises a check on the actions of the others, preventing too great a concentration of power in any one person or group of persons

Each of the major decision-making bodies of American government possesses important *checks and balances* (see Figure 7-1) over the decisions of the others. No bill can become law without the approval of both the House and the Senate. The president shares in legislative power through the veto and the responsibility of the office to "give to the Congress information of the State of the Union, and recommend to their consideration such measures as he shall judge necessary and expedient." The president can also convene sessions of Congress. But the president's powers to make appointments and treaties are shared by the Senate. Congress can also override executive vetoes. The president must execute the laws, but to do so he or she must rely on the executive departments, and they must be created by Congress. Moreover, the executive branch cannot spend money that has not been appropriated by Congress.

Federal judges, including members of the Supreme Court, must be appointed by the president, with the consent of the Senate. Congress must create lower and intermediate courts, establish the number of judges, fix the jurisdiction of lower federal courts, and make "exceptions" to the appellate jurisdiction of the Supreme Court.

## JUDICIAL REVIEW

**judicial review**
power of the Supreme Court or any court to declare federal or state laws unconstitutional

Perhaps the keystone of the system of checks and balances is the idea of *judicial review*, an original contribution by the nation's Founders to the science of government. Judicial review is the power of the courts to strike down laws that

**FIGURE 7-1**

CHECKS AND BALANCES IN THE U.S. GOVERNMENT

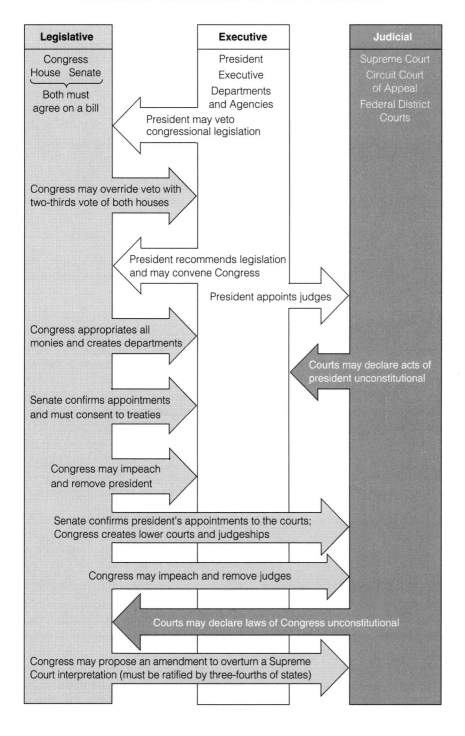

they believe conflict with the Constitution. Article VI grants federal courts the power of judicial review of *state* decisions, specifying that the Constitution and the laws and treaties of the national government are the supreme law of the land, superseding anything in any state laws or constitutions. However, nowhere does the Constitution specify that the Supreme Court has power of judicial review of *executive* action or of laws enacted by *Congress*. This principle was instead established in the case of *Marbury* v. *Madison* in 1803, when Chief Justice John Marshall argued convincingly that the Founders had intended the Supreme Court to have the power of invalidating not only state laws and constitutions, but also any laws of Congress or executive actions that came into conflict with the Constitution of the United States. Thus, the Supreme Court stands as the final defender of the constitutional principles against the encroachments of popularly elected legislatures and executives.

# FEDERALISM AND THE GROWTH OF POWER IN WASHINGTON

**sources of growing national power:**

Over the nation's 200-year history, power has flowed toward the national government and away from the states. Major developments in the history of American federalism have contributed to national power:

## EXPANSION OF IMPLIED NATIONAL POWER

**1. broad interpretation of national power in the Constitution**

Chief Justice John Marshall added immeasurably to national power in *McCulloch* v. *Maryland* (1819) when he broadly interpreted the "necessary and proper" clause of Article I, Section 8, of the Constitution. In approving the establishment of a national bank (a power not specifically delegated to the national government in the Constitution), Marshall wrote:

> *Let the end be legitimate, let it be within the scope of the Constitution, and all means which are appropriate, which are plainly adopted to that end, which are not prohibited but consistent with the letter and the spirit of the Constitution, are constitutional.*

Since then, the "necessary and proper" clause has been called the "implied powers" clause or even the "elastic" clause, suggesting that the national government can do anything not specifically prohibited by the Constitution. Given this tradition, the courts are unlikely to hold an act of Congress unconstitutional simply because no formal constitutional grant of power gives Congress the power to act.

## NATIONAL VICTORY IN THE CIVIL WAR

**2. national military force**

The Civil War was the nation's greatest crisis in federalism. Did a state have the right to oppose federal action by force of arms? This issue was decided in the nation's bloodiest war. (Combined military and civilian casualties in the Civil War exceeded U.S. casualties in World War II, even though the U.S. population in 1860 was only one-quarter of the population in 1940.) The same issue was at stake when the federal government sent troops to Little Rock, Arkansas, in 1957; to Oxford, Mississippi, in 1962; and to Tuscaloosa, Alabama, in 1963, to enforce desegregation; however, in these confrontations it was clear which side held the military advantage.

## GROWTH OF INTERSTATE COMMERCE

The growth of national power under the interstate commerce clause is also an important development in American federalism. The Industrial Revolution created a national economy governable only by a national government. Yet, until the 1930s, the Supreme Court placed many obstacles in the way of government regulation of the economy. Finally, in *National Labor Relations Board* v. *Jones & Laughlin Steel Corporation* (1937), the Supreme Court recognized the principle that Congress could regulate production and distribution of goods and services for a national market under the interstate commerce clause. As a result, the national government gained control over wages, prices, production, marketing, labor relations, and all other important aspects of the national economy.

**3. broad interpretation of interstate commerce**

## FEDERAL CIVIL RIGHTS ENFORCEMENT

Over the years, the U.S. Supreme Court has built a national system of civil rights based on the Fourteenth Amendment. This amendment rose out of the Civil War: "No State shall . . . deprive any person of life, liberty, or property, without due process of law; nor deny to any person within its jurisdiction the equal protection of the laws." In early cases, the Supreme Court held that the general guarantee of *liberty* in the first phrase (the "due process" clause) prevents states from interfering with free speech, press, religion, and other personal liberties. Later, particularly after *Brown* v. *Board of Education of Topeka* in 1954, the Supreme Court also used the "equal protection" clause to ensure fairness and equality of opportunity throughout the nation.

**4. development of national system of civil rights enforceable in federal courts**

## FEDERAL GRANTS-IN-AID MONEY

Money and power go together. The income tax (established in 1913) gave the federal government the authority to raise large sums of money, which it spent for the "general welfare," as well as for defense. Gradually the federal government expanded its power in states and communities by use of *grants-in-aid*. During the Great Depression of the 1930s, the national government used its taxing and spending powers in a number of areas formerly reserved to states and communities. Congress began grants-in-aid programs to states and communities for public assistance, unemployment compensation, employment services, child welfare, public housing, urban renewal, highway construction, and vocational education and rehabilitation.

**5. growth of federal grants-in-aid money**

**federal grants-in-aid** payments of funds from the national government to state or local governments, usually with conditions attached to their uses

# FEDERALISM TODAY

Today federal grants-in-aid are the principal source of federal power over states and communities. Approximately one-fifth of all state and local government revenues are from federal grants. These grants almost always come with detailed conditions regarding how the money can be used. "Categorical" grants specify particular projects or particular individuals eligible to receive funds; "block" grants provide some discretion to state or local officials in using the money for a particular governmental function, such as law enforcement. Federal grant money is distributed in hundreds of separate programs, but welfare (including Assistance to Needy Families) and health (including Medicaid) account for nearly two-thirds of federal aid money (see Figure 7-2).

**federal mandates**
directions to state and local governments from the national government

*Federal mandates* to state and local governments also centralize power in Washington. Often the federal government by law requires state and local governments to perform functions or undertake tasks that Congress deems in the public interest. Many of these federal mandates are "unfunded"—that is, Congress does not provide any money to carry out these mandated functions or tasks even though they impose costs on states and communities. For example, environmental protection laws passed by Congress require local governments to provide specified levels of sewage treatment; the Americans with Disabilities Act requires state and local governments to build ramps and alter curbs in public streets and buildings.

In its 1985 *Garcia* decision the U.S. Supreme Court removed all constitutional barriers to direct federal legislation in matters traditionally "reserved" to the states.[3] The case arose when Congress mandated that state and local

## FIGURE 7-2

### PURPOSES OF FEDERAL GRANTS-IN-AID TO STATE AND LOCAL GOVERNMENTS

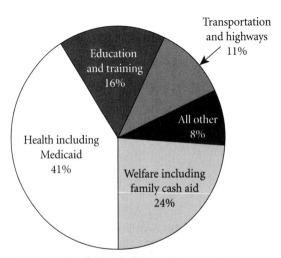

SOURCE: *Budget of the United States Government 1998*

governments pay federal minimum wages to their own employees. The Supreme Court dismissed arguments that the "reserved power clause" of the Tenth Amendment prevented Congress from directly legislating in state and local affairs. The Court said that the only protection for state powers was to be found in the states' role in electing U.S. House and Senate members and the president—a concept known as *representational federalism.*

**representational federalism**
the Supreme Court's argument that there are no constitutional barriers to Congress's legislating in state affairs, and the only protection for states is their role in electing Congress members and the president

## DEVOLUTION?

Over the years various efforts have been made to return power to states and communities. President Ronald Reagan was partially successful in his "New Federalism" efforts; many categorical grant programs were consolidated into block grants with greater discretion given to state and local governments. But today state and local government reliance on federal aid remains high; about 25 percent of all state-local revenue comes from federal grants-in-aid.

Recently, Congress has considered the "devolution" of many governmental responsibilities from the national government to the states and their local governments. So far, welfare cash assistance is the only major federal program to "devolve" back to the states. Since Franklin Delano Roosevelt's New Deal, with its federal guarantee of cash Aid to Families with Dependent Children (AFDC), low-income mothers and children had enjoyed a legal "entitlement" to welfare payments. But welfare reform in 1996, by devolving responsibility for determining eligibility to the state, ended this sixty-year federal entitlement. This is a major change in federal social welfare policy (see Chapter 11) and may become a model for future shedding of federal entitlement programs.

# PRESIDENTIAL POWER

Americans look to their president for "greatness." Great presidents are those associated with great events—George Washington with the founding of the nation, Abraham Lincoln with the preservation of the Union, Franklin D. Roosevelt with the nation's emergence from economic depression and victory in World War II (see Focus, "Rating the Presidents"). People tend to believe that the president is responsible for "peace and prosperity" as well as "change." They expect their president to present a "vision" of America's future and to symbolize the nation.

## THE SYMBOLIC PRESIDENT

The president personifies American government for most people. People expect the president to act decisively and effectively to deal with national problems. They expect the president to be "compassionate"—to show concern for problems confronting individual citizens. The president, while playing these

**FOCUS**
Rating the
Presidents

From time to time, historians and political scientists have been asked to rate U.S. presidents. The ratings given the presidents have been remark-

ably consistent. Abraham Lincoln, George Washington, Franklin Roosevelt, Woodrow Wilson, and Thomas Jefferson are universally recognized as the

| Schlesinger (1948) | Schlesinger (1962) | Dodder (1970) | Murray (1982) | Ridings & McIver (1996) |
|---|---|---|---|---|
| **Great** | **Great** | **Accomplishments of Administration** | **Presidential Rank** | **Overall Ranking** |
| 1. Lincoln | 1. Lincoln | 1. Lincoln | 1. Lincoln | 1. Lincoln |
| 2. Washington | 2. Washington | 2. F. Roosevelt | 2. F. Roosevelt | 2. F. Roosevelt |
| 3. F. Roosevelt | 3. F. Roosevelt | 3. Washington | 3. Washington | 3. Washington |
| 4. Wilson | 4. Wilson | 4. Jefferson | 4. Jefferson | 4. Jefferson |
| 5. Jefferson | 5. Jefferson | 5. T. Roosevelt | 5. T. Roosevelt | 5. T. Roosevelt |
| 6. Jackson | **Near Great** | 6. Truman | 6. Wilson | 6. Wilson |
| **Near Great** | 6. Jackson | 7. Wilson | 7. Jackson | 7. Truman |
| 7. T. Roosevelt | 7. T. Roosevelt | 8. Jackson | 8. Truman | 8. Jackson |
| 8. Cleveland | 8. Polk | 9. L. Johnson | 9. J. Adams | 9. Eisenhower |
| 9. J. Adams | Truman (tie) | 10. Polk | 10. L. Johnson | 10. Madison |
| 10. Polk | 9. J. Adams | 11. J. Adams | 11. Eisenhower | 11. Polk |
| **Average** | 10. Cleveland | 12. Kennedy | 12. Polk | 12. L. Johnson |
| 11. J. Q. Adams | **Average** | 13. Monroe | 13. Kennedy | 13. Monroe |
| 12. Monroe | 11. Madison | 14. Cleveland | 14. Madison | 14. J. Adams |
| 13. Hayes | 12. J. Q. Adams | 15. Madison | 15. Monroe | 15. Kennedy |
| 14. Madison | 13. Hayes | 16. Taft | 16. J. Q. Adams | 16. Cleveland |
| 15. Van Buren | 14. McKinley | 17. McKinley | 17. Cleveland | 17. McKinley |
| 16. Taft | 15. Taft | 18. J. Q. Adams | 18. McKinley | 18. J. Q. Adams |
| 17. Arthur | 16. Van Buren | 19. Hoover | 19. Taft | 19. Carter |
| 18. McKinley | 17. Monroe | 20. Eisenhower | 20. Van Buren | 20. Taft |
| | | | 21. Hoover | 21. Van Buren |

These ratings result from surveys of scholars ranging in numbers from 55 to 950.
SOURCES: Arthur Murphy, "Evaluating the Presidents of the United States," *Presidential Studies Quarterly* 14 (1984): 117–26; William J. Ridings, Jr., and Stuart B. McIver, *Rating the Presidents* (Secaucus, N.J.: Citadel Press, 1997).

roles, is the focus of public attention and is the nation's leading celebrity. Presidents receive more media coverage than any other person in the nation, for everything from their policy statements to their favorite foods.

## MANAGING CRISES

In time of crisis, the American people look to their president to take action, to provide reassurance, and to protect the nation and its people. It is the president, not the Congress nor the courts, who is expected to speak on behalf of the people in time of national triumph and tragedy. The president greatest American presidents.

It is more difficult for historians to rate recent presidents; the views of historians are influenced by current political controversies. Often the passage of time allows scholars to make more objective evaluations. Richard Nixon may be evaluated higher by future historians than he is today. How would you rate Ronald Reagan, George Bush, and Bill Clinton?

| Schlesinger (1948) | Schlesinger (1962) | Dodder (1970) | Murray (1982) | Ridings & McIver (1996) |
|---|---|---|---|---|
| **Average** | **Average** | **Accomplishments of Administration** | **Presidential Rank** | **Overall Ranking** |
| 19. A. Johnson | 18. Hoover | 21. A. Johnson | 22. Hayes | 22. Bush |
| 20. Hoover | 19. B. Harrison | 22. Van Buren | 23. Arthur | 23. Clinton |
| 21. B. Harrison | 20. Arthur | 23. Arthur | 24. Ford | 24. Hoover |
| **Below Average** | Eisenhower (tie) | 24. Hayes | 25. Carter | 25. Hayes |
| 22. Tyler | 21. A. Johnson | 25. Tyler | 26. B. Harrison | 26. Reagan |
| 23. Coolidge | **Below Average** | 26. B. Harrison | 27. Taylor | 27. Ford |
| 24. Fillmore | 22. Taylor | 27. Taylor | 28. Tyler | 28. Arthur |
| 25. Taylor | 23. Tyler | 28. Buchanan | 29. Fillmore | 29. Taylor |
| 26. Buchanan | 24. Fillmore | 29. Fillmore | 30. Coolidge | 30. Garfield |
| 27. Pierce | 25. Coolidge | 30. Coolidge | 31. Pierce | 31. B. Harrison |
| **Failure** | 26. Pierce | 31. Pierce | 32. A. Johnson | 32. Nixon |
| 28. Grant | 27. Buchanan | 32. Grant | 33. Buchanan | 33. Coolidge |
| 29. Harding | **Failure** | 33. Harding | 34. Nixon | 34. Tyler |
|  | 28. Grant |  | 35. Grant | 35. W. Harrison |
|  | 29. Harding |  | 36. Harding | 36. Fillmore |
|  |  |  |  | 37. Pierce |
|  |  |  |  | 38. Grant |
|  |  |  |  | 39. A. Johnson |
|  |  |  |  | 40. Buchanan |
|  |  |  |  | 41. Harding |

gives expression to the nation's pride in victory. The nation's heroes are welcomed and its championship sports teams are feted in the White House Rose Garden. The president also gives expression to the nation's sadness in tragedy and strives to help the nation go forward.

## PROVIDING POLICY LEADERSHIP

The president is expected to set policy priorities for the nation. Most policy initiatives originate in the White House and various departments and agencies of the executive branch, then are forwarded to Congress with the president's

*The president gives expression to a nation's sadness in tragedy. Here, President Clinton and his wife Hillary attend the funeral service for the victims of the Oklahoma City bombing. Some mourners hold teddy bears to symbolize the children who perished in the blast.*

approval. Presidential programs are submitted to Congress in the form of messages, including the president's annual State of the Union Address, and the Budget of the United States Government, which the president presents each year to Congress.

As a political leader, the president is expected to mobilize political support for policy proposals. It is not enough for the president to send policy proposals to Congress. The president must rally public opinion, lobby members of Congress, and win legislative battles. To avoid being perceived as weak or ineffective, presidents must get as much of their legislative proposals through Congress as possible. Presidents use the threat of a veto to prevent Congress from passing bills they oppose; when forced to veto a bill, they fight to prevent an override of the veto. The president thus is responsible for "getting things done" in the policy arena.

## MANAGING THE ECONOMY

The American people hold the president responsible for maintaining a healthy economy. Presidents are blamed for economic downturns, whether or not government policies had anything to do with market conditions. The president is expected to "Do Something!" in the face of high unemployment, declining personal income, high mortgage rates, rising inflation, or even a stock market crash. Herbert Hoover in 1932, Gerald Ford in 1976, Jimmy Carter in 1980, and George Bush in 1992—all incumbent presidents defeated for reelection during recessions—learned the hard way that the general public holds the president responsible for hard economic times. Presidents must have an economic "game plan" to stimulate the economy—tax incentives to spur investments, spending proposals to create jobs, plans to lower interest rates. In today's economy, they must also develop programs to improve America's international "competitiveness."

Presidents themselves are partly responsible for these public expectations. Incumbent presidents have been quick to take credit for economic growth, low inflation, low interest rates, and low unemployment. And presidential candidates in recessionary times invariably promise "to get the economy moving again."

However, public expectations far exceed presidential power to ensure prosperity for all. The U.S. economy is not easily manipulated by *anything* the government does (see Chapter 6), whether changes in taxing, spending, or interest rates. The American economy also is increasingly influenced by global forces—oil prices, recessions in other nations, trade restrictions—beyond the direct control of the U.S. government. Finally, the president must share control with Congress on issues of taxing and spending and with an independent Federal Reserve Board on issues of interest rates.

## Managing the Government

As the chief executive of a mammoth federal bureaucracy with 2.8 million civilian employees, the president is responsible for implementing policy— that is, for achieving policy goals. Policy making does not end when a law is passed. Policy implementation involves issuing orders, creating organizations, recruiting and assigning personnel, disbursing funds, overseeing work, and evaluating results. It is true that the president cannot perform all of these tasks personally. But the ultimate responsibility for implementation—in the words of the Constitution, "to take Care that the Laws be faithfully executed"—rests with the president. Or as the sign on Harry Truman's desk put it: "THE BUCK STOPS HERE."

## The Global President

Nations strive to speak with a single voice in international affairs; for the United States, the global voice is that of the president. As commander-in-chief of the armed forces of the United States, the president is a powerful voice in foreign affairs. Efforts by Congress to speak on behalf of the nation in foreign affairs and to limit the war-making power of the president have been generally unsuccessful. It is the president who orders American troops into combat. It is the president's finger that rests on the nuclear trigger.

## COMMANDER-IN-CHIEF

Global power derives primarily from the president's role as commander-in-chief of the armed forces of the United States. Presidential command over the armed forces is not merely symbolic; presidents may issue direct military orders to troops on the field. As president, Washington personally led troops to end the Whiskey Rebellion in 1794; Abraham Lincoln issued direct orders to his generals in the Civil War; Lyndon Johnson personally chose bombing targets in Vietnam; and George Bush personally ordered the Gulf War cease-fire after 100 hours of ground fighting. All presidents, whether they are experienced in world affairs or not, soon learn after taking office that their influence throughout the world is heavily dependent upon the command of capable military forces.

## MODEST CONSTITUTIONAL POWERS

Popular expectations of presidential leadership far exceed the formal constitutional powers granted to the president. Compared with the Congress, the president has only modest constitutionally expressed powers (see Table 7-1). Nevertheless, presidents over the years have consistently exceeded their specific grants of power in Article II, from Thomas Jefferson's decision to double the land area of the United States in the Louisiana Purchase, to William Jefferson Clinton's decision to send U.S. troops to keep the peace in Bosnia.

## LIMITS ON PRESIDENTIAL POWER

Despite the great powers of the office, no president can monopolize policy making. The president functions within an established political system and can exercise power only within its framework. The president cannot act outside existing political consensus, outside the "rules of the game." (See the Case Study, "Watergate and the Limits of Presidential Power.")

# THE POWER OF CONGRESS

What are the powers of Congress in the American political system? Policy proposals are usually initiated *outside* Congress; it is the role of Congress to respond to proposals from the president, executive agencies, and interest groups. Congress does not merely ratify or "rubber-stamp" decisions; it plays an independent role in the policy-making process. But this role is essentially a deliberative one in which Congress accepts, modifies, or rejects the policies initiated by others. Congress functions as an *arbiter* rather than an *initiator* of public policy.

**Congress as arbiter rather than initiator of policy**

**TABLE 7-1**

## CONSTITUTIONAL POWERS OF THE PRESIDENT

**Chief Administrator**

Implement policy: "take Care that the Laws be faithfully executed" (Article II, Section 3)

Supervise executive branch of government

Appoint and remove executive officials (Article II, Section 2)

Prepare executive budget for submission to Congress (by law of Congress)

**Chief Legislator**

Initiate policy: "give to the Congress Information of the State of the Union, and recommend to their Consideration such Measures as he shall judge necessary and expedient" (Article II, Section 3)

Veto legislation passed by Congress, subject to override by a two-thirds vote in both houses

Convene special session of Congress "on extraordinary Occasions" (Article II, Section 3)

**Chief Diplomat**

Make treaties "with the Advice and Consent of the Senate" (Article II, Section 2)

Exercise the power of diplomatic recognition: "receive Ambassadors" (Article II, Section 3)

Make executive agreements (by custom and international law)

**Commander-in-Chief**

Command U.S. armed forces: "The president shall be Commander in Chief of the Army and Navy" (Article II, Section 2)

Appoint military officers

**Chief of State**

"The executive Power shall be vested in a President" (Article II, Section 1)

Grant reprieves and pardons (Article II, Section 2)

Represent the nation as chief of state

Appoint federal court and Supreme Court judges (Article II, Section 2)

## DOMESTIC AFFAIRS

Congress is more influential in *domestic* than in foreign and military affairs. It is much freer to reject presidential proposals regarding business, labor, agriculture, education, welfare, urban affairs, civil rights, taxation, and appropriations. The president and executive departments must go to Congress for needed legislation and appropriations. Congressional committees can exercise power in domestic affairs by giving or withholding the appropriations and the legislation these executive agencies want.

**Congress more influential in domestic policy than foreign or military affairs**

**CASE STUDY**
Watergate and the
Limits of
Presidential Power

Election to the nation's highest office, even by an overwhelming majority, does not entitle the president to govern alone. It only gives the president the opportunity to engage in consultation, accommodation, and compromise with other elites. Richard Nixon was the only president ever to resign from office. His forced resignation in 1974 was not merely a product of specific misdeeds; it also grew out of his failure to cooperate with Congress and the courts, and his disregard for the general "rules of the game."

On the night of June 17, 1972, five men with burglary and wiretapping tools were arrested in the offices of the Democratic National Committee in the Watergate apartments in Washington, together with E. Howard Hunt and G. Gordon Liddy, who directed the break-in. All pleaded guilty and were convicted, but U.S. District Court Judge John J. Sirica believed that the defendants were shielding whoever had ordered and paid for the bugging and break-in. Judge Sirica threatened the defendants with heavy sentences, and soon James W. McCord confessed to secret payments and a cover-up.

The Senate formed a Special Select Committee on Campaign Activities—the so-called Watergate Committee—headed by Sen. Sam J. Ervin, to delve into Watergate and related activities. The national press, led by "investigative reporters" Bob Woodward and Carl Bernstein of the *Washington Post*, launched a series of damaging stories, reported nightly on the national television networks, involving Nixon's campaign director and former Attorney General John Mitchell, White House chief of staff H. R. Haldeman, and White House adviser John Ehrlichman.

President Nixon might have been able to stay in office if he had publicly repented his own actions and cooperated in the Watergate investigation by Congress and the courts. But Nixon increasingly viewed the Watergate affair as a test of his own strength and character; he perceived it as a conspiracy among liberal opponents in Congress and the news media to reverse the 1972 election outcome; he

## FOREIGN AND MILITARY AFFAIRS

In the Constitution, the president and Congress share power over foreign and military affairs. The president is "Commander in Chief of the Armed Forces," but Congress "declares war." The president "sends and receives ambassadors" and "makes treaties," but the Senate must confirm appointments and "advise and consent" to treaties. Nevertheless, strong presidents have generally led the nation in both war and peace. (See the Case Study in Chapter 8, "Vietnam: A Political History," and the Case Study in Chapter 14, "American Military Power: 'Desert Storm.'")

## WAR POWERS ACT

Until Vietnam, no congressional opposition to undeclared war was evident. But military failure and public opposition to the war in Vietnam led Congress to try to curtail the war power of the president. Congress passed the controversial became rigid in his stance on withholding information.

When the Senate Watergate Committee learned that the president regularly taped conversations in the Oval Office, it issued subpoenas for tapes that would prove or disprove charges of a cover-up. In response President Nixon chose to argue that the constitutional separation of powers permitted the president to withhold information from both Congress and the courts. But the Supreme Court, in *The United States* v. *Richard M. Nixon,* denied the president the power to withhold information that was essential to a criminal investigation. President Nixon publicly released the transcripts of the subpoenaed White House tapes in a national television broadcast in which he claimed innocence of any wrongdoing.

The conversations on the tapes are rambling and inconclusive but the most common interpretation is that President Nixon approved a payoff to silence the convicted burglars.

The Judiciary Committee of the House of Representatives was convened in the spring of 1974 to consider a series of articles of impeachment against President Nixon. The committee passed two articles of impeachment: one accused the president of obstructing justice in the Watergate investigation; the other accused the president of misusing his executive power and disregarding his constitutional duties to take care that the laws be faithfully executed. Shortly thereafter, Nixon was informed by congressional leaders of his own party that impeachment by a majority of the House and re-

moval from office by two-thirds of the Senate was assured. On August 9, 1974, President Nixon resigned his office—the first U.S. president ever to do so.

On September 8, 1974, new President Gerald R. Ford pardoned former President Richard Nixon "for all offenses against the United States which he, Richard Nixon, has committed or may have committed or taken part in" during his presidency. In accepting the pardon, Nixon expressed remorse over Watergate and acknowledged grave errors of judgment, but he did not admit personal guilt. President Ford stated that his purpose in granting the pardon was to end "bitter controversy and divisive national debate."

War Powers Act in 1973 over a weakened President Nixon's veto. The act specifies that if the president sends U.S. troops into combat, this must be reported to Congress within forty-eight hours. American forces can remain in a combat situation for only sixty days unless Congress by specific legislation authorizes their continued engagement. The act also states that Congress can withdraw troops at any time by passing a resolution in both houses, and the president cannot veto a resolution. Obviously the War Powers Act raises very serious constitutional questions, but they may never be tested in court. The U.S. Constitution makes the president, not Congress, commander-in-chief of the armed forces, and commanders may order their troops to go anywhere at any time. The act did not prevent President Ford from sending troops to Cambodia during the *Mayaguez* incident; or President Carter from attempting a military rescue of the Iranian-held U.S. hostages; or President Reagan from sending U.S. troops to Lebanon and Grenada; or President Bush from sending military forces to Panama and ordering U.S. forces into "Operation Desert Storm" to liberate Kuwait; or President Clinton from ordering U.S. forces into Haiti and Bosnia.

**War Powers Act**
Congress's effort to limit presidential war-making power

## CONTROVERSIES IN SOCIAL SCIENCE
Should We Limit the Terms of Congress Members?

At the Constitutional Convention of 1787, delegate Roger Sherman commented that Congress should be composed of "citizen-legislators" who would be expected to "return home and mix with the people." He feared that "by remaining at the seat of government, they would acquire the habits of the place, which might differ from those of their constituents." But after brief consideration, the Convention dropped the idea of limiting congressional terms. The president's term was not constitutionally limited until the adoption of the Twenty-second Amendment in 1951. This amendment was passed largely in reaction to Franklin D. Roosevelt's election to four terms in office, breaking the tradition of a two-term presidency set by George Washington. In addition, some twenty-five states restrict governors to two terms, and four additional states restrict them to one term.

Proponents of *term limits* argue that citizen-legislators have largely been replaced by career professional politicians. Long-time professional officeholders become isolated from the lives and concerns of average citizens; they acquire an "inside the Beltway" (the circumferential interstate highways surrounding Washington) mentality. They respond to the media, to polls, and to interest groups, but have no direct feeling for how their constituents live. Term limits, proponents argue, would force politicians to return home and live under the laws that they make.

Proponents also argue that term limits would increase competition in the electoral system. By creating "open seat" races on a regular basis, term limits would encourage more people to seek public office. Incumbents do not keep winning because they are the most qualified people in their districts, but rather because of the many electoral advantages granted by incumbency—name recognition, campaign contributions from special interests, pork barrel and casework opportunities, free mailing, office staff, and so on.

Opponents of term limits argue that limits infringe on the voters' freedom of choice. If voters are upset about the performance of Congress or their state legislature, they can always "throw the rascals out." But if voters wish to keep popular, able, experienced, and hard-working legislators in office, they should be permitted to do so. Experience is a valuable asset in Washington. Voters may legitimately desire to be represented by members of Congress with knowledge and experience in public affairs.

Opponents further argue that inexperienced legislators would be forced to rely more on the policy information supplied by bureaucrats, lobbyists, and staff people. Term limits, thus, would weaken the institution of Congress, leaving it less capable of checking the power of special interests. But proponents of term limits counter by observing that close relationships have developed between lobbyists and senior members of Congress who have interacted professionally and socially over the years. They also note that the most powerful lobbying groups in Washington strongly oppose term limits.

Term limits are currently very popular with voters. Referenda votes in a number of states have shown overwhelming support for limiting members of both the House of Representatives and the Senate.

However, the Supreme Court ruled in 1995 that the states cannot limit terms of their members of Congress, that Congressional term limits can only be imposed by amending the constitution.* (The House also failed to muster the necessary two-thirds vote to send such an amendment to the states for ratification.) The Court argued that age, citizenship, and residency—the only eligibility requirements mentioned in the Constitution—were the only qualifications intended by the Founders.

*U.S. Term Limits v. Thornton (1995).

# THE POWER OF THE COURTS

The Founders of the United States viewed the federal courts as the final bulwark against threats to individual liberty. Since *Marbury* v. *Madison* first asserted the Supreme Court's power of judicial review over congressional acts, the federal courts have struck down more than eighty congressional laws and uncounted state laws that they believed conflicted with the Constitution. *Judicial review and the right to interpret the meaning and decide the application of the Constitution and laws of the United States* are great sources of power for judges.

## KEY COURT DECISIONS

Some of the nation's most important policy decisions have been made by courts rather than by executive or legislative bodies. The federal courts took the lead in eliminating racial segregation in public life, ensuring the separation of church and state, defining relationships between citizens and law enforcers, and guaranteeing voters equal voice in government. Today the federal courts grapple with the most controversial issues facing the nation: abortion, affirmative action, the death penalty, religion in schools, the rights of criminal defendants, and so on. Courts are an integral component of America's governmental system, for sooner or later most important policy questions are brought before them.

**key policy decisions by federal courts**

eliminating racial segregation

ensuring separation of church and state

guaranteeing voters equal voice

establishing abortion rights

defining affirmative action

determining rights of criminal defendants

## DEMOCRACY AND THE SUPREME COURT

The undemocratic nature of judicial review has long been recognized in American politics. Nine Supreme Court justices—who are not elected to office, whose terms are for life, and who can be removed only for "high crimes and misdemeanors"—possess the power to void the acts of popularly elected presidents, Congresses, governors, and state legislators. Why should the views of an appointed court about the meaning of the Constitution prevail over the views of *elected* officials? Presidents and members of Congress are sworn to uphold the Constitution, and it can reasonably be assumed they do not pass laws they believe to be *un*constitutional. Why should the Supreme Court have judicial review of the decisions of these bodies?

**judicial review of federal laws**

The answer appears to be that the Founders distrusted both popular majorities and elected officials who might be influenced by popular majorities. They believed government should be limited so it could not attack principle and property, whether to do so was the will of the majority or not. So the courts were deliberately *insulated* against popular majorities; to ensure their independence, judges were not to be elected, but appointed for life terms. Only in this way, the writers of the Constitution believed, would they be sufficiently protected from the masses to permit them to judge courageously and responsibly. Insulation is, in itself, another source of judicial power.

**insulation of the courts**

appointed, not elected

judges serve life terms

*Custom, rather than the Constitution, dictates a nine-member Supreme Court of the United States.*

## JUDICIAL RESTRAINT

**judicial restraint**
judges should defer to the decision of elected representatives unless it is in clear conflict with the plain meaning of the Constitution

The power of the courts, especially the U.S. Supreme Court, is limited only by the justices' own judicial philosophy. The doctrine of *judicial restraint* argues that because justices are not popularly elected, the Supreme Court should defer to the decisions of Congress and the president unless their actions are in clear conflict with the plain meaning of the Constitution. Justice Felix Frankfurter once wrote: "The only check upon our own exercise of power is our own sense of self-restraint. For the removal of unwise laws from the statute books, appeal lies not with the Courts but to the ballot and to the processes of democratic government."[4] One should not confuse the wisdom of a law with its constitutionality; the courts should decide only the constitutionality of laws, not the wisdom or fairness.

**stare decisis**
reliance on precedent to give stability to the law

A related limitation on judicial power is the principle of *stare decisis,* which means the issue has already been decided in earlier cases. Reliance on precedent is a fundamental notion in law; it gives stability to the law. If every decision ignored past precedents and created new law, no one would know what the law is from day to day.

## JUDICIAL ACTIVISM

**judicial activism**
judges may interpret the meaning of the Constitution to fit the needs of contemporary society

However, much of the history of the Supreme Court has been one of *judicial activism,* not restraint. The dominant philosophy of the Supreme Court under Chief Justice Earl Warren (1953–1969) was that judges should interpret the meaning of the Constitution to fit the needs of contemporary society. By viewing the Constitution as a broad and flexible document, the nation can avoid new constitutional amendments and still accomplish changes in society. Precedents can be overturned as society grows and changes.

Judicial activism was reflected in the Supreme Court's famous *Brown v. Board of Education of Topeka* decision in 1954 that declared that racially segregated schools violated the equal protection clause of the Fourteenth Amendment. The Supreme Court also overturned precedent in requiring that the states apportion their legislatures so as to guarantee equal voter representation in *Baker* v. *Carr* in 1962. It struck down long-established practices of prayer and Bible reading in public schools in *Engle* v. *Vitale,* also in 1962. The Court under Earl Warren also greatly expanded the rights of criminal defendants.

The Supreme Court under President Richard Nixon's appointee, Chief Justice Warren Burger (1969–1986), was only slightly less activist. The Court's 1973 decision in *Roe* v. *Wade,* declaring that abortion was a constitutional right of women, was perhaps the most sweeping reinterpretation of individual liberty in the Court's history.

Presidents Ronald Reagan and George Bush sought to strengthen the doctrine of judicial restraint in their appointments to the Supreme Court. Chief Justice William Rehnquist (first appointed to the Court by President Nixon in 1971 and later elevated to chief justice by President Reagan in 1986) has been less activist than his predecessors. However, none of the major decisions of the Warren or Burger Courts has been reversed.

Liberals worried that the appointment of conservative Clarence Thomas by President Bush in 1991 would result in an emergence of a conservative majority on the Supreme Court. But despite the fears of liberals, no solid conservative majority emerged on the Court. Rather, moderates (including Sandra Day O'Connor, David Souter, and Anthony Kennedy) appeared to prevail in key cases over conservatives (Rehnquist, Scalia, Thomas). For example, in the important abortion case of *Planned Parenthood* v. *Casey,* Sandra Day O'Connor led the Court in upholding *Roe* v. *Wade* abortion rights while at the same time allowing state restrictions that do not "unduly burden" women in the exercise of their rights[5] (see Chapter 10). President Clinton's appointments of Ruth Bader Ginsburg (the second woman to serve on the Court) and Stephen Breyer further strengthen the moderate to liberal voice of the current Supreme Court (see Table 7-2).

## POLITICAL BEHAVIOR IN THE UNITED STATES

Popular participation in the political system is the very definition of democracy. Individuals in a democracy may run for public office; participate in marches and demonstrations; make financial contributions to political candidates and causes; attend political meetings, speeches, and rallies; write letters to public officials and newspapers; belong to organizations that support or oppose particular candidates and take stands on public issues; wear political buttons and place bumper stickers on their cars; attempt to influence friends

**TABLE 7-2**

MEMBERS OF THE U.S. SUPREME COURT

|  | Law school from which graduated | President who appointed |
| --- | --- | --- |
| Rehnquist, William Hubbs* | Stanford | Nixon (1971)<br>Reagan (1986) |
| Stevens, John Paul | Chicago | Ford (1975) |
| O'Connor, Sandra Day | Stanford | Reagan (1981) |
| Scalia, Antonin | Harvard | Reagan (1986) |
| Kennedy, Anthony McLeod | Harvard | Reagan (1988) |
| Souter, David H. | Harvard | Bush (1990) |
| Thomas, Clarence | Yale | Bush (1991) |
| Ginsburg, Ruth Bader | Columbia | Clinton (1993) |
| Breyer, Stephen G. | Harvard | Clinton (1994) |

*Rehnquist was nominated to the U.S. Supreme Court in 1971 by Richard Nixon; he was nominated as chief justice by Ronald Reagan in 1986.

**forms of political participation**

while discussing candidates and issues; vote in elections; or merely follow an issue or campaign in the mass media. This list of activities constitutes a ranking of the *forms of political participation*, in inverse order of their frequency. The activities at the beginning of the list require greater expenditure of time and energy and greater personal commitment; consequently, far fewer people engage in those activities (see Figure 7-3). Fully one-third of the population are politically apathetic: they do not vote, and they are largely unaware of and indifferent to the political life of the nation.

## VOTER TURNOUT

Voter turnout is greatest in presidential elections, but even in those contests turnout is only about 50–55 percent of eligible people. "Off-year" congressional elections—congressional elections held in years in which there is no presidential election—attract only 35 or 40 percent of eligible people to the polls. Yet in these "off-year" contests the nation chooses all of its U.S. representatives, one-third of its U.S. senators, and about one-half of its governors. Local government elections—for mayor, council members, school board, and so forth—frequently attract only one-quarter to one-third of eligible voters.

## NONVOTING

Who votes and who doesn't? Some groups of people are more likely to vote than others. Education appears to be the most important determinant of voter turnout. It may be that schooling promotes an interest in politics, instills the ethic of citizen participation, or gives people a better awareness of public affairs and an understanding of the role of elections in a democracy. Education is associated with a sense of confidence and political "efficacy"—the feeling that one can indeed have a personal impact on public affairs.

Age is another factor affecting voter participation. Perhaps because young people have more distractions, more demands on their time in schooling, work, or new family responsibilities, nonvoting is greatest among those age eighteen to twenty-one. In contrast, older Americans are politically influential in part because candidates know they turn out at the polls.

High-income people are more likely to vote than are low-income people. Most of this difference is a product of the fact that high-income people are more likely well educated and older. But poor people may also feel alienated from the political system. The poor may lack a sense of political efficacy—they may feel they have little control over their own lives, let alone over public affairs. Or the poor may simply be so absorbed in the problems of life that they have little time or energy to spend on registering and voting.

Historically, race was a major determinant of nonvoting. Black voter turnout, especially in the South, was markedly lower than white voter turnout. But today, blacks and whites at the *same* educational and income levels register and vote with the same frequency. The greatest racial disparity in voter turnout is between Hispanics and others. Low voter participation by Hispanics may be a product of language differences, lack of cultural assimilation, or noncitizenship status.

## THE VOTER DECIDES

Perhaps no other area of political science has been investigated so thoroughly—by political candidates, campaign strategists, and political scientists—as the *reasons behind the voters' choices* at the polls. Voters cast ballots for and against candidates for a variety of reasons, including their party affiliation, their membership in social and economic groups, their positive and negative evaluations of the images of the candidates, their view of the goodness or badness of the times (especially the economy), and sometimes even the positions of the candidates on important issues.

**reasons behind voters' choices**
party affiliation
group membership
candidate image
nature of the times, especially the economy
issues

Although party ties have weakened somewhat over time, party affiliation remains an important influence over voter choice. People who identify themselves as Democrats or Republicans usually vote for their party's candidate (see "Politics" in Table 7-3). Membership in various social and economic groups also affects voting; for example, black voters regularly give much greater support to Democratic candidates (see "Race" in Table 7-3).

Candidates spend a great deal of time and money during a campaign trying to project a favorable image of themselves (or a negative image of their opponent) through television and the press. (See the Focus, "Media Power:

## FIGURE 7-3

### POLITICAL PARTICIPATION

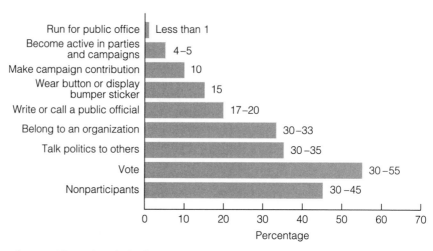

The Presidential Debates.") Challengers attack the record of *incumbents* seeking reelection, holding them responsible for anything bad that happened during their term, especially any weaknesses that developed in the economy. Incumbents are more likely to be reelected when the nation enjoys "peace and prosperity." Relatively few voters cast their ballot exclusively on a particular policy position of a candidate, although some "hot button" issues—abortion, for example—influence the choice of some voters.

**incumbent**

a candidate currently in office seeking reelection

## DEMOCRATS AND REPUBLICANS— WHAT'S THE DIFFERENCE?

Democracy is ultimately based on majority rule, and one function of political parties is to *put majorities together*. Political parties organize voters for effective political expression at the polls. Voters, in turn, use party labels to help them identify the general political viewpoints of the candidates.

Because American parties are necessarily rather loose coalitions of interests, they do not command the total loyalty of every officeholder elected under a party's banner. The fact that candidates run under a Republican or Democratic label does not clearly indicate where they will stand on every public issue. Even so, these coalitions do have considerable cohesion and historical continuity. The party label *discloses the coalition of interests and the policy views* with which candidates have generally associated themselves. At the least, the party label tells more about a candidate's politics than would a strange name, with no party affiliation, on the ballot.

Especially in two-party systems, such as we have in the United States, parties also *structure the choice of candidates* for public office and thus relieve

**functions of political parties**

organize majorities

identify candidate's coalition of interests

structure choices

define issues

criticize officeholders

**TABLE 7-3**

## VOTING BY GROUPS IN RECENT PRESIDENTIAL ELECTIONS

| | | 1984 | | 1988 | |
|---|---|---|---|---|---|
| | | Democrat Mondale | Republican Reagan | Democrat Dukakis | Republican Bush |
| **National** | | **41%** | **59%** | **46%** | **54%** |
| Gender | Male | 37 | 61 | 42 | 58 |
| | Female | 42 | 57 | 49 | 51 |
| Race | White | 34 | 66 | 40 | 60 |
| | Nonwhite | 90 | 9 | 90 | 10 |
| Age | Under 30 years | 41 | 58 | 47 | 53 |
| | 30–49 | 42 | 58 | 46 | 54 |
| | 50 years & older | 36 | 63 | 48 | 52 |
| Religion | Protestants | 26 | 73 | 38 | 62 |
| | Catholics | 44 | 55 | 54 | 46 |
| Politics | Republicans | 7 | 92 | 8 | 92 |
| | Democrats | 73 | 26 | 83 | 17 |
| | Independents | 35 | 63 | 43 | 57 |

| | | 1992 | | | 1996 | | |
|---|---|---|---|---|---|---|---|
| | | Democrat Clinton | Republican Bush | Independent Perot | Democrat Clinton | Republican Dole | Independent Perot |
| **National** | | **43%** | **38%** | **19%** | **49%** | **41%** | **8%** |
| Gender | Male | 41 | 38 | 21 | 43 | 44 | 10 |
| | Female | 46 | 37 | 17 | 54 | 38 | 7 |
| Race | White | 39 | 41 | 20 | 43 | 46 | 9 |
| | Nonwhite | 82 | 11 | 7 | 84 | 12 | 4 |
| Age | Under 30 years | 44 | 34 | 22 | 53 | 34 | 10 |
| | 30–49 | 42 | 38 | 20 | 48 | 41 | 9 |
| | 50 years & older | 45 | 40 | 15 | 48 | 41 | 9 |
| Religion | Protestants | 33 | 46 | 12 | 41 | 50 | 8 |
| | Catholics | 44 | 36 | 20 | 53 | 32 | 9 |
| Politics | Republicans | 10 | 73 | 17 | 13 | 80 | 6 |
| | Democrats | 77 | 10 | 13 | 84 | 10 | 5 |
| | Independents | 38 | 32 | 30 | 43 | 35 | 17 |

SOURCE: Based on data from the *Gallup Poll* surveys.

voters of the task of choosing among dozens of contending candidates on election day. The preliminary selecting and narrowing of candidates, by conventions and primary elections, are indispensable in a large society.

Political parties help *define the major problems and issues* confronting society. In attempting to win a majority of the voters, parties inform the public about the issues facing the nation. The comparisons parties make during

## FOCUS
Media Power:
The Presidential
Debates

Presidential debates attract
more viewers than any other
campaign activity. They produce vastly greater audiences
than the candidates could gar-
ner by any other means. Most
campaign activities—speeches,
rallies, motorcades—reach only
supporters. Such activities may
inspire supporters to go to the
polls, contribute money, and
even work to get others to vote
their way. But televised debates
reach undecided voters as well
as supporters, and they allow
candidates to be seen by supporters of their opponent. Debates allow people to directly
compare the responses of each
candidate. Even if issues are
not really discussed in depth,
people see how presidential
candidates react as human beings under pressure.

### Kennedy-Nixon

Televised presidential debates
began in 1960 when John F.
Kennedy and Richard M.
Nixon confronted each other
on a bare stage before an
America watching on black-
and-white TV sets. Nixon was
the vice-president in the popu-

lar presidential administration
of Dwight Eisenhower; he was
also an accomplished college
debate team member. He prepared for the debates as if they
were college debates, memoriz-
ing facts and arguments. But
he failed to realize that image
triumphs over substance on
television. Nixon was shifty-
eyed and clearly in need of a
shave or more makeup to hide
his pronounced "five o'clock
shadow." By contrast, Kennedy
was handsome, cool, confident;
whatever doubts the American
people may have had regarding
his youth and inexperience
were dispelled by his polished
manner. Radio listeners tended
to think that Nixon won, and
debate coaches scored him the
winner. But television viewers
preferred the glamorous young
Kennedy. The polls shifted in
Kennedy's direction after the
debate, and he won in a very
close general election. Nixon
blamed his makeup man.

### Carter-Ford

President Lyndon Johnson
avoided debating in 1964, and
Nixon, having learned his lesson, declined to debate in 1968
and 1972. Thus televised presidential debates did not resume
until 1976, when incumbent
President Gerald Ford, perceiv-
ing that he was behind in the
polls, agreed to debate chal-

lenger Jimmy Carter. Ford
made a series of verbal slips—
saying, for example, that the
nations of eastern Europe were
free from Soviet domination.
In that same year, the first vice-
presidential debate was held. In
it, Republican Robert Dole's
biting comments appeared
mean-spirited in contrast to
Democrat Walter Mondale's
"Boy Scout" image. Both Carter
and Mondale were widely perceived as having "won" their
debates, and they went on to
victory in the general election.

### Reagan-Carter and
### Reagan-Mondale

It was Ronald Reagan who
demonstrated the true power
of television. Reagan had lived
his life in front of a camera. It
was the principal tool of both
of his trades—actor and politi-
cian. In 1980, incumbent President Jimmy Carter attempted
to portray Reagan as a mean-
spirited conservative ideologue
who was a threat to peace.
Carter talked rapidly and seriously about programs, figures,
and budgets. But Reagan was
master of the stage; he was relaxed, confident, joking. He appeared to treat the president of
the United States as an overly
aggressive, impulsive younger
man, regrettably given to exag-
geration ("There you go
again."). When it was all over, it

SOURCE: Thomas R. Dye, *Politics in America,* 2nd ed. (New York: Prentice-Hall, 1997), pp. 276–277.

was clear to most viewers that Carter had been bested by a true professional in media skills.

However, in the first of two televised debates with Walter Mondale in 1984, Reagan's skills of a lifetime seemed to desert him. He stumbled over statistics and groped for words. Mondale was respectful of the presidency, somewhat stiff and ill-at-ease before the cameras but nevertheless clearheaded in his responses. Reagan's poor performance raised the only issue that might conceivably defeat him—his age. The president had looked and sounded *old*.

In preparation for the second debate, Reagan decided, without telling his aides, to lay the perfect trap for his questioners. When asked about his age and capacity to lead the nation, he responded with a serious deadpan expression to a hushed audience and waiting America: "I want you to know that I will not make age an issue in this campaign. I am not going to exploit for political purposes [pause] my opponent's youth and inexperience." The studio audience broke into uncontrolled laughter. Even Mondale had to laugh. With a classic one-liner, the president buried the age issue and won not only the debate but the election.

### Bush-Dukakis

In 1988, Michael Dukakis ensured his defeat with a cold, detached performance in the presidential debates, beginning with the very first question. When CNN anchor Bernard Shaw asked: "Governor, if Kitty Dukakis were raped and murdered, would you favor an irrevocable death penalty for the killer?" The question demanded an emotional reply. Instead, Dukakis responded with an impersonal recitation of his stock positions on crime, drugs, and law enforcement. Bush seized the opportunity to establish an intimate, warm, and personal relationship with the viewers: "I do believe some crimes are so heinous, so brutal, so outrageous . . . I do believe in the death penalty." Voters responded to Bush, electing him.

### Clinton-Bush-Perot

The three-way presidential debates of 1992 drew the largest television audiences in the history of presidential debates. In the first debate, Ross Perot's Texas twang and down-home folksy style stole the show. Chided by his opponents for having no governmental experience, he shot back: "Well, they have a point. I don't have any experience in running up a $4 trillion debt. I don't have any experience in gridlock government. I don't have any experi-

ence in creating the worst public school system in the industrialized world, the most violent crime-ridden society in the industrialized world. But I do have a lot of experience in getting things done." Perot's popularity in the polls, hardly visible at all following his earlier abrupt withdrawal from the race, suddenly sprang to life again.

But it was Bill Clinton's smooth performance in the second debate, with its talk-show format, that seemed to wrap up the election. Ahead in the polls, Clinton appeared at ease walking about the stage and responding to audience questions with sympathy and sincerity. By contrast, George Bush appeared stiff and formal, and somewhat ill-at-ease with the "unpresidential" format. Bush made a modest comeback in the third and final debate with hard-hitting attacks on Clinton as a "waffler," but his modest recovery was too little and too late.

### Clinton-Dole

A desperate Bob Dole, running 20 points behind, faced a newly "presidential" Bill Clinton in their two 1996 debates. (Perot's poor standing in the polls led to his exclusion.) Dole tried to counter his image as a grumpy old man in the first encounter; his humor actually won more

*(Continued)*

**FOCUS**

Media Power:
The Presidential
Debates
*(Continued)*

In the 1996 presidential debates, Bob Dole's humor helped counter his image as a grumpy old man, but was not enough to sway voters away from the more polished and "presidential" Bill Clinton.

laughs from the audience than the president's more stately comments. Dole injected more barbs in the second debate, complaining of "ethical problems in the White House" and repeating the mantra "I keep my word," suggesting that Clinton did not. But Clinton remained cool and comfortable, ignoring the challenger and focusing on the nation's economic health. Viewers, most of whom were already in Clinton's court, judged him the winner of both debates.

political campaigns have an important educational value: voters come to "know" the opposing candidates for public office, and the problems of national interest are spotlighted.

Finally, the party *out* of office performs an important function for democratic government by *criticizing officeholders*. Moreover, the very existence of a recognized party outside the government helps make criticism of government legitimate and effective.

## PARTY DIFFERENCES

**evidence of party differences**

differing coalitions of voter groups

differing views of party leaders

differing voting records in Congress

It is sometimes argued that there are few significant differences between the two main American parties. It is not uncommon in European nations to find authoritarian parties competing with democratic parties, capitalist parties with socialist parties, Catholic parties with secular parties, and so on. However, within the context of American political experience, the Democratic and Republican parties can be clearly differentiated. There are at least three ways in which to discern the differences: (1) by examining differences in the *coalitions of voters* supporting each party, (2) by examining differences in the *policy views of the leaders* in each party, and (3) by examining differences in the *voting records of the representatives and senators* of each party.

## SOCIAL GROUP DIFFERENCES IN PARTY SUPPORT

In ascertaining party differences according to support from different groups of voters, we must note first that major groups are seldom *wholly* within one party or the other. For example, in presidential elections all major social groups divide their votes between the parties. Yet differences between the parties are revealed *in the proportions of votes given by each major group to each party.* Thus, the Democratic party receives a disproportionate amount of support from Catholics, Jews, blacks, lower-income groups, blue-collar workers, union members, and big-city residents. The Republican party receives disproportionate support from Protestants, whites, higher-income groups, professionals and managers, white-collar workers, nonunion members, and rural and small-town residents.

## DIFFERENCES IN VIEWS OF PARTY LEADERS

The second way of discerning Democratic and Republican party differences involves an examination of the political opinions of the leaders of each party. Political scientists have studied party differences by presenting a series of policy questions to the delegates to the Democratic and Republican national conventions. They have found substantial differences of opinion between Democratic and Republican leaders on important public issues. Political scientist Herbert McClosky concludes:

> *Democratic leaders typically display the stronger urge to elevate the low-born, the uneducated, the deprived minorities, and the poor in general; they are also more disposed to employ the nation's collective power to advance humanitarian and social welfare goals (e.g., Social Security, immigration, racial integration, a higher minimum wage, and public education). They are more critical of wealth and big business and more eager to bring them under regulation. Theirs is the greater faith in the wisdom of using legislation for redistributing the national product and for furnishing social services on a wide scale. Of the two groups of leaders, the Democrats are more "progressively" oriented toward social reform and experimentation. The Republican leaders, while not uniformly differentiated from their opponents, subscribe in greater measure to the symbols and practices of individualism, laissez-faire, and national independence. They prefer to overcome humanity's misfortunes by relying upon personal effort, private incentives, frugality, hard work, responsibility, self-denial (for both men and government), and the strengthening rather than the diminution of the economic and status distinctions that are the "natural" rewards of the differences in human character and fortunes.[6]*

## Party Differences in Congressional Voting

**party votes**

roll-call votes in Congress in which a majority of Democrats oppose a majority of Republicans

The third indication of party differences in the United States is the roll-call voting behavior of the representatives and senators of each party on controversial issues. About half of all roll-call votes in Congress are *party votes*—votes in which a majority of Democrats oppose a majority of Republicans. Party votes occur most frequently on well-publicized, high-conflict issues (see Table 7-4). Party voting also occurs on presidential recommendations, with the president's party in Congress supporting the president's position and the opposition party opposing it. Bipartisan votes, those roll calls in which party majorities are found on the same side, usually occur on less-publicized, low-conflict issues. On many issues, voting follows party lines during roll calls on preliminary amendments but swings to a bipartisan vote on the final legislation. This occurs when the parties disagree on certain aspects of a bill but compromise on its final passage.

### TABLE 7-4

### Party Conflict on Selected Roll-Call Votes

| | House votes | | | |
| --- | --- | --- | --- | --- |
| | Republicans | | Democrats | |
| | yes | no | yes | no |
| Reagan income tax cuts (1981) | 189 | 1 | 48 | 196 |
| Clinton budget and tax increase (1993) | 0 | 175 | 218 | 38 |
| Brady law, gun control (1993) | 56 | 116 | 182 | 70 |
| Balanced Budget Constitutional Amendment* (1995) | 228 | 2 | 72 | 129 |
| Ban late-term abortions† (1996) | 218 | 15 | 70 | 121 |
| Welfare reform (1996) | 226 | 4 | 30 | 165 |

| | Senate votes | | | |
| --- | --- | --- | --- | --- |
| | Republicans | | Democrats | |
| | yes | no | yes | no |
| Reagan income tax cuts (1981) | 51 | 0 | 20 | 26 |
| Clinton budget and tax increase (1993) | 0 | 44 | 50 | 6 |
| Brady law, gun control (1993) | 16 | 28 | 47 | 8 |
| Balanced Budget Constitutional Amendment* (1995) | 52 | 1 | 14 | 33 |
| Ban late-term abortions† (1996) | 45 | 6 | 12 | 35 |
| Welfare reform (1996) | 51 | 1 | 23 | 33 |

*Requires two-thirds vote for passage. Dole vote shown as "yes" although officially cast as "no" to preserve option of calling for another vote.

†Vote to override President Clinton's veto; fails to win necessary two-thirds vote of both houses.

SOURCE: *Congressional Quarterly Weekly Report,* "Key Votes," in various issues.

# NOTES

1. Harold Lasswell, *Politics: Who Gets What, When and How* (New York: McGraw-Hill, 1936).
2. *The Federalist Papers* were a series of essays by James Madison, Alexander Hamilton, and John Jay, written in 1787 and 1788 to explain and defend the new Constitution during the struggle over its ratification. (*The Federalist*, New York: Modern Library, 1937).
3. *Garcia* v. *San Antonio Metropolitan Transit Authority* 469 U.S. 528 (1985).
4. *West Virginia State Board of Education* v. *Barrett* 319 U.S. 624 (1943).
5. *Planned Parenthood* v. *Casey* 505 U.S. 199 (1992).
6. Herbert J. McClosky et al., "Issue Conflict and Consensus Among Party Leaders and Followers," *American Political Science Review* 54 (June 1960): 595.

# ABOUT THIS CHAPTER

The power of government is truly awesome. Government power influences every facet of our lives "from the cradle to the grave." We eat government-inspected foods, which have been transported on government-regulated railroads and highways and grown on government-subsidized farms. We live in government-inspected homes, paid for by government-subsidized mortgages from government-regulated banks. We attend government-subsidized schools, or work in government-inspected shops, or manage government-regulated businesses. The awesome powers of government have worried people for centuries. How can governmental power be limited? How can we enjoy the benefits and protections of government yet not become slaves to it? How can government leaders be restrained? How can we guarantee that our personal liberties will not be threatened by governments?

These questions are the province of political science, and in this chapter we have examined the answers that political science provides. Now that you have read Chapter 7, you should be able to

- discuss the meaning of *democracy*—its underlying values and rules of decision making
- describe the separation of powers in American government and the system of checks and balances, and discuss the reasons the Founders designed these amendments
- discuss the meaning of *federalism,* and describe how and why power has flowed through Washington over the years
- describe the growth of presidential power as well as the limits on such power

- contrast the power of Congress in foreign and domestic affairs, and outline the arguments for and against term limits
- define the power of judicial review and discuss judicial activism and judicial restraint
- define the principal forms of political participation in American government
- identify differences between the Democratic and Republican parties
- discuss the impact of television on presidential elections

# DISCUSSION QUESTIONS

1. Define *political science* and describe its areas of concern.
2. Describe John Locke's views on constitutionalism and constitutional government, natural law, and the social contract. Discuss the influence of Locke's ideas on the authors of the U.S. Constitution.
3. Define *democracy.*
4. What are the foundations of national power, and how does the Constitution define and limit them? Contrast *expressed* (delegated) powers with *implied* powers and identify the clause on which implied powers are based.
5. Define *federalism* and discuss the changes that have taken place in the American federal structure. Include in your discussion a definition of *grants-in-aid.*
6. Discuss the rationale the Founders used for structuring the government around a separation of powers. Identify the separate power structures the Constitution created. Describe the principal checks and balances each structure exercises over the others.
7. Discuss the sources of presidential power and the factors contributing to the growth of that power in the twentieth century. Briefly describe how Richard Nixon overstepped the boundaries or limitations of presidential power.
8. Define *judicial review* and explain why the nation's Founders were in favor of this principle. Describe how and why the courts are "insulated." Contrast the arguments for "judicial restraint" and "judicial activism."
9. Discuss participation and nonparticipation in democracy. Who participates, and how is it possible to participate? What are the principal forms of participation? What groups of people are more likely to vote?
10. Describe the functions of political parties. How is it possible to identify real party differences in America?
11. What has been the impact of television on politics, especially presidential elections?

Chapter 8

# Power
# and History

## HISTORY AND SOCIAL SCIENCE

Can history inform the social sciences? The purpose of this chapter is not to teach American history, but rather to examine the work of historians to see what contribution they can make to our understanding of power and the social sciences.

*History* refers to all *past human actions and events.* The study of history is the *recording, narrating, and interpreting of these events.* History includes the discovery of facts about past events, as well as the interpretation of the events. Many historians contend that their primary responsibility is the reporting of facts about the past: the accurate presentation of what actually happened, unbiased by interpretive theories or philosophies.

But however carefully historians try to avoid bias, they cannot report *all* the facts of human history. Facts do not select and arrange themselves. The historians must select and organize facts that are worthy of interest, and this process involves personal judgment of what is important about the past. The historian's judgment about the past is affected by present conditions and by

**history**
the recording, narrating, and interpreting of all past human actions and events

personal feelings about the future. So the past is continually reinterpreted by each generation of historians. History is "an unending dialogue" between the present and the past; it is "what one age finds worthy of note in another."

In selecting and organizing their facts, historians must consider the causes of wars and revolutions, the reasons for the rise and fall of civilizations, the consequences of great events and ideas. They cannot marshal their facts without some notion of *interrelations* among human events. Because they must consider what forces have operated to shape the past, they become involved in economics, sociology, psychology, anthropology, and political science. Historian Henry Steele Commager has observed that "no self-respecting modern historian is content merely with recording what happened; he wants to explain why it happened."[1] Thus, history and social science are intimately related.

## HISTORY AND THE AMERICAN EXPERIENCE

There is a great temptation to romanticize national history. Many national histories are self-congratulating, patriotic exercises. Many historical biographies paint their subjects as larger-than-life figures, free of the faults of common people, who shape the course of events themselves rather than merely respond to the world in which they live. National leaders of the past—Washington, Jefferson, Jackson, Lincoln, Franklin D. Roosevelt—are portrayed as noble people superior in character and wisdom to today's politicians. Even with the myth of the cherry tree discarded, generations of historians have looked with awe on the gallery of national heroes.

Some national histories do not rely on "great man" explanations, but instead emphasize the origin and growth of democratic institutions. Democracy is traced from its ancient Greek beginnings, through English constitutional development, to the colonies and the American constitutional system. Frequently these national histories reinforce reverence for existing political and governmental institutions.

But historians have also been critical of American institutions. At the beginning of the twentieth century, reform politicians and muckraking journalists brought a new skepticism to American life. The Progressive era was critical of the malfunctioning of many governmental institutions that had become sacred over time, and even of the Olympian position of the nation's Founders. In 1913 Charles A. Beard created an uproar by suggesting that economic motives played a part in leading the Founders to write the Constitution. (See Controversies in Social Science, "Charles Beard and the Economic Interpretation of the Constitution.")

Nevertheless, for the most part the quest for the American past has been carried on in a spirit of sentiment and nostalgia, rather than of critical analysis. Historical novels, fictionalized biographies, pictorial collections, and books on American regions all appeal to our fondness for looking back to what we believe was a better era. Americans have a peculiar longing to recapture the past, to try to recover what seems to have been lost.

**approaches to American history**

the "great man" approach

the democratic institutions approach

critical approaches

## CONTROVERSIES IN SOCIAL SCIENCE
Charles Beard and the Economic Interests of the Founders

Charles Beard, historian and political scientist, provided the most controversial historical interpretation of the origin of American national government in his landmark book, *An Economic Interpretation of the Constitution.*[a] Beard argued that to understand the Constitution we must understand the economic interests of the national elite, which included the writers of the document:

*Did the men who formulated the fundamental law of the land possess the kinds of property which were immediately and directly increased in value or made more secure by the results of their labors in Philadelphia? Did they have money at interest [loans outstanding]? Did they own public securities [government bonds]? Did they hold Western lands for appreciation? Were they interested in shipping and manufactures?*[b]

Beard was *not* charging that the Founders wrote the Constitution exclusively for their own

benefit. But he argued that they personally benefited immediately from its adoption and that they did not act only "under the guidance of abstract principles of political science." Beard closely studied old unpublished financial records of the U.S. Treasury Department and the personal letters and financial accounts of the fifty-five delegates to the Philadelphia convention. The table summarizes his findings of the financial interests of the nation's Founders.

Beard then turned to an examination of the *Constitution* itself, in the original form in which it emerged from the Convention, to observe the *relationship between economic interests and political power.*

The first, and perhaps the most important, enumerated power is the power to "lay and collect taxes, duties, imposts, and excises." The *taxing power* was of great benefit to the holders of government bonds, particularly when it was combined with the provision in Article VI that "all debts contracted and engagements entered into, before the adoption of this Constitution, shall be as valid against the United States under this Constitution, as under the Confederation." This meant that the national government would be obliged to pay off all

those investors who held bonds of the United States, and the taxing power would give the national government the ability to do so on its own.

Following the power to tax and spend, to borrow money, and to regulate commerce in Article I, there is a series of *specific powers designed to enable Congress to protect money and property.* Congress is given the power to make bankruptcy laws, to coin money and regulate its value, to fix standards of weights and measures, to punish counterfeiting, to establish post offices and post roads, to pass copyright and patent laws to protect authors and inventors, and to punish piracies and felonies committed on the high seas. Each of these powers is a specific asset to bankers, investors, merchants, authors, inventors, and shippers.

The Constitution provided an explicit advantage to slaveholders in Article IV, Section 2 (later altered by the Thirteenth Amendment, which abolished slavery):

*No person held to Service or Labour in one State, under the Laws thereof, escaping into another, shall, in Consequence of any Law or Regulation therein, be discharged from such Service or Labour, but shall be delivered up on Claim of the Party to*

---

[a]Charles Beard, *An Economic Interpretation of the Constitution* (New York: Macmillan, 1913).
[b]Ibid., p. 73.

*whom such Service or Labour may be due.*

Many historians disagree with Beard's emphasis on the economic motives of the Founders. For example:

*The Constitution was adopted in a society which was fundamentally democratic, not undemocratic; and it was adopted by people who were primarily middle-class property owners, especially farmers who owned realty, not just by the owners of personalty. . . . The Constitution was not just an economic document, although economic factors were undoubtedly important. Since most of the people were middle-class and had private property, practically everybody was interested in the protection of property.[c]*

Moreover, in the struggle over ratification of the new Constitution, influential anti-Federalists deplored its undemocratic features, and their criticism about the omission of a Bill of Rights led directly to the inclusion of the first ten amendments.

## BEARD'S CLASSIFICATION OF THE FOUNDERS OF THE AMERICAN NATION BY ECONOMIC INTERESTS

| Public security interests (owners of U.S. bonds) | | Real estate and land speculation | Lending and banking investments | Mercantile, manufacturing, and shipping interests | Plantations and slaveholdings |
|---|---|---|---|---|---|
| Major | Minor | | | | |
| Baldwin | Bassett | Blount | Bassett | Broom | Butler |
| Blair | Blount | Dayton | Broom | Clymer | Davie |
| Clymer | Brearley | Few | Butler | Ellsworth | Jenifer |
| Dayton | Broom | FitzSimons | Carroll | FitzSimons | A. Martin |
| Ellsworth | Butler | Franklin | Clymer | Gerry | L. Martin |
| FitzSimons | Carroll | Gerry | Davie | King | Mason |
| Gerry | Few | Gilman | Dickinson | Langdon | Mercer |
| Gilman | Hamilton | Gorham | Ellsworth | McHenry | C. C. Pinckney |
| Gorham | L. Martin | Hamilton | Few | Mifflin | C. Pinckney |
| Jenifer | Mason | Mason | FitzSimons | G. Morris | Randolph |
| Johnson | Mercer | R. Morris | Franklin | R. Morris | Read |
| King | Mifflin | Washington | Gilman | | Rutledge |
| Langdon | Read | Williamson | Ingersoll | | Spaight |
| Lansing | Spaight | Wilson | Johnson | | Washington |
| Livingston | Wilson | | King | | Wythe |
| McClurg | Wythe | | Langdon | | |
| R. Morris | | | McHenry | | |
| C. C. Pinckney | | | Mason | | |
| C. Pinckney | | | C. C. Pinckney | | |
| Randolph | | | C. Pinckney | | |
| Sherman | | | Randolph | | |
| Strong | | | Read | | |
| Washington | | | Washington | | |
| Williamson | | | Williamson | | |

[c]Robert E. Brown, *Charles Beard and the Constitution* (Princeton, N.J.: Princeton University Press, 1956), p. 200.

# POWER AND CHANGE OVER TIME

Our own bias about the importance of power in society leads us to focus attention on *changing sources of power over time* in American history and on the characteristics of the people and groups who have acquired power. We contend that the Constitution, and the national government it established, reflected the beliefs, values, and interests of the people of power— the elite—of the new republic. If we are to have a true understanding of the Constitution, we must investigate the political interests of the Founders and the historical circumstances surrounding the Philadelphia convention in 1787.

## CHANGES IN POWER OVER TIME

Power structures change over time. To understand power in society we have to explore the historical development of power relationships. Any society, to maintain stability and avoid revolution, must provide opportunities for talented and ambitious individuals to acquire power. As an expanding economy created new sources of wealth, power in the United States shifted to those groups and individuals who acquired the new economic resources. Western expansion and settlement, industrialization, immigration, urbanization, technological innovation, and new sources of wealth created new bases of power and new powerholders.

But power in the United States has changed slowly, without any serious break in the ideas and values underlying the American political and economic system. The nation has never experienced a true revolution, in which national leadership is formally replaced by groups or individuals who do not share the values of the system itself. Instead, *changes have been slow and incremental.* New national leaders have generally accepted the national consensus about private enterprise, limited government, and individualism.

**incremental change**
slow and continuous rather than rapid or revolutionary

Historian Richard Hofstadter argues effectively that many accounts of the American past overemphasize the political differences in every era:

> *The fierceness of the political struggles has often been misleading; for the range of vision embraced by the primary contestants in the major parties has always been bounded by the horizons of property and enterprise. However much at odds on specific issues, the major political traditions have shared a belief in the rights of property, the philosophy of economic individualism, the value of competition; they have accepted the economic virtues of capitalist culture as necessary qualities of man. Even when some property right has been challenged—as it was by followers of Jefferson and Jackson—in the name of the rights of man or the rights of the community, the challenge, when translated into practical policy, has actually been urged on behalf of some other kind of property.[2]*

**American beliefs shared over time**
individualism

private property

enterprise

competition

# THE RISE OF WESTERN ELITES

As we have noted, power relationships change over time. Industrialization, urbanization, technological change, and new sources of wealth create new bases of power and new powerholders. The governmental structure of society must provide for changes in the distribution of power or suffer the threat of instability and even revolution. The political system must provide for the "circulation of the elite" as new bases of power and new powerholders emerge in society.

According to historian Frederick Jackson Turner, "The rise of the New West was the most significant fact in American history."[3] Certainly the American West had a profound impact on the political system of the new nation. People went west because of the vast wealth of fertile lands that awaited them there; nowhere else in the world could one acquire wealth so quickly. Because landed families of the eastern seaboard seldom had reason to migrate westward, the western settlers were mainly middle- or lower-class immigrants. With hard work and good fortune, a penniless migrant could become a rich plantation owner or cattle rancher in a single generation. Thus, the West meant rapid upward social mobility.

**influence of the West on American history**
new wealth and opportunity

upward social mobility

more open elite system

## JACKSONIAN DEMOCRACY

A new elite arose in the West and had to be assimilated into America's governing circles. This assimilation had a profound effect on the character of America's elite. No one exemplifies the new entrants better than Andrew Jackson. Jackson's victory in the presidential election of 1828 was not a victory of the common man over the propertied classes, but a victory of the new western elite over established leadership in the East. It forced the established elite to recognize the growing importance of the West and to open their ranks to the new rich who were settling west of the Alleghenies.

Because Jackson was a favorite of the people, it was easy for him to believe in the wisdom of the masses. But *Jacksonian Democracy* was by no means a philosophy of leveling egalitarianism. The ideal of the frontier society was the self-made individual, and wealth and power won by *competitive skill* were much admired. Wealth and power obtained through special privilege offended the frontierspeople. They believed in a *natural aristocracy,* rather than an aristocracy by birth, education, or special privilege. It was *not* absolute equality that Jacksonians demanded but a *more open elite system—* a greater opportunity for the rising middle class to acquire wealth and influence through competition.

**Jacksonian Democracy**
"natural aristocracy" of self-made individuals

universal white male suffrage

no property restrictions on voting or office-holding

presidential nominations by party conventions

presidential electors chosen by popular vote

## SEEKING MASS SUPPORT

In their struggle to open America's elite system, the Jacksonians appealed to mass sentiment. Jackson's humble beginnings, his image as a self-made man, his military adventures, his frontier experience, and his rough, brawling style endeared him to the masses. As beneficiaries of popular support, the new western elite developed a strong faith in the wisdom and justice of popular decisions. The new western states that entered the Union granted universal white male suffrage, and gradually the older states fell into step. The rising elite, themselves often less than a generation away from the masses, saw in a widened electorate a chance for personal advancement they could never have achieved under the old regime. Therefore, the Jacksonians became noisy and effective advocates of the principle that all free men should have the right to *vote* and that no restrictions should be placed on *office-holding*. They also launched a successful attack on the congressional caucus system of nominating presidential candidates, substituting instead nomination by national party conventions. In 1832, when the Democrats held their first national convention, Andrew Jackson was renominated by acclamation.

Jacksonian Democracy also brought changes in the method of selecting presidential electors. The Constitution left to the various state legislatures the right to decide how presidential electors should be chosen, and in most cases the legislatures themselves chose the electors. But after 1832 all states elected their presidential electors by popular vote. In most states the people voted for electors who were listed under the name of their party and their candidate.

# THE CIVIL WAR AND THE DIVISION OF THE ELITE

**division among the elite**

Social scientists can gain insight into societal conflict and *the breakdown of elite consensus* through the study of history, particularly the history of the American Civil War. America's elite were in substantial agreement about the character and direction of the new nation during its first sixty years. In the 1850s, however, the role of African Americans in American society—the most divisive issue in the history of American politics—became an urgent question that drove a wedge between the elite groups and ultimately led to the nation's bloodiest war. The political system was unequal to the task of negotiating a peaceful settlement to the problem of slavery because America's elite were deeply divided over the question.

## SOUTHERN ELITES

**southern elites**
plantation owners dependent on slave labor

It was the white southern elite and not the white masses who had an interest in the slave and cotton culture. On the eve of the Civil War probably not more than one in four southern families held slaves, and many of those families held only one or two slaves each. The number of great planters (men who owned fifty or more slaves and large holdings of land) was probably not more than 7,000. Yet the views of these planters dominated southern politics.

*The costs of preserving the Union. This photo, taken after the battle of Antietam, shows the "Bloody Lane" where two Union regiments trapped Confederates in a barrage of rifle fire. The photo was taken by the famous Civil War photographer Matthew Brady, whose images were the first that Americans had ever seen of the horrors of war.*

The Library of Congress

## Northern Elites

The northern elite consisted of merchants and manufacturers who depended on wage labor. However, the northern elite had no direct interest in the abolition of slavery in the South. Some northern manufacturers were making good profits from southern trade, and with higher tariffs they stood a chance to make even better profits. Abolitionist activities imperiled trade relations between North and South and were often looked on with irritation in northern social circles.

**northern elite**
manufacturers dependent on wage labor

## Elite Conflict over Western Land

Both the northern and the southern elite realized that control of the West was the key to future dominance of the nation. The northern elite wanted a West composed of small farmers who produced food and raw materials for the industrial and commercial East and provided a market for eastern goods. But southern planters feared the voting power of a West composed of small farmers and wanted western lands for the expansion of the cotton and slave culture. Cotton ate up the land, and because it required continuous cultivation and monotonous rounds of simple tasks, cotton growing was suited to slave labor. Thus, to protect the cotton economy, it was essential to expand westward and to protect slavery in the West. The conflict over western land eventually precipitated the Civil War.

## ATTEMPTS AT COMPROMISE

**underlying elite consensus: attempts at compromise**

Missouri Compromise of 1820

Compromise of 1850

Kansas-Nebraska Act

Yet despite such differences, the underlying consensus of the American elite was so great that compromise after compromise was devised to maintain unity. Both the northern and the southern elite displayed a continued devotion to the principles of constitutional government and the protection of private property. In the *Missouri Compromise* of 1820, the land in the Louisiana Purchase exclusive of Missouri was divided between free territory and slave territory at 36°30'; and Maine and Missouri were admitted to the Union as free and slave states, respectively. After the war with Mexico, the elaborate *Compromise of 1850* caused one of the greatest debates in American legislative history, with Senators Henry Clay, Daniel Webster, John C. Calhoun, Salmon P. Chase, Stephen A. Douglas, Jefferson Davis, Alexander H. Stephens, Robert Toombs, William H. Seward, and Thaddeus Stevens all participating. Cleavage within the elite was apparent, but it was not yet so divisive as to split the nation. A compromise was achieved, providing for the admission of California as a free state; for the creation of two new territories, New Mexico and Utah, out of the Mexican cession; for a drastic fugitive slave law to satisfy southern planters; and for the prohibition of the slave trade in the District of Columbia. Even the *Kansas-Nebraska Act of 1854* was intended to be a compromise; each new territory was supposed to decide for itself whether it should be slave or free, the expectation being that Nebraska would vote free and Kansas slave. Gradually, however, the spirit of compromise gave way to divergence and conflict.

## ELITE CONSENSUS BREAKS DOWN

Beginning in 1856, proslavery and antislavery forces fought it out in "bleeding Kansas." Senator Charles Sumner of Massachusetts delivered a condemnation of slavery in the Senate and was beaten almost to death on the Senate floor by Congressman Preston Brooks of South Carolina. Intemperate language in the Senate became commonplace, with frequent threats of secession, violence, and civil war. In 1857 a southern-dominated Supreme Court decided, in *Dred Scott* v. *Sanford,* that the Missouri Compromise was unconstitutional because Congress had no authority to forbid slavery in any territory. Slave property, said Chief Justice Roger B. Taney, was as much protected by the Constitution as was any other kind of property. In 1859 John Brown and his followers raided the U.S. arsenal at Harper's Ferry, as a first step to freeing the slaves of Virginia by force. Brown was captured by Virginia militia under the command of Colonel Robert E. Lee, tried for treason, found guilty, and executed. Southerners believed that northerners had tried to incite the horror of slave insurrection, whereas northerners believed that Brown died a martyr.

## LINCOLN'S VIEWS AND SLAVERY

Abraham Lincoln never attacked slavery in the South; his exclusive concern was to halt the spread of slavery in the western territories. He wrote in 1845: "I hold it a paramount duty of us in the free States, due to the Union of the States, and perhaps to liberty itself (paradox though it may seem), to let the slavery of the other states alone."[4] Throughout his political career Lincoln consistently held this position. On the other hand, with regard to the western territories, he said: "The whole nation is interested that the best use shall be made of these territories. We want them for homes and free white people. This they cannot be, to any considerable extent, if slavery shall be planted within them."[5] In short, Lincoln wanted the western territories to be tied economically and culturally to the northern system. As for Lincoln's racial views, as late as 1858 he said:

> I will say, then, that I am not, nor ever have been, in favor of bringing about in any way the social and political equality of the white and black races: that I am not, nor ever have been, in favor of making voters or jurors of negroes, nor of qualifying them to hold office, nor to intermarry with white people. . . .
>
> And inasmuch as they cannot so live, while they do remain together there must be the position of superior and inferior, and I as much as any other man am in favor of having the superior position assigned to the white race.[6]

## PRESERVING THE UNION

Historian Richard Hofstadter believed that Lincoln's political posture was essentially conservative: he wished to preserve the long-established order and consensus that had protected American principles and property rights so successfully in the past. He was not an abolitionist, and he did not seek the destruction of the southern elite or the rearrangement of the South's social fabric. His goal was to bring the South back into the Union, to restore orderly government, and to establish the principle that states cannot resist national authority with force. At the beginning of the Civil War, Lincoln knew that a great part of conservative northern opinion was willing to fight for the Union but might refuse to support a war to free slaves. Lincoln's great political skill was his ability to gather all the issues of the Civil War into one single overriding theme: *the preservation of the Union.* However, he was bitterly attacked throughout the war by radical Republicans who thought he had "no antislavery instincts."

As the war continued and casualties mounted, opinion in the North became increasingly bitter toward southern slaveowners. Many Republicans joined the abolitionists in calling for emancipation of the slaves simply to punish the "rebels." They knew that the power of the South was based on the labor of slaves. Lincoln also knew that if he proclaimed to the world that the war was being fought to free the slaves, there would be less danger of foreign intervention.

## THE EMANCIPATION PROCLAMATION

On September 22, 1862, Lincoln issued his preliminary Emancipation Proclamation. Claiming his right as commander-in-chief of the army and navy, he promised that "on the first day of January, . . . 1863, all persons held as slaves within any State or designated part of a State the people whereof shall then be in rebellion against the United States shall be then, thenceforward, and forever free." Thus, one of the great steps forward in human freedom in this nation, the Emancipation Proclamation, did not come about as a result of demands by the people, and certainly not as a result of demands by the slaves themselves. (See the Focus, "Reconstruction and African-American History.") Hofstadter contended that *the Emancipation Proclamation was a political action taken by the president for the sake of helping to preserve the Union.* It was not a revolutionary action but a conservative one.

# POWER AND THE INDUSTRIAL REVOLUTION

**the rise of the industrial elite**

The importance of the Civil War for the power structure of the United States lay in the commanding position that the new industrial capitalists won during the course of that struggle. Even before 1860, northern industry had been altering the course of American life; the economic transformation of the United States from an agricultural to an industrial nation reached the crescendo of a revolution in the second half of the nineteenth century. Canals and steam railroads had been opening up new markets for the growing industrial cities of the East. The rise of corporations and of stock markets for the accumulation of capital upset old-fashioned ideas about property. The introduction of machinery in factories revolutionized the conditions of labor and made the masses dependent on industrial capitalists for their livelihood. Civil War profits compounded the capital of the industrialists and placed them in a position to dominate the economic life of the nation. Moreover, when the southern planters were removed from the national scene, the government in Washington became the exclusive domain of the new industrial leaders.

## SOCIAL DARWINISM

**social Darwinism**
competition selects the best; a philosophy justifying great accumulations of wealth

The new industrial elite found a new philosophy to justify its political and economic dominance. Drawing an analogy from Darwinian biology, Herbert Spencer undertook to demonstrate that, just as an elite was selected in nature

*The growth of industry, such as the mass production of automobiles, brought many people to urban areas.*

Brown Brothers

through evolution, so also society would near perfection as it allowed a natural *social* elite to be selected by *free competition*. Spencer hailed the accumulation of new industrial wealth as a sign of "the survival of the fittest." The *social Darwinists* found in the law of survival of the fittest an admirable defense for the emergence of a ruthless ruling elite, an elite that defined its own self-interest more narrowly, perhaps, than any other in American history. It was a philosophy that permitted the conditions of the masses to decline to the lowest depths in American history.

## Reconstruction and African-American History

Consciously or unconsciously, all historians are biased. There is bias in their choice of subject, in their selection of material, in their organization and presentation of the material, and, inevitably, in their interpretation of it.

Let us consider the historical interpretation of the African-American experience in America, particularly of the black experience in the Reconstruction era following the Civil War. Traditionally historians viewed the Reconstruction Congress as vindictive. The period as a whole was considered destructive, oppressive, and corrupt. Military rule was imposed on the South. "Carpetbaggers" and "scalawags" confiscated the property of helpless southerners and retarded the economic progress of the South for decades. Maladministration and corruption in the federal government were portrayed as being greater than ever before in American history. The accomplishments of African Americans during this period were overlooked. Finally, it was suggested that the separation of the races—segregation—

was the "normal" pattern of southern life. The belief was fostered that blacks and whites in the South had never known any other pattern of life than slavery and segregation.

A new awareness of African-American history in recent years has resulted in a thoroughgoing reinterpretation of the Reconstruction era. Historian C. Vann Woodward's work led the way in bringing new light to this important period. Woodward recorded the progress of blacks during Reconstruction, described the good-faith efforts of the Reconstruction Congress to secure equality for African Americans, and explained the reimposition of segregation in terms of class conflict among whites. (Alex Haley's popular book *Roots,* together with the dramatic television series based on it, is another example of historical interpretation. Whereas many older histories of the pre–Civil War South romanticized plantation life, *Roots* described the cruelties and brutality of slavery.)

### A Revised View of Reconstruction: African-American Progress

When the Republicans gained control of Congress in 1867, African Americans momentarily seemed destined to attain their full rights as U.S. citizens. Under military rule

southern states adopted new constitutions that awarded the vote and other civil liberties to blacks. Black men were elected to state legislatures and to the U.S. Congress. In 1865 nearly 10 percent of all federal troops were black.[a]

The accomplishments of the Reconstruction Congress were considerable. Even before the Republicans gained control, the Thirteenth Amendment, which abolished slavery, had become part of the Constitution. But it was the Fourteenth and Fifteenth Amendments and the important Civil Rights Act of 1875 that attempted to secure a place for the blacks in the United States equal to that of whites.

The Civil Rights Act of 1875 declared that all persons were entitled to the full and equal enjoyment of all public accommodations, inns, public conveniences, theaters, and other places of public amusement. In this act the Reconstruction Congress committed the nation to a policy of nondiscrimination in all aspects of public life.

But by 1877 support for Reconstruction policies began to crumble. In what has been described as the "Compromise of 1877," the national government agreed to end military occupation of the South, thereby giving up its efforts to rearrange southern society and lending tacit approval to white supremacy in that region. In return, the southern states pledged their support for the Union, accepted national supremacy, and enabled the Republican candidate, Rutherford B. Hayes, to assume the presidency following the much-disputed election of 1876, in which his opponent, Samuel Tilden, had received a majority of the popular vote.

### The Development of the White Supremacy Movement

The withdrawal of federal troops from the South in 1877 did not bring about an instant change in the status of the blacks. Southern blacks voted in large numbers well into the 1880s and 1890s. Certainly we do not mean to suggest that discrimination was nonexistent during that period. Perhaps the most debilitating of all segregation—that in the public schools—appeared immediately after the Civil War under the sanction of Reconstruction authorities. Yet segregation took shape only gradually.

The first objective of the *white supremacy movement* was to disenfranchise blacks. The standard devices developed for achieving this feat were the literacy test, the poll tax, the white primary, and various forms of intimidation. Following the disenfranchisement of African Americans, the white supremacy movement established segregation and discrimination as public policy by the adoption of a large number of "Jim Crow" laws, designed to prevent the mingling of whites and blacks (Jim Crow was a stereotypical African American in a nineteenth-century song-and-dance show). Between 1900 and 1910, laws were adopted by southern state legislatures requiring segregation of the races in streetcars, hospitals, prisons, orphanages, and homes for the aged and indigent. In 1913 the federal government itself adopted policies that segregated the races in federal office buildings, cafeterias, and restroom facilities. Social policy followed (indeed, exceeded) public policy. Little signs reading "White Only" or "Colored" appeared everywhere, with or without the support of law.

### Response of Blacks to Segregation

Many early histories of Reconstruction paid little attention to the response of blacks to the imposition of segregation.

*This Ku Klux Klan cross-burning is meant to intimidate.*

AP /Wide World Photos

*(Continued)*

But there were at least three distinct types of response: (1) accommodation to a subordinate position in society, (2) the formation of a black protest movement, and (3) migration out of the South to avoid some of the consequences of white supremacy.

The foremost African-American advocate of accommodation to segregation was the well-known educator Booker T. Washington. Washington enjoyed wide popularity among both white and black Americans. He was an adviser to two presidents (Theodore Roosevelt and William Howard Taft) and was highly respected by white philanthropists and government officials. In his famous Cotton States' Exposition speech in Atlanta in 1895, Washington assured whites that blacks were prepared to accept a separate position in society:

*In all things that are purely social we can be as separate as the fingers, yet one as the hand in all things essential to mutual progress.*[b]

Booker T. Washington's hopes for African Americans lay in a program of self-help through education. He himself had attended Hampton Institute in Virginia, where the curriculum centered around practical trades for blacks. Washington obtained some white philanthropic support in establishing his own Tuskegee Institute in Tuskegee, Alabama, in 1881. His first students helped build the school. Training at Tuskegee emphasized immediately useful vocations, such as farming, preaching, and blacksmithing. Washington urged his students to stay in the South, to acquire land, and to build homes, thereby helping to eliminate ignorance and poverty among their fellow African Americans. One of Tuskegee's outstanding faculty members was George Washington Carver, who researched and developed uses for southern crops. Other privately and

publicly endowed black colleges were founded that later developed into major universities, including Fisk and Howard (both started by the Freedmen's Bureau) and Atlanta, Hampton, and Southern.

While Washington was urging blacks to make the best of segregation, a small band of blacks were organizing themselves behind a declaration of black resistance and protest that would later rewrite American public policy. The leader of this group was W. E. B. Du Bois, a brilliant historian and sociologist at Atlanta University. In 1905 Du Bois and a few other African-American intellectuals met in Niagara Falls, Canada, to draw up a black platform intended to "assail the ears" and sear the consciences of white Americans. In rejecting moderation and compromise, the Niagara statement proclaimed: "We refuse to allow the impression to remain that the Negro American assents to inferiority, is submissive under oppression and apologetic before insults." The platform listed the major injustices perpetrated against blacks since

## Industrialists Acquire Political Power

After the Civil War, industrialists became more prominent in Congress than they had ever been. They had little trouble in voting high tariffs and hard money, both of which heightened profits. Very little effective regulatory legislation was permitted to reach the floor of Congress. After 1881 the Senate

Reconstruction: the loss of voting rights, the imposition of Jim Crow laws and segregated public schools, the denial of equal job opportunities, the existence of inhumane conditions in southern prisons, the exclusion of blacks from West Point and Annapolis, and the failure on the part of the federal government to enforce the Fourteenth and Fifteenth Amendments. Out of the Niagara meeting came the idea for a nationwide organization dedicated to fighting for blacks, and on February 12, 1909, the one-hundredth anniversary of Abraham Lincoln's birth, the National Association for the Advancement of Colored People (NAACP) was founded.

Du Bois himself was on the original board of directors of the NAACP, but a majority of the board consisted of white liberals. In the years to follow, most of the financial support and policy guidance for the association was provided by whites rather than blacks. However, Du Bois was the NAACP's first director of research and the editor of its magazine, *Crisis*. The NAACP began a long and eventually successful campaign to establish black rights through legal action. Over the years, hundreds of court cases were brought at the local, state, and federal court levels on behalf of blacks denied their constitutional rights.

World War I provided an opportunity for restive blacks in the South to escape the worst abuses of white supremacy by migrating en masse to northern cities. In the years 1916 to 1918, an estimated half-million blacks moved to the North to fill the labor shortage caused by the war effort. Most migrating blacks arrived in big northern cities only to find more poverty and segregation. But at least they could vote and attend better schools, and they did not encounter laws requiring segregation in public places.

The progressive "ghettoization" of African Americans—their migration from the rural South to the urban North and their increasing concentration in central-city ghettos—had profound political, as well as social, implications. The ghetto provided an environment conducive to political action. Even as early as 1928, the black residents of Chicago were able to elect one of their own to the House of Representatives. The election of Oscar de Priest, the first African-American congressman from the North, signaled a new turn in American urban politics by announcing to white politicians that they would have to reckon with the black vote in northern cities. The black ghettos would soon provide an important element in a new political coalition that was about to take form: namely, the Democratic party of Franklin Delano Roosevelt.

[a]For a general history of Reconstruction politics, see C. Vann Woodward, *Reunion and Reaction* (Boston: Little, Brown, 1951), and *The Strange Career of Jim Crow* (New York: Oxford University Press, 1957).
[b]Quoted in Henry Steele Commager, ed., *The Struggle for Racial Equality: A Documentary Record* (New York: Harper & Row, 1967), p. 19.

came under the spell of Nelson Aldrich, son-in-law of John D. Rockefeller, who controlled Standard Oil. Aldrich served thirty years in the Senate. He believed that geographical representation in that body was old-fashioned and openly advocated a Senate manned officially by representatives from the great business "constituencies"—steel, coal, copper, railroads, banks, textiles, and so on.

## The Rise of the Modern Corporation

The *corporate form of business* facilitated the amassing of capital by limiting the liability of capitalists to their actual investments and thereby keeping their personal fortunes safe in the event of misfortunes to their companies. The corporate form also encouraged capitalists to take risks in expanding industrial capital through the stock market. "Wall Street," the address of the nation's busiest securities market, the New York Stock Exchange, became a synonym for industrial capitalism. The markets for corporation stocks provided a vast and ready money source for new enterprises or for the enlargement and consolidation of old firms.

## The New Deal and the Emergence of the "Liberal Establishment"

**Impact of the Great Depression**

The *economic collapse of the Great Depression* undermined the faith of both rich and poor in the idea of social Darwinism. Following the stock market crash of October 1929, and in spite of assurances by President Herbert Hoover that prosperity lay "just around the corner," the American economy virtually stopped. Prices dropped sharply, factories closed, real estate values declined, new construction practically ceased, banks went under, wages were cut drastically, unemployment figures mounted, and welfare rolls swelled.

**new era in elite thinking**
reform and welfare to preserve American democracy

The election of Franklin D. Roosevelt to the presidency in 1932 ushered in a new era in American political philosophy. The Great Depression did *not* bring about a revolution; it did *not* result in the emergence of a new elite; but it did have an important impact on the *thinking* of America's governing circles. The economic disaster that had befallen the nation caused the elite to consider the need for economic reform. The Great Depression also reinforced the notion that the elite must acquire a greater public responsibility. The victories of fascism in Germany and communism in the Soviet Union and the growing restlessness of the masses in the United States made it plain that *reform and regard for the public welfare* were essential to the continued maintenance of the American political system and the dominant place of the elite in it.

### The New Deal

**Roosevelt and the New Deal**
to reform capitalism, not replace it

Roosevelt sought to elaborate a *New Deal philosophy* that would permit government to devote much more attention to the public welfare than did the philosophy of Hoover's somewhat discredited "rugged individualism." The New Deal was not a revolutionary system but rather a necessary *reform* of the existing capitalist system. In the New Deal, the American elite accepted the principle that the entire community, through the agency of the national government, has a *responsibility for mass welfare*. Roosevelt's second inaugural address called attention to "one-third of a nation, ill housed, ill clad,

*President Franklin D. Roosevelt signs the Social Security Bill in 1935.*

UPI/Corbis-Bettmann

ill nourished." Roosevelt succeeded in preserving the existing system of private capitalism and avoiding the threats posed to the established order by fascism, socialism, communism, and other radical movements.

Historian Richard Hofstadter commented on Roosevelt's liberal, public-regarding philosophy:

> At the beginning of his career he took to the patrician reform thought of the progressive era and accepted a social outlook that can best be summed up in the phrase "noblesse oblige." He had a penchant for public service, personal philanthropy, and harmless manifestos against dishonesty in government; he displayed a broad easy-going tolerance, a genuine liking for all sorts of people; he loved to exercise his charm in political and social situations.[7]

Roosevelt's personal philosophy was soon to become the prevailing ethos of the new liberal establishment.

## THE ORIGINS OF LIBERALISM

Thus, *liberalism* in the United States today is a product of elite response to economic depression at home and the rising threats of fascism and communism abroad. Its historical origin can be traced to elite efforts to *preserve* the existing political and economic system through reform. This historical perspective on the liberal tradition gives us a better understanding of the origins of change and reform within society.

## CASE STUDY
Vietnam:
A Political History

Histories of the Vietnam War, like all histories, reflect the historian's judgment about what facts are most important and how they should be interpreted. Perhaps the Vietnam experience is still too recent to expect dispassionate explanations—why it happened and why it turned out so badly for so many people. Histories of the war continue many of the same controversies that occurred during the war itself.

The account of the Vietnam War presented here reflects the writer's view that the war was a political, not a military, defeat, and that responsibility for the tragic results lies with the nation's political leadership— their failure to set forth clear objectives in Vietnam, to develop a strategy to achieve those objectives, and to rally mass support behind the effort.

Initially the United States sought to resist communist aggression from North Vietnam and ensure a strong and independent democratic South Vietnamese government. President John F. Kennedy sent a force of more than 12,000 advisers and counterinsurgency forces to assist in every aspect of training

and support for the Army of the Republic of Vietnam (ARVN). President Kennedy personally inspired the development and deployment of Special Forces ("Green Berets") to deal directly with a guerrilla enemy and help "win the hearts and minds" of the Vietnamese people.

By 1964 units of the North Vietnamese Army (NVA) had begun to supplement the communist guerrilla forces (Vietcong) in the South. President Lyndon B. Johnson, informed that the South Vietnamese government was on the "verge of collapse," authorized major increases in U.S. supporting forces and began planning for a U.S. combat role.

In February 1965 President Lyndon B. Johnson ordered U.S. combat troops into South Vietnam and authorized a gradual increase in air strikes against North Vietnam. Marines landing on the beaches near Da Nang on March 8 in full battle gear were greeted by young girls selling flowers, souvenirs, and themselves; the heavy fighting would come later.

The fateful decision to commit U.S. ground combat forces to Vietnam was made without any significant effort to mobilize American public opinion, the government, or the economy, for war. On the contrary, President Johnson minimized the U.S. military effort, placed numerical limits on U.S. troop strength in Vietnam, limited

bombing targets, and underestimated North Vietnam's military capabilities, as well as expected U.S. casualties. No U.S. ground troops were permitted to cross into North Vietnam, and only once (in Cambodia in 1970) were they permitted to attack NVA forces elsewhere in Indochina.

By late 1967 more than 500,000 U.S. troops were committed to Vietnam. Washington committed these military forces to a war of attrition, a war in which U.S. firepower was expected to inflict sufficient casualties on the enemy to force them to negotiate a settlement. U.S. forces stressed mobility, and the helicopter became a principal instrument of U.S. ground forces in carrying troops into battle, waging war at treetop levels, and evacuating the wounded. But the enemy retained the initiative throughout the war. The enemy could attack, then quickly melt into the civilian population, hide in tunnels, or retreat back to "sanctuaries" in Cambodia and Laos. With attrition defined as the military objective, the enemy "body count" became notoriously unreliable.

The failure of the nation's leadership to set forth a clear military objective in Vietnam made "victory" impossible. The failure to achieve any decisive military victories eroded support for the war among both elites and masses. The *Pentagon*

*Marines landing by helicopter off the coast of Vietnam. The U.S. forces in Vietnam stressed mobility.*

AP/Wide World Photos

*Papers,[a]* composed of official memos and documents of the war, reveal increasing disenchantment with military results throughout 1967 by Secretary of Defense Robert McNamara and others who had originally initiated U.S. military actions. But President Johnson sought to rally support for the war by claiming that the United States was "winning." The U.S. commander in Vietnam, General William Westmoreland, was brought home to tell Congress that there was light at the end of the tunnel. But these pronouncements only helped set the stage for the enemy's great political victory—the Tet offensive.

On January 30, 1968, Vietcong forces blasted their way into the U.S. embassy compound in Saigon and held the courtyard for six hours. The attack was part of a massive, coordinated Tet offensive against all major cities of South Vietnam. The offensive caught the United States and ARVN forces off guard. The ancient city of Hue was captured and held by Vietcong for nearly three weeks. But U.S. forces responded and inflicted very heavy casualties on the Vietcong. The Vietcong failed to hold any of the positions they captured, the people did not rise up to welcome them as "liberators," and their losses were high. By any *military* measure, the Tet offensive was a "defeat" for the enemy and a "victory" for U.S. forces.

Yet the Tet offensive was Hanoi's greatest political victory. "What the hell is going on?" asked a shocked television anchorman, Walter Cronkite. "I thought we were winning the war."[b] Television pictures of bloody fighting in Saigon and Hue seemed to mock the administration's reports of an early end to the war. The media, believing they had been duped by Johnson and Westmoreland, launched a long and bitter campaign against the war effort. Elite support for the war plummeted.

Deserted by the very elite who had initiated American involvement in the war, hounded by hostile media, and confronting a bitter and divisive presidential election, Lyndon Johnson made a dramatic announcement on national television on March 31, 1968: he halted the bombing of North Vietnam and asked Hanoi for peace talks, and concluded: "I shall not seek, and I will not accept, the nomination of my party for another term as your president."

American objectives in Vietnam shifted again with the arrival in Washington of the new president, Richard M. Nixon, and his national security adviser, Henry A. Kissinger. Nixon and Kissinger knew the war must be ended. But they sought to end it "honorably." The South Viet-

---

[a]*New York Times, The Pentagon Papers* (New York: Bantam Books, 1971).
[b]George C. Herring, *America's Longest War* (New York: Random House, 1979), p. 188.

*(Continued)*

**CASE STUDY**

Vietnam:
A Political History
(Continued)

namese could not be abruptly abandoned without threatening the credibility of American commitments everywhere in the world. They sought a peace settlement that would give South Vietnam a reasonable chance to survive. They hoped that "détente" with the Soviet Union, and a new relationship with communist China, might help to bring about "peace with honor" in Vietnam. But even in the absence of a settlement, they began the withdrawal of U.S. troops under the guise of "Vietnamization" of the war effort.

Unable to persuade Hanoi to make even the slightest concession at Paris, President Nixon sought to demonstrate American strength and resolve. He wished to make clear to Hanoi that he would not necessarily be bound by his predecessors' restraints. In the spring of 1970 Nixon authorized an attack on an NVA sanctuary inside the territory of Cambodia—an area known as the Parrot's Beak—not far from Saigon. The Cambodian operation was brief and probably achieved very little militarily. But it mobilized the antiwar movement in the United States. Demonstrations centered on American cam-

puses, and four students were killed in an angry confrontation with National Guardsmen at Kent State University.

When North Vietnam launched a new, massive, conventional invasion of the South in March 1972, Nixon authorized the heaviest bombing campaign of the war, as well as a naval blockade of North Vietnam and the mining of its Haiphong Harbor. The NVA suffered heavy casualties, and the attack was thrown back.

Meanwhile, National Security Adviser Henry Kissinger and Hanoi's Le Duc Tho had begun meeting secretly in Paris, away from the formal negotiations, to work out "the shape of a deal." U.S. prisoners of war were a major bargaining chip for Hanoi. In the presidential election of 1972, the war became a partisan issue. Democratic candidate George McGovern had earlier stated that he would "crawl on his hands and knees to Hanoi" for peace, while Nixon continued his "peace with honor" theme. Nixon's landslide reelection strengthened his position in negotiations.

The United States unleashed a devastating air attack directly on Hanoi for the first time in December 1972. U.S. B-52s from Guam joined with bombers based in Thailand to destroy factories, power plants, and transportation facilities in Hanoi itself. Critics at home la-

beled Nixon's action "the Christmas bombing," and congressional doves planned to end the war by law. But when negotiations resumed in Paris in January, the North Vietnamese quickly agreed to peace on the terms that Kissinger and Le Duc Tho had worked out earlier. Both Nixon and Kissinger contended that the Christmas bombing secured the final peace.[c]

The Paris Peace Agreement of 1973 called for a cease-fire in place, with NVA troops remaining in their areas of control in the South. The South Vietnamese government and its troops also remained in place. All U.S. forces were withdrawn from South Vietnam and U.S. prisoners returned.

The South Vietnamese government lasted two years after the Paris Agreement. Congress refused to provide significant military aid to the South Vietnamese. The Watergate affair forced Nixon's resignation in August 1974. In early 1975 Hanoi decided that the Americans would not "jump back in," and therefore "the opportune moment" was at hand. President Gerald Ford never gave serious consideration to the use of U.S. military forces to repel the new invasion, and his requests to Congress for emergency military aid to the South Vietnamese fell on deaf ears. U.S. Ambassador Graham Martin, embarrassed by his government's abandonment of Vietnam, delayed implementation of escape plans until the last moment. The United States abandoned hundreds of thousands of loyal Vietnamese who had fought alongside the Americans for years.[d] The spectacle of U.S. Marines using rifle butts to keep desperate Vietnamese from boarding helicopters on the roof of the U.S. embassy "provided a tragic epitaph for twenty-five years of American involvement in Vietnam."[e]

America's humiliation in Vietnam had lasting national and international consequences. The United States suffered 47,378 battle deaths and missing-in-action among the 2.8 million who fought in Vietnam. Perhaps one million Vietnamese, military and civilian, in both the North and South, were killed during the war years. But the "peace" was more bloody than the war. In Cambodia more than two million people were murdered by victorious communist forces in genocidal "killing fields." More than 1.5 million South Vietnamese were forcibly relocated to harsh rural areas and "reeducation camps." Nearly one-half million "boat people" tried to flee their country; eventually the United States took in nearly 250,000 Vietnamese refugees. Unlike past wars, there were no victory parades, and no one could answer the question of the mother whose son was killed in Vietnam: "What did he die

*On the Vietnam memorial in Washington, D.C., are engraved the names of all those Americans who died in combat during the Vietnam War.*

Ellen Shub/Impact Visuals

SOURCE: Taken from Thomas R. Dye and Harmon Zeigler, *The Irony of Democracy*, 7th. ed. (Pacific Grove, Calif.: Brooks/Cole, 1987), pp. 78–88.

[c]Henry Kissinger, *The White House Years* (Boston: Little, Brown, 1979), p. 1461; Richard Nixon, *RN: The Memoirs of Richard Nixon*, vol. 2 (New York: Warner Books, 1978), p. 251.
[d]Frank Snepp, *Decent Internal* (New York: Random House, 1977).
[e]Herring, *America's Longest War*, p. 262.

# NOTES

1. Henry Steele Commager, *The Study of History* (Columbus, Ohio: Merrill, 1965), p. 79.
2. Richard Hofstadter, *The American Political Tradition and the Men Who Made It* (New York: Vintage Books, 1956), p. viii.
3. Frederick Jackson Turner, "The West and American Ideals," in *The Frontier in American History* (New York: Holt, 1921).
4. Hofstadter, *American Political Tradition,* 109.
5. Turner, "The West and American Ideals," 113.
6. Ibid., 116.
7. Hofstadter, *American Political Tradition,* 323–324.

# ABOUT THIS CHAPTER

History is the recording, narrating, and interpreting of past human actions and events. History is not always considered a social science; but when historians seek to go beyond recording and narrating the human experience and try to explain relationships among human events, they become involved in the social sciences. And certainly the social sciences can learn a great deal from history.

Over the ages, history seems to have had a variety of meanings for people:

*So very difficult a matter is it to trace and find out the truth of anything by history.*
—Plutarch (46–120)

*History is little else than a picture of human crimes and misfortunes.*
—Voltaire (1694–1778)

*Peoples and governments never have learned anything from history, or acted on principles derived from it.*
—Hegel (1770–1831)

*The history of the world is but the biography of great men.*
—Thomas Carlyle (1795–1881)

*The subject of history is the life of peoples and of humanity. To catch and pin down in words . . . to describe directly the life, not only of humanity, but even of a single people, appears to be impossible.*
—Tolstoy (1828–1910)

Despite these somewhat gloomy views, we believe it is possible to learn something from history, and we hope

you will agree. After you have read this chapter, you should be able to

- describe briefly the various approaches to American history
- describe historian Charles Beard's "economic interpretation" of the Constitution
- describe changes in the power elite of various periods of American history, from the Revolution through the New Deal
- discuss the historical reinterpretation of the African-American experience during the Reconstruction era
- discuss the reasons for U.S. involvement in the Vietnam War and why the U.S. effort failed
- discuss how the Jacksonian period in American History helped to advance our institutions of democracy.

# DISCUSSION QUESTIONS

1. Describe the various approaches to studying history. Comment on the strengths or weaknesses of each.
2. What were Charles Beard's two main approaches to understanding the Constitution? Describe briefly how the following constitutional provisions were of immediate benefit to the nation's elite: taxing power; interstate commerce clause; congressional powers to protect money and property; Article IV, Section 2, which required the return of runaway slaves and indentured servants; prevention of laws impairing obligation of contracts. Discuss the criticisms of Beard's interpretation of the Constitution.
3. Describe how the power elite was changed by expansion into the American West. What factors contributed to the emergence of this elite, and what was its power base? Describe the philosophy of this new elite and the impact it had on both the elite system and the electoral system.
4. Describe the economic interests of the northern and southern elite on the eve of the Civil War. What were their points of conflict and of agreement? Discuss at least one of the compromises they attempted. Describe Lincoln's attitude toward slavery and his attempts at preserving consensus. Why was the Emancipation Proclamation a conservative, rather than a revolutionary, document?
5. Describe the new elite that emerged in the aftermath of the Civil War. What factors contributed to the rise of this elite? Discuss the philosophy this elite adopted, as well as the influence this elite had on Congress.

6. Discuss the impact the Great Depression had on both elite and nonelite philosophy and the kind of elite thinking that developed in this era. What foreign influences had an impact on this new thinking? Briefly describe Franklin Delano Roosevelt's New Deal philosophy.

7. Show how historical interpretations of the same historical events can radically differ by contrasting earlier interpretations of the Reconstruction era with the more recent interpretations of historian C. Vann Woodward.

8. What were the U.S. objectives in Vietnam? How did these objectives change over time? Do you agree with the author that America's political leadership was responsible for our nation's defeat?

9. In chapter 14, Power among Nations, you will find a case study, "American Military Power: 'Desert Storm.'" Describe differences in military strategies and outcomes between the Vietnam war and Persian Gulf war.

# The Uses of Power

## PART THREE

**I**n Part 3 we shall explore the major social problems confronting society. These problems are inter-disciplinary in nature, not confined to any of the social science disciplines. The problem of crime and violence, for example, is of as much interest and concern to the psychologist as it is to the sociologist. Because it is a question of human behavior and its consequences, it is also of concern to the political scientist, the historian, the economist, and the anthropologist. Each of these social scientists would approach the study of crime and violence from a somewhat different perspective. Our unifying perspective will continue to be power in society, but our main focus here will be on how power can be used to confront the crises that afflict human societies, for the betterment or detriment of humanity.

In Chapter 9 we shall explore the power of ideology and some of the major ideological conflicts in the twentieth century. In Chapter 10 we shall examine powerlessness and discrimination on the bases of race and gender and the power of the protest movements by which blacks and women have gained some measure of equality. In Chapter 11 we shall look at the problem of poverty in an affluent nation and at governmental efforts to alleviate, prevent, or cure this type of powerlessness. In Chapter 12 we shall explore the ways in which the United States has struggled to maintain a balance between the exercise of its police powers and the safeguarding of individual freedom, and we shall look at the continuous role that violence has played in American struggles for power. In Chapter 13 we shall examine some of the problems that affect the quality of life in the nation's large metropolitan areas and how power is exercised at the community level. In Chapter 14 we shall consider the global struggle for power and the attempts to maintain peace in international relations.

# Chapter 9

# Power and Ideology

## The Power of Ideas

Ideas have power. People are coerced by ideas—beliefs, symbols, doctrines—more than they realize. Indeed, whole societies are shaped by systems of ideas that we frequently refer to as *ideologies*. An *ideology* is an integrated system of ideas that provides society and its members with rationalizations for a way of life, guides for evaluating "rightness" and "wrongness," and emotional impulses to action. Power and ideology are intimately related. Ideology rationalizes and justifies the exercise of power. By providing a justification of power, ideology itself becomes a source of control over people. Without the added *legitimacy* provided by ideology, powerholders would be confronted by an aroused populace who strongly resented what they regarded as the naked power exercised over them. Nothing could be more dangerous to the stability of a power system. Yet the very ideology that legitimizes power also governs the *conduct of powerholders*. Once an ideology is deeply rooted in a society, powerholders themselves are bound by it if they wish to retain power.

**ideology**
an integrated system of ideas that rationalizes and justifies the exercise of power

## FUNCTIONS OF IDEOLOGY

**the functions of ideology**

describes human character and society

rationalizes and justifies a way of life

provides standards of right and wrong

motivates people to social and political action

Ideologies control people's behavior in several ways: (1) Ideologies affect perception. Ideas influence what people "see" in the world around them. Ideologies frequently describe the character of human beings in society; they help us become aware of certain aspects of society but often impair our ability to see other aspects. Ideologies may distort and oversimplify in their effort to provide a unified and coherent account of society. (2) Ideologies rationalize and justify a way of life and hence provide legitimacy for the structure of society. An ideology may justify the status quo, or it may provide a rationale for change, or even for revolution. (3) Ideologies provide normative standards to determine "rightness" and "wrongness" in the affairs of society. Ideologies generally have a strong moral component. Occasionally, they even function as "religions," complete with prophets (Marx), scriptures (the *Communist Manifesto*), saints (Lenin, Stalin, Mao), and visions of utopia (a communist society). (4) Ideologies provide motivation for social and political action. They give their followers a motive to act to improve world conditions. Ideologies can even "convert" individuals to a particular social or political movement and arouse them to action.

## THE RISK OF OVERSIMPLIFICATION

It is difficult to summarize a modern ideology in a few brief paragraphs. The risk of oversimplification is great. And because ideologies themselves are oversimplifications, the problem is compounded. Moreover, ideologies are constantly changing. When old utopian hopes are disappointed, they are frequently revised or replaced by new ones. New ideologies compete with older ones in various stages of revision. To unravel the ideological forces operating in society at any given time is a highly complex affair. With these warnings in mind, however, let us consider some of the major ideologies that influence our contemporary world.

## CLASSICAL LIBERALISM: THE LEAST GOVERNMENT IS THE BEST GOVERNMENT

**classical liberalism**

asserting the dignity of the individual and limited government

Historically, *liberalism* has asserted the worth and dignity of the *individual*. It has emphasized the rational ability of human beings to determine their own destinies, and it has rejected ideas, practices, and institutions that submerge individuals into a larger whole and deprive them of their essential dignity. Liberalism grew out of eighteenth-century Enlightenment, the Age of Reason in which great philosophers such as John Locke and Adam Smith affirmed their faith in reason, virtue, and common sense. Liberalism originated as an attack on hereditary prerogatives and distinctions of a feudal society, the monarchy, the privileged aristocracy, the state-established church, and the restrictions on individual freedom associated with the feudal order.

## CLASSICAL LIBERAL IDEAS

Classical liberalism helped motivate America's Founders to declare their independence from England, to write the American Constitution, and to establish the Republic. It rationalized their actions and provided ideological legitimacy for the new nation. John Locke, the English political philosopher whose writings most influenced the Founders of the United States, argued that even in a "state of nature"—that is, a world in which there were no governments—an *individual* possesses *inalienable rights* to life, liberty, and property. Locke spoke of a *natural law,* or moral principle, that guaranteed every person these rights. They were not given to the individual by government, and no government could legitimately take them away. Locke believed that the very purpose of government was to protect individual liberty. Human beings form a *social contract* with one another to establish a government to protect their rights; they agree to accept governmental authority in order to better protect life, liberty, and property. Implicit in the social contract and the liberal notion of freedom is the belief that governmental activity and restrictions over the individual should be kept to a minimum.

Thus, classical liberalism included a belief in *limited government.* Because government is formed by the consent of the governed to protect individual liberty, it logically follows that government cannot violate the rights it was established to protect.

Classical liberalism also affirmed the equality of all human beings. The Declaration of Independence expressed the conviction that "all men are created equal." The Founders believed in equality for all *before the law,* notwithstanding the accused's circumstances. Over time, the notion of equality has also come to include *equality of opportunity* in all aspects of life—social, educational, and economic. Each person should have an equal chance to develop individual capacities to his or her natural limits; there should be no artificial barriers to personal advancement. It is important to remember, however, that classical liberalism has always stressed *equality of opportunity* and not *absolute equality.* Thomas Jefferson recognized a "natural aristocracy" of talent, ambition, and industry, and classical liberals have always accepted inequalities that are a product of individual merit and hard work. Absolute equality, or "leveling," is *not* a part of classical liberalism.

## CLASSICAL LIBERALISM AND CAPITALISM

Classical liberalism as a *political* ideology is closely related to *capitalism* as an *economic* ideology. Capitalism asserts the individual's right to own private property and to buy, sell, rent, and trade in a free market. The economic version of freedom is the freedom to make contracts, to bargain for one's services, to move from job to job, to join labor unions, to start one's own business. Capitalism and classical liberal democracy are closely related as economic and political systems. Capitalism stresses individual rationality in economic matters; freedom of choice in working, producing, buying, and selling; and limited governmental intervention in economic affairs. Liberal democracy

**classical liberal ideas:**

**inalienable individual rights**

**natural law**

**social contract**

**limited government**

**equality of opportunity but not absolute equality**

**political freedom and economic freedom related**

emphasizes individual rationality in voter choice; freedoms of speech, press, and political activity; and limitations on governmental power over individual liberty. In liberal politics, individuals are free to speak out, to form political parties, and to vote as they please—to pursue their political interests as they think best. In liberal economics, individuals are free to find work, to start businesses, and to spend their money as they please—to pursue their economic interests as they think best. The role of government is restricted to protecting private property, enforcing contracts, and performing only those functions and services that cannot be performed by the private market.

# Modern Liberalism: Governmental Power to "Do Good"

**modern liberalism**
governmental power, a positive force in protecting the individual

Modern liberalism rationalizes and justifies much of the growth of governmental power in the United States in the twentieth century. Modern liberalism emphasizes the importance of the social and economic security of a whole population as a prerequisite to individual self-realization and self-development. Classical liberalism looked with suspicion on government as a potential source of "interference" with personal freedom, but modern liberalism looks on the *power of government as a positive force* to be used to contribute to the elimination of social and economic conditions that adversely affect people's lives and impede their self-development. Modern liberals approve of the use of governmental power to ensure the general social welfare and to correct the perceived ills of society. They believe they can change people's lives through the exercise of governmental power: end discrimination, abolish poverty, eliminate slums, ensure employment, uplift the poor, eliminate sicknesses, educate the masses, and instill humanitarian values in everyone. The prevailing impulse is to *do good,* to perform public services, and to assist the least fortunate in society, particularly minorities and the poor.

## Reforming Capitalism

Modern liberalism is frequently critical of certain aspects of capitalism, but it proposes to *reform* capitalism rather than replace it with socialism. Modern liberalism continues to recognize the individual's right to own private property, but it imposes on the property owner many social and economic obligations. It assumes that business will be privately owned but will be subject to considerable governmental regulation. Thus, the government intervenes to ensure fair labor standards, minimum wages, healthy working conditions, consumer protection, environmental protection, and so forth.

## A Larger Role for Government

Modern liberals are also committed to a significant *enlargement of the public (governmental) sector of society* in matters having to do with education, welfare, housing, the environment, transportation, urban renewal, medicine, employment, child care, and so on. Modern liberalism envisions a larger role for government in the future: setting new goals, managing the economy, meeting popular wants, and redirecting national resources from private wants toward public needs.

## REDUCTION OF INEQUALITIES

Modern liberalism defines equality somewhat differently than classical liberalism. Classical liberalism stresses the value of *equality of opportunity*: individuals should be free to make the most of their talents and skills, but differences in wealth or power that are a product of differences in talent, initiative, risk taking, and skill are accepted as natural. In contrast, modern liberalism contends that individual dignity and equality of opportunity depend in some measure on *reduction of absolute inequality* in society. Modern liberals believe that true equality of opportunity cannot be achieved where significant numbers of people suffer from hunger, remediable illness, or extreme hardships in the conditions of life. Thus, modern liberalism supports government efforts to reduce inequalities in society.

## MODERN CONSERVATISM: INDIVIDUALISM AND TRADITIONAL VALUES

In the United States today, *conservatism* is associated with classical liberalism (see the Focus, "How to Tell If You're Liberal or Conservative"). Conservatives in this country retain the early liberal commitment to individual freedom from governmental controls; maximum personal liberty; reliance on individual initiative and effort for self-development, rather than on governmental programs and projects; a free-enterprise economy with a minimum of governmental intervention; and rewards for initiative, skill, risk, and hard work, in contrast to government-imposed "leveling" of income. These views are consistent with the early classical liberalism of Locke, Jefferson, and the nation's Founders. The result, of course, is a confusion of ideological labels: conservatives today charge modern liberals with abandoning the principles of individualism, limited government, and free enterprise, and today's conservatives claim to be the true "liberals" in society.

**modern conservatism**
classical liberalism
tradition
evolutionary change
morality

## LAW AND TRADITION

Modern conservatism does indeed incorporate much of classical liberalism, but conservatism also has a distinct ideological tradition of its own. Conservatism is not as optimistic as liberalism about human nature. Traditionally, conservatives realized that human nature includes elements of irrationality, intolerance, extremism, ignorance, prejudice, hatred, and violence. Thus, they were more likely to place their faith in *law* and *tradition* than in the popular emotions of mass movements. Without the protection of law and tradition, people and societies are vulnerable to terror and violence. The absence of law does not mean freedom, but rather, exposure to the tyranny of terrorism and violence.

## Preference for Evolutionary Change

Conservatism sets forth an *evolutionary* view of social progress. Revolutionary change is far more likely to set society back than to improve it. But over time, people can experiment in small ways with incremental changes; continued from generation to generation, this process of evolutionary change leads to a progressive improvement in the condition of humanity. No government possesses the wisdom to resolve all problems, but the cumulative experience of society does produce certain workable arrangements for the amelioration of social ills. Gradual progress is possible, but only if people do not destroy the painfully acquired wisdom of the past in favor of new, untried utopian solutions that jeopardize the well-being of society.

## Tradition, Family, and Church as Guides

**tradition and morality as guides**

**family, church, and community**

Conservatives hold that people are rational beings, but that they are also victims of passion. Without the guidance of *law, tradition,* and *morality,* people would soon come to grief by the unruliness of their passions, destroying both themselves and others in pursuit of selfish gain. Rationalism is far from a sufficient guide to action; law, tradition, and morality are also needed for the realization of human purposes. Strong institutions—*family, church,* and *community*—are needed to repress individuals' selfish and irrational impulses and to foster civilized ways of life.

## How Americans Describe Themselves

The terms *liberal* and *conservative* have been used with different meanings over the years, so it is difficult to know whether Americans are really liberal or conservative on the issues. One way of determining their stance is to ask questions such as "How would you describe your own political philosophy— conservative, moderate, or liberal?" As can be seen from the following results of recent surveys, self-described conservatives outnumber liberals, although it is important to note that many Americans prefer "moderate" and many others decline to label themselves at all (see figure).

What do Americans mean when they label themselves "liberal," "moderate," or "conservative"? There is no clear answer to this question. People who called themselves "conservatives" did not consistently oppose social welfare programs or government regulation of the economy. People who called themselves "liberals" did not consistently support social welfare programs or government regulation of the economy.

**FOCUS**
How to Tell If
You're Liberal or
Conservative

| | YOU ARE **LIBERAL** IF YOU AGREE THAT | YOU ARE **CONSERVATIVE** IF YOU AGREE THAT |
|---|---|---|
| Economic Policy | Government should regulate business to protect the public interest<br>The rich should pay higher taxes to support public services for all<br>Government spending for social welfare is a good investment in people | Free-market competition is better at protecting the public than government regulation<br>Taxes should be kept as low as possible<br>Government welfare programs destroy incentives to work |
| Crime | Government should place primary emphasis on alleviating the social conditions (poverty, joblessness, etc.) that cause crime | Government should place primary emphasis on providing more police and prisons and stop courts from coddling criminals |
| Social Policy | Government should protect the right of women to choose abortion and fund abortions for poor women<br>Government should pursue affirmative action programs on behalf of minorities and women in employment, education, etc.<br>Government should keep religious prayers and ceremonies out of schools and public places | Government should restict abortion and not use taxpayer money for abortions<br>Government should not grant preferences to anyone based on race or gender<br><br>Government should allow prayers and religious observances in schools and public places |
| National Security Policy | Government should support "human rights" throughout the world<br>Military spending should be reduced now that the Cold War is over | Government should pursue the "national interest" of the United States<br>Military spending must reflect a variety of new dangers in this post–Cold War period |
| YOU GENERALLY DESCRIBE YOURSELF AS: | "caring"<br>"compassionate"<br>"progressive" | "responsible"<br>"moderate"<br>"sensible" |
| AND YOU DESCRIBE YOUR POLITICAL OPPONENTS AS: | "extremists"<br>"right-wing radicals"<br>"reactionaries" | "knee jerks"<br>"bleeding hearts"<br>"left-wing radicals" |

SOURCE: Adapted from Thomas R. Dye, *Politics in America*, 2nd ed. (New York: Prentice-Hall, 1997).

## FIGURE 9-1

### HOW AMERICANS DESCRIBE THEMSELVES

*Question*: How would you describe your views on most political matters?
Generally, do you think of yourself as liberal, moderate, or conservative?

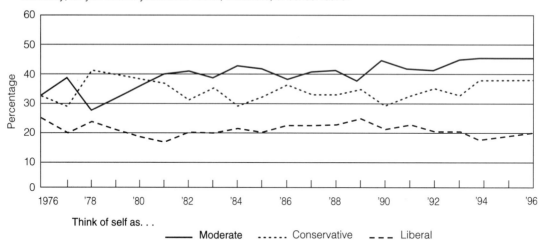

Think of self as. . .

———— Moderate    ····· Conservative    – – – Liberal

SOURCES: Surveys by CBS News/*New York Times* as reprinted in *The American Enterprise*
(March/April 1993): 84; and *Voter News Exit Survey,* November 8, 1994, and November 8, 1996.

# FASCISM: THE SUPREMACY OF RACE AND NATION

**fascism**
the supremacy of the nation over the individual

Fascism is an ideology that asserts *the supremacy of the nation or race over the interests of individuals.* In the words of the former Italian fascist dictator, Benito Mussolini, "Everything for the state; nothing against the state; nothing outside of the state." The state is the embodiment of a unifying, ethical "ideal" that stands above the materialistic class interest of a Marxist or the selfish individualism of the liberals.

## THE ORGANIC STATE

**Hitler, *Mein Kampf***

Fascism perceives the state as not merely a governmental bureaucracy but *the organic life* of a whole people. According to Mussolini, "The Italian nation is an organism having ends, life, and means of action superior to those of the separate individuals or groups of individuals which compose it." In *Mein Kampf,* written before his assumption of power in Germany in the 1930s, Adolf Hitler added to the concept of an organic state, with his idea of the *Volk* (people), in which race and nation are united.

**Volk**
race and nation united

## FASCIST GOALS

**the goal of the fascist state**
a superior race of human beings

The *goal of the fascist state* is not the welfare of the mass of people but the *development of a superior race of human beings.* The goal is the cultivation of bravery, courage, creativity, genius, intelligence, and strength. Fascism values the superior individual who rises out of the mire of mass mediocrity, and the superior nation that rises above the vast anthill of humankind. If life is a struggle for existence in which the fittest survive, then strength is the ultimate virtue and weakness is a fault. Good is that which survives and wins; bad is that which fails. War frequently brings out the best in a nation: unity, bravery, strength, and courage.

## Merger of Nationalism and Socialism

Fascism offers itself as a *merger of nationalism and socialism.* Before World War II, fascism in Italy and Germany put itself forward as a socialist regime adopted to national purposes. The party of Adolf Hitler was the National Socialist, or "Nazi," party. Under fascism the nation is an organic whole; therefore, the economy ought to be *cooperative* rather than competitive. Every class and every interest ought to work together for the *good of the nation.* Against the rights of liberty or equality, national socialism established the duties of *service, devotion,* and *discipline.*

## Totalitarian Power Structure

*The power structure of a fascist regime is totalitarian.* The unity of the fascist state requires "one people, one party, one leader." The fascist believes that a natural, superior, self-made leadership will emerge to provide intelligence and direction to the nation. At the head of the fascist elite is the leader—*Il Duce* in Italy or *Der Fuehrer* in Germany—in whose name everything is done, who is said to be "responsible" for all, but whose acts can nowhere be called into question. The leader is neither a scholar nor a theorist, but a charismatic man of action. Fascism strives for a *totality of power* in which all sectors of society—education, labor, art, science—are incorporated into the state and serve the purposes of the state.

**totalitarianism**
incorporating all sections of society into the state

## Anti-Semitism

The origins of *anti-Semitism*—hatred and prejudice directed against Jews—go back many centuries in Europe—through persecutions, exclusions, ghettoization, and attacks (pogroms) against Jewish communities. But the racial theories developed under fascism brought anti-Semitism to a historically unprecedented scale of horror. In *Mein Kampf* Hitler depicts the Jews as defilers of German racial purity—not human beings, but "maggots" "contaminating" the nation and state. The Nazis exploited anti-Semitism in their rise to power, encouraging discrimination, exclusion from schools and businesses, forced ghettoization, and violent attacks against Jews and Jewish-owned property. Later Hitler implemented his "final solution" to the "Jewish problem"—the mass murder of an entire people or *genocide.*

**anti-Semitism**
hatred and prejudice against Jews

**genocide**
mass murder of an entire people

*At the Belsen, Germany, concentration camp, liberating troops discovered a mass grave—a scene they would encounter again at each concentration camp.*

UPI/Corbis-Bettmann

## GENOCIDE

Almost six million European Jews were systematically murdered during World War II, along with millions of other peoples styled as "inferior" by Nazi ideology. The killing began with mass shootings by special *Einsatzgruppen* squads and later escalated into the systematic transportation of millions of Jews and others to a huge network of death camps including Auschwitz, Belsen, Buchenwald, and Dachau. Huge gas chambers and furnaces for the burning of corpses enabled SS troops to kill many thousands in a single day; many others died from starvation, beatings, disease, and cruel medical experimentation. Evidence of this *Holocaust* is preserved in photos, artifacts, documents, and personal accounts at the Yad Vashem memorial in Jerusalem, Israel, as well as the records of the International Military Tribunal held in Nuremberg, Germany, after the war to try Nazi war criminals.

Neofascism today can be observed in some extremist movements in Germany, France, Great Britain, and the United States. "Skinheads," often emblazoned with Nazi swastikas, preach and practice violence against nonwhites, Jews, and foreigners. Extremist parties and politicians frequently echo fascist themes in their aggressive patriotism, opposition to racial and ethnic minorities, and calls for national and racial unity.

**Holocaust**
the murder of millions of Jews and others in Nazi death camps during World War II

*Fascist ideas are preserved in some extremist movements today. These "Skin-heads" are emblazoned with Nazi swastikas.*

# Marxism: "Workers of the World, Unite"

Communism is a violent strain of the larger ideological movement of social-ism. Both socialism and communism arose out of the Industrial Revolution and the "social evils" it generated. Even though the Industrial Revolution led to a rapid rise in standards of living in western Europe, what impressed many early observers of this revolution was the economic inequalities it engen-dered. Throughout much of the nineteenth century, the real beneficiaries of the new industrialism seemed to be the successful manufacturers, bankers, merchants, and speculators; the lot of the slum-dwelling working classes showed little improvement. This was a bitter disappointment to the human-itarian hopes of many who had earlier embraced liberalism in the expecta-tion that the rewards of economic progress would be shared by everyone. It appeared that liberalism and capitalism had simply substituted an aristoc-racy of wealth for an aristocracy of birth.

## Karl Marx

Like many other socialists, Karl Marx (1818–1883) was an upper-middle-class intellectual. When his radicalism barred academic advancement, he turned to journalism and moved from Berlin to Paris. There he met Friedrich Engels, a wealthy young intellectual who supported Marx financially and col-laborated with him on many of his writings. The *Communist Manifesto* (1848) was a political pamphlet—short, concise, and full of striking phrases,

**Communist Manifesto**
political pamphlet describing Marxism and calling for world revolution

such as "Workers of the world, unite. You have nothing to lose but your chains." It provided an ideology to what had previously been no more than scattered protest against injustices. The *Manifesto* set forth the key ideas of Marxism, which would be developed twenty years later in great detail in a lengthy work, *Das Kapital.*

## ECONOMIC DETERMINISM

**economic determinism**
the nature of the economy determines the social structure

Communists believe that the nature of the economy, or "mode of production," is basic to all the rest of society. The mode of production determines the class structure, the political system, religion, education, family life, law, and even art and literature. The economic structure of capitalism creates a class structure of a wealthy *bourgeoisie* (a property-owning class of capitalists) who control the government and exercise power over the *proletariat* (the propertyless workers).

## CLASS STRUGGLE

**class struggle**
the basic conflict in any society is between economic classes; capitalists versus proletariat

The first sentence of the *Communist Manifesto* exclaims, "The history of all hitherto existing society is the history of class struggles." The class that owns the mode of production is in the dominant position and *exploits* the other classes. Such exploitation creates antagonism, which gradually increases until it bursts into revolution. The capitalist exploits the worker to the point at which the worker is forced to revolt against the oppressors and overthrow the capitalist state.

*Cuba's Fidel Castro is one of the last communist dictators in the world.*

Reuters/Corbis-Bettmann

## INEVITABILITY OF REVOLUTION

Marx asserted that the proletariat revolution was inevitable. As capitalists try to maximize their profits, the rich become richer and the poor become poorer. As capitalists drive wages down to maximize profits, capitalism becomes plagued by a series of crises or depressions, each one worse than the one before. The result of these "internal contradictions" in capitalism is a great deal of human misery, which eventually explodes in revolution. Thus, in their drive for profit, capitalists really dig their own graves by bringing the revolution ever closer.

**inevitability of revolution**
by exploiting the workers, capitalism inspires revolution

## DICTATORSHIP OF PROLETARIAT

Although Marx claimed that the coming of the revolution was inevitable, he nonetheless urged workers to organize for revolutionary action. The capitalists will never peacefully give up their ruling position. Only a violent revolution will place the proletarians in power. When the proletarians come to power, they, like ruling classes before them, will set up a state of their own—a dictatorship of the proletariat—to protect their class interests. This proletariat dictatorship will seize the property of the capitalists and place ownership of the mode of production in the hands of the proletariat. The bourgeoisie will be eliminated as a class.

**dictatorship of the proletariat**
violent revolution will give all power to the workers and eliminate the bourgeoisie

## THE CLASSLESS SOCIETY

After the revolution, as a result of *common ownership* of everything, a *classless* society will emerge. Because the purpose of government is to assist the ruling class in exploiting and oppressing other classes, once a classless society is established the government will have no purpose and will gradually "wither away." In the early stages of the revolution, the rule of distribution will be "from each according to his ability, to each according to his work." But after the victory of communism and the establishment of a full classless society, the rule of distribution will be "from each according to his ability, to each according to his need." (See the Case Study, "The Rise and Fall of Communism in Russia.")

**withering away of the state**
after the revolution, a classless society will emerge; the need for government will disappear

# SOCIALISM: GOVERNMENT OWNERSHIP, CENTRAL PLANNING

There are a bewildering variety of definitions of *socialism.* Occasionally critics of governmental programs in the United States label as "socialist" any program or policy that restricts free enterprise in any way. But fundamentally, socialism means *public ownership of the means of production,*

**socialism**
collective ownership of the means of production, distribution, and service

The task fell to Lenin to reinterpret Marxism as a revolutionary ideology, to carry out a successful communist revolution, and to construct a communist state in the Soviet Union after the 1917 Revolution. Lenin contributed a great deal to communist ideology, so much so that contemporary communist ideology is frequently referred to as *Marxism–Leninism.*

Marx believed the communist revolution would occur when capitalism itself had produced a class of factory workers that would be large enough to overcome its capitalist rulers. But this theory did not apply in 1917 in Russia, which was still a semifeudal society of peasants and landlords, with only a small number of factory workers and an even smaller number of capitalists. Lenin, however, believed that Russia could skip the capitalist stage of revolution and move directly from a feudal order to a communist society.

### The Totalitarian Party

According to Lenin, the *key to a successful revolution* was the creation of a new and revolutionary type of totalitarian political party composed of militant professional revolutionaries. This party would be organized and trained like an army to obey the commands of superior officers. While western European socialist parties were gathering millions of supporters in relatively democratic organizations, Lenin constructed a small, exclusive, well-disciplined, elitist party. According to Lenin, the Communist party is the true "vanguard of the proletariat"—the most advanced and class-conscious sector of the proletariat—which has an exclusive right to act as spokesperson for the proletariat as a whole and to exercise the dictatorial powers of the proletariat over the rest of society.

### Communism in One Country

After Lenin came to power in the Soviet Union in 1917, he found himself no longer in the position of revolutionary leader; he was the leader of a nation. Gradually abandoning their original hopes for an immediate world revolution, Lenin and his successor, Stalin, turned to the task of creating "communism in one country." With the Communist party more centrally disciplined than ever, the Soviet leaders turned to the achievement of rapid industrialization through a series of five-year plans designed to convert a backward agrarian country into a modern industrial nation. The sweeping industrialization, brought about by the repression and terror of a totalitarian regime, came at great cost to the people.

### The Police State

The Stalinist period saw brutality, oppression, imprisonment, purges, and murders—later officially admitted by the Soviet leaders. The Soviet regime held down the production of consumer goods in order to concentrate on the development of heavy industry. In part, the ideology of communism made it possible to call on the people for tremendous sacrifices for the good of the communist state.

Neither Marx nor Lenin proved successful as a political prophet. The state never withered away in communist Russia. Indeed, to maintain the communist government, a massive structure of coercion—informants, secret police, official terrorism, and a giant prison system—was erected. (The brutality of the system is described by Nobel Prize–winning author and former Soviet political prisoner Aleksandr Solzhenitsyn in *The Gulag Archipelago.*)

### Militarism

Following the "Great Patriotic War"—the Russian name for

*This statue of Lenin, a symbol of communist rule, was torn down by the people of Riga, Latvia.*

Reuters,/Corbis-Bettmann

running for and winning elective office.

Gorbachev also reached agreements with the United States and western European nations on the reduction of both nuclear and conventional forces (see Chapter 14). Most importantly, he renounced the use of Soviet military force to keep communist governments in power in eastern Europe. As a result of this decision, communist governments were ousted in Poland, Czechoslovakia, Hungary, Bulgaria, Romania, and East Germany in 1989. The Berlin Wall was torn down and Germany was unified in 1990.

World War II, in which more than 20 million Soviet citizens were killed and Nazi Germany was defeated—Stalin and his successors directed the Soviet economy primarily toward military purposes. The Soviets maintained the world's largest and most heavily armed military forces, and they built a nuclear missile force that surpassed that of the United States in size and numbers. (Their rapid progress in heavy missiles allowed them to place the first satellite in orbit in 1957 and the first man in space in 1962.) But the huge military establishment was a heavy economic burden; consumer goods in the Soviet Union were generally shoddy and always in short supply. Long waiting lines at state-run stores became the symbol of the Soviet economy.

### Perestroika and Glasnost

Mikhail Gorbachev ascended to power in the Soviet Union in 1985, committed to *perestroika* ("restructuring")—the reform and strengthening of communism in the nation. Gorbachev deviated from many of the earlier interpretations of Marxism-Leninism. He encouraged greater decentralization in industry and less reliance on centralized state direction. At the same time, he called for *glasnost* ("openness") in Soviet life and politics, removing many restrictions on speech, press, and religion and permitting elections with noncommunist candidates

### The Collapse of Communism

Gorbachev's economic and political reforms threatened powerful interests in the Soviet state—the Communist party "apparatchniks" (bureaucrats) who were losing control over economic enterprises; the military leaders, who opposed the withdrawal of Soviet troops from Germany and eastern Europe; the KGB police, whose terror tactics were increasingly restricted; and central government officials, who were afraid of losing power to the republics. When these hard-liners attempted the forcible removal of Gorbachev in August 1991, the democratic forces rallied to

*(Continued)*

**CASE STUDY**
The Rise and Fall
of Communism
in Russia
*(Continued)*

his support. Led by Boris
Yeltsin, the first elected president of the Russian Republic,
thousands of demonstrators
took to the streets, Soviet
military forces stood aside,
and the coup crumbled.
Gorbachev was temporarily
restored as president, but
Yeltsin emerged as the most
influential leader in the nation. The failed coup hastened
the demise of the Communist
party.

**The Disintegration of the
Soviet Union**

Strong independence move-
ments in the republics of the
former Union of Soviet Socialist Republics (USSR) emerged
as the authority of the centralized Communist party in
Moscow waned. Lithuania, Estonia, and Latvia—nations that
had been forcibly incorporated
into the Soviet Union in
1939—led the way to independence in 1991. Soon all of the
fifteen republics of the USSR
declared their independence,
and the USSR officially ceased
to exist after December 31,
1991. Its president, Mikhail
Gorbachev, no longer had a
government to preside over.
The red flag with its hammer

and sickle atop the Kremlin in
Moscow was replaced with the
flag of the Russian Republic.

**The Difficult Transition to
Democracy and Capitalism**

Today Russia, Ukraine,
Byelorusse, and the other
smaller republics of the former
Soviet Union are struggling to
overcome the disastrous effects
of seventy-five years of communist rule. Their economies
are shattered, and their experience in democratic politics is
limited. They are trying to de-
vise a new form of association,
a Commonwealth of Independent States, which will achieve
cooperation among republics
yet avoid domination by a central authority.

*distribution, and service.* Socialists agree on one point: private property in
land, buildings, factories, and stores must be transformed into social or
collective property. The idea of *collective ownership* is the core of socialism.

## Opposition to Capitalism

**socialism and communism**
condemnation of capitalism

Socialism shares with communism a *condemnation of the capitalist system* as
exploitive of the working classes. Communists and socialists agree on the
evils of industrial capitalism: the exploitation of labor, the concentration of
wealth, the insensitivity of the profit motive to human needs, the insecuri-
ties and sufferings brought on by the business cycle, the conflict of class
interests, and the propensity of capitalist nations to involve themselves in
war. (See the Cross-National Perspective, "Capitalism and Socialism in the
World," on page 240.) In short, most socialists agree with the criticisms of
the capitalist system set forth by Marx.

## COMMITMENT TO DEMOCRACY

However, socialists are committed to the *democratic process* as a means of replacing capitalism with collective ownership of economic enterprise. They generally reject the desirability of violent revolution as a way to replace capitalism and instead advocate peaceful constitutional roads to socialism. Moreover, socialists have rejected the idea of a socialist "dictatorship"; they contend that the goal of socialism is a *free society* embodying the democratic principles of freedom of speech, press, assembly, association, and political activity. They frequently claim that socialism in the economic sector of society is essential to achieving democracy and equality in the political sector of society. In other words, they believe that true democracy cannot be achieved until wealth is evenly distributed and the means of production are commonly owned.

**democratic socialism**
replacing capitalism through democratic processes

## GOVERNMENT OWNERSHIP

Wealth must be redistributed so that all persons can share in the benefits created by society. Redistribution means a transfer of ownership of all substantial economic holdings to the government. But the transfer must be accomplished in a democratic fashion, rather than by force or violence; and a socialist society must be governed as a true democracy.

**government ownership of property**

## CENTRAL PLANNING

Socialism relies on central planning by government bureaucrats to produce and distribute goods and services. Free markets are either outlawed or restricted to a few consumer items. Government bureaucrats decide how many shirts, televisions, autos, and so on, should be produced. Factories are given quotas to meet, and their output is shipped to government stores. Workers' wages are also determined by government planners, as are decisions about new investments and developments. Government planners rely on their own judgment about what is needed, rather than relying on market demand. Planners set goals for each sector of the economy, usually in five-year plans.

**central planning of economic activity**

## NATIONALIZATION

Socialists envision a gradual change from private to public ownership of property. Thus, socialists may begin by "nationalizing" the railroads, the steel industry, the automobile industry, privately owned public utilities, or other specific segments of the economy. Nationalization involves governmental seizure of these industries from private owners.

**nationalization**
government seizure of industries from private owners

In reality all modern economies use some combination of capitalist and socialist economic organization. In primarily capitalist countries like the United States, the government protects private property, provides some public goods, and regulates and taxes business. In socialist countries, government ownership and central control of the economy exist side by side with a small but often significant free market.

The figure presents a rough classification of current world governments according to their reliance on capitalist or socialist economic organization. Hong Kong has long been among the most free and prosperous market systems in the world. (In 1997 this British colony was returned by treaty to the People's Republic of China, an avowedly socialist state. The Chinese government has pledged to allow capitalism to continue in Hong Kong.) The Japanese economy is dominated by large private corporations, although social custom and government persuasion result in a high degree of central coordination. Approximately 35 percent of the gross national product of the United States is produced by governments—federal, state, and local combined. European nations generally have larger public sectors than the United States. Government in Sweden and Israel produces over half of the output of these nations.

The collapse of communism in eastern Europe has led to the introduction of market reforms in all of the nations of the former Soviet empire. Russia under President Boris Yeltsin is committed to market reforms, and that nation's economy is moving away from a centralized socialist system. In the past, 85 to 90 percent of the Russian economy was government-owned. China initiated market reforms in its agricultural sector as early as 1978, but movement toward a market economy in that nation has slowed since 1989. Communist Cuba and North Korea remain as socialist systems, wherein most private economic activity is suppressed by the government.

# WHY COMMUNISM COLLAPSED

Speculation about the causes of communism's collapse is risky. The fact that before 1989 very few western social scientists had predicted these revolutionary events suggests that we do not fully understand their causes. Yet we can suggest some interesting hypotheses about the current crisis of communism.

## DETERIORATING LIVING STANDARDS

*Socialist economies cannot provide an adequate standard of living* for their people. The democratic revolutions in eastern Europe and the Soviet Union were inspired principally by the realization that free market capitalism was providing much higher standards of living in the western world. The economies of the socialist-bloc nations were falling further and further behind the

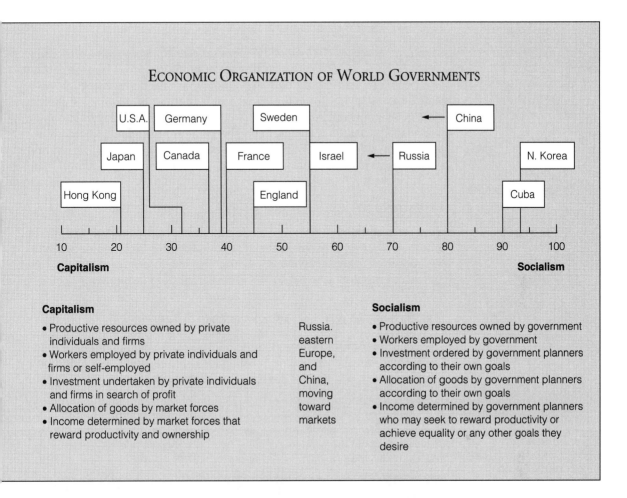

economies of the capitalist nations of the West. Similar comparative observations of the successful economies of the free market "Four Dragons"— South Korea, Taiwan, Singapore, and Hong Kong—inspired Chinese leaders to experiment with market forces.

## INEFFICIENCIES AND SHORTAGES

*Socialist bureaucracies cannot determine production and allocate goods and services as effectively as free markets.* In a socialist system, central bureaucracies, not consumers, determine production. Production for elite goals (principally, a strong military) comes first; production for individual needs comes last. People serve the system instead of the other way around. Consumer goods are shoddily made and always in short supply. This results in long lines at stores, rampant black marketeering, and frequent bribery of bureaucrats and managers to obtain necessary consumer items.

## LACK OF INDIVIDUAL INCENTIVES

*Socialism destroys the individual's incentive to work, produce, innovate, invent, save, and invest in the future.* The absence of profit incentives leads to extravagant waste by enterprise managers. Employees have no incentives to work hard or to satisfy customers. Official prices are low, but shortages prevent workers from improving their standard of living. A common refrain among workers in socialist systems is: "The government pretends to pay me, and I pretend to work." Bureaucrats try to order innovation, but innovation requires individual creativity and reward, not conformity to a central plan.

## POPULAR DISTRUST AND CYNICISM

Over time, *socialist systems lose the trust of the people.* Because the system promised a worker's paradise, the economic hardship imposed on the people inspires widespread *cynicism.* Because the system promised equality, the power and privilege enjoyed by the bureaucratic elite inspire resentment.

## ABSENCE OF POLITICAL AND ECONOMIC FREEDOMS

The concentration of both economic and political decision making in the hands of a central government bureaucracy is *incompatible with democracy.* Democracy requires limited government, individual freedom, and dispersal

*Can an individual confront the power of an authoritarian state? A lone citizen in Beijing, China, temporarily halted a column of tanks. Later, authoritarian rule was reimposed following a massacre of civilians in Tiananmen Square.*

Reuters/Corbis-Bettmann

of power in society. In socialist nations, the government exercises virtually *unlimited power over economic as well as political affairs,* individual economic freedoms are curtailed, and great power is accumulated by the government bureaucracy. In contrast, in capitalist nations, governmental intervention in the marketplace is limited, individuals are free to make their own economic decisions, and power is dispersed among many groups and institutions: governments, corporations, unions, press and television, churches, interest groups, and so forth.

## Communism's Incompatibility with Democracy

Thus, democracy is closely tied to capitalism. Capitalism does not *ensure* democracy; some capitalist nations are authoritarian. But capitalism is a necessary condition for democracy. *All existing democracies have free market economies, and no socialist system is a democracy.* In other words, capitalism is a necessary, although not a sufficient, condition for democracy.

Above all, the socialist system denies individual freedom, political pluralism, and democracy. Force, repression, and indoctrination can be effective over many years. But at some point, the universal human aspiration for personal freedom and dignity emerges to challenge the socialist order.

## About This Chapter

When commanded by authority they perceive as legitimate, ordinary human beings may inflict extreme pain and suffering on their fellow humans. It is difficult for us to comprehend the atrocities of World War II—six million Jews murdered; entire villages of Europe eradicated in acts of indiscriminate retaliation; millions of men, women, and children condemned to slave labor; untold numbers suffering the horrors of concentration camps; still others suffering hideous "medical experiments." Incredibly enough, these were the acts of human beings. Not all of them could have been monsters. Many of them pleaded that they were just obeying "orders." Others revealed that despite their Nazi indoctrination, they felt a certain human aversion to their work. One German officer who had been in charge of an "extermination gang" testified at Nuremberg that to relieve the "psychological burden" on his men, he had had them fire as a group, never as individuals, so they could avoid "personal responsibility."*

*William L. Shirer, *The Rise and Fall of the Third Reich* (New York: Simon and Schuster, 1960), p. 959.

How is authority invested with such legitimacy that it has the power to command ordinary people to commit acts of such unthinkable brutality and inhumanity? At least part of the answer, but by no means all, may be found in the power of ideology. Ideology, it should be noted, may be used to further humanitarian as well as nonhumanitarian goals, but regardless of the purpose for which it is used, ideology can be an extremely powerful weapon. In this chapter we have examined the nature of that power and described some of the major ideological conflicts in the contemporary world. Now that you have read Chapter 9, you should be able to

- define *ideology* and describe its power to influence people's behavior
- compare and contrast classical liberalism, modern liberalism, and modern conservatism
- discuss fascism, socialism, and communism
- describe the development of Marxism–Leninism in the Soviet Union and its subsequent collapse
- describe the relationships between capitalism, socialism, and democracy
- discuss the crisis of communism and the possible reasons for the collapse of communist regimes in eastern Europe

# DISCUSSION QUESTIONS

1. Define *ideology* and describe its relationship to power. Discuss the ways in which ideology can control people's behavior. Identify the characteristics of modern ideologies.
2. Compare and contrast classical liberalism and modern liberalism. What is the attitude of each of these ideologies toward the individual? What is their approach to governmental power, the concept of equality, and the capitalist system?
3. Explain the confusion that arises from the ideological labels of "conservative" and "classical liberal."
4. Describe the goals of the fascist state. What is genocide?

5. Trace the development of socialism and communism. Discuss what Marx meant by economic determinism, class struggle, the inevitability of revolution, the dictatorship of the proletariat, and the "withering away" of the state.
6. Define *socialism* and discuss how this ideology differs from capitalism. How does democratic socialism differ from communism?
7. Describe how Lenin adapted the ideology of Marxism to conditions in the Soviet Union. Describe Lenin's totalitarian party and his theory of imperialism. How was the ideology of communism used during Stalin's regime? What changes did Mikhail Gorbachev introduce?
8. What explanations might be given for the collapse of communist regimes in eastern Europe?

Chapter 10

# Power,
# Race, and Gender

## RACISM IN AMERICAN HISTORY

Race has been a central issue in American society throughout the nation's history. African slaves were introduced to the earliest colonial settlements in 1619. In 1863 the Emancipation Proclamation, issued by President Abraham Lincoln in the midst of the Civil War, applied to slaves living in the Confederate states, and slavery was constitutionally abolished in the United States by the Thirteenth Amendment in 1865. But within a generation, racial segregation replaced slavery as a means of subjugation (see the Focus, "Reconstruction and African-American History" in Chapter 8). Segregation won constitutional approval by the U.S. Supreme Court in 1896; not until the historic *Brown* v. *Board of Education* case in 1954 did the Supreme Court formally reverse itself and declare segregation unconstitutional. Slavery and segregation left social scars that remain visible in American society today.

Following the Civil War, Congress passed, and the states ratified, the Fourteenth Amendment to the U.S. Constitution, declaring that

> *no State shall make or enforce any law which shall abridge the privileges or immunities of citizens of the United States; nor shall any*

*State deprive any person of life, liberty, or property, without due process of law; nor deny to any person within its jurisdiction the equal protection of the laws.*

The language and historical context leave little doubt that the purpose of the Fourteenth Amendment was to secure for blacks a place in American society equal to that of whites. Yet for a full century these promises went unfulfilled. Segregation became the social instrument by which blacks were "kept in their place," that is, denied social, economic, educational, and political equality.

Segregation was enforced by a variety of private sanctions, from the occasional lynching mobs to country club admission committees. But government was a principal instrument of segregation both in the southern and in the border states of the nation. (School segregation laws in the United States in 1954 are shown in Figure 10-1.) In the northern states government was seldom used to enforce segregation, but it was also seldom used to prevent it. The results were often quite similar.

The constitutional argument made on behalf of segregation—that the phrase "equal protection of the laws" did not prohibit the enforced separation of races so long as the races were treated equally—became known as the *separate-but-equal doctrine.* In 1896 the Supreme Court, in *Plessy v. Ferguson,* made this doctrine the official interpretation of the equal protection clause, thus giving segregation constitutional approval.

The initial goal of the civil rights movement was the elimination of direct *legal segregation.* Discrimination and segregation practiced by governments

**separate but equal**

interpreting the equal protection clause of the Fourteenth Amendment to allow segregation of the races if facilities were equal (1896–1954)

**initial civil rights goal**

elimination of segregation by law

*Before the historic decision in Brown v. Board of Education in 1954, Jim Crow laws separated blacks and whites.*

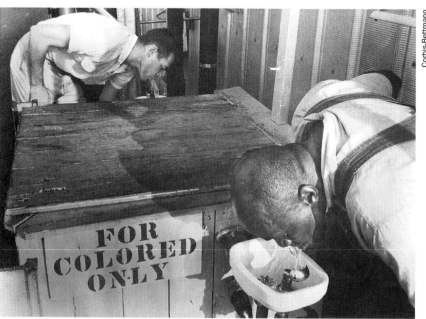

Corbis-Bettmann

**FIGURE 10-1**

SEGREGATION LAWS IN THE UNITED STATES IN 1954

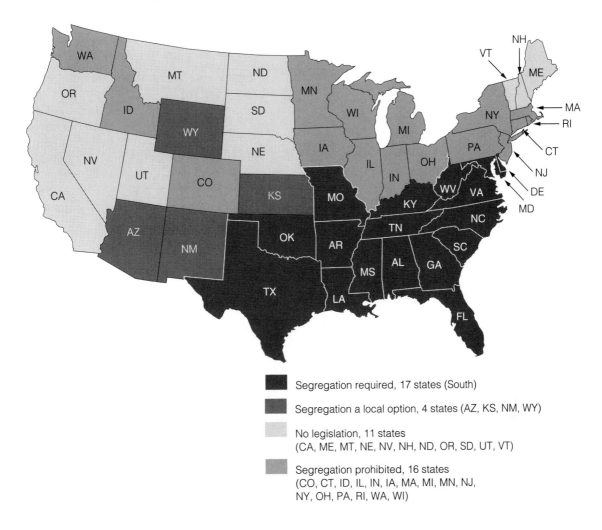

Segregation required, 17 states (South)

Segregation a local option, 4 states (AZ, KS, NM, WY)

No legislation, 11 states
(CA, ME, MT, NE, NV, NH, ND, OR, SD, UT, VT)

Segregation prohibited, 16 states
(CO, CT, ID, IL, IN, IA, MA, MI, MN, NJ,
NY, OH, PA, RI, WA, WI)

had to be prohibited, particularly in voting and public education. Led by Roy
Wilkins, executive director of the National Association for the Advancement
of Colored People (NAACP), and Thurgood Marshall, chief counsel for the
NAACP (who was later to become the first African-American Supreme Court
justice), the newly emerging civil rights movement of the 1950s pressed for
a court decision that direct lawful segregation violated the guarantee of
"equal protection of the laws" of the Fourteenth Amendment. The civil rights
movement sought a complete reversal of the separate-but-equal interpretation of *Plessy* v. *Ferguson;* it wanted a decision that laws separating the races
were *unconstitutional.*

**Brown v. Board of Education of Topeka, Kansas**
landmark Supreme Court decision declaring that segregation itself violates the equal protection clause of the Fourteenth Amendment (1954)

On May 17, 1954, the Court rendered its historic *Brown* v. *Board of Education of Topeka, Kansas*:

> *Segregation of white and colored children in public schools has a detrimental effect upon the colored children. The impact is greater when it has the sanction of law, for the policy of separating the races is usually interpreted as denoting the inferiority of the Negro group.*[1]

The Supreme Court's decision in *Brown* was symbolically very important. Although it would be many years before any significant number of black children would attend previously all-white schools, the decision by the nation's highest court stimulated black hopes and expectations. Indeed, *Brown* started the modern civil rights movement. The African-American psychologist Kenneth Clark wrote: "This [civil rights] movement would probably not have existed at all were it not for the 1954 Supreme Court school desegregation decision which provided a tremendous boost to the morale of blacks by its *clear* affirmation that color is irrelevant to the rights of American citizens."[2]

# THE CIVIL RIGHTS MOVEMENT

**private discrimination**

As long as the civil rights movement was combating *governmental* discrimination, it could employ the U.S. Constitution as a weapon in its arsenal, and rely on *judicial* action to accomplish its objective. But when the civil rights movement turned its attention to combating *private discrimination,* it had to carry its fight into the *legislative* branch of government. *Only* Congress could restrict discrimination practiced by private owners of restaurants, hotels, and motels; private employers; and other individuals who were not government officials.

**the civil rights movement**

In the early 1960s, the civil rights movement stepped up its protests and demonstrations and attracted worldwide attention with organized sit-ins, freedom rides, picketing campaigns, boycotts, and mass marches. After the massive "March on Washington" in August 1963, led by Martin Luther King, Jr., President Kennedy asked Congress for the most comprehensive civil rights legislation it had ever considered. The Civil Rights Act of 1964 finally passed both houses of Congress by better than a two-thirds vote and with the overwhelming support of members of both the Republican and Democratic parties. It can be ranked with the Emancipation Proclamation, the Fourteenth Amendment, and *Brown* v. *Board of Education* as one of the most important steps toward full equality for blacks in America.

**Civil Rights Act of 1964 provisions:**
prohibits discrimination in public accommodations

prohibits discrimination in programs receiving federal funds

prohibits discrimination in employment

establishes EEOC to enforce its provisions

The Act includes the following key provisions:

- It is unlawful to discriminate against or segregate persons on the grounds of race, color, religion, or national origin in any place of public accommodation, including hotels, motels, restaurants, movies, theaters, sports arenas, entertainment houses, and other places offering to serve the public.
- Each federal department and agency shall take appropriate action to end discrimination in all programs or activities receiv-

ing federal financial assistance in any form. These actions may include the termination of assistance.

- It shall be unlawful for any firm or labor union to discriminate against any individual in any fashion because of his or her race, color, religion, sex, or national origins; an Equal Employment Opportunity Commission shall be established to enforce this provision by investigation, conference, conciliation, or civil action in federal court.

In 1965, following an organized march from Selma to Montgomery to protest voting inequities, Congress enacted the *Voting Rights Act of 1965,* which authorized the attorney general, upon evidence of voter discrimination in southern states, to replace local registrars with federal examiners, who were authorized to abolish literacy tests, waive poll taxes, and register voters under simplified federal procedures. The impact of the Voting Rights Act of 1965 was observed in increased black voter registration figures in the South and election of African Americans to state legislatures in every southern state and to many city and county offices as well. **Voting Rights Act of 1965**

On April 4, 1968, Martin Luther King, Jr., was shot and killed in Memphis, Tennessee. The murder of the nation's leading advocate of nonviolence was a tragedy affecting all Americans. Before his death, King had campaigned in Chicago and other northern cities for an end to de facto segregation of blacks in ghettos and for the passage of legislation prohibiting discrimination in the sale or rental of houses and apartments. "Fair housing" legislation had consistently failed in Congress; there was no mention of discrimination in housing even in the comprehensive Civil Rights Act of 1964; and the prospects of a national fair housing law at the beginning of 1968 were not promising. With the assassination of Martin Luther King, Jr., however, the mood of the nation and of Congress changed dramatically. Congress passed a fair housing law as a tribute to the slain civil rights leader.

The *Civil Rights Act of 1968* prohibited the following forms of discrimination: **Civil Rights Act of 1968**

- refusal to sell or rent a dwelling to any person because of race, color, religion, or national origin
- discrimination against a person in the terms, conditions, or privileges of the sale or rental of a dwelling
- indication of a preference or discrimination on the basis of race, color, religion, or national origin in advertising the sale or rental of a dwelling

## CONTINUING INEQUALITIES

Despite progress toward equality in law, social and economic inequalities between blacks and whites persist. Median income of black families is only about 60 percent of that of white families, and this ratio has not improved

## MASTERS OF SOCIAL THOUGHT
Martin Luther King, Jr., and the Power of Protest

*Martin Luther King, Jr., addresses a crowd of 70,000 people in Chicago.*

AP/Wide World Photos

The civil rights movement invented new techniques for minorities to gain power and influence in American society. *Mass protest* is a technique by which groups seek to obtain a bargaining position for themselves that can induce desired concessions from established powerholders. It is a means of acquiring a bargaining leverage for those who would otherwise be powerless.

The nation's leading exponent of *nonviolent* protest was Dr. Martin Luther King, Jr. Indeed, King's contributions to the development of a philosophy of nonviolent, direct-action protest on behalf of African Americans won him international acclaim and the Nobel Peace Prize in 1964. King first came to national prominence in 1955, when he was only twenty-five years old;

he led a year-long bus boycott in Montgomery, Alabama, to protest discrimination in seating on public buses. In 1957 he formed the Southern Christian Leadership Conference (SCLC) to provide encouragement and leadership to the growing nonviolent protest movement in the South.

In 1963 a group of Alabama clergymen petitioned Martin Luther King, Jr., to call off mass demonstrations in Birmingham, Alabama. King, who had been arrested in the demon-

strations, replied in his famous "Letter from Birmingham Jail":

*One may well ask, "How can you advocate breaking some laws and obeying others?" The answer is found in the fact that there are* unjust *laws. I would be the first to advocate obeying just laws. One has not only a legal but a moral responsibility to obey just laws. Conversely, one has a moral responsibility to disobey unjust laws. . . .*

*One who breaks an unjust law must do it openly, lovingly*

over the past two decades (see Table 10-1). The black poverty percentage is three times higher than the white poverty percentage. Blacks have made notable progress in education but the proportion of college graduates is still smaller than that of the white population. Female-headed households have increased among both whites and blacks, but today nearly 46 percent of all black households are headed by a woman with no spouse present. Life

*. . . and with a willingness to accept the penalty. I submit that an individual who breaks a law that conscience tells him is unjust, and willingly accepts the penalty by staying in jail to arouse the conscience of the community over its injustice, is in reality expressing the very highest respect for law.[a]*

*Nonviolent direct action* is mass action directed against laws regarded as unjust. Mass demonstrations, sit-ins, and other nonviolent direct-action tactics often involve disobedience to state and local laws. The political purpose of nonviolent direct action and civil disobedience is to call attention or "to bear witness" to the existence of injustices. Only laws regarded as unjust are broken, and they are broken openly, without hatred or violence. Punishment is actively sought rather than avoided because punishment will further emphasize the injustices of the law. The object of nonviolent civil disobedience is to stir the conscience of an apathetic majority and to win support for measures that will eliminate the injustices. By accepting punishment for the violation of an unjust law, persons practicing civil disobedience demonstrate their sincerity. They hope to shame the majority and to make it ask itself how far it will go to protect the status quo.

Perhaps the most dramatic application of nonviolent direct action occurred in Birmingham, Alabama, in the spring of 1963. Under the direction of Martin Luther King, Jr., thousands of African Americans, including schoolchildren, staged protest marches. In response, police and firefighters, under the direction of Police Chief "Bull" Connor, attacked the demonstrators with fire hoses, cattle prods, and police dogs, all in clear view of national television cameras. Pictures of police brutality were flashed throughout the nation and the world, doubtless touching the consciences of many white Americans. The demonstrators conducted themselves in a nonviolent fashion. Thousands were dragged off to jail, including King. (It was at this time that King wrote his "Letter from Birmingham Jail," explaining and defending nonviolent direct action.)

The most massive application of nonviolent direct action was the great "March on Washington" in August 1963, during which more than 200,000 black and white marchers converged on the nation's capital. The march ended in a formal program at the Lincoln Memorial in which Martin Luther King, Jr., delivered his most eloquent appeal, entitled "I Have a Dream."

*I still have a dream. It is a dream deeply rooted in the American dream. I have a dream that one day this nation will rise up and live out the true meaning of its creed: "We hold these truths to be self-evident, that all men are created equal."*

[a]A public letter by Martin Luther King, Jr., Birmingham, Alabama, April 16, 1963.

expectancy among blacks lags behind that of whites, although the gap is closing over time. The infant mortality rate for blacks remains twice as high as for whites.

The civil rights movement opened many new opportunities for African Americans. But equality of *opportunity* is not the same as equality of *results*. What public policies should be pursued to achieve greater equality

**TABLE 10-1**

## CONTINUING RACIAL INEQUALITIES

|  |  | White | Black |
|---|---|---|---|
| Median family income | 1970 | $10,236 | $6,279 |
|  | 1995 | $40,884 | $24,698 |
| Poverty (percentage below poverty line) | 1970 | 9.9% | 33.5% |
|  | 1995 | 10.7% | 29.3% |
| College education (percentage of population 25 years and over) | 1970 | 11.3% | 4.4% |
|  | 1995 | 24.0% | 13.2% |
| Female household, with children, no spouse present (percentage of all families with children) | 1970 | 9% | 33% |
|  | 1995 | 21% | 58% |
| Life expectancy (years) | 1970 | 71.7 | 64.1 |
|  | 1995 | 76.4 | 69.6 |
| Infant mortality (deaths per 1,000 live births) | 1970 | 17.8 | 32.6 |
|  | 1993 | 6.8 | 16.5 |

SOURCE: U.S. Bureau of the Census, *Statistical Abstract of the United States 1996.*

**affirmative action**

compensatory or preferential treatment of minorities

between the races? Is it sufficient that government eliminate discrimination, guarantee equality of opportunity, and apply "colorblind" standards to both blacks and whites? Or should government undertake *affirmative action*—preferential or compensatory treatment of minorities—to narrow the gap between whites and blacks in employment, education, and income? (See Controversies in Social Science: "Affirmative Action and the Constitution.")

# HISPANIC POWER

**Hispanic**

referring to Spanish-speaking ancestry and culture

The term *Hispanic* refers to Mexican Americans, Puerto Ricans, Cubans, and others of Spanish-speaking ancestry and culture. In the 1990 census there were an estimated twenty-two million Hispanics, or 9.0 percent of the U.S. population. (There were thirty million African Americans, or 12.1 percent of the population; see Table 10-2.) The largest subgroup is Mexican Americans. Some are descendants of citizens who lived in the Mexican territory annexed to the United States in 1848, but most have come to the United States in accelerating numbers in recent years. The largest Mexican-American populations are found in Texas, Arizona, New Mexico, and California. Puerto Ricans constitute the second-largest Hispanic subgroup. Many still retain ties to the commonwealth and move back and forth from the island to New York. Cubans make up the third-largest subgroup; most have fled from Castro's Cuba and live mainly in the Miami metropolitan area.

Each of these Hispanic groups has encountered a different experience in American life. Indeed, there is some evidence that these groups identify

**TABLE 10-2**

## Minorities in America

| | Number (in thousands) | Percentage of Population |
|---|---|---|
| African Americans | 29,986 | 12.1 |
| Hispanic Americans | 22,354 | 9.0 |
|   Mexican Americans | 13,496 | 5.4 |
|   Puerto Rican Americans | 2,728 | 0.9 |
|   Cuban Americans | 1,044 | 0.4 |
|   Other | 5,086 | 1.4 |
| Asian or Pacific Islander Americans | 7,274 | 2.9 |
|   Chinese Americans | 1,645 | 0.7 |
|   Filipino Americans | 1,407 | 0.6 |
|   Japanese Americans | 848 | 0.3 |
|   Indian Americans | 815 | 0.3 |
|   Korean Americans | 799 | 0.3 |
|   Vietnamese Americans | 615 | 0.2 |
|   Hawaiian Americans | 211 | 0.1 |
|   Samoan Americans | 63 | * |
|   Guamanian Americans | 49 | * |
|   Other | 822 | 0.3 |
| Native Americans | 1,959 | 0.8 |
|   American Indians | 1,878 | 0.8 |
|   Eskimos | 57 | * |
|   Aleuts | 24 | * |

*Less than 0.1 percent.

SOURCE: Data from 1990 census in *Statistical Abstract of the United States 1996* (Washington, D.C.: U.S. Government Printing Office, 1996).

themselves separately, rather than as Hispanics.[3] Many Cuban Americans, especially early refugees from Castro's revolution in 1959, were skilled professionals and businesspeople who rapidly set about rebuilding Miami's dormant economy. On the whole, Cuban Americans today are better educated and enjoy higher incomes than other Hispanic groups (see Table 10-3). In politics Cuban Americans tend to vote Republican; they have succeeded in electing Cuban Americans to state and local office in Florida and to the U.S. Congress.

**Cuban Americans**

The Mexican-American population in the southwestern United States is growing very rapidly; it doubled in size between 1980 and 1990. For many years agricultural business encouraged immigration of Mexican farm laborers willing to endure harsh conditions for low pay. Many others came to the United States as undocumented or illegal aliens. In the Immigration Reform Act of 1987 Congress offered amnesty to all undocumented workers who had entered the United States prior to 1982. But the Act also required employers, under threat of penalties, to hire only people who could provide documentation of their legal status in the country. But the

**Mexican Americans**

## CONTROVERSIES IN SOCIAL SCIENCE
Affirmative Action and the Constitution

The civil rights movement has opened new opportunities for minorities and women in America. But equality of *opportunity* is not the same as equality of *results*. The early emphasis of government policy was, of course, nondiscrimination. Over time, however, the goal of public policy shifted from the traditional aim of equality of opportunity through nondiscrimination, to equality of results through "goals and timetables" established by affirmative action. Although carefully avoiding the term *quota*, the notion of affirmative action tests the success of equal opportunity by observing whether minorities and women achieve admissions, jobs, and promotions in proportion to their numbers in the population.

However, a *constitutional* question arises as to whether affirmative-action programs discriminate against whites and males and therefore violate the equal protection clause of the Fourteenth Amendment. The U.S. Supreme Court has wrestled with this question in several important cases.

### The Bakke Case[a]

After several years of premedical courses and volunteer work in a hospital, Allan Bakke, a thirty-two-year-old white male who was also a Vietnam veteran, applied to the University of California at Davis Medical School. He was rejected two years in a row. He later learned that his college grades and medical aptitude test scores ranked well above those of many who had been accepted. All who had been accepted with lower scores were African or Mexican American. Bakke filed a lawsuit arguing that the university had discriminated against him because of race—a violation of the Fourteenth Amendment's guarantee of "equal protection of the laws." The university, which accepted one hundred applicants to medical school per year, admitted that it set aside sixteen places for "disadvantaged students," a category that never included any whites. Candidates for those sixteen positions were placed in a separate admissions pool and competed only against each other. White applicants with grade point averages below 2.5 (out of a possible 4.0) were always rejected, but many minority students were accepted with averages as low as 2.1 and 2.2. Bakke's average was 3.5.

The university argued that using race as a favorable criterion was in the best interest of the state and the nation. By increasing the number of minority students, the university hoped eventually to improve medical care among the poor and the black. Minority doctors would also provide "role models" for young African and Mexican Americans, giving them something to aspire to in their career development. The university contended that its separation of black and white candidates was "benign" discrimination (meant to help) rather than "invidious" (meant to hurt).

The Supreme Court held that the affirmative-action program at the University of California at Davis Medical School violated Allan Bakke's rights to "equal protection of the laws" under the Fourteenth Amendment. The Court ordered the university to admit Bakke to medical school.

The Supreme Court was careful to specify the discriminatory aspects of the university's affirmative-action program:

*The Davis special admission program involves the use of an explicit racial classification. . . . No matter how strong their qualifications . . . they [whites] are never afforded the chance to compete with applicants from the preferred groups for the special admission seats.*

However, the Supreme Court went on to describe how an affirmative-action program *could* be constitutional:

*Race or ethnic background may be deemed a "plus" in a particular applicant's file, . . . [as long as] it does not insulate the individual from comparison with all other candidates for the available seats.*

The Supreme Court generally approved of the goal of achieving racial and ethnic diversity in the student body. Thus, the *Bakke* case set some limits on affirmative-action programs, but it still permitted schools to consider race as a "plus" factor in competition for admission.

Since *Bakke*, the Supreme Court has considered many challenges to affirmative-action plans on a case-by-case basis. No clear or consistent policy has emerged. In some cases, racial quota systems have been upheld as constitutional, and in other cases they have been struck down as violations of the U.S. Constitution or the Civil Rights Act. Many of these cases have been decided by close 5-to-4 votes of the justices.

### Strict Scrutiny

In 1995, the Supreme Court held that racial classifications in law must be subject to "strict scrutiny." This means that race-based actions by government—any disparate treatment of the races by federal, state, or local public agencies—must be found necessary to remedy past proven discrimination, or to further clearly identified, compelling, and legitimate government objectives. Moreover, it must be "narrowly tailored" so as not to adversely affect the rights of individuals. In striking down a federal construction contract "set-aside" program for small businesses owned by racial minorities, the Court expressed skepticism about governmental racial classifications: "There is simply no way of determining what classifications are 'benign' and 'remedial' and what classifications are in fact motivated by illegitimate notions of racial inferiority or simple racial politics."[b]

### The California Civil Rights Initiative

Opposition to racial and gender preferences inspired a citizen's initiative to be placed on the ballot in California in 1996. The California Civil Rights Initiative added the following key phrase to that state's constitution:

*Neither the state of California nor any of its political subdivisions or agents shall use race, sex, color, ethnicity or national origin as a criterion for either discriminating against, or granting preferential treatment to, any individual or group in the operation of the State's system of public employment, public education or public contracting.*

Supporters argued that this initiative leaves all existing federal and state civil rights protections intact. It simply extends the rights of specially protected groups to all of the state's citizens. The initiative was approved by 54 percent of California's voters.

Opponents argue that it sets back the civil rights movement, that it will end the progress of minorities in education and employment. And indeed, minority admission to universities in California dropped dramatically following the elimination of racial preferences. Opponents also argued that it was a violation of the U.S. Constitution's equal protection clause in that it denied minorities and women the opportunity to seek the assistance and protection of government. But a federal Court of Appeals upheld the decision of California's voters to ban racial and gender preferences. "Impediments to preferential treatment do not deny equal protection. . . . That the Constitution permits rare race-based or gender-based preferences hardly implies that the state cannot ban them altogether."[c]

[a] *Regents of the University of California* v. *Bakke*, 438 U.S. 265 (1978).
[b] *Aderand Construction* v. *Pena*, 132 L. Ed. 158 (1995).
[c] *Coalition for Economic Equity et al.* v. *Pete Wilson et al.*, Ninth Circuit Court of Appeals, April 1997.

**TABLE 10-3**

SOCIAL CHARACTERISTICS OF VARIOUS HISPANIC GROUPS
IN THE UNITED STATES*

| | Percentage of males over 16 in labor force | Percentage of college graduates | Percentage of families below poverty line | Median family income |
|---|---|---|---|---|
| Total population | 74.8 | 23.7 | 10.4 | $32,191 |
| Mexican Americans | 82.2 | 8.4 | 24.9 | $21,025 |
| Puerto Rican Americans | 69.6 | 11.3 | 30.8 | $18,932 |
| Cuban Americans | 76.3 | 23.8 | 16.9 | $26,858 |

*Data for 1990.

SOURCE: U.S. Bureau of the Census, *The Hispanic Population of the United States* (Washington, D.C.: U.S. Government Printing Office, 1992).

result has been a booming business in counterfeit green cards (employment) and Social Security cards. Economic conditions in Mexico and elsewhere in Central America continue to fuel immigration, legal and illegal, to the United States. Mexican Americans appear to work more than most groups; over 82 percent of adult Mexican-American males are in the workforce, compared to only 75 percent of the general population of adult males. But with lower educational levels, average incomes of Mexican-American families are lower and the poverty rate is higher than the general population. While Mexican Americans have served as governors of Arizona and New Mexico and won election to the U.S. Congress, their political power does not yet match their population percentages. Mexican-American voter turnout is lower than other ethnic groups, perhaps because many are resident aliens or illegal immigrants not eligible to vote, or perhaps because of cultural factors that discourage political participation.[4]

**Puerto Ricans**     Residents of Puerto Rico are American citizens. Puerto Rico is a commonwealth of the United States with a government that resembles that of a state with a constitution and elected governor and legislature. However, Puerto Rico has no voting members of the U.S. Congress and no electoral votes for president. Median family income in Puerto Rico is higher than anywhere else in the Caribbean but only half that of the poorest state in the United States. As citizens, Puerto Ricans can move anywhere in the United States; many have immigrated to New York City. But Puerto Ricans in the United States have not fared as well economically as other Hispanic groups: Puerto Ricans have lower median family incomes and higher poverty percentages, perhaps in part because of lower workforce participation. One explanation centers on the history of access to federal welfare programs on the island, and the resulting social dependency it fostered among some Puerto Rican families.[5]

# IMMIGRATION TO AMERICA

The United States accepts more immigrants than all other nations of the world combined. The vast majority of immigrants in recent years come from less-developed nations of Asia and Latin America (see Figure 10-2). Most immigrants come to the United States for economic opportunity. Most personify the traits we typically think of as American: opportunism, ambition, perseverance, initiative, and a willingness to work hard. As immigrants have always done, they frequently take dirty, low-paying, thankless jobs that other Americans shun. When they open their own businesses, they often do so in blighted, crime-ridden neighborhoods long since abandoned by other entrepreneurs.

## CULTURAL CHANGE?

The politics of immigration center on both cultural and economic issues. The nation's business and corporate leaders tend to view immigration in economic terms, principally as an increase in the supply of low wage workers in the United States. Most middle-class Americans view immigration in cultural terms, principally its impact on the ethnic composition of their

**FIGURE 10-2**

SOURCES OF LEGAL IMMIGRATION

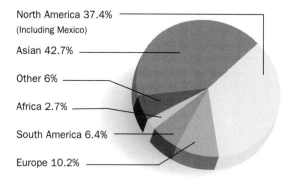

North America 37.4%
(Including Mexico)

Asian 42.7%

Other 6%

Africa 2.7%

South America 6.4%

Europe 10.2%

communities. Population projections based on current immigration and fertility (birth) rates suggest that the ethnic character of the nation will shift dramatically over time (see Figure 10-3).

## LEGAL IMMIGRATION

Immigration policy is a responsibility of the national government. It was not until 1882 that Congress passed the first legislation restricting entry into the United States of persons alleged to be "undesirable" as well as virtually all Asians. Following the end of World War I, Congress passed a comprehensive Immigration Act of 1921 which established maximum numbers of new immigrants each year and set a quota for each foreign country at three percent (later reduced to two percent) of the number of that nation's foreign born living in the United States in 1890. These restrictions reflected anti-immigration feelings that were generally directed at the large wave of southern and eastern European, Catholic and Jewish immigrants (Poland, Russia, Hungary, Italy, Greece) who had entered the United States prior to World War I. It was not until the Immigration and Nationality Act of 1965 that national origin quotas were abolished, replaced by preference categories for relatives and family members and professional and highly skilled persons (see Figure 10-4).

Immigration "reform" was the announced goal of Congress in the Immigration Reform and Control Act of 1986, also known as the Simpson-Mazzoli Act. It sought to control immigration by placing principal responsibility on employers; it set fines for knowingly hiring an illegal alien, with prison terms for repeat offenders. However, it allowed employers to accept many different forms of easily forged documentation, and subjected them to penalties for dis-

**FIGURE 10-3**

PROJECTED ETHNIC CHANGES IN
THE UNITED STATES OVER TIME

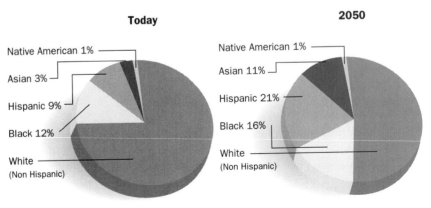

**Today**

Native American 1%
Asian 3%
Hispanic 9%
Black 12%
White
(Non Hispanic)

**2050**

Native American 1%
Asian 11%
Hispanic 21%
Black 16%
White
(Non Hispanic)

**FIGURE 10-4**

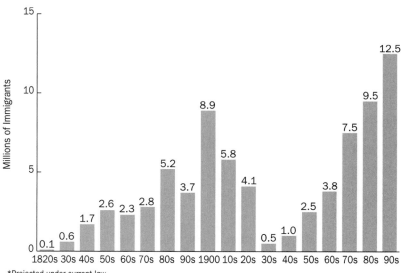

IMMIGRATION TO THE UNITED STATES
BY DECADES

*Projected under current law.

criminating against legal foreign-born residents. To win political support, the Act granted amnesty to illegal aliens who had lived in the United States since 1982. But the Act failed to reduce the flow of either legal or illegal immigrants.

## CURRENT IMMIGRATION POLICY

Today, roughly one million people per year are admitted *legally* to the United States as "lawful permanent residents" (persons who have relatives who are U.S. citizens are lawful permanent residents, or who have needed job skills); or as "refugees" or "asylees" (persons with "a well-founded fear of persecution" in their country of origin). In addition, over twenty million people are awarded visas each year to enter the United States for study, pleasure, or business. Federal law recognizes the following categories of non-citizens admitted into the United States:

- *Legal immigrants* (also "lawful permanent residents" or "permanent resident aliens"). These immigrants are admitted to the United States under a ceiling of 675,000 per year, with some admitted on the basis of job skills but most coming as family members of persons legally residing in the United States. Legal immigrants may work in the United States, and apply for citizenship after five years of continuous residence; they are eligible for all federal assistance programs.

- *Refugees and asylees.* These are persons admitted to the United States because of "a well-founded fear of persecution because of race, religion, nationality, political opinion, or membership in a social group." (Refugees are persons not yet in the United States; asylees are persons who have already arrived and apply for refugee protection.) They may work in the United States and are eligible for all federal assistance programs.
- *Parolees* (or persons enjoying "temporary protected status"). These are persons admitted to the United States for humanitarian or medical reasons or whose countries are faced with natural or man-made disasters.
- *Legalized aliens* (also called "amnesty aliens"). These formerly illegal aliens were given legal status (amnesty) under the Immigration Reform and Control Act of 1986. To qualify, they must show some evidence of having resided in the United States since 1982. They may work in the United States and are eligible for all federal assistance programs after five years.
- *Non-immigrants* (also "nonresident legal aliens"). Over twenty million people are awarded visas to enter the United States for pleasure and business. Time limits are placed on these visas usually by stamping a passport. Additionally, students, temporary workers and trainees, transient aliens, and foreign officials are eligible for temporary visas.

## ILLEGAL IMMIGRATION

The United States is a free and prosperous society with over 5,000 miles of borders (2,000 with Mexico) and hundreds of international air and sea ports. In theory, a sovereign nation should be able to maintain secure borders, but in practice the United States has been unwilling and unable to do so. Estimates of illegal immigration vary wildly, from the official U.S. Immigration and Naturalization Service (INS) estimate of 400,000 per year (about 45 percent of the legal immigration), to unofficial estimates ranging up to three million per year. The INS estimates that about four million illegal immigrants currently reside in the United States; unofficial estimates range up to ten million or more. Many illegal immigrants slip across U.S. borders, or enter port with false documentation, while many more overstay tourist or student visas (and are not counted by the INS as illegal immigrants).[6]

As a free society, the United States is not prepared to undertake massive roundups and summary deportations of millions of illegal residents. The Fifth and Fourteenth Amendments to the U.S. Constitution require that every *person* (not just *citizen*) be afforded "due process of law." The INS may turn back persons at the border or even hold them in detention camps. The Coast Guard may intercept boats at sea and return persons to their country of origin.[7] Aliens have no constitutional right to come to the United States. However, *once in the United States, whether legally or illegally, every person is entitled to due process of law and equal protection of the laws.* People are entitled to a fair hearing prior to any government attempt to deport them. Aliens are entitled to apply for asylum and present evidence at a hearing of their "well-founded fear of persecution" if returned to their country. Localized experiments in border enforcement have indicated that illegal immigration can be reduced by half or more with significant increases in INS personnel and technology.

A national bipartisan commission on immigration reform, chaired by former Texas Democratic Congresswoman Barbara Jordan, recommended the enforcement of existing federal laws barring the hiring of illegal aliens by establishing a national computerized verification system that employers could easily access when considering job applicants. But industry groups managed to bury the recommendation in Congress. A weakened immigration reform bill was passed by Congress in 1996 that increased the number of U.S. Border Patrol guards and expedited deportation procedures for illegal aliens convicted of a crime.

In 1994 California voters set off a renewed debate over immigration by approving a referendum that denies nonemergency health care and social welfare benefits to illegal aliens. Washington's reaction to the message sent by Californians was reflected in Congress's welfare reform act in 1996. The act denies most federal welfare benefits to *illegal* immigrants, and allows the states to deny federal welfare, Medicaid, and social services to *legal* immigrants if they wish to do so. Refugees and those granted asylum are exempt from these restrictions, and both legal and illegal immigrants are entitled to emergency medical care. President Clinton has pledged to repeal the restrictions on aid to legal immigrants, and federal courts may also act to block these restrictions. Nonetheless, in anticipation of the new restrictions, more immigrants applied for citizenship in 1996 (over 1.2 million) than any previous year in history.

# NATIVE AMERICANS: AN HISTORICAL OVERVIEW

Christopher Columbus, having erred in his estimate of the circumference of the globe, believed he had arrived in the Indian Ocean when he first came to the Caribbean. He mistook the Arawaks for people of the East Indies, calling them "Indios," and this Spanish word passed into English as *Indians*—a word that came to refer to all Native-American peoples. But at the time of the first European contacts, these peoples had no common ethnic identity; there were hundreds of separate cultures and languages thriving in the Americas. Although estimates vary, most historians believe that seven to twelve million people lived in the land that is now the United States and Canada; twenty-five million more lived in Mexico; and as many as sixty to seventy million in all lived in the western hemisphere, a number comparable to Europe's population at the time.

In the centuries that followed, the native population of the Americas was devastated by warfare, famine, and, most of all, by epidemic diseases brought from Europe. Overall, the native population fell by 90 percent, the greatest human disaster in world history. Smallpox was the Europeans' most effective weapon, followed by measles, bubonic plague, influenza, typhus, diphtheria, and scarlet fever. Superior military technology, together with skill in exploiting hostilities between tribes, gradually overcame native resistance. By 1910, there were only 210,000 Native Americans in the United States. Their population has slowly recovered to the current 1.8 million.

## THE TRAIL OF BROKEN TREATIES

**Intercourse Act of 1790**
recognized Indian nations
land concessions by treaty with U.S. government

In the Northwest Ordinance of 1787, Congress, in organizing the western territories of the new nation, declared that: "The utmost good faith shall always be observed toward the Indians. Their lands and property shall never be taken from them without their consent." And later in the Intercourse Act of 1790, Congress declared that public treaties between the United States government and the independent Indian "nations" would be the only legal means of obtaining Indian land. As president, George Washington forged a treaty with the Creeks: in exchange for land concessions, the U.S. pledged to protect the boundaries of the "Creek Nation" and allow the Creeks themselves to punish all violators of their laws within these boundaries. This semblance of legality was reflected in hundreds of treaties to follow. (And indeed, in recent years some Indian tribes have successfully sued in federal court for reparations and return of lands obtained in violation of the Intercourse Act of 1790 and subsequent treaties.) Yet Indian lands were constantly invaded by whites. Indian resistance would typically lead to wars that would ultimately result in great loss of life among warriors and their families and the further loss of tribal land. The cycle of invasion, resistance, military defeat, and further land concessions continued for a hundred years.

## "INDIAN TERRITORIES"

Following the purchase of the vast Louisiana territory in 1801, President Thomas Jefferson sought to "civilize" the Indians by promoting farming in "reservations" offered to eastern tribes west of the Mississippi River. But soon Indians who had been forced to move from Ohio to Missouri were forced to move again to survive the relentless white expansion. In 1815 President James Monroe designated as "Indian Territory" most of the Great Plains west of the Missouri River. Indians increasingly faced three unattractive choices: assimilation, removal, extinction.

**forced land concessions**

In 1814 the Creeks, encouraged by the British during the War of 1812 to attack American settlements, faced an army of Tennessee volunteer militia led by Andrew Jackson. At the Battle of Horseshoe Bend, Jackson's cannon fire decimated the Creek warriors. In the uneven Treaty of Fort Jackson, the Creeks, Choctaws, and Cherokees were forced to concede millions of acres of land.

*"Sitting Bull Returns at the Drive-in." This 1976 painting by Willard Midgette contrasts Native Americans' experience during the time of Sitting Bull with their current plight. The oil on canvas work was a gift of Donald B. Anderson to the National Museum of American Art, Washington, D.C.*

National Museum of American Art, Washington, D.C./Art Resource

By 1830 the "Five Civilized Tribes" of the southeastern United States (Choctaws, Cherokees, Creeks, Chickasaws, and Seminoles) had ceded most but not all of their lands. When gold was discovered on Cherokee land in northern Georgia in 1829, whites invaded their territory. Congress, at the heeding of the old Indian fighter Andrew Jackson, passed a Removal Act, ordering the forcible relocation of the tribes to "Indian Territory" (now Oklahoma). The Cherokees tried to use the white man's law to defend their land, bringing their case to the U.S. Supreme Court. When Chief Justice John Marshall held that the tribe was a "domestic dependent nation" that could not be forced to give up its land, President Jackson replied scornfully, "John Marshall has made his decision. Now let him enforce it." A 7,000-man army pursued Seminoles into the huge Florida Everglades swamp and forced 16,000 Seminoles, Cherokees, and other Indians on the infamous "Trail of Tears" march to Oklahoma in 1838.

Encroachment upon the "Indian Territory" of the Great Plains was not long in coming. First, the territory was crossed by the Santa Fe and Oregon trails and a series of military forts built to protect travelers. In 1854, under pressure from railroad interests, the U.S. government abolished much of the

*Cherokee Nation* v. *Georgia* **(1831)**

**"Trail of Tears"**
forced march to Oklahoma

original Indian Territory to create the Kansas and Nebraska territories that were immediately opened to white settlers. The tribes in the land—including Potawatomis, Kickapoos, Delawares, Shawnees, Miamis, Omahas, and Missouris—were forced to sign treaties accepting vastly reduced land reservations. But large buffalo-hunting tribes remained in the northern Dakotas and western Great Plains: the Sioux, Cheyennes, Arapahos, Comanches, and Kiowas. (Other smaller tribes inhabited the Rockies to California and the Pacific Northwest; and sedentary tribes—Pueblos, Hopis, Pimas—and migrating tribes—Apaches and Navahos—occupied the Southwest.) The Plains Indians took pride in their warrior status, often fighting among themselves.

## INDIAN WARS

The "Indian Wars" were fought between the Plains Indian tribes and the U.S. Army between 1864 and 1890. Following the Civil War, the federal government began to assign boundaries to each tribe and created a Bureau of Indian Affairs (BIA) to "assist and protect" Indian peoples on their "reservations." But the reservations were repeatedly reduced in size until subsistence by hunting became impossible. Malnutrition and demoralization of the native peoples were aided by the mass slaughter of the buffalo; vast herds, numbering perhaps as many as seventy million, were exterminated over the years. The most storied engagement of the long war occurred at the Little Big Horn River in South Dakota on June 25, 1876, where Civil War hero General George Armstrong Custer led elements of the U.S. Seventh Cavalry to destruction at the hands of Sioux and Cheyenne warriors led by Chief Crazy Horse, Chief Sitting Bull, and Chief Gall. But Custer's Last Stand inspired renewed army campaigns against the Plains tribes; the following year Crazy Horse was forced to surrender. In 1881 destitute Sioux under Sitting Bull returned from exile in Canada to surrender themselves to reservation life. Among the last tribes to hold out were the Apaches, whose famous warrior Geronimo finally surrendered in 1886. Sporadic fighting continued to 1890 when a small malnourished band of Lakota Sioux was wiped out at Wounded Knee Creek.

## THE ATTEMPTED DESTRUCTION OF TRIBAL LIFE

**Dawes Act of 1887**
attempted forced assimilation

The Dawes Act of 1887 governed federal Indian policy for decades. The thrust of the policy was to break up tribal lands, allotting acreage for individual homesteads in order to assimilate Indians into the white agricultural society. Farming was to replace hunting, and tribal life and traditional customs were to be shed for English language and schooling. But this effort to destroy Indian culture never really succeeded. While Indian peoples lost over half of their 1877 reservation land, they neither lost their communal ties nor accumulated much private property. The Dawes Act remained federal policy until 1934 when Congress finally reversed itself and reaffirmed tribal ownership of land.

Life on the reservations was often desperate. Indians suffered the worst poverty of any group in the nation, with high rates of infant mortality, alcoholism, and other diseases. The BIA, notoriously corrupt and mismanaged, encouraged dependency, and regularly interfered with Indian religious affairs and tribal customs.

# The New Deal

The New Deal under President Franklin D. Roosevelt came to Native Americans in the form of the Indian Reorganization Act of 1934. This act sought to restore tribal structures by recognizing tribes as instruments of the federal government. Tribal land ownership was restored and elected tribal councils were recognized as legal governments. Efforts to force assimilation were largely abandoned. The BIA became more sensitive to Indian culture and began employing Indians in larger numbers.

**Indian Reorganization Act of 1934**
recognized tribes as legal governments

Yet the BIA remained "paternalistic," frequently interfering in tribal "sovereignty." Moreover, in the 1950s Congress initiated a policy of "termination" of sovereignty rights for specific tribes that consented to relinquish their lands in exchange for cash payments. Only a few tribes chose this course, but the results were often calamitous: after the one-time cash payments were spent, Indian peoples became dependent upon state social welfare services and often slipped further into poverty and alcoholism.

# The American Indian Movement

The civil rights movement of the 1960s inspired a new activism among Native-American groups. The American Indian Movement (AIM) was founded in 1968 and attracted national headlines by occupying Alcatraz Island in San Francisco Bay. Violence flared in 1972 when AIM activists took over the site of the Wounded Knee battle and fought with FBI agents. Several tribes succeeded in federal courts and the Congress to win back lands and/or compensation for lands taken in treaty violations. Indian culture was revitalized, and Vine Deloria's *Custer Died for Your Sins* and Dee Brown's *Bury My Heart at Wounded Knee* became national bestsellers.

In the 1990 census about 1.8 million people—less than 1 percent of the nation's population—identified themselves as American Indians. About 800,000 of these people lived on tribal reservation and trust land, the largest of which is the Navaho and Hopi enclave in the southwestern United States (see Figure 10-5). Yet these peoples remain the poorest and least healthy in America, with high incidences of infant mortality, suicide, and alcoholism. Approximately half of all Indians live below the poverty line.

## FIGURE 10-5

### NATIVE AMERICANS' SETTLEMENTS

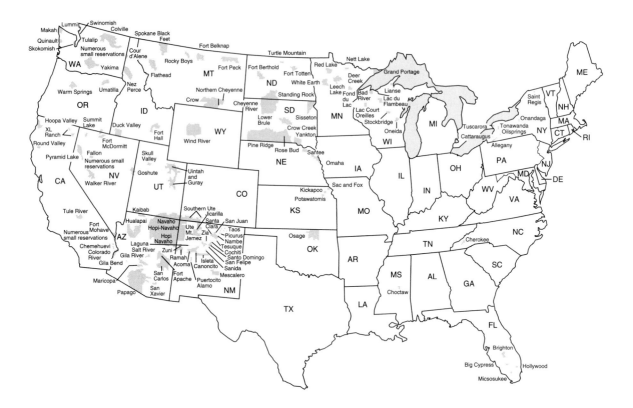

# POWER AND GENDER

Gender roles involve power relationships. The traditional American family was patriarchal, and many cultural practices continue to reflect male dominance. (See Chapter 3.) Men still hold most of the major positions in industry, finance, academia, the military, politics, and government. Authority in many families still rests with the man. Today more than half of all married women work; more than half of women with children under six years of age work. Nonetheless, stereotyped gender roles continue to assign domestic service and child care to women, whether they work or not, and human achievement, interest, and ambition to men.

Despite increases in the number and proportion of working women, the nation's occupational fields are still divided between traditionally male and female jobs. Women continue to dominate the traditional "pink-collar" jobs (see Table 10-4). Women have made important inroads in traditionally male white-collar occupations—doctors, lawyers, and engineers, for example—although men still remain in the majority in these professions. However,

**TABLE 10-4**

## WOMEN'S WORK

| | | Percentage female | |
| --- | --- | --- | --- |
| | | 1960 | 1994 |
| "White collar" | Women are increasingly entering white-collar occupational fields traditionally dominated by men: | | |
| | Architects | 3 | 17 |
| | Computer analysts | 11 | 31 |
| | College and university teachers | 28 | 43 |
| | Engineers | 1 | 8 |
| | Lawyers and judges | 4 | 25 |
| | Physicians | 10 | 22 |
| "Pink collar" | Women continue to be concentrated in occupational fields traditionally dominated by women: | | |
| | Nurses | 97 | 93 |
| | Elementary school teachers | 89 | 84 |
| | Secretaries | 98 | 98 |
| | Receptionists | 97 | 97 |
| | Waitresses/Waiters | 91 | 78 |
| "Blue collar" | Women continue to be largely shut out of blue-collar occupational fields traditionally dominated by men: | | |
| | Carpenters | 1 | 1 |
| | Mechanics | 1 | 1 |
| | Firefighters | 0 | 3 |
| | Police officers | 1 | 11 |
| | Truck drivers | 1 | 5 |
| | Bartenders | 21 | 55 |

SOURCE: U.S. Bureau of the Census, *Statistical Abstract of the United States 1996* (Washington, D.C.: U.S. Government Printing Office, 1996), pp. 411–413.

women have only begun to break into the "blue-collar" occupations traditionally dominated by men. Blue-collar jobs usually pay more than pink-collar jobs. This circumstance accounts for much of the earnings gap between men and women that we examined in Chapter 3. (See the Cross-National Perspective, "The Earnings Gap.")

# GENDER INEQUALITY: CULTURE OR BIOLOGY?

How much of male dominance can be attributed to *biology* and how much to *culture*? Many scholars deny that biological differences necessitate any distinctions between male and female in domestic service or child-care responsibilities, authority in the family, economic roles in society, or political or legal rights. They contend that *existing gender differences are culturally imposed on women from earliest childhood.* The very first item in personality formation is the assignment of gender roles (you are a boy, you are a girl) and the encouragement of

**inequality as a product of cultural conditioning**

In recent decades women have entered the labor force in all of the advanced industrial nations. In some western nations, notably Sweden, there is a long tradition of women holding jobs outside of the home. In other nations, like Japan, women in the workforce are a more recent development. Nonetheless, an earnings gap between men and women workers exists in *all* of the industrialized nations (see table).

The earnings gap—the ratio of median weekly earnings of women to men in the workforce—in the United States in 1992 was .75. Thus, we can say that for every dollar an American man earns in a week, an American woman earns an average of seventy-five cents. In many advanced democracies the earnings gap is significantly smaller. In France, for example, women's wages are estimated to be 82 percent of men's wages. However, in Japan, women's earnings relative to men are much worse than in the United States: the average weekly wage of women in Japan is only half that of men.

### WOMEN'S MEDIAN WEEKLY WAGE AS A PERCENTAGE OF MEN'S

| | | | |
|---|---|---|---|
| Iceland | 91 | Belgium | 75 |
| Australia | 88 | Norway | 75 |
| Denmark | 83 | United States | 75 |
| France | 82 | Germany | 73 |
| New Zealand | 81 | Czechoslovakia | 70 |
| Sweden | 81 | United Kingdom | 70 |
| Italy | 80 | Switzerland | 67 |
| Austria | 78 | Greece | 65 |
| Netherlands | 77 | Luxembourg | 63 |
| Finland | 76 | Canada | 63 |
| Portugal | 76 | Ireland | 62 |
| | | Japan | 50 |

SOURCES: International Labor Organization, *We're Number One* (New York: Vintage Books, 1992), p. 111; *Statistical Abstract of the United States 1993*, p. 426.

"masculine" and "feminine" traits. Aggression, curiosity, intelligence, initiative, and force are encouraged in the boy; passivity, refinement, shyness, and virtue are encouraged in the girl. Girls are supposed to think in terms of domestic and child-care roles, whereas boys are urged to think of careers in industry and the professions. Deeply ingrained symbols, attitudes, and practices are culturally designated as masculine or feminine ("What a big boy!" "Isn't she pretty!").

There are masculine and feminine subjects in school: science, technology, and business are male; teaching, nursing, and secretarial studies are female. Boys are portrayed in roles in which they master their environment; girls, in roles in which they admire the accomplishments of men. It is this *cultural* conditioning that leads a woman to accept a family- and child-centered life and an inferior economic and political role in society—not her *physiology.*

Many writers have deplored the *sociopsychological barriers* to a woman's full human development. There is a double standard of sexual guilt in which women are subject to greater shame for any sexual liaison, whatever the circumstances. Yet, while denied sexual freedom herself, the woman is usually obliged to seek advancement through the approval of men. She may try to overcome her powerlessness by using her own sexuality, perhaps at the cost of her dignity and self-respect. The prevailing male attitude is to value women for their sexual traits rather than for their qualities as human beings. Women are frequently portrayed as "sex objects" in advertising, magazines, and literature. They are supposed to entertain, please, gratify, and flatter men with their sexuality; it is seldom the other way around. There is even evidence of self-rejection among women that is similar to that encountered among minority groups: female children are far more likely to wish they had been born boys than male children are to wish they had been born girls.[8] The power aspects of gender roles are also ingrained in male psychology. Young men are deemed feminine (inferior) if they are not sufficiently aggressive, physical, or violent.

In contrast to these arguments about *culturally* imposed gender roles, other observers have contended that *physiological differences* between men and women account for differential gender roles. The woman's role in the reproduction and care of the young is biologically determined. To the extent that she seeks to protect her young, she also seeks family arrangements that will provide maximum security and support for them. Men acquire dominant positions in industry, finance, government, and so forth, largely because women are preoccupied with family and child-care tasks. Men are physically stronger than women, and their role as economic providers is rooted in this biological difference. Whether there are any biologically determined mental or emotional differences between men and women is a disputed point, but the possibility of such differences exists. Thus, differential gender roles may be partly physical in origin.

**inequality as a product of sociopsychological barriers**

**inequality as a product of physiological differences**

# The Long History of Women's Protests

The movement for women's rights in America is nearly as old as the nation itself. In 1776, Abigail Adams wrote to her husband John Adams at the Second Continental Congress while it was debating whether to declare American independence:

> *If particular care and attention is not paid to the ladies, we are determined to foment a rebellion and will not hold ourselves bound by any laws in which we have no voice or representation.*[9]

The political movement forecast by Abigail Adams did not really emerge until a generation later, however. The origins of the women's rights movement lie in the pre–Civil War antislavery crusade in which women played the major role. (See the Focus, "A Declaration of Women's Rights, 1848.") The first generation of feminists, including Lucretia Mott, Elizabeth Cady Stanton, Lucy Stone, and Susan B. Anthony, learned to organize, to hold public meetings, and to conduct petition campaigns as abolitionists. After the Civil War, the feminist movement concentrated on winning civil rights and the franchise for women. The suffragettes employed mass demonstrations, parades, picketing, and occasional disruptions and civil disobedience—tactics similar to those of the civil rights movement of the 1960s. The more moderate wing of the American suffrage movement became the League of Women Voters; in addition to the women's vote, they sought protection of women in industry, child welfare laws, honest election practices, and the elimination of laws discriminating against the rights of women.

**political equality**
Nineteenth Amendment (1920)

The culmination of the early feminist movement was the passage in 1920 of the Nineteenth Amendment to the Constitution:

> *The right of citizens of the United States to vote shall not be denied or abridged by the United States or by any State on account of sex.*

The movement was also successful in changing many state laws that abridged the property rights of the married woman and otherwise treated her as the "chattel" (property) of her husband. But active feminist politics declined after the goal of women's voting rights had been achieved.

**equality in employment**
Civil Rights Act of 1964

Renewed interest and progress in women's rights came with the civil rights movement of the 1960s. The Civil Rights Act of 1964 prevents discrimination on the basis of gender, as well as of race, in employment, salary, promotion, and other conditions of work. The Equal Employment Opportunity Commission (EEOC), the federal agency charged with eliminating discrimination in employment, has established guidelines barring stereotyped classifications of "men's jobs" and "women's jobs." State laws and employer practices that differentiate between men and women in terms of hours, pay, retirement age, and so on, have been struck down. Under active lobbying from feminist organizations, federal agencies, including the U.S. Office of Education and the Office of Federal Contract Compliance, have established affirmative-action guidelines for government agencies, universities, and private businesses doing work for the government. These guidelines set goals and timetables for employers to alter their workforce to achieve higher percentages of women at all levels.

**ERA**
Equal Rights Amendment

For many years feminist activity focused on the Equal Rights Amendment (ERA) to the Constitution, which would have struck down *all* existing legal inequalities in state and federal laws between men and women. The proposed amendment stated simply:

> *Equality of rights under the law shall not be denied or abridged by the United States or by any State on account of sex.*

The ERA passed the Congress easily in 1972 and was sent to the states for the necessary ratification by three-fourths (thirty-eight) of them. The

**FOCUS**

A Declaration of
Women's Rights,
1848

When a delegation of American
women was excluded from the
World Anti-Slavery Convention
in London in 1840, they realized that the cause of emancipation affected them as well as
slaves. On July 19, 1848, they
met in Seneca Falls, across the
New York border in Canada,
to draw up "The Seneca Falls
Declaration of Sentiments and
Resolutions." The Resolution
parallels the Declaration of Independence and reads in part:

*We hold these truths to be
self-evident: that all men and
women are created equal; that
they are endowed by their Creator
with certain inalienable rights;
that among these are life, liberty,
and the pursuit of happiness . . . .*

*The history of mankind is a
history of repeated injuries and
usurpations, on the part of man
toward woman, having in direct
object the establishment of an
absolute tyranny over her. To*

*prove this, let facts be submitted
to a candid world.*

*He has never permitted her to
exercise her inalienable right to
the elective franchise.*

*He has compelled her to sub-
mit to laws, in the formation of
which she had no voice. . . .*

*Having deprived her of this
first right of a citizen, the elective franchise, thereby leaving
her without representation in
the halls of legislation, he has
oppressed her on all sides.*

*He has made her, if married,
in the eye of the law, civilly dead.*

*He has taken from her all
rights in property, even to the
wages she earns. . . .*

*He has monopolized nearly all
the profitable employments, and
from those she is permitted to follow, she receives but a scanty re-
muneration. He closes against
her all the avenues to wealth and
distinction which he considers
most honorable to himself. As a
teacher of theology, medicine, or
law, she is not known.*

*He has denied her the facili-
ties for obtaining a thorough education, all colleges being closed
against her.*

*He allows her in Church, as
well as State, but a subordinate*

*position, claiming Apostolic au-
thority for her exclusion from the
ministry, and, with some exceptions, from any public participation in the affairs of the Church.*

*He has created a false public
sentiment by giving to a world a
different code of morals for men
and women, by which moral
delinquencies which exclude
women from society, are not
only tolerated, but deemed of little account in man. . . .*

*He has endeavored, in every
way that he could, to destroy her
confidence in her own powers, to
lessen her self-respect and to
make her willing to lead a dependent and abject life.*

*Now, in view of this entire
disfranchisement of one-half the
people of this country, their social and religious degradation—
in view of the unjust laws above
mentioned, and because women
do feel themselves aggrieved, oppressed, and fraudulently deprived of their most sacred
rights, we insist that they have
immediate admission to all the
rights and privileges which belong to them as citizens of the
United States.*

amendment won quick ratification by half of the states, but a developing
"Stop-ERA" movement slowed progress after 1976. Both the ERA and Stop-
ERA movements were led by women; they fought their battles over ratifica-
tion in state legislatures across the nation. Despite an extension of time by
Congress, ERA fell three states short of the necessary thirty-eight in 1982.
Throughout the debates over ratification of ERA, opinion polls reported that
a large majority of Americans favored it. Opponents argued that it might

eliminate many legal protections for women: financial support by husbands, an interest in the husband's property, exemption from military service, and so forth. In addition to these specific objections, the opponents of the ERA and the feminist movement also charged that it would weaken the family institution and demoralize women who wish to devote their lives to their family and children. Supporters of the ERA argue that only a constitutional amendment can guarantee women full equality and that such a guarantee should be a part of the fundamental laws of the land.

**changing mores and medical advances**

Women are also acquiring greater power over their own lives through a series of *social and medical developments*. Advances in birth control techniques, including "the pill," have freed women's sexuality from the reproductive function. Abortions are now a recognized constitutional right. Women can determine for themselves whether and when they will undertake childbirth and child rearing.

## SEXUAL HARASSMENT AND THE LAW

In recent years the women's movement has succeeded in placing the issue of sexual harassment on the national agenda. This effort was aided by the nationally televised Senate Judiciary Committee hearings in 1991 on the confirmation of Clarence Thomas to the U.S. Supreme Court. Title VII of the Civil Rights Act of 1964 protects employees from sexual discrimination "with respect to compensation, terms, conditions, or privileges of employment." The Supreme Court held in 1986 that "discriminatory intimidation" of employees could be "sufficiently severe" to alter the "conditions" of employment and therefore violate Title VII.

Sexual harassment may take various forms. There seems to be little doubt that it includes (1) conditioning employment or promotion or privileges of employment on the granting of sexual favors by an employee and (2) "tangible" acts of touching, fondling, or forced sexual relations. But sexual harassment has also been defined to include (3) a "hostile working environment." This phrase may include offensive utterances, sexual innuendoes, dirty jokes, the display of pornographic material, and unwanted proposals for dates. Several problems arise with this definition. First, it would appear to include speech and hence raise First Amendment questions regarding how far speech may be curtailed by law in the workplace. Second, the definition depends more on the subjective feelings of the individual employee about what is "offensive" and "unwanted" rather than on an objective standard of behavior that is easily understood by all. The Supreme Court wrestled with the definition of a "hostile work environment" in *Harris* v. *Forklift* in 1993. It held that a plaintiff need not show that the utterances caused psychological injury but only that a "reasonable person" would perceive the work environment to be hostile or abusive. Presumably a single incident would not constitute harassment; rather, courts should consider "the frequency of the discriminatory conduct," "its severity," and whether it "unreasonably interferes with an employee's work performance."

# ABORTION AND THE LAW

Abortion is not an issue that can be easily compromised. The arguments touch on fundamental moral and religious principles. Proponents of abortion, who generally refer to themselves as "pro-choice," argue that a woman should be permitted to control her own body and should not be forced by law to have unwanted children. They cite the heavy toll in lives lost because of criminal abortions and the psychological and emotional pain of an unwanted pregnancy. Opponents of abortion, who often refer to themselves as "pro-life," base their belief on the sanctity of life, including the life of the unborn child, which they insist deserves the protection of law—"the right to life." Many believe that the killing of an unborn child for any reason other than the preservation of the life or health of the mother is murder.

One of the most controversial decisions in the Supreme Court's history was its ruling in *Roe* v. *Wade* (1973), which recognized abortion as a *constitutional* right of women. In this historic decision the Court determined that a fetus is not a "person" within the meaning of the Constitution, and therefore a fetus's right to life is not guaranteed by law. Moreover, the Court held that the "liberty" guaranteed by the Fifth and Fourteenth Amendments encompassed the privacy right of a woman to decide whether or not to terminate her pregnancy. The Supreme Court decided that during the first three months of pregnancy the abortion decision must be left wholly to the woman and her physician; that during the second three months of pregnancy the state may not prohibit abortion, but only regulate procedures in ways reasonably related to a woman's health; and that only in the final three months of pregnancy may the state prohibit abortion except when abortion is necessary for the preservation of life or health of the mother.

**Roe v. Wade**
abortion as a constitutional right

The Supreme Court's decision did not end the controversy over abortion. Congress banned the use of federal funds under Medicaid (medical care for the poor) for abortions except to protect the life of a woman (and later in cases of rape and incest as well). The Supreme Court upheld the constitutionality of federal and state *laws denying tax funds for abortions.* Although women retained the right to an abortion, the Court held that there was no constitutional obligation for government to pay for abortions:[10] the decision about whether to pay for abortion from tax revenues was left to Congress and the states.

**no constitutional right to tax-funded abortion**

**incidence of abortion**

**constitutionally allowable restrictions on abortion**

About 1.5 million abortions are performed each year in the United States. This is about 43 percent of the number of live births. Most of these abortions are performed in the first three months; about 10 percent are performed after the third month.

Opponents of abortion won a victory in *Webster* v. *Reproductive Health Services* (1989), when the Supreme Court upheld a Missouri law placing restrictions on abortion. The right to abortion under *Roe* v. *Wade* was not overturned but was narrowed in application. The Court held that Missouri could deny public funds for abortions that were not necessary for saving the life of the woman and could deny the use of public facilities or employees in performing or assisting in abortions. More importantly, the Court upheld the requirement for a test of "viability" (capability of living outside of the mother's womb) and a prohibition on abortion of a viable fetus except to save a woman's life. The Court recognized the state's interest in the protection of human life when "viability is possible."

**reaffirming constitutional right to abortion; no undue burdens on women's right**

In *Planned Parenthood* v. *Casey* (1992), the Supreme Court reaffirmed *Roe v. Wade*'s holding that abortion was a personal liberty of women protected by the U.S. Constitution. However, the Court upheld Pennsylvania's requirements for physician counseling prior to an abortion, a twenty-four-hour waiting period, and parental notification when minors seek an abortion. It struck down a spousal notification requirement as too burdensome. Justice Sandra Day O'Connor wrote the Court's opinion, reaffirming a woman's constitutional right to obtain an abortion, but also upholding a state's power to protect any fetus that reached "viability." Her opinion went on to establish a new standard for constitutionally evaluating state restrictions on abortion: they must not impose an "undue burden" on women seeking abortion. Despite outcries from both pro-choice and pro-life forces, the *Casey* decision appears to place the Supreme Court's position on abortion almost exactly where public opinion polls suggest most Americans are: generally supporting a woman's right to choose an abortion but also supporting reasonable restrictions on the exercise of that right.

Violence at abortion clinics, including the murders of physicians who performed abortions, inspired Congress to pass federal legislation in 1994 restricting demonstrations at these sites. Federal laws now supplement state and local laws prohibiting interference in access to abortion clinics.

# NOTES

1. *Brown* v. *Board of Education of Topeka, Kansas*, 347 U.S. 483 (1954).
2. Kenneth B. Clark, *Dark Ghetto: Dilemmas of Social Power* (New York: Harper & Row, 1965), p. 75.
3. Rudolpho O. de la Garza et al., *Latino Voices: Mexican, Puerto Rican, and Cuban Perspectives on American Politics* (Boulder: Westview Press, 1992).
4. See F. Chris Garcia, *Latinos in the Political System* (Notre Dame, Ind.: University of Notre Dame Press, 1988).
5. Linda Chavez, "Tequila Sunrise: The Slow but Steady Progress of Hispanic Immigrants," *Policy Review* (Spring 1989): 64–67.
6. American Security Council, *The Illegal Immigration Crisis* (Washington D.C.: ASC, 1994).
7. *Sale* v. *Haitian Centers* Council 125 L. Ed. 2nd 128 (1993).
8. Goodwin Watson, "Psychological Aspects of Sex Roles," in *Social Psychology, Issues, and Insights* (Philadelphia: Lippincott, 1966), p. 477.
9. Quoted in Jay M. Shafritz, *The HarperCollins Dictionary of American Politics* (New York: HarperCollins, 1992), p. 620.
10. *Harris* v. *McRae*, 448 U.S. 297 (1980).

# ABOUT THIS CHAPTER

The United States has a long history of protest. The nation was in fact born as a protest against the injustices of colonialism—against powerlessness and the lack of a "voice" in controlling its own affairs. Despite that heritage, America's women and racial minorities have had a long and continuing fight against the inequalities imposed on them by their nation's laws and customs.

In 1776 Abigail Adams wrote to her husband John, who was then a delegate to the Continental Congress, cautioning him and his fellow delegates that when framing the new nation's laws they should "Remember the Ladies. . . . Do not put such unlimited power into the hands of the Husbands."* The "Ladies" did not find their voice until 1920, when the Nineteenth Amendment finally guaranteed women the right to vote. And the struggle for sexual equality continues today.

In this chapter we explored the struggles and triumphs of African Americans, Hispanics, Native Americans, and women in the United States, as well as some of the continuing inequalities these groups suffer. Now that you have read it, you should be able to

- discuss the civil rights movement of the 1950s and 1960s and the changes that it brought about in the Constitution and laws of the United States
- describe the philosophy of nonviolent direct action advocated by Martin Luther King, Jr.
- discuss the constitutional controversy over "affirmative action"
- describe the separate Hispanic groups in America
- describe the history of U.S. governmental policies toward Native Americans
- describe economic inequality between the sexes and various theories purporting to explain sexual inequality
- describe the various forms of sexual harassment and their status under civil rights law
- describe the Supreme Court's reasoning in *Roe* v. *Wade* regarding the constitutionality of abortion, as well as the Court's current approach toward abortion laws in the states

*L. H. Butterfield, Marc Friedlander, and Mary-Jo Kline, eds., *The Book of Abigail and John* (Cambridge, Mass.: Harvard University Press, 1975), p. 121.

# DISCUSSION QUESTIONS

1. Identify the initial goal of the civil rights movement. Discuss the Supreme Court case that marked the first step in attaining that goal and the constitutional amendment upon which the civil rights movement based its arguments. Why was the Supreme Court unable to implement its decision by itself?
2. Identify the key provisions of the Civil Rights Act of 1964.
3. Describe *nonviolent direct action* as advocated by Martin Luther King, Jr., its political purpose, and factors important to its success.
4. Describe how King and his followers were instrumental in the passage of the Voting Rights Act of 1965 and the Civil Rights Act of 1968. Briefly describe the content of each act.
5. Describe the purpose of affirmative-action programs. How does affirmative action differ from "colorblind" standards? What is the constitutional status of affirmative-action programs?
6. Describe the separate experiences of various Hispanic groups in American society.
7. Describe the cycle of broken treaties with Native-American tribes. Describe the historical occurrences of the Trail of Tears march, the battle at the Little Big Horn River, and the massacre at Wounded Knee Creek.
8. Discuss the "cultural" and "biological" explanations of male dominance in society. Describe some of the important landmarks for women's protest movements.
9. Define various forms of sexual harassment. What federal law has been interpreted to ban sexual harassment?
10. What did the U.S. Supreme Court decide in *Roe* v. *Wade?* What restrictions on abortion has the Court allowed?

# Chapter 11

# Poverty and Powerlessness

## Poverty as Powerlessness

**powerlessness**
the inability to control the events that shape one's life

*Powerlessness* is the inability to control the events that shape one's life. The poor lack economic resources and are hence largely dependent on others for the things they need. Their lack of power derives from their *dependency*. But powerlessness is also an attitude, a feeling that no matter what one does it will have little effect on one's life. An *attitude* of powerlessness *reinforces* the *condition* of powerlessness. Persistent poverty generates a lack of motivation and feelings of meaninglessness, hopelessness, distrust, and cynicism. Constant defeat causes many of the poor to retreat into a self-protective attitude characterized by indifference and a pervasive sense of futility.

**alienation**
a feeling of separation from society

The poor often feel *alienated*—separated from society—because of their lack of success in obtaining important life goals. Persons who are blocked consistently in their efforts to achieve life goals are most likely to express powerlessness and alienation. These attitudes in turn become barriers to effective self-help, independence, and self-respect. Persistent poverty can lead to apathy, aimlessness, and a lack of motivation.

To be *both* black and poor in a predominantly white, affluent society often magnifies feelings of powerlessness and alienation. Social psychologists are not always certain about the processes by which social inequalities are perceived or how these perceptions influence attitudes and behaviors. But African-American psychologist Kenneth B. Clark has provided some interesting insights into "the psychology of the ghetto."[1]

Clark argues that human beings who live apart from the rest of society, who do not share in society's affluence, and who are not respected or granted the ordinary dignities and courtesy accorded to others will eventually begin to doubt their own worth. All human beings depend on their experiences with others for clues to how they should view and value themselves. Black children who consistently see whites in a superior position begin to question whether they, or their family, or blacks in general really deserve any more respect from the larger society than they receive. These doubts, Clark maintains, become the seeds of "a pernicious self- and group-hatred."[2]

**self-hatred and self-doubt**
victims of poverty begin to blame themselves and see themselves as inferior

But all human beings search for self-esteem. According to Clark, teenage inner-city males often pretend to knowledge about illicit activities and to sexual experiences that they have not really had. Many use as their models the petty criminals of the ghetto, with their colorful, swaggering style of cool bravado. The inability to succeed by the standards of the wider society leads to a peculiar fascination with individuals who successfully defy society's norms. Some young African-American men seek their salvation in aggressive and self-destructive behavior. Because the larger society has rejected them, they reject—or at least appear to reject—the values of that society.

**the search for self-esteem**
a poor environment leads to aggressive and self-destructive behavior

Clark believes that the explanation for violence and crime in the inner city lies in the conscious or unconscious belief of many young African Americans that they cannot hope to win meaningful self-esteem through the avenues available to middle-class whites, so they turn to "hustling"—pimping, prostitution, gambling, or drug dealing. They are frequently scornful of what they consider the hypocrisy and dishonesty of the larger society. They point to corruption among respected middle-class whites, including the police force.

## POVERTY IN THE UNITED STATES

How much poverty really exists in America? According to the U.S. Bureau of the Census, in 1994 there were about 38 million poor people (those below the official poverty level) in the United States, or approximately 14 percent of the population (see Figure 11-1). The official poverty level is derived by calculating the minimum cash income required to maintain families of different sizes. The dollar amounts change each year to take into account the effect of inflation.

This official definition of poverty emphasizes *subsistence levels;* it seeks to describe poverty objectively as the lack of enough income to acquire the minimum necessities of life. Liberals frequently view the subsistence definition of poverty as insensitive to a variety of needs, including entertainment, recreation, and the relief of monotony. Items that were "luxuries" a generation ago are

**official definition of poverty**
government estimates each year of the minimum cash income required for families of various sizes to subsist

**liberal objections to official definition of poverty**

**FIGURE 11-1**

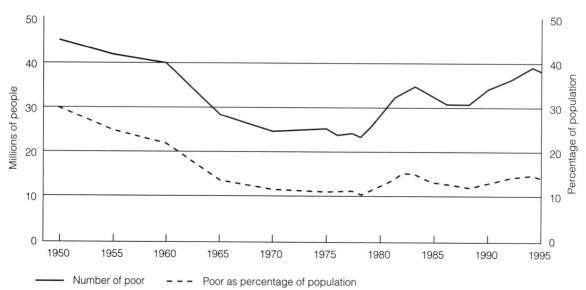

POVERTY IN THE UNITED STATES

——— Number of poor    – – – Poor as percentage of population

SOURCE: *Statistical Abstract of the United States 1997* (Washington, D.C.: U.S. Government Printing Office, 1997).

now considered "necessities." Liberals also note that the official definition *includes* cash income from welfare and Social Security. Without this government assistance, the number of poor would be higher.

**conservative objections to official definition of poverty**

Conservatives also challenge the official definition of poverty: it does not include the value of family assets. People (usually older people) who own their own houses and automobiles may have incomes below the poverty line yet not suffer any real hardship. (More than 50 percent of the official "poor" own their own homes and more than 65 percent own automobiles.) Many persons who are ranked as poor do not think of themselves as "poor people"—students, for example. More important, the official definition of poverty *excludes* "in-kind" (noncash) benefits provided by government, benefits that include, for example, free medical care under Medicaid and Medicare, food stamps, public housing, and school lunches. If these benefits were "costed out" (that is, calculated as cash income), there might be fewer persons classified as poor.

# Is There a Culture of Poverty?

**the culture-of-poverty thesis**
the idea that a lifestyle of poverty, alienation, and apathy is passed on from one generation to another

It is sometimes argued that the poor have a characteristic lifestyle or *culture of poverty* that assists them in adjusting to their world. (See the Focus, "Who Are the Poor?") Like other aspects of culture it is passed on to future gen-

## FOCUS
## Who Are the Poor?

Poverty occurs in many kinds of families and in all races and ethnic groups. However, some groups experience poverty in proportions that are greater than the national average. The following statistics indicate the percentage of Americans in various groups who were living below the poverty level in 1995 (see table).

| | |
|---|---|
| Total population | 14.0% |
| Husband–wife families | 6.1 |
| Families with female heads | 38.6 |
| White | 11.6 |
| African American | 30.6 |
| Hispanic | 30.7 |
| Over age 65 | 11.7 |
| Under age 18 | 21.8 |

Poverty is most common among female-headed families. In 1995 the incidence of poverty among these families was 38.6 percent, compared with only 6.1 percent for married couples. These women and their children constitute over two-thirds of all of the persons living in poverty in the United States. These figures describe the "feminization of poverty" in America. Clearly, poverty is closely related to family structure. Today the disintegration of the traditional husband–wife family is the single most influential factor contributing to poverty.

Blacks experience poverty in much greater proportions than whites. Over the years the poverty rate among blacks in the United States has been almost three times higher than the poverty rate among whites. Poverty among Hispanics is also significantly greater than among whites.

The aged in America experience *less* poverty than younger people. The aged are not poor, despite the popularity of the phrase "the poor and the aged."

The poverty rate for persons over sixty-five years of age is *below* the national average. Moreover, the aged are much wealthier than younger age groups. They are more likely than younger people to own homes with paid-up mortgages. Medicare pays a large portion of their medical expenses. With fewer expenses, the aged, even with relatively smaller cash incomes, experience poverty in a different fashion than a younger mother with children. The declining poverty rate among the aged is a relatively recent occurrence. Continuing increases in Social Security benefits over the years are largely responsible for this singular "victory" in the war against poverty.

Finally, we should note that about one of every five children in the United States lives in poverty.

erations, setting in motion a self-perpetuating cycle of poverty. The theory of the poverty cycle is as follows: deprivation in one generation leads, through cultural impoverishment, indifference, apathy, or misunderstanding of their children's educational needs, to deprivation in the next generation. Lacking the self-respect that comes from earning an adequate living, some young men cannot sustain responsibilities of marriage, and so they hand down to their children the same burden of family instability and female-headed households that they themselves carried. Children born into a culture of alienation, apathy, and lack of motivation learn these attitudes themselves. Thus, the poor are prevented from exploiting any opportunities that are available to them.

## POVERTY AS SUBCULTURE

It is probably more accurate to talk about a *subculture* of poverty. The prefix *sub* is used because most of the poor subscribe to the "middle-class American way of life," at least as a cultural ideal and even as a personal fantasy. Most poor people do not reject American culture but strive to adapt its values to the realities of economic deprivation and social disorganization in their own lives.

**the culture of poverty as present-orientedness**
the inability to plan or sacrifice for the future

Another view of the culture of poverty emphasizes the *present-orientedness* of many poor people. It is argued that the culture of poverty is produced primarily by present-orientedness rather than a lack of income or wealth. Individuals caught up in the culture of poverty are unable to plan for the future, to sacrifice immediate gratifications in favor of future ones, or to exercise the discipline that is required to get ahead. It is true that some people experience poverty because of involuntary unemployment, prolonged illness, death of the breadwinner, or some other misfortune. But even when severe, this kind of poverty is not self-perpetuating. It ends once the external cause no longer exists. Other people will be poor no matter what their "external" circumstances are. They live in a culture of poverty that continues for generations because they are psychologically unable to provide for the future. Increased income is unlikely to change their way of life; the additional money will be spent quickly on nonessential or frivolous items. This culture of poverty may involve no more than a small portion of all families who live below the poverty line, but it generally continues regardless of what is done in the way of remedial action.[3]

## POVERTY AS ECONOMIC DEPRIVATION

**poverty**
a result of current social and economic conditions, or parental transmission of values and beliefs?

Opponents of the idea of a culture of poverty argue that this notion diverts attention from the *conditions* of poverty that foster family instability, and present-orientedness. The question is really whether the conditions of poverty create a culture of poverty or vice versa. Reformers are likely to focus on the economic deprivation as the fundamental cause of the social pathologies that afflict the poor. They note that the idea of a culture of poverty can be applied only to groups who have lived in poverty for several generations. It is not relevant to those who have become poor during their lifetime because of sickness, accident, or old age. The cultural explanation basically involves *parental transmission of values and beliefs,* which in turn determines behavior of future generations. In contrast, the situational explanation of poverty involves social conditions—differences in financial resources—that operate directly to determine behavior. Perhaps the greatest danger in the idea of a culture of poverty is that poverty in this light can be seen as an unbreakable, puncture-proof cycle, which may lead to a relaxation of efforts to ameliorate the conditions of poverty. In other words, it is feared that the "culture of poverty" idea may become an excuse for inaction.

*Extreme poverty can also be found in rural America.*

James Holland/Stock Boston

# Government and Social Welfare

Public welfare has been a recognized responsibility of government in English-speaking countries for many centuries. As far back as the Poor Relief Act of 1601, the English Parliament provided workhouses for the "able-bodied poor" (the unemployed) and poorhouses for widows and orphans, the aged, and the handicapped. Today nearly one-third of the U.S. population receives some form of government benefit: Social Security, Medicare or Medicaid, disability insurance, unemployment compensation, government employee retirement, veterans' benefits, food stamps, school lunches, job training, public housing, and cash public assistance payments (see Table 11-1). Thus, the "welfare state" now encompasses a very large part of our society.

## Social Insurance

In the Social Security Act of 1935 the federal government undertook to establish a basic framework for social welfare policies at the federal, state, and local levels in America. The *social insurance* concept was designed to *prevent* poverty resulting from individual misfortune—unemployment, old age,

**social insurance**
compulsory savings for all with legal entitlement to benefits

**TABLE 11-1**

## MAJOR GOVERNMENT SOCIAL INSURANCE
## AND PUBLIC ASSISTANCE PROGRAMS

Social Insurance Programs

| Social Security | Beneficiaries (millions) |
|---|---|
| Retirement | 29.9 |
| Survivors | 7.4 |
| Disabled | 5.6 |
| Total | 42.9 |
| **Unemployment Compensation** | |
| Total | 7.9 |

Public Assistance Programs

| Cash Aid | Beneficiaries (millions) |
|---|---|
| Family assistance | 14.0 |
| SSI | 6.3 |
| General assistance | 0.9 |
| Income tax credit | 37.8 |
| **Medical Care** | |
| Medicaid | 35.0 |
| Veterans | 0.8 |
| Maternal and child health services | 11.6 |
| **Food Benefits** | |
| Food stamps | 26.6 |
| School lunches | 25.6 |
| Women, infants, children | 6.9 |
| Nutrition for elderly | 2.1 |
| **Housing Benefits** | |
| Total | 4.1 |
| **Education Aid** | |
| Stafford Loans | 3.8 |
| Pell Grants | 3.8 |
| Head Start | 0.7 |
| Work study | 0.8 |
| Educational opportunity grants | 0.9 |
| **Job Training** | |
| Total | 1.8 |

SOURCE: U.S. Bureau of the Census, *Statistical Abstract of the United States 1996*, pp. 117, 186, 371,

death of the family breadwinner, or physical disability. Social insurance was based on the same notion as private insurance: the sharing of risks, the setting aside of money for a rainy day, and legal entitlement to benefits on reaching retirement or on occurrence of specific misfortunes. Social insurance was *not* to be charity or public assistance. Instead, it relied on people's (compulsory) financial contribution through payroll deductions to their own protection.

**major social insurance programs**
Social Security
unemployment compensation
Medicare

The key feature of the Social Security Act is the Old-Age, Survivors, Disability Insurance program; this is a compulsory social insurance program

How does the United States compare to other nations in its distribution of income to its lowest income families? It is important to realize that *all* advanced industrialized democracies distribute income more equally than less developed agricultural societies. As nations modernize and industrialize, the conditions of the poor improve and extremes of inequality are lessened.

But there is some evidence that the United States lags behind other advanced democracies in income equality. The figures in the table report the percentage of each nation's total income going to the lowest 20 percent of families. In the United States, in 1997, 4.7 percent of total income went to the lowest income group. Most other advanced democracies managed to distribute larger shares of national income to their lowest income group. In Japan, for example, the lowest income group received 8.7 percent of national income.

### CROSS-NATIONAL PERSPECTIVE
Income of the Poor in Advanced Democracies

| | Percentage of total income received by lowest 20% of families |
|---|---|
| Japan | 8.7 |
| Netherlands | 8.2 |
| Sweden | 8.0 |
| Belgium | 7.9 |
| Germany | 7.0 |
| Italy | 6.8 |
| Norway | 6.2 |
| Israel | 6.0 |
| United Kingdom | 5.8 |
| Canada | 5.7 |
| France | 5.6 |
| Denmark | 5.4 |
| Switzerland | 5.2 |
| United States | 4.7 |

SOURCE: Data derived from the World Bank, *World Development Report 1997* (New York: Published for the World Bank by Oxford University Press, 1997).

financed by regular deductions from earnings, which gives individuals the legal right to benefit in the event that their income is reduced by old age, death of the head of the household, or permanent disability. It is not public charity but a way of compelling people to provide insurance against loss of income. Another feature of the Social Security Act was that it induced states to enact unemployment compensation programs. Unemployment compensation is also an *insurance* program, only in this case the costs are borne solely by the employer. In 1965 Congress amended Social Security to add comprehensive health insurance for persons over sixty-five—Medicare. Medicare provided for prepaid hospital insurance for the aged under Social Security and for low-cost voluntary medical insurance for the same group under federal administration. Medicare, too, is based upon the insurance principle: individuals pay for their medical insurance during their working years and enjoy its benefits after age sixty-five. Thus, the program resembles private medical hospital insurance, except that it is compulsory.

## PUBLIC ASSISTANCE

**social insurance versus public assistance**

**social insurance**
contributions required
all are entitled to benefits

**public assistance**
financed out of tax revenues
benefits paid only to persons who are poor

**major public assistance cash programs**
SSI
TANF
general assistance

The distinction between the *social insurance* program and a *public assistance* (welfare) program is an important one that has on occasion become a major political issue. If the beneficiaries of a government program are required to have made contributions to it before claiming any of its benefits, and if they are entitled to the benefits regardless of their personal wealth, the program is said to be financed on the *social insurance* principle. If the program is financed out of general tax revenues, and if the recipients are required to show that they are poor before claiming its benefits, the program is said to be financed on the *public assistance* principle.

The purpose of public assistance is clearly *alleviative;* the idea is simply to provide a minimal level of subsistence to certain categories of needy persons. The federal government, under its Supplemental Security Income (SSI) program, directly aids three categories of recipients: the aged, the blind, and the disabled. The federal government, under its Temporary Assistance to Needy Families (formerly Aid to Families with Dependent Children) program, gives money to the states to assist them in providing welfare payments to families with children under eighteen. Welfare aid to persons who do not fall into any of these categories but who, for one reason or another, are poor is referred to as *general assistance* and is paid for entirely from state funds.

## IN-KIND WELFARE BENEFITS

**major public assistance in-kind programs**
food stamps
school lunches
Medicaid
public housing

The federal government also provides many *in-kind (noncash) welfare benefits.* The Food Stamp program was begun in 1965; originally the poor were allowed to purchase food stamps at large discounts and use the stamps to buy food at stores; after 1977 the stamps were distributed free. Free school lunches (and in some cities breakfasts as well) are made available to children of the poor by federal payments to school districts. In 1965 Congress also authorized federal funds to enable states to guarantee medical services to all public assistance recipients. This program is known as Medicaid. Unlike Medicare, Medicaid is a welfare program designed for needy persons; no prior contributions are required, but recipients of Medicaid must be eligible for welfare assistance. In other words, they must be poor. Finally, the federal government assists in providing job training and low-cost public housing for the poor and educational programs for needy students.

## WELFARE REFORM

In 1996 Congress passed and President Clinton signed a welfare reform act that ended the sixty-one-year-old guarantee of federal cash assistance to needy families with children. (The Social Security Act of 1935 had established Aid to Families with Dependent Children, AFDC, as a federal "entitlement," a guarantee of benefits to anyone who meets eligibility requirements set by law.) The Welfare Reform Act replaced AFDC with a block grant of federal money to the states to assist them in providing their own cash welfare aid. States were given wide discretion to determine eligibility for cash assistance. But the focus of welfare reform was on "welfare to work"—moving welfare recipients off public aid and into jobs. Among major provisions of welfare reform:

**entitlement**
a guarantee of benefits to anyone who meets eligibility requirements set by law

WORK REQUIREMENTS  Adults receiving welfare benefits will be required to begin working within two years of receiving aid. States could exempt from this work requirement a parent of a child twelve months of age or younger. However, a parent will receive this exemption only for a total of twelve months, regardless of whether they are consecutive. States will be required to have at least 25 percent of their welfare caseload engaged in work in fiscal 1997, rising to 50 percent by 2002.

RESTRICTIONS ON AID  Block grant funds cannot be used for adults who have *received welfare for more than five years*, although state and local funds could be used. States can exempt up to 20 percent of their caseload from this time limit. States can also opt to impose a shorter time limit on benefits. None of the funds can be used for adults who do not work *after receiving welfare for two years*. In addition, states will have the option to:

> Deny welfare assistance to children born to welfare recipients. Deny welfare to unwed parents under age eighteen unless they live with an adult and attend school.

MEDICAID  States will be required to continue to offer Medicaid coverage for one year to welfare recipients who lose ther welfare benefits because of increased earnings.

STATE FLEXIBILITY  States are permitted to align their food stamp program with other revamped welfare programs. They can establish a single set of eligibility and work requirements for food stamps, welfare checks, and other welfare programs.

**CASE STUDY**
Senior Power

Senior citizens are the most politically powerful age group in the population. They constitute 28 percent of the voting-age population, but more important, because of their high voter turnout rates, they constitute over one-third of the voters on election day. Persons over sixty-five average a 68-percent turnout rate in presidential elections; this compares, for example, with a turnout rate of 36 percent for persons eighteen to twenty-one years old. In short, the voting power of senior citizens is twice that of young people. The American Association of Retired People (AARP) is the largest organized interest group in American politics and one of the most powerful in Washington. No elected officials can afford to offend the seniors, and seniors strongly support generous Social Security benefits.

**The Graying of America**
The "baby boom" from 1945 to 1960 produced a large generation of people who crowded

schools and colleges in the 1960s and 1970s and encountered stiff competition for jobs in the 1970s and 1980s. This baby-boom generation will be retiring beginning in 2010, and by 2030 they will constitute nearly 20 percent of the population (see the figure). Changes in lifestyle—less smoking, more exercise, better weight control—may increase the aged population even more. So, too, may medical advances extend life expectancy.

**A Generational Compact?**
Today's generation of workers is paying for the benefits of the last generation, and it is hoped that this generation's benefits will be financed by the next generation of workers. Taxing current workers to pay benefits to current retirees may be viewed as a *compact between generations.* Each generation of workers in effect agrees to pay benefits to an earlier generation of retirees, in the hope that the next generation will pay for their own retirement. But low birthrates (reducing the number of workers), longer life spans (increasing the number of re-

tirees), and very generous benefits are straining workers' ability to pay. The generation compact is likely to break before today's younger workers reach retirement. Many of them, for good reason, have lost their confidence and trust in the system to support them in their old age.

**The "Dependency Ratio"**
Because current workers must pay for the benefits of current retirees and other beneficiaries, the *dependency ratio* becomes an important component of evaluating the future of Social Security. The dependency ratio for Social Security is the number of recipients in relation to the number of contributing workers. Americans are living longer, thereby increasing the dependency ratio. In the early years of Social Security, there were ten workers supporting each retiree—a dependency ratio of 10 to 1. But today, as the U.S. population grows older—because of lower birthrates and longer life spans—there are only three workers for each retiree, and by 2020 the dependency ratio will be two workers for each retiree. Virtually every

AID TO IMMIGRANTS *Illegal* immigrants are denied most federally funded benefits including cash aid and food stamps. Exceptions include emergency medical care. *Legal* immigrants are denied cash aid under the Supplemental Security Income (SSI) program as well as food stamps. States can choose to deny them family assistance, Medicaid, and other social services.

## THE GRAYING OF AMERICA

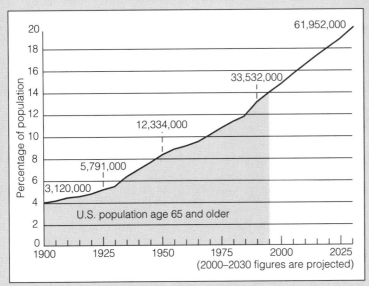

SOURCE: U.S. Bureau of the Census, *Statistical Abstract of the United States 1996* (Washington, D.C.: U.S. Government Printing Office, 1996), pp. 21, 25.

family with two wage earners will be compelled to support one retiree!

### Wealthy Retirees

Social Security benefits are paid to all eligible retirees, regardless of whatever other income they receive. There is no means test for benefits. The result is that large numbers of affluent Americans receive government checks each month. Of course, they paid into Social Security during their working years, and they can claim these checks as a legal "entitlement" under the insurance principle. But currently their benefits far exceed their previous payments. However, because the aged experience *less* poverty than today's workers (see the Focus, "Who Are the Poor?") and possess considerably more wealth, Social Security benefits constitute a "negative" redistribution of income, that is, a transfer of income from poorer to richer people. The elderly are generally better off than the people supporting them!

### The "Third Rail" of American Politics

Social Security is the single most expensive program in the federal budget and also the most politically sacrosanct. Politicians regularly call it the "third rail" of American politics—touch it and die. Virtually everyone acknowledges that controlling the costs of "entitlements" in the federal budget is the only way to reduce annual deficits. Social Security is the largest entitlement program. In theory, Congress could reform Social Security by limiting cost-of-living increases for retirees, or by introducing means tests to deny benefits to high-income retirees, or by increasing the age at which Social Security benefits begin. But politically these reforms are very unlikely. As long as senior citizens remain politically powerful and unified in support of government benefits, Social Security will remain unchanged.

PROSPECTS FOR SUCCESS   Welfare rolls declined dramatically in 1996–97 from roughly fourteen million recipients of family aid to twelve million. Part of this decline can be atrributed to a strong economy, but certainly the tightening of eligibility requirements and the new emphasis on training and work in the states contributed to the decline. Many states, anticipating federal welfare

## CONTROVERSIES IN SOCIAL SCIENCE
### Do Welfare Programs Cause Poverty?

Does the government itself create poverty by fashioning social welfare programs and policies that destroy incentives to work, encourage families to break up, and condemn the poor to social dependency? Does the current social welfare system unintentionally sentence to a life of poverty many people who would otherwise form families, take low-paying jobs, and perhaps, with hard work and perseverance, gradually pull themselves and their children into the mainstream of American life?

Poverty in America steadily *declined* from 1950, when about 30 percent of the population was officially poor, to 1970, when about 13 percent of the population was poor. During this period of progress toward the elimination of poverty, government welfare programs were minimal. There were small AFDC (Aid to Fam-

ilies with Dependent Children) programs for women who lived alone with their children; eligibility was restricted, and welfare authorities checked to see if an employable male lived in the house. Further, there were federal payments for the aged, blind, and disabled poor. Welfare rolls were modest; only about 1 to 2 percent of Americans received AFDC payments.

The downward trend in poverty ended with the addition of many new Great Society welfare programs in the 1960s. Indeed, the number and proportion of the population living in poverty began to move upward (see Figure 11-1). This was a period in which AFDC eligibility rules were relaxed and AFDC rolls grew to 5 to 6 percent of all Americans. The Food Stamp program was initiated in 1965 and became a major new welfare benefit. Medicaid was initiated in the same year and by the late 1970s became the costliest welfare program. Federal aid to the aged, blind, and disabled was merged into a new Supplemental Security Income (SSI) program. The number of recipients of this program quadrupled. Did

poverty increase in spite of, or because of, these new social welfare programs?

According to social scientist Charles Murray, the persons hurt most by welfare programs are the poor themselves. In his well-titled yet controversial book *Losing Ground,* he argues that current social welfare policy provides many disincentives to family life.[a] Nearly everyone agrees that the breakup of the family is closely associated with poverty. Murray argues that generous welfare programs encourage poor young women to start families before they have sufficient job skills to support them, and poor young men are allowed to escape their family responsibilities. Surveys show that the poor prefer work over welfare, but welfare payments may subtly affect the behavior of the poor. Persons unwilling to take minimum-wage jobs may never acquire the work habits required to move into better-paying jobs later in life. Welfare may even help create a dependent and defeatist subculture, lowering personal self-esteem and contributing further to joblessness, illegitimacy, and broken families.

Murray's policy prescription

reform, had initiated "workfare" programs even before Congress enacted welfare reform. But a substantial portion of welfare recipients have handicaps—physical problems, chronic illnesses, emotional problems, learning disabilities, alcohol or drub abuse problems—that prevent them from holding a job. Many is a drastic one. He recommended

*scrapping the entire federal welfare and income-support structure for working-age persons. It would leave the working-age person with no recourse whatever except the job market, family members, friends, and public or private locally funded services . . . cut the knot, for there is no way to untie it.[b]*

The result, he argued, would be less poverty, less illegitimacy, more upward mobility, freedom, and hope for the poor. "The lives of large numbers of poor people would be radically changed for the better." The obstacle to this solution is not only the army of politicians and bureaucrats who want to keep their dependent clients but, more important, the vast majority of generous and well-meaning middle-class Americans who support welfare programs because they do not understand how badly these programs injure the poor.

But Murray's opponents note that half of all welfare recipients are only temporarily on welfare rolls. They are encountering difficulties in life that temporarily reduce their income. Researchers who have traced family-income changes over time report the following events associated with falling below the poverty line:[c]

| | |
|---|---|
| Divorce/separation | 45% |
| Unmarried woman bears a child | 30 |
| Unemployment/earnings decline of female family head | 12 |
| Unemployment/earnings decline of male family head | 3 |
| All other (including unidentified) | 9 |

For the *temporarily* poor, welfare provides a short-term safety net that tides them over the difficult events in life.

At best, Murray's view that government welfare programs contribute to poverty would apply only to the *persistently* poor—those who are dependent upon welfare for two to five years or more. These people, most of whom are women with children, comprise about half of all welfare recipients. Many of these long-term welfare recipients have physical or mental problems, learning disabilities, and alcohol and drug dependencies that preclude finding or holding a job. To become employable, many would require extensive training; they have difficulty in meeting time schedules and responding to orders from others. Most lack a high school education. They have no means of transportation to work. And child-care arrangements would require more government assistance. The costs of putting these people to work—counseling, job training, transportation, child care, etc.—exceed costs of welfare benefits.

Recent welfare reforms, including a time limit on cash benefits, and a five-year lifetime limit, reflect Congress's concern that long-term welfare benefits may indeed encourage dependency and continued poverty. Perhaps Murray's work helped shape welfare reform. But it is not yet clear whether welfare reform will succeed.

[a] Charles Murray, *Losing Ground* (New York: Basic Books, 1984).

[b] Ibid., 227–228.

[c] Data from University of Michigan Panel Study of Income Dynamics, courtesy of Greg J. Duncan and Saul D. Hoffman. See Greg J. Duncan, *Years of Poverty, Years of Plenty* (Ann Arbor: University of Michigan Press, 1984).

have no prior work experience. Over half have children under six, making child-care arrangements a major obstacle. Finally, there might not be the necessary five to ten million jobs available for largely unskilled former welfare recipients. Cutting off aid may place millions of children at risk.

# Homelessness in America

The most visible social welfare problem in America is the nation's homeless "street people," suffering exposure, alcoholism, drug abuse, and chronic mental illness while wandering the streets of the nation's larger cities.

**homeless**

persons living in streets and public places

persons accepting housing in public shelters

The term *homeless* is used to describe many different situations.[4] There are the street people who sleep in subways, bus stations, parks, or the streets. Some of them are temporarily traveling in search of work; some have left home for a few days or are youthful runaways; others have roamed the streets for months or years. There are the sheltered homeless who obtain housing in shelters operated by local governments or private charities. As the number of shelters has grown in recent years, the number of sheltered homeless has also grown. But most of the sheltered homeless come from other housing, not the streets. These are people who have been recently evicted from rental units or have previously lived with family or friends. These sheltered homeless often include families with children; the street homeless are virtually all single persons.

## Street People

The ranks of the street homeless expand and contract with the seasons.[5] These homeless are difficult subjects for systematic interviewing; many do not wish to admit to alcoholism, drug dependency, or mental illness. (The television networks often sensationalize the topic, exaggerate the number of homeless, and incorrectly portray the homeless as middle-class white families victimized by economic misfortune and the high cost of housing.) Serious studies indicate that close to half of the street homeless are chronic alcohol and drug abusers, and an additional one-fourth to one-third are mentally ill.[6] The alcohol and drug abusers, especially "crack" cocaine users, are the fastest-growing groups among the homeless. Moreover, the alcohol and drug abusers and mentally ill among the homeless are likely to remain on the streets for long periods of time. Among the 15 to 25 percent of the homeless who are neither mentally ill nor dependent on alcohol or drugs, homelessness is more likely to be temporary.

## Deinstitutionalization

**deinstitutionalization**

release of mental patients who pose no threat to others

Deinstitutionalization was a reform advanced by mental health care professionals and social welfare activists in the 1960s and 1970s to release chronic mental patients from state-run mental hospitals. It was widely recognized that aside from drugs, no psychiatric therapies have much success among the long-term mentally ill. Drug therapies can be administered on an outpatient basis; they usually do not require hospitalization. So it was argued that no one could be rightfully kept in a mental institution against his or her will; people who had committed no crimes and who posed no danger to others

*Homeless families seek temporary shelter, and sometimes live in
their car; others sleep in the streets.*

Mary Ellen Mark/Library

should be released. The nation's mental hospitals were emptied of all but the
most dangerous mental patients. The population of mental hospitals
declined from about 500,000 in 1960 to about 100,000 in 1990.

## DECRIMINALIZATION

Vagrancy (homelessness) and public intoxication have been decriminalized.
Involuntary confinement has been abolished for the mentally ill and for the
substance abuser unless such a person is adjudged in court to be "a danger
to himself or others." This means a person must commit a serious act of violence before the courts will intervene. For many homeless this means the
freedom to "die with their rights on." The homeless are victimized by cold,
exposure, hunger, the availability of alcohol and illegal drugs, and violent
street crimes perpetrated against them, in addition to the ravages of illness
itself.

**decriminalization**
abolishing confinement for
vagrancy or public intoxication
of persons who pose no danger
to others

## OUTSIDE THE SOCIAL WELFARE SYSTEM

Social welfare programs are frequently irrelevant to the plight of the chronic
mentally ill persons and alcohol and drug abusers in the streets. Most are
"uncooperative"; they are isolated from society; they have no family members,

doctors, or counselors to turn to for help. The nation's vast social welfare system provides them little help. They may lose their Social Security, welfare, and disability checks because they have no permanent address. They cannot handle forms, appointments, or interviews; the welfare bureaucracy is intimidating. Welfare workers seldom provide the "aggressive care management" and mental health care these people need.

## NOTES

1. Kenneth B. Clark, *Dark Ghetto: Dilemmas of Social Power* (New York: Harper & Row, 1965).
2. Ibid., 67.
3. Edward C. Banfield, *The Unheavenly City* (Boston: Little, Brown, 1968), ch. 6.
4. Robert C. Ellickson, "The Homelessness Muddle," *The Public Interest* (Spring 1990): 45–60.
5. No one knows the total number of homeless, but the systematic estimate is 250,000 to 350,000.
6. As reported in a survey of twenty-seven cities conducted by the U.S. Conference of Mayors. See *U.S. News & World Report,* January 15, 1990, 27–29.

## ABOUT THIS CHAPTER

Captain John Smith's ultimatum to his starving band of settlers in Jamestown in 1609 that "he who would not work must not eat" is probably the first recorded American welfare policy statement. It was not until the western frontier had finally closed and the Great Depression of the 1930s had reduced many of the prosperous to the ranks of the paupers that there was any discernible change in the American attitude toward poverty. When poverty exists in the midst of plenty, it is more difficult for the poor to bear.

In this chapter we have explored various definitions of poverty, as well as some recent efforts to lift the poor from their position of powerlessness. Now that you have read it, you should be able to

- discuss various definitions of poverty and describe the characteristics of the poor
- discuss the theory of a subculture of poverty
- describe the relationship between poverty and powerlessness
- discuss how government policies might contribute to poverty

- identify major social insurance and public assistance programs and distinguish between the two types of programs
- describe the changing age composition of the American population and how this will affect Social Security in the future
- discuss the causes of homelessness

## DISCUSSION QUESTIONS

1. Discuss the criteria used by the U.S. Social Security Administration to define the poverty line. Describe the emphasis of this official definition of poverty on subsistence levels. What are the criticisms of this definition of poverty?
2. Identify the groups of people who experience poverty in greater proportions than the national average.
3. Discuss the relationship between poverty and feelings of powerlessness. What are the feelings of the poor about themselves? What are their attitudes toward the larger society? Describe some of the forms of personal adjustment to poverty and the effect of poverty and discrimination on family life.
4. What is meant by the expression *culture of poverty?* Comment on the view of the culture of poverty as "present-orientedness." What are the policy implications of a culture of poverty? Discuss the arguments of those who oppose the idea of a culture of poverty.
5. Differentiate between social insurance programs and public assistance programs in terms of who pays, who benefits, and when they benefit. Give examples of each type of program and specify the type of strategy each expresses.
6. Why might government programs designed to remedy poverty actually contribute to continuing poverty? Discuss the criticisms of current public assistance programs.
7. What changes are occurring in the age composition of the nation's population? What do these changes mean for Social Security? How can the Social Security program be preserved?
8. What "reforms" may have contributed to homelessness in America?

# Chapter 12

# Power, Crime, and Violence

## POWER AND INDIVIDUAL FREEDOM

For centuries people have wrestled with the question of balancing social power against individual freedom. How far can individual freedom be extended without undermining the stability of a society, threatening the safety of others, and risking anarchy? The early English political philosopher Thomas Hobbes (1588–1679) believed that society must establish a powerful "Leviathan"—the state—in order to curb the savage instincts of human beings. A powerful authority in society was needed to prevent people from attacking each other for personal gain—"war of every man against every man" in which "notions of right and wrong, justice and injustice, have no place." According to Hobbes, without law and order there is no real freedom. The fear of death and destruction permeates every act of life: "Every man is enemy to every man"; "Force and fraud are the two cardinal virtues"; and "The life of man [is] solitary, poor, nasty, brutish, and short." Freedom, then, is not the absence of law and order. On the contrary, law and order are required if there is to be any freedom in society at all.[1]

**Thomas Hobbes**
Freedom is not the absence of law; law is required to protect individual freedom. Governments are formed for collective self-protection.

# THE PROBLEM OF CRIME

**crime rates**
reported serious crimes per 100,000 people

**FBI classification, serious crimes**
criminal homicide
forcible rape
robbery
aggravated assault
burglary
larceny
auto theft

*Crime rates* are the subject of a great deal of popular discussion. Very often they are employed to express the degree of social disorganization or even the effectiveness of law enforcement agencies. Crime rates are based on the Federal Bureau of Investigation's *Uniform Crime Reports,* but the FBI reports themselves are based on figures supplied by state and local police agencies. The FBI has established a *uniform classification* of the number of serious crimes per 100,000 people that are known to the police—murder and nonnegligent manslaughter, forcible rape, robbery, aggravated assault, burglary, larceny, and theft, including auto theft. These serious crimes are totaled and divided by the population in order to ascertain crime rates. But these crimes are only a small portion of all crimes (see the Focus: "It's a Real Crime!").

We should be cautious in interpreting official crime rates. They are really a function of several factors: the willingness of victims to report crime to the police, the adequacy of the system for reporting and tabulating crime, and the amount of crime itself.

## CHANGES IN CRIME RATES

The official FBI crime rate has risen dramatically in the United States over recent decades. Increases occurred in both violent crime—murder, rape, robbery, and assault (see Table 12-1)—and property crime—burglary, larceny, and theft. Certainly some of the increase was a result of improved reporting. As more people insure their property, they file more police reports in order to make insurance claims. The introduction of the 911 emergency phone number across the United States may also have increased reported crimes. The introduction of computers and sophisticated police data collection systems may also have contributed to the increases. But unquestionably crime itself was also on the rise.

**TABLE 12-1**

### CRIME RATES
Offenses Reported to Police per 100,000 Population

| | 1960 | 1970 | 1980 | 1985 | 1990 | 1995 |
|---|---|---|---|---|---|---|
| *Violent Crimes* | 160 | 360 | 581 | 557 | 732 | 689 |
| Murder | 5 | 8 | 10 | 8 | 9 | 8 |
| Forcible Rape | 9 | 18 | 36 | 37 | 41 | 37 |
| Robbery | 60 | 172 | 244 | 209 | 257 | 221 |
| Assault | 85 | 162 | 291 | 303 | 424 | 423 |
| *Property Crimes* | 1,716 | 3,599 | 5,319 | 4,651 | 4,903 | 4,611 |

SOURCE: Federal Bureau of Investigation, *Uniform Crime Reports* (annual).

In the early 1980s crime rates declined slightly. Many commentators attributed this success to the changing age structure of the population: the most "crime-prone" age group, persons fifteen to twenty-four years old, was no longer increasing as a percentage of the population. But then crime rates surged upward again. The new crime wave appeared to be related to the expanding use of "crack" cocaine. About one-half of all crimes today are drug-related.

Since peaking in the early 1990s, crime rates have actually declined (see Figure 12-1). Law enforcement officials attribute recent successes in crime-fighting to police "crackdowns," more aggressive "community policing," and longer prison sentences for repeat offenders, including "three strikes you're out" laws. (All are discussed later in this chapter.) In support of this claim, they observe that the greatest reductions in crime have occurred in the nation's largest cities, especially those such as New York that have adopted tougher law enforcement practices. However, while overall crime rates are down, juvenile crime is on the rise. So it is by no means certain that crime rates will not rise again in future years.

## VICTIMIZATION

How much crime is there in America today? We know that the FBI official crime rate understates the real amount of crime. Many crimes are not reported to the police and therefore cannot be counted in the official crime rate. In an effort to learn the real amount of crime in the nation, the U.S. Justice Department regularly surveys a national sample of people, asking whether they have been a victim of a crime during the past year.[2] These surveys reveal that the *victimization rate* is many times greater than the official crime rate. The number of forcible rapes is three to five times greater than the number reported to police, the number of unreported burglaries is three times greater,

**victimization rates**
national survey responses to the question of whether one has been the victim of a crime in the past year

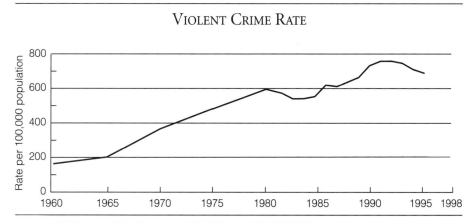

**FIGURE 12-1**

VIOLENT CRIME RATE

SOURCE: U.S. Bureau of the Census, *Statistical Abstract of the United States 1994*, p. 198.

FOCUS
It's a Real Crime!

Crimes are often divided into two categories: felonies—crimes punishable by more than one year in prison—and misdemeanors—crimes punishable by less than one year. Most people who are convicted and incarcerated for a felony are sent to state prisons (or federal prison for federal felonies), while most people jailed for misdemeanors serve their sentence in city or county jails, which also hold people awaiting trial. All of the FBI uniform classified serious crimes are felonies; most other nonserious crimes are misdemeanors, although federal and most state laws define the sale and manufacturing of illegal drugs as felonies.

## SERIOUS CRIMES
### (crimes used to calculate crime rates)

### Violent

**Criminal Homicide:** (a) murder and nonnegligent manslaughter (the willful killing of one human being by another); deaths caused by negligence, attempts to kill, assaults to kill, suicides, accidental deaths, and justifiable homicides are excluded; (b) manslaughter by negligence (the killing of another person through gross negligence; traffic fatalities are excluded)
**Forcible Rape:** the carnal knowledge of a female forcibly and against her will; includes rapes by force and attempts to rape, but excludes statutory offenses (no force used and victim under age of consent)
**Robbery:** the taking or attempting to take anything of value from the care, custody, or control of a person or persons by force or threat of force and/or by putting the victim in fear
**Aggravated Assault:** an unlawful attack by one person upon another to inflict severe bodily injury; usually involves use of a weapon or other means likely to produce death or great bodily harm. Simple assaults are excluded.

### Property

**Burglary:** unlawful entry, completed or attempted, of a structure to commit a felony or theft
**Larceny-Theft:** unlawful taking, completed or attempted, of property from another's possession that does not involve force, threat of force, or fraud; examples include thefts of bicycles or car accessories, shoplifting, pocket-picking

and the number of robberies is over twice that of the reported rate. Only auto theft and murder statistics are reasonably accurate, indicating that most people call the police when their car is stolen or someone is murdered. (See the Cross-National Perspective, "Murder and Homicide.")

Why do people fail to report crime to the police? The most common reason interviewees give is the feeling that police cannot be effective in dealing with the crime. Other reasons included the feeling that the crime was "a private matter" or that the victim did not want to harm the offender. Fear of reprisal was mentioned much less frequently, usually in cases of assaults and family crimes.

**Motor Vehicle Theft:** theft or attempted theft of self-propelled motor vehicle that runs on the surface and not on rails; excluded are thefts of boats, construction equipment, airplanes, and farming equipment

**Arson:** willful burning or attempt to burn a dwelling, public building, personal property, etc.

## Other Crimes

**Simple Assaults:** assaults and attempted assaults involving no weapon and not resulting in serious injury

**Forgery and Counterfeiting:** making, altering, uttering, or possessing, with intent to defraud, anything false in the semblance of that which is true

**Fraud:** fraudulent obtaining of money or property by false pretense; included are confidence games and bad checks

**Embezzlement:** misappropriation of money or property entrusted to one's care or control

**Stolen Property:** buying, receiving, and possessing stolen property, including attempts

**Vandalism:** willful destruction or defacement of public or private property without consent of the owner

**Weapons:** carrying, possessing, etc. All violations of regulations or statutes controlling the carrying, using, possessing, furnishing, and manufacturing of deadly weapons or silencers. Attempts are included.

**Prostitution and Commercialized Vice:** sex offenses such as prostitution and procuring

**Sex Offenses:** statutory rape and offenses against common decency, morals, etc.; excludes forcible rape and prostitution and commercial vice

**Drug Abuse:** unlawful possession, sale, use, growing, and manufacturing of drugs

**Gambling**

**Offenses Against the Family and Children:** nonsupport, neglect, desertion, or abuse of family and children

**Driving Under the Influence**

**Liquor Laws:** state/local liquor law violations, except drunkenness and driving under the influence

**Drunkenness**

**Disorderly Conduct:** breach of the peace

**Vagrancy:** vagabonding, begging, loitering, etc.

**All Other Offenses:** all violations of state/local laws, except as above and traffic offenses

**Curfew and Loitering Laws:** persons under age 18

**Runaways:** persons under age 18

SOURCE: Federal Bureau of Investigation, 1995.

# THE CONSTITUTIONAL RIGHTS OF DEFENDANTS

Society needs the protection of police. But it is equally important in a free society to protect individuals *from* the police. Arbitrary searches and arrests, imprisonment without trial, forced confessions, beatings and torture, secret trials, excessive punishments, and other human rights violations are all too common throughout the world. The U.S. Constitution—especially the Fourth, Fifth, Sixth, and Eighth Amendments (see Table 12-2)—limits the powers of police and protects the rights of accused persons.

*[handwritten annotations in top margin: "96.1 million convicted of felony. 2/3 to prison or jail. 98  99 prevalent"]*

*[handwritten annotations in left margin: "Community Policing = everyone works together and Police is there to help. 98"]*

*[handwritten annotations: "assault = ↓  Gun rates = ↓"]*

The U.S. Constitution limits the powers of police and protects the rights of accused persons. Here, a Los Angeles police officer frisks teenagers in a line-up along Hollywood Boulevard.

Dorothy Littell/Stock Boston

*[handwritten annotation: "59% have HD in prison"]*

## Guarantee of the Writ of Habeas Corpus

**habeas corpus**
police may not hold a defendant without showing cause before a judge

An ancient right in English common law is the right to *obtain a writ of habeas corpus,* a court order directing police who are holding a person in custody to bring the prisoner into court to explain the reasons for the confinement. Police must bring persons held before a judge as soon as possible, or release them upon their written pledge to appear in court. If a judge finds that the prisoner is being unlawfully detained, or that there is not sufficient evidence that a crime has been committed or that the prisoner committed it, the judge orders the prisoner's immediate release.

*[handwritten annotation: "2/3 where employed before prison."]*

*[handwritten annotations in left margin: "Crime rate since 1984 = ↓  Homicide is lower than since 1964  Rape - no change  Robbery - same"]*

## Prohibition of Bills of Attainder and of Ex Post Facto Laws

**bill of attainder**
a legislative act that inflicts punishment without a trial

**ex post facto law**
making an act criminal after it is committed or retroactively increasing punishment

Protection against bills of attainder and against ex post facto laws was, like the guarantee of habeas corpus, considered so fundamental to individual liberty that it was included in the original text of the Constitution. A *bill of attainder* is a legislative act that inflicts punishment without judicial trial. An *ex post facto law* is a retroactive criminal law that works to the detriment of the accused—for example, a law that makes an act a criminal one *after* the act is committed, or a law that increases the punishment for a crime and applies it *retroactively.*

*[handwritten annotation: "Car Stealing"]*

**TABLE 12-2**

## CONSTITUTIONAL LIMITS ON POLICE POWERS

| Criminal justice process | Individual rights |
|---|---|
| Investigation by law enforcement officers<br>Expectation that police act lawfully | Fourth Amendment: Protection against unreasonable searches and seizures<br>Warranted searches for sworn "probable cause"; exceptions: consent searches, safety searches, car searches, and searches incident to a valid arrest; evidence "in plain view" may be seized<br>Fifth Amendment: Protection against self-incrimination<br>Miranda rules |
| Arrest<br>Arrests based on warrants issued by judges and magistrates<br>Arrests based on crimes committed in the presence of law enforcement official<br>Arrests for "probable cause" | Habeas Corpus<br>Police holding a person in custody must bring the person before a judge with cause to believe that a crime was committed and the prisoner committed it |
| Hearing and bail<br>Preliminary hearing where prosecutor presents testimony that a crime was committed and probable cause for charging the accused | Eighth Amendment: No excessive bail<br>Defendant considered innocent until proven guilty; release on bail and amount of bail depend on seriousness of crime, trustworthiness of defendant, and safety of community |
| Indictment<br>Prosecutor, or a grand jury in federal cases, issues formal document naming the accused and specifying the charges | Fifth Amendment: Grand jury (federal)<br>Federal prosecutors (but not necessarily state prosecutors) must convince a grand jury that a reasonable basis exists to believe that the defendant committed a crime and he or she should be brought to trial |
| Arraignment<br>Judge reads indictment to the accused and ensures that the accused understands charges and rights and has counsel<br>Judge asks defendant to choose a plea: guilty, *nolo contendere* (no contest), or not guilty; if defendant pleads guilty or no contest, a trial is not necessary and defendant proceeds to sentencing | Sixth Amendment: Right to counsel<br>Begins in investigation stage, when officials become "accusatory," extends throughout criminal justice process<br>Free counsel for indigent defendants |
| Trial<br>Impartial judge presides as prosecuting and defense attorneys present witnesses and evidence relevant to guilt or innocence of defendant and make arguments to the jury; jury deliberates in secret and issues a verdict | Sixth Amendment: Right to a fair public and speedy trial<br>Impartial jury<br>Right to confront witnesses<br>Right to compel favorable witnesses to testify<br>Fourth Amendment: Exclusionary rule<br>Illegally obtained evidence cannot be used against defendant |
| Sentencing<br>If the defendant is found not guilty, the process ends; defendants who plead guilty or no contest and defendants found guilty by jury are sentenced by fine, imprisonment, or both by the judge | Eighth Amendment: Protection against cruel or unusual punishment |
| Appeal<br>Defendants found guilty may appeal to higher courts for reversal of verdict or a new trial based on errors made anywhere in the process | Fifth Amendment: Protection against double jeopardy<br>Government cannot try a defendant again for the same offense |

Domestic violence ∴ 20-39 is majority of victims.

## CROSS-NATIONAL PERSPECTIVE
### Murder and Homicide

The United States is one of the more violent societies in the world. Crimes of violence—murder, homicide, rape, robbery, and assault—appear to be more common in the United States than in other advanced nations. Indeed, in acts of violence per capita, the United States resembles many troubled, less developed nations.

The murder rate in the United States is about twice as high as that in most European nations and almost ten times higher than Japan's (see table). It is little wonder that many Japanese consider the United States a very dangerous place to visit. Victimization surveys, reporting the percent of respondents who say they have been victims of a crime in the last year, appear to confirm that the United States is the most crime-ridden of the advanced nations of the world. Over three times as many Americans as Japanese report that they have been victimized by crime. There are more people behind bars in the United States than in any other nation. With nearly 1 million prisoners, the nation's incarceration rate (prisoners in relation to the population) is over four times higher than other advanced nations.

| | Victimization rate[*] | | Murder rate[†] | | Incarceration rate[‡] |
|---|---|---|---|---|---|
| United States | 28.8 | United States | 9.4 | United States | 426 |
| Canada | 28.1 | Sweden | 7.2 | United Kingdom | 97 |
| Australia | 27.8 | Canada | 5.5 | Germany | 85 |
| Netherlands | 26.8 | France | 4.6 | France | 81 |
| Spain | 24.6 | Australia | 4.5 | Spain | 76 |
| Germany | 21.9 | Germany | 4.2 | Finland | 73 |
| France | 19.4 | Belgium | 2.8 | Switzerland | 73 |
| United Kingdom | 19.4 | Spain | 2.3 | Australia | 72 |
| Belgium | 17.7 | Switzerland | 2.3 | Denmark | 68 |
| Norway | 16.5 | Italy | 2.2 | Belgium | 65 |
| Finland | 15.9 | Norway | 2.0 | Italy | 60 |
| Switzerland | 15.6 | United Kingdom | 2.0 | Norway | 48 |
| Japan | 9.3 | Japan | 1.2 | Japan | 45 |

[*]Percentage of population who say they have been victims of a crime in the last year.
[†]Murders reported to the police per 100,000 population.
[‡]Prisoners per 100,000 population.

SOURCES: Data from Jan J. M. van Dijk, *Experience of Crime Across the World,* 2nd ed. (Netherlands: Klower, 1991); and Andrew J. Shapiro, *We're Number One* (New York: Vintage Books, 1992).

## PROHIBITION OF "UNREASONABLE" SEARCHES AND SEIZURES

**unreasonable search**
search without lawful warrant by judge, unless "incident to a lawful arrest"

The Fourth Amendment provides: "The right of the people to be secure in their persons, houses, papers, and effects, against unreasonable searches and seizures, shall not be violated, and no warrants shall issue, but upon probable cause, supported by oath or affirmation, and particularly describing the place to be searched, and the persons or things to be seized." The requirement that the things to be seized must be described in the warrant is meant to prevent "fishing expeditions" into an individual's home and personal effects on the possibility that some evidence of unknown illegal activity might crop up. An exception to the requirement for a warrant is made if the search is "incident to a lawful arrest." A "lawful arrest" can be made by the police if they have "probable cause" to believe a person has committed a crime; a search of the person and the person's property is permitted without a warrant at the time of such an arrest.

## FREEDOM FROM SELF-INCRIMINATION

Although the Fifth Amendment establishes a number of procedural guarantees, perhaps the most widely quoted clause of that amendment guarantees that no person "shall be compelled in any criminal case to be a witness against himself." The sentence "I refuse to answer that question on the ground that it might tend to incriminate me" is, today, a household expression. Freedom from self-incrimination has its origins in English resistance against torture and confession. It now embodies the ideas that individuals should not be forced to contribute to their own prosecution and that the burden of proof of guilt is on the state. The constitutional protection against self-incrimination applies not only to accused persons in their own trials but also to witnesses testifying in any public proceedings, including criminal trials of other persons, civil suits, congressional hearings, or other investigations. The silence of an accused person cannot be interpreted as guilt; the burden of proving guilt rests with the prosecution.

**freedom from self-incrimination**
no physical or psychological force can be used to obtain confession or incriminating evidence from a defendant

## GUARANTEE OF A FAIR JURY TRIAL

Trial by jury is guaranteed in both the original text of the Constitution and the Sixth Amendment: "In all criminal prosecutions, the accused shall enjoy the right to a speedy and public trial, by an impartial jury ... and to be informed of the nature and cause of the accusation; to be confronted with the witnesses against him; to have compulsory process for obtaining witnesses in his favor. ..." The requirement of a *speedy* trial protects the accused from long pretrial waits; but the accused may ask for postponements in order to prepare a defense. A *public* trial prevents secret proceedings, and *impartial* means that each juror must be able to judge the case objectively. Discrimination in the selection of the jury is forbidden. The guarantee of a fair trial can be violated if sensational pretrial publicity or an unruly courtroom hinders the jury from making an unbiased verdict. By tradition a jury consisted of twelve persons, and the vote of the jurors had to be unanimous. This is still the requirement in most cases, but recently the Supreme Court indicated that unanimity might not be required in some cases.

**fair jury trial**
speedy
public
impartial

**unanimous jury not required in all cases**

*The burden of proof rests with the prosecution.* It is up to the prosecution to convince a jury "beyond reasonable doubt" that the accused is guilty.

**burden of proof on prosecution**
"beyond reasonable doubt"

Witnesses must appear in person against the accused. The accused or the counsel for the accused has the right to cross-examine those witnesses and may present witnesses on behalf of his or her own case. The accused may even obtain a "summons" to compel people to testify at the trial. If a guilty verdict is rendered, the defendant may appeal any errors in the trial to a higher court.

## PROTECTION AGAINST DOUBLE JEOPARDY

**no double jeopardy**
if found not guilty, a person cannot be tried again for the same crime

The Fifth Amendment states: "Nor shall any person be subject for the same offense to be twice put in jeopardy of life or limb. . . ." Once a person has been tried for a particular crime and the trial has ended in a decision of not guilty, that person cannot be tried again for the same crime. However, this right does not prevent a new trial if the jury cannot agree on a verdict (a "hung jury"), or if the verdict is reversed by an appeal to a higher court because of a procedural error. Moreover, an individual may be tried by federal and state courts on charges stemming from the same act.

## PROTECTION AGAINST EXCESSIVE BAIL AND CRUEL AND UNUSUAL PUNISHMENTS

**bail**
money held by court to ensure that defendant will appear for trial

Arrested persons are considered innocent until tried and found guilty. They are entitled to go free prior to trial unless their freedom would unreasonably endanger society or unless there is reason to believe that they would not appear for trial. Bail is supposed to ensure that the accused will appear. Bail may be denied for major crimes, but most accused persons are entitled to be released on bail pending their trial. The Eighth Amendment states that bail must not be "excessive," although there are no fixed standards for determining what "excessive" is. It also prohibits "cruel and unusual punishments," but it does not define this phrase (see Case Study, "The Death Penalty and the Constitution").

## THE RIGHT TO COUNSEL

**right to counsel**
the right to an attorney in all criminal cases

right to free counsel for indigent defendants

counsel provided at beginning of investigation

defendants must be informed of rights upon arrest

The Sixth Amendment states: "In all criminal prosecutions, the accused shall enjoy . . . the assistance of counsel for his defense." In a series of cases in the 1960s, the Supreme Court, under the leadership of Chief Justice Earl Warren, greatly strengthened the Sixth Amendment's guarantee of the right to counsel:

- *Gideon* v. *Wainwright* (1963)—Ruling that equal protection under the Fourteenth Amendment requires that free legal counsel be appointed for all indigent defendants in all criminal cases.
- *Escobedo* v. *Illinois* (1964)—Ruling that a suspect is entitled to confer with counsel as soon as police investigation focuses on him or her, or once "the process shifts from investigatory to accusatory."

- *Miranda* v. *Arizona* (1966)—Ruling that police, before questioning a suspect, must inform the suspect of all his or her constitutional rights, including the right to counsel, appointed free if necessary, and the right to remain silent (see Figure 12-2). Although the suspect may knowingly waive these rights, the police cannot question anyone who at any point asks for a lawyer or indicates "in any manner" that he or she does not wish to be questioned. If the police commit an error in these procedures, the accused goes free, regardless of the evidence of guilt.

## The Exclusionary Rule

The exclusionary rule prevents illegally obtained evidence from being used in a criminal case. The rule, unique to the courts in the United States, was adopted by the U.S. Supreme Court in *Mapp* v. *Ohio* in 1961. Although illegally seized evidence may prove the guilt of the accused, it cannot be used in court, and the accused may go free because the police committed a procedural error.

Many trial proceedings today are not concerned with the guilt or innocence of the accused, but instead center on possible procedural errors by police or prosecutors. If the defendant's attorney can show that an error was committed, the defendant goes free, regardless of his or her guilt or innocence.

**FIGURE 12-2**

## The "Miranda Card"

*Used by San Francisco police to inform suspects of their rights at the time of arrest.*

| DEFENDANT | LOCATION |
|---|---|

SPECIFIC WARNING REGARDING INTERROGATIONS

1. You have the right to remain silent.
2. Anything you say can and will be used against you in a court of law.
3. You have the right to talk to a lawyer and have him present with you while you are being questioned.
4. If you cannot afford to hire a lawyer one will be appointed to represent you before any questioning, if you wish one.

SIGNATURE OF DEFENDANT                    DATE

WITNESS                    TIME

☐ REFUSED SIGNATURE          SAN FRANCISCO POLICE DEPARTMENT          PR.9.1.4

## CASE STUDY
The Death Penalty
and the
Constitution

One of the more emotional debates in correctional policy today concerns capital punishment. Opponents of the death penalty argue that it is "cruel and unusual punishment," and is thus in violation of the Eighth Amendment of the Constitution. In contrast, there is a strong sense of justice among many Americans that demands retribution for heinous crimes—a life for a life.

For nearly 200 years there was general agreement that death was not "cruel" or "unusual" unless it was carried out in a particularly bizarre or painful fashion. Most executions were by hanging; the electric chair was introduced in the 1920s as a "humane" alternative, and the gas chamber followed in some states. Today, some states employ a "lethal injection." Before 1972 the death penalty was officially approved by thirty states; only fifteen states had abolished capital punishment. Federal laws also retained the death penalty.

However, in *Furman* v. *Georgia* (1972) the Supreme Court ruled that capital punishment *as then imposed* violated the Eighth and Fourteenth Amendments in that it constituted cruel and unusual punishment and denied due process of law. The decision was made by a 5-to-4 vote of the justices, and the reasoning in the case is very complex. Only two justices declared that capital punishment itself is cruel and unusual. The other three justices in the majority felt that death sentences had been applied unfairly; a few individuals were receiving the death penalty for crimes for which many others were receiving lighter sentences. These justices left open the possibility that capital punishment would be constitutional if it were specified for certain kinds of crime and applied uniformly. After this decision, a majority of states rewrote their death penalty laws to try to ensure fairness and uniformity of application. Generally, these laws mandate the death penalty for murders committed during rape, robbery, hijacking, or kidnapping; murders of prison guards; murder with torture; and multiple murders.

In a series of cases in 1976 (*Gregg* v. *Georgia, Profitt* v. *Florida, Jurek* v. *Texas*), the Supreme Court held that "the punishment of death does not invariably violate the Constitution." The Court upheld the death penalty with the following rationale: the men who drafted the Bill of Rights accepted death as a common sanction of crime. It is true that the Eighth Amendment prohibition against cruel and unusual punishment must be interpreted in a dynamic fashion, reflecting changing moral values. But the decisions of more than half of the nation's state legislatures to reenact the death penalty since 1972, as well as the decisions of juries to impose the death penalty under these new laws, were evidence that "a large proportion of American society continues to regard it as an appropriate and necessary criminal sanction." Moreover, said the Court, the social purposes of retribution and deterrence justify the use of the death penalty. This ultimate sanction is "an expression of society's moral outrage at particularly offensive conduct."

The Court upheld the death penalty in states where the trial was a two-part proceeding, the second part of which provided the judge or jury with relevant information and standards for deciding whether to impose the death penalty. The Court approved the consideration of "aggravating and mitigating circumstances." The Court also required automatic review of all death sentences by state supreme courts to ensure

*The gas chamber was introduced in the 1920s as an alternative to execution by electric chair.*

Kevin Moloney/Gamma-Liaison

that the sentences were not imposed under the influence of passion or prejudice, that aggravating factors were supported by the evidence, and that the sentences were not disproportionate to the crimes.

Today there are over two thousand prisoners nationwide on "death row," that is, persons convicted and sentenced to death. But only ten to twenty-five executions are actually carried out each year. The strategy of death-row prisoners and their lawyers, of course, is to delay indefinitely the imposition of the death penalty with stays and appeals. So far the strategy has been successful for all but a few luckless murderers. As trial judges and juries continue to impose the death penalty and appellate courts continue to grant stays of execution, the number of prisoners on death row grows. The few who have been executed have averaged ten years of delay between trial and execution.

The death penalty as it is employed today—inflicted on so few after so many years following the crime—has little deterrent effect. Nonetheless, proponents say the death penalty serves several purposes. It gives prosecutors some leverage in plea bargaining with murder defendants. The defendants may choose to plead guilty in exchange for a life sentence when confronted with the possibility that the prosecutor may win a conviction and the death penalty in a jury trial. Most importantly, however, the death penalty is symbolic of the value society places on the lives of innocent victims. The death penalty dramatically signifies that society does not excuse or condone the taking of innocent lives. It symbolizes the potential for society's retribution against heinous crime. Public opinion favors the death penalty by three to one.

Supreme Court Justice Felix Frankfurter wrote many years ago: "The history of liberty has largely been the history of procedural safeguards." These safeguards protect us all from the abuse of police powers. But Chief Justice Warren Burger attacked the exclusionary rule for "the high price it extracts from society—the release of countless guilty criminals."[3] Why should criminals go free because of police misconduct? Why not punish the police directly, perhaps with disciplinary measures imposed by courts that discover procedural errors, instead of letting guilty persons go free? Releasing criminals because of police misconduct punishes society, not the police.

## Plea Bargaining

Most convictions are obtained by guilty pleas. Indeed, about 90 percent of the criminal cases brought to trial are disposed of by guilty pleas before a judge, not trial by jury. The Constitution guarantees trial by jury (Sixth Amendment) and protects against self-incrimination (Fifth Amendment). All defendants have the right to a trial by jury to determine guilt or innocence. But guilty pleas outnumber jury trials by ten to one.[4]

**plea bargaining**
criminal defendants agree to plead guilty and forgo a jury trial in exchange for reduced charges or lighter penalties

"Plea bargaining," in which the prosecution reduces the seriousness of the charges, drops some but not all charges, or agrees to recommend lighter penalties, in exchange for a guilty plea by the defendant, is very common. Some critics of plea bargaining view it as another form of leniency in the criminal justice system that reduces its deterrent effects. Other critics view plea bargaining as a violation of the Constitution's protection against self-incrimination and guarantee of a fair jury trial. Prosecutors, they say, threaten defendants with serious charges and stiff penalties in order to force a guilty plea. Still other critics see plea bargaining as an "under-the-table" process that undermines respect for the criminal justice system.

Although the decision to plead guilty or go to jury trial rests with the defendant, the decision is strongly influenced by the policies of the prosecutor's office. A defendant may plead guilty and accept the certainty of conviction with whatever reduced charges the prosecutor offers, or accept the prosecutor's pledge to recommend a lighter penalty, or both. Or the defendant may go to trial, confronting serious charges with stiffer penalties with the hope of being found innocent. However, the possibility of an innocent verdict in a jury trial is only one in six. This apparently strong record of conviction comes about because prosecutors have already dismissed charges in cases where the evidence is weak or illegally obtained. Thus, most defendants confronting strong cases against them decide to "cop a plea."

It is very fortunate for the nation's court system that most defendants plead guilty. The court system would quickly break down from overload if any substantial proportion of defendants insisted on jury trials.

*Cocaine use spread from upper-middle-class recreational use to wider street use with the introduction of smokable "crack."*

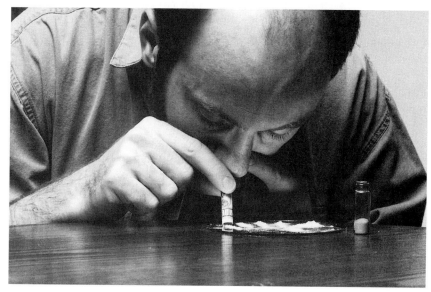

Joel Gordon

# CRIME AND DRUGS

It is difficult to estimate the various forms of drug use. According to the U.S. National Institute on Drug Abuse, there are twelve to fourteen million "problem drinkers," or about 6 percent of the population. There are an estimated forty-seven million cigarette smokers, or about 28 percent of the adult population (significantly less than the 45 percent of the population who smoked cigarettes in the 1940s and 1950s). An estimated twelve million, or about 6 percent of the population, are current users of marijuana, although many more have smoked it at least once.[5] The medical evidence on the health effects of marijuana is mixed; conflicting reports have been issued about whether or not it is more dangerous than alcohol.[6] Referenda votes in California and Arizona in 1996 indicate that voters approve of the use of marijuana for therapeutic purposes, but the U.S. government still outlaws its sale.

It is difficult to estimate drug use, to measure whether it is rising or falling over time, or to assess the effectiveness of antidrug efforts. The U.S. National Institute on Drug Abuse (NIDA) annually surveys households in the United States, asking respondents whether they have used drugs in the past month, the past year, or ever in their lifetime. Past-month, or "current," use is the most widely cited NIDA statistic. Based on this survey evidence, overall drug use has declined over the last decade, although this decline may have ended recently (see Figure 12-3). The NIDA also sponsors a national high school survey. It suggests that student drug use has increased in recent years.

**FIGURE 12-3**

## Declines in Reported Drug Use

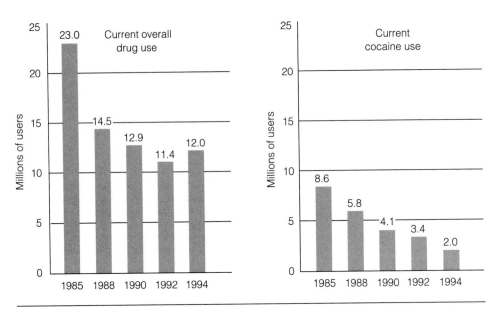

SOURCE: National Institute on Drug Abuse, *National Drug Control Strategy* (Washington, D.C.: U.S. Government Printing Office, February 1996).

## Drug Trafficking

Crime associated with drug trafficking is a serious national problem, whatever the health effects of various drugs. The world of drug trafficking is fraught with violence. Sellers rob and murder buyers and vice versa; neither can seek the protection of police or courts in their dealings with the other. Although some citizens might want simply to allow dealers to wipe each other out, the frequency with which innocent bystanders are killed must be considered.

It is very difficult to estimate the total size of the drug market, but $20 to $25 billion per year is a common figure. This would suggest that the drug business is comparable in size to one of the ten largest U.S. industrial corporations. More important, perhaps, drugs produce huge profit margins: a kilo of cocaine sold in Colombia may cost only $3,600; when sold in the United States, that kilo may retail for $80,000 to $120,000.[7] The price of smuggling a single, easily concealable kilo may run to $15,000. These huge profits allow drug traffickers to corrupt police and government officials as well as private citizens in the United States and other nations.

## FOCUS
## Getting High

Drugs that affect behavior or consciousness or mood are referred to as *psychoactive drugs*. The table below lists the most commonly used and abused drugs and their intended and unintended effects.

*Drug dependence,* or "addiction," is said to occur when the user experiences (1) increased tolerance (user must take more and more to achieve the same effect), (2) withdrawal symptoms (when use is discontinued, the user experiences unpleasant physical or psychological reactions, or (3) compulsive use (the user cannot control use and expends unwonted time and resources in obtaining and using the drug).

*Drug abuse* does not necessarily imply dependence, but means that the user impairs his or her functioning in life (repeated accidents, inability to work or concentrate, marital problems, etc.)

| Drug | Intended Effects | Unintended Effects |
|---|---|---|
| Alcohol<br>Sources: fermentation of grains and fruits | Lightheadedness ("buzz"); relaxation; release of inhibitions. | Slurred speech; poor coordination; anger and aggressiveness or moroseness; physical and psychological dependence; fetal alcohol syndrome in newborns. |
| Opiates<br>codeine, morphine, heroin<br>Source: poppy seeds | Pain relief; thrill ("rush"); experience of intense pleasure; euphoria; absence of anxiety and worry. | Death from overdose; serious physical discomforts with withdrawal (chills, sweating, vomiting, cramps, headaches); deterioration of social and personal life; infections including AIDS associated with sharing drug needles; abnormalities in fetus and newborn infants. |
| Stimulants<br>Amphetamines:<br>"speed," "uppers," "bennies";<br>Cocaine including "crack" (smoked), powdered (inhaled), solution (injected into vein)<br>Source: coca leaf | Increased alertness; reduction in fatigue and boredom, enhanced endurance; increased energy and self-confidence. | Increase in tolerance; anguish and extreme depression following brief euphoria; hallucinations and moving flashes of light; crawling sensation under the skin ("coke bugs"); and abnormalities in fetus and newborn infants. |
| Hallucinogens (psychedelics)<br>LSD ("acid")<br>mescaline<br>PCP ("angel dust")<br>Sources: mescaline from cactus; mushrooms and laboratory processed | Changed perceptions, including dramatic sounds and colors; time perception altered; auditory and visual hallucinations; mystical, semireligious experiences. | Extremely unpleasant reactions ("bad trip"); flashback hallucinations long after use; panic; irrational behavior (e.g., jumping from high places), disorientation; comatose condition. |
| Cannabis<br>marijuana<br>hashish<br>Source: dried marijuana leaves; hashish from squeezed resin | Euphoria and sense of well-being; relaxation; improved tolerance of discomforting medical treatments. | Decreased alertness, coordination, and physical performance; sleepiness and lethargy; short-term memory loss; mild anxiety and irritability upon withdrawal. |

# THE WAR ON DRUGS

Federal antidrug efforts can be divided into three categories: interdiction, enforcement, and education. *Interdiction:* Efforts to seal U.S. borders against the importation of drugs have been frustrated by the sheer volume of smuggling. Each year increasingly larger drug shipments are intercepted by the U.S. Drug Enforcement Administration, the U.S. Customs Service, the Coast Guard, and state and local agencies. Yet each year the volume of drugs entering the country seems to increase. Drug "busts" are considered just another cost of business to the traffickers. It is not likely that the use of U.S. military forces to augment other federal agencies can succeed in sealing our borders. American pressure against Latin American governments to destroy coca crops and assist in interdiction has already resulted in strained relationships. Our neighboring countries wonder why the U.S. government directs its efforts at the suppliers, when the demand for drugs arises within the United States itself. *Enforcement:* The federal Drug Enforcement Administration (DEA), together with the FBI and state and local law enforcement agencies, already devote great effort to combating drugs; an estimated 40 percent of all arrests in the United States are drug-related. Federal and state prisons now hold a larger percentage of the nation's population than ever before. Sentences have lengthened for drug trafficking, and prisons are overcrowded as a direct result of drug-related convictions. Drug testing in government and private employment is increasing, but unless it is random it is not very useful, and some courts have prevented random testing of individuals without their consent. *Education:* Efforts at educating the public about the dangers of drugs have inspired many public and private campaigns, from former First Lady Nancy Reagan's "Just say no" to Jesse Jackson's "Up with hope, down with dope," and police-community-school D.A.R.E. programs. But it is difficult to evaluate the effects of these efforts.

As a nation the United States is both wealthy and free, two conditions that make it a perfect market for illicit drugs. The costs of truly effective enforcement, both in terms of dollar expenditures and, more important, in terms of lost individual liberty, may be more than our society wishes to pay. (See Controversies in Social Science, "Should Drugs Be Legalized?")

# AN ECONOMIC PERSPECTIVE ON CRIME

Crime is not only a major concern of citizens, but also a topic of great interest to social scientists. Each of the social sciences brings a slightly different perspective to crime.

Economists tend to view crime as a product of people's rational calculations of the expected benefits and expected costs of criminal acts. They believe that the reason we have so much crime is that crime *pays*—that is, its benefits outweigh its costs. The economic approach to criminal justice emphasizes *deterrence*—that is, convincing potential lawbreakers that the certainty and severity of punishment will impose costs on them far in excess of any benefit they might derive from criminal acts.

## CONTROVERSIES IN SOCIAL SCIENCE
### Should Drugs Be Legalized?

Public opinion polls show that the vast majority of Americans support strong law enforcement efforts to halt illegal drug use in America. But the high costs of drug law enforcement, prisons overcrowded with drug law violators, the violence associated with drug trafficking, and the threats to civil liberties posed by antidrug wars all combine to inspire some observers to propose the legalization of drugs and government control of their production and sale.

"Prohibition" failed earlier in the century to end alcohol consumption, and the crime, official corruption, and enormous cost of futile efforts to stop drinking eventually forced the nation to end Prohibition. Similarly, it is argued that the legalization of drugs would end organized crime's profit monopoly over the drug trade, raise billions of dollars by legally taxing drugs, end the strain on relations with Latin American nations caused by efforts to eradicate drugs, and save additional billions in enforcement costs that could be used for education and treatment.[a] If drugs were legally obtainable under government supervision, it is argued that many of society's current problems would be alleviated: the crime and violence associated with the drug trade, the corruption of public officials, the spread of diseases associated with drug use, and the many infringements of personal liberty associated with antidrug wars.

But even the suggestion of drug legalization concerns Americans who believe that legalization would greatly expand drug use in the country. Cheap, available drugs would increase the numbers of addicted persons, creating a "society of zombies" that would destroy the social fabric of the nation. Cocaine and heroin are far more habit-forming than alcohol, and legalization would encourage the development of newer and even more potent and addictive synthetic drugs. Whatever the health costs of drug abuse today, it is argued that legalization would produce public health problems of enormous magnitude.[b] Cocaine is very cheap to produce; the current $5 to $10 cost of a "hit" is mostly drug-dealer profit; legalization even with taxation might produce a 50¢ "hit." Whatever the damages to society from drug-related crime and efforts to prohibit drugs, the damages to society from cheap, available drug use might be far greater.

[a]Ethan A. Nadelmann, "The Case for Legalization," *The Public Interest* (Summer 1988): 3–31.
[b]John Kaplan, "Taking Drugs Seriously," *The Public Interest* (Summer 1988): 32–50.

## REQUIREMENTS FOR DETERRENCE

If law enforcement is to be a deterrent to crime, punishment must be *perceived* as: (1) fairly certain, (2) swift enough to establish a link between the crime and its consequences, and (3) severe enough to outweigh the benefits of the crime. These criteria for an effective deterrent policy are ranked in the order of their probable importance. It is most important that punishment for crime is certain in the minds of potential criminals. The severity of the punishment is probably less important than its certainty or swiftness.

**deterring crime in theory** punishment must be certain, swift, and severe enough to outweigh benefits

## FAILURE OF DETERRENCE

But the current system of criminal justice is certainly no serious deterrent to crime. The best available estimates of the ratio between crime and punishment suggest that the likelihood of an individual's being jailed for a serious crime is less than one in a hundred (see Figure 12-4). Many crimes are not even reported by the victim. Police are successful in clearing fewer than one in five reported crimes by arresting the offender. The judicial system convicts fewer than half of the persons arrested and charged; others are not prosecuted, are handled as juveniles, are found not guilty, or are permitted to plead guilty to a lesser charge and released. Only about one-fourth of convicted felons are given prison sentences.

Thus, economists would argue that crime in the United States has risen in part because people realize that they have little chance of being caught or punished. Crime may be more prevalent among young rootless males because the prospect of jail is perceived to be less costly for them than for older men with jobs and families to lose.

But a great deal of crime may be "irrational"—that is, the criminal does not stop to weigh the benefits against potential costs before committing the act. Violent criminal behavior, perhaps more than property crime, often shows little sign of rational calculation.

### FIGURE 12-4

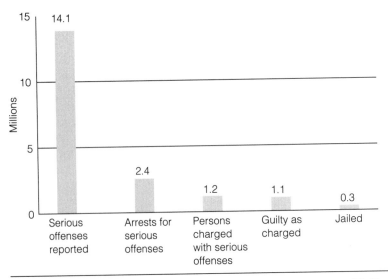

LAW ENFORCEMENT IN RELATION TO REPORTED CRIME

*(Actual crime is estimated to be two and a half times the reported offenses.)*

SOURCE: U.S. Bureau of the Census, *Statistical Abstract of the United States 1996* (Washington, D.C.: U.S. Government Printing Office, 1996).

# A Psychological Perspective on Crime— the Antisocial Personality

Some crimes are committed by individuals suffering various personality disorders. These people are not "insane" (see Case Study, "The Insanity Defense"), but they exhibit long-standing patterns of maladaptive behavior—inappropriate ways of coping with stress, solving problems, and relating to others. Personality disorders may have their origin in either genetic or environmental factors.

## The Antisocial Personality

Psychologists have identified an antisocial personality disorder that is often associated with criminal behavior. (Antisocial personalities are sometimes referred to as "psychopaths" or "sociopaths"; a "pathology" is a disease leading to death.) Individuals with antisocial personalities have little sense of responsibility for their action, little concern for others, and little or no sense of morality. It can be said that they lack a conscience. They behave impulsively, they seek immediate gratification, and they cannot tolerate frustration.

**antisocial personality**
long-standing patterns of maladaptive behavior; lack of concern for others and no sense of guilt

The behavioral characteristics used to identify the antisocial personality are (1) a lack of empathy and concern for others, and (2) a lack of shame or guilt or remorse for their own actions however harmful they may be.

Antisocial personalities sometimes develop in children who first show signs of attention deficit disorder (ADD). ADD is diagnosed when children have significant problems in maintaining attention and consistently display impulsive uncontrolled behavior. Their disruptive behavior may lead to rejection by teachers, playmates, and even parents, thus leading to even more disruptive and aggressive behavior and eventually antisocial personality disorder.

**attention deficit disorder (ADD)**
difficulty maintaining attention; impulsive uncontrolled behavior

## Genetic Explanations

A genetic cause of antisocial personality disorder is revealed in studies of criminal behavior across generations and among identical twins. For example, the criminal records of adopted sons have been found to be more similar to the record of their biological fathers than their adopted fathers. The criminal records of identical twins are much closer to each other than those of fraternal twins.

## Environmental Influences

Not all children with genetic predisposition to antisocial personality disorder or to criminal behavior develop these characteristics. Parental conduct is a better predictor of the emergence of antisocial personality than genetics. Disruptive children who are unsupervised or poorly supervised are much more likely to develop a pattern of delinquent behavior than children

How should society deal with a mentally ill person who commits a crime? Should the mentally ill be held responsible for their actions in the same fashion as everyone else? Or should criminal law recognize that the mentally ill may not be able to control their conduct?

In an historic nineteenth-century case, a mentally ill Scotsman, M'Naghten, attempted to assassinate the English Prime Minister Robert Peel, but instead shot his secretary. The trial judge was convinced by M'Naghten's senseless rambling and para-

noid delusions that the defendant was insane and he was sent to a mental hospital. But Queen Victoria was unsatisfied with the verdict; she asked the House of Lords to review the decision. The result was the *M'Naghten Rule*—that a defendant may be found not guilty by reason of insanity if he did not know at the time what he was doing or did not know that what he was doing was wrong.

Later American courts expanded on the M'Naghten Rule, holding that people are not responsible for a crime if, as a result of a mental disease or defect, they lack the capacity to appreciate the wrongfulness of their conduct or the ability to conform their conduct to the law. The word *appreciate* is considered a looser term than

"know" in the original M'Naghten Rule, implying that the defendant must have some understanding of the moral and legal consequences of his or her behavior.

Perhaps the most publicized successful insanity defense in American history was that of John Hinckley, Jr. Accused in a Washington, D.C., court of attempting to assassinate President Ronald Reagan in 1981, Hinckley was found not guilty by virtue of insanity. Many Americans were outraged by the verdict and the insanity defense came under attack in Congress. Congress responded by enacting the Insanity Defense Reform Act of 1984, designed to make it more difficult to successfully employ the insanity defense.

of parents who are involved in their everyday life. Parents who closely monitor ADD and intervene consistently to overcome it can help children avoid the development of antisocial and criminal behaviors.

Genetic and environmental factors often combine to cause antisocial personality disorder. Maternal drug use, maternal exposure to toxic agents, and low birth weight are associated with childhood problems of irritability, impulsiveness, inattention, and slow learning. These children are difficult to care for and they are at risk for abuse and neglect. Both genetic and adverse home factors tend to contribute to aggressive behaviors in children, especially hitting.

## SOCIAL AND CULTURAL PERSPECTIVES ON CRIME

**deviance**
the failure to conform to social norms

Sociologists view crime as a form of deviance—the failure to conform to social norms. *Deviance* may range from the trivial (vulgar language) to the acute (serial murders). Not all deviance involves lawbreaking. While norms

The act stipulates that the defendant's mental disease or defect must be "severe" in order to avoid guilt. The intent is to exclude nonpsychotic disorders such as antisocial personality. The act also shifted the burden of proof of insanity to the defendant; the prosecution need not prove that the person was sane beyond a reasonable doubt. And the defendant must prove insanity with "clear and convincing evidence."

Some states have adopted the use of the verdict "guilty but mentally ill." This verdict may be rendered when the jury decides that a mental disorder significantly impacted the judgment of the defendant at the time of the crime or his or her capacity to recognize reality. The verdict allows a judge to impose a sentence that may be served either in a mental hospital or in prison or both. The intent is to keep a mentally ill dangerous person off the streets.

Mental illness also intrudes into the criminal justice process early in the legal process when a judge declares that a defendant is not mentally competent to stand trial. After reviewing the psychological evidence, a judge may determine that a defendant is *not competent to stand trial* if he or she is unable to understand the charges and unable to cooperate with a lawyer in preparing his or her defense. The judge's decision is based on the constitutional right to a fair trial; it is separate from the question of whether the defendant was insane *at the time the crime was committed*. The judge may drop criminal charges and commit the person to a psychiatric facility. Psychiatrists can later release the person after determining that he or she is no longer mentally incompetent.

Defendants have a better chance of convincing a judge that they are incompetent to stand trial than they have to convince a jury that they are not guilty by reason of insanity. Most juries hold individuals responsible for their criminal acts. Fewer than one percent of defendants charged with serious crimes are found not guilty by reason of insanity. Most defense attorneys consider the insanity defense a last resort.

may differ from one society to another, all societies have norms and all societies impose some forms of punishment on those who violate norms. Not all sociologists who study deviance focus on crime (*criminology*), but those who do are generally referred to as criminologists.

A sociological perspective on crime emphasizes its presumed "root causes"—poverty, unemployment, lack of opportunity, inequality, and discrimination. It shows how crime rates vary with gender, race, age, mobility, and other social characteristics of populations.

**criminology**
the scientific study of crime, criminals, and punishment

## CRIME AND GENDER

Crime rates for women are much lower than those for men. Men account for about 86 percent of violent crime and 73 percent of property crime. Sociologists offer a variety of explanations for this differential: males are socialized to be active, assertive, and dominant, traits conducive to criminal behavior, while females are socialized to be more gentle and nurturing. Parents often impose a "double standard" of morality, monitoring their daughters' behavior more closely than their sons', providing more opportunities for males to commit crimes. Some research indicates that girls feel more strongly attached to families than boys and are more likely to value their parents' norms. If men's crime rates were as low as women's, crime in the United States would not be a major social problem.

## CRIME AND RACE

Crime disproportionately victimizes poor and black Americans. A black male is almost eight times more likely to be murdered than a white male. And the poor and black are disproportionately represented among persons arrested and sentenced for crime. Blacks comprise 12.6 percent of the nation's population, yet comprise 34.6 percent of all arrests for serious crimes, 46.9 percent of state prison inmates, and 41.6 percent of prisoners under sentence of death.

There are a variety of sociological explanations of racial differences on crime statistics, all of them controversial. (Indeed, some social scientists and some texts avoid mentioning these statistics or discussing possible explanations for them.) The higher rate of father-absent households among African-American families may result in less supervision and discipline of young males and fewer positive role models. Economic deprivation and conditions in inner-city neighborhoods where African Americans are concentrated are frequently cited as contributing to higher rates of crime.

## AGE AND CRIME

Crime is closely related to age. Crime is primarily a young man's activity. Men between the ages of sixteen and thirty-four commit most of the crimes in the nation. Indeed, overall arrests by age category show that about 9 percent involve persons under sixteen, 36 percent involve persons sixteen to twenty-five, and 30 percent involve persons twenty-six to thirty-four. In contrast, only 16 percent of arrests involve persons thirty-five to forty-four, only 7 percent involve persons forty-five to sixty-four, and only 1 percent involve persons over sixty-five.

Sociologists cite a variety of factors influencing the "crime-prone" age group: peer influences and the urge to assert independence are greatest among adolescents. Young men who have not yet acquired full-time jobs or gotten married or fathered children are less likely to have acquired a stake in conformity to social norms. Maturity usually brings greater control over one's compulsions. Risk-taking behavior becomes less attractive. Sociologists note that all other things being equal, an increase or decrease in the proportion of the population in the most crime-prone age category of sixteen to twenty-five should result in increases and decreases in crime.

## SUBCULTURAL EXPLANATION

Crime is much more prevalent in urban areas. One explanation for the concentration of crime in the inner city centers on the subculture of the streets.[8] A disproportionate number of female-headed households among poor black families inspires young males to seek masculine identities through peer-group associations in gangs. The gangs develop a subculture of "toughness," exaggerated masculinity, demands for respect, and danger and thrill-seeking. These values lead young males to respond violently to remarks, gestures, and actions that most others would ignore. A reputation for violence brings respect, and symbols of violence, including guns, are marks of distinction. Arrest and imprisonment is sometimes regarded as a "coming of age." At the same time, these young males aspire to the wealth and material well-being of the larger culture. But economic opportunities are limited; drugs are a thriving business in the streets and drug dealers provide role models. The gap between aspirations and opportunities creates the frustration that leads to crime.

But the problem with the criminal subculture thesis is that *most young males in the inner city do not turn to violence or crime.* While crime rates can be correlated with poverty, unemployment, age, and race, these conditions quite obviously do not cause crime, inasmuch as the majority of poor, unemployed, young, and black do *not* have criminal records. The overwhelming majority of children raised in single-parent households turn out to be law-abiding citizens. Sociological and cultural perspectives on crime, while helpful in identifying the factors associated with high crime rates and "deviant" behavior, fail to provide a policy remedy.[9]

# VIOLENCE IN AMERICAN HISTORY

Violence is not uncommon in American society. The nation itself was founded in armed revolution, and violence has been a *source of power* and a *stimulus to social change* ever since. Violence has been associated with most of the important movements in American history: the birth of the nation (revolutionary violence), the freeing of the slaves and the preservation of the union (Civil War violence), the westward expansion of the nation (Indian Wars), the establishment of law and order in frontier society (vigilante violence), the organization of the labor movement (labor-management violence), the civil rights movement (racial violence), and attempts to deal with the problems of cities (urban violence). History reveals that the patriot, the humanitarian, the pioneer, the lawman, the laborer, the African American, and the urban dweller have all used violence as a source of power. Despite pious pronouncements against it, Americans have frequently employed violence even in their most idealistic endeavors.

**violence as a source of power and change**

**major instances of violence in American history**
guerrilla warfare in the Revolution
Shays's Rebellion
violence of the Civil War era
the Indian Wars
vigilante violence
labor-management violence
racial violence
political violence—assassinations

## THE REVOLUTIONARY WAR

Perhaps the most famous act of organized mob violence occurred in 1773 when a group of "agitators" in Boston, Massachusetts, illegally destroyed 342 chests of tea. The early Revolutionary War fighting in 1774 and 1775, including the battles of Lexington and Concord, was really a series of small guerrilla skirmishes designed more to intimidate Tories than to achieve national independence. The old American custom of tarring and feathering was a product of the early patriotic campaign to root out Tories. Aside from the regular clash of Continental and British armies, a great deal of violence and guerrilla strife occurred during the Revolution. Savage guerrilla forays along the eastern coast resulted in the killing of thousands of Tory families and the destruction of their property. The success of this violence enshrined it in our traditions.

## SHAYS'S REBELLION

After the Revolutionary War many armed farmers and debtors resorted to violence to assert their economic interests. If taxes owed to the British government and debts owed to British merchants could be denied, why not the taxes owed to state governments and the debts owed to American merchants? In several states debtors had already engaged in open rebellion against tax collectors and sheriffs. The most serious rebellion broke out in the summer of 1786 in Massachusetts, when a band of insurgents, composed of farmers and laborers, captured courthouses in several western districts of that state and momentarily held the city of Springfield. Led by Daniel Shays, a veteran of Bunker Hill, the insurgent army posed a direct threat to the governing elite of the new nation. Shays's Rebellion, as it was called, was put down by a small mercenary army paid for by well-to-do citizens who feared that a wholesale attack on property rights was imminent. The growing domestic violence in the states contributed to the momentum leading to the Constitutional Convention of 1787, where propertied men established a new central government with the power to "ensure domestic tranquility," guarantee "the republican form of government," and protect "against domestic violence." Thus, the Constitution itself reflects a concern of the nation's Founders about domestic violence.

## THE CIVIL WAR

The Civil War was the bloodiest war the United States ever fought. Total casualties of the northern and southern armies equaled American casualties in World War II; but when the Civil War occurred, the nation was only one-third as large as it was during the latter conflict. There were few families that did not suffer the loss of a loved one during the Civil War. In addition to military casualties, the toll in lives and property among civilians was enormous. A great deal of domestic violence also occurred both before and after the war. Beginning in 1856, proslavery and antislavery forces fought in "bleeding Kansas." In 1859 John Brown led a raid at Harper's Ferry, meant to start the freeing of the slaves in Virginia. Brown's capture, trial for treason, and execution made him a hero to many abolitionists, though Southerners believed that he had tried to incite slave uprisings. The guerrilla war that took place in the West during the Civil War has seldom been equaled for savagery; the fearsome Kansas Jayhawkers traded brutalities with Confederate guerrillas headed by William Quantrell. Later, western bandits, including Frank and Jesse James and the Younger brothers, who had fought as Confederate guerrillas, continued their forays against banks and railroads and enjoyed considerable popular prestige and support. Moreover, after the war, racial strife and Ku Klux Klan activity became routine in the old Confederate states. The Ku Klux Klan was first used to intimidate the Republicans of the Reconstruction era by violence and threats, and later to force blacks to accept the renewed rule of whites.

## THE INDIAN WARS

Unquestionably the longest and most brutal violence in American history was that between whites and Native Americans. It began in 1607 and continued with only temporary truces for nearly three hundred years, until the final battle at Wounded Knee, South Dakota, in 1890. The norms of Indian warfare were generally more barbaric than those in other types of warfare, if such a thing is possible. Women and children on both sides were deliberately and purposefully killed. Torture was accepted as a customary part of making war. Scalping was a frequent practice on both sides.

## VIGILANTES

Vigilante violence (taking the law into one's own hands) arose as a response to a typically American problem: the absence of effective law and order in the frontier region. Practically every state and territory west of the Appalachians had at one time or another a well-organized vigilante movement. The first vigilante movement appeared in 1767–1769 in South Carolina, where the vigilantes were known as *regulators*—a term later used by San Francisco vigilantes in the 1850s. Vigilantes were frequently backed by prominent men; many later became senators, representatives, governors, judges, businessmen, and even clergy. Like Indian-fighters, vigilantes became great popular heroes. Antitheft and antirustling associations flourished in the West until World War I. Vigilantes often undertook to establish law and order and to regulate the morals of the citizens—punishing drunks, vagrants, ne'er-do-wells, and occasional strangers.

## LABOR VIOLENCE

Violence was also a constant companion of the early labor movement in the United States. Both management and strikers resorted to violence in the struggles accompanying the Industrial Revolution. In 1887, in the bitter railroad strike in Pittsburgh, Pennsylvania, an estimated sixteen soldiers and fifty strikers were killed, and locomotives, freight cars, and other property were destroyed. The famous Homestead strike of 1892 turned Homestead, Pennsylvania, into an open battlefield. The Pullman strike of 1893 in Chicago resulted in twelve deaths and the destruction of a great deal of railroad property. In 1914, Ludlow, Colorado, was the scene of the famous Ludlow Massacre, in which company guards burned a miner tent city and killed nearly a hundred persons, including women and children. The Molly Maguires were a secret organization of Irish miners who fought their employers with assassination and mayhem. The last great spasm of violence in the history of American labor came in the 1930s with the strikes and plant takeovers ("sit-down strikes") that accompanied the successful drive to unionize the automobile, steel, and other mass-production industries.

## Racial Violence

The long history of racial violence in the United States continues to plague the nation. Slavery itself was accompanied by untold violence. It is estimated that one-third to one-half of those captured in African slave raids never survived the ordeal of forced marches to the sea, with thirst, brutalities, and near starvation the rule; the terrible two-month voyage in filthy holds packed with squirming and suffocating humanity; and the brutal "seasoning" whereby African blacks were turned into slaves. Nat Turner's slave insurrection in 1831 resulted in the deaths of fifty-seven white persons and the execution of Turner and his followers. Following the end of slavery the white supremacy movement employed violence to reestablish the position of whites in the southern social system. Racial violence directed against blacks—whippings, torture, and lynching—was fairly common from the 1870s to the 1930s. During World War II serious racial violence erupted in Detroit. Black and white mobs battled each other in June 1943, causing thirty-five deaths and hundreds of injuries, more than a thousand arrests, and finally the dispatching of federal troops to restore order.

## Assassinations

Political assassinations have not been uncommon. Four presidents (Lincoln, Garfield, McKinley, and Kennedy) have fallen to assassins' bullets, and others were the intended objects of assassination. Only Lincoln was the target of a proven assassination conspiracy; the other presidential victims were the prey of presumably freelance assassins in varying states of mental instability. In the 1930s Senator Huey P. Long of Louisiana was murdered, and a bullet narrowly missed President Franklin Delano Roosevelt and killed Mayor Anton Cermak of Chicago, who was standing near the president. The wave of political assassinations and assassination attempts in more recent years, which cut down John F. Kennedy, Robert

F. Kennedy, and Martin Luther King, Jr.; crippled George C. Wallace; and threatened the life of Ronald Reagan, may represent a "contagion phenomenon," unstable individuals being motivated to violence by highly publicized and dramatic acts of violence. But an even grimmer possibility is that political assassination may become a persistent feature of American society.

# NOTES

1. Thomas Hobbes, *Leviathan,* ed. Michael Oakeshott (New York: Crowell-Collier, 1962).
2. U.S. Department of Justice, *Criminal Victimization in the United States* (Washington, D.C.: Bureau of Justice Statistics, published annually).
3. Chief Justice Warren E. Burger, address on the State of the Federal Judiciary to the American Bar Association, August 10, 1970.
4. U.S. Department of Justice, Bureau of Labor Statistics, *The Prevalence of Guilty Pleas* (December 1984).
5. National Institute on Drug Abuse, *National Survey on Drug Abuse 1986 and 1990* (Washington, D.C.: U.S. Government Printing Office).
6. For a summary of this evidence and references to the relevant health literature, see Richard C. Schroeder, *The Politics of Drugs,* 2nd ed. (Washington, D.C.: Congressional Quarterly, 1980).
7. Ethan A. Nadelmann, "U.S. Drug Policy," *Foreign Policy* 70 (Spring 1988): 83–108.
8. Erich Goode, *Deviant Behavior,* 3rd ed. (Englewood Cliffs, N.J.: Prentice-Hall, 1990).
9. See James Q. Wilson, *Thinking About Crime,* rev. ed. (New York: Basic Books, 1983).

# ABOUT THIS CHAPTER

More than 2,000 years ago Aristotle wrote of the problem of crime that "the generality of men are naturally apt to be swayed by fear rather than by reverence, and to refrain from evil rather because of the punishment that it brings, than because of its own foulness." Power must be exercised by society for the very basic purposes of maintaining order and protecting the citizenry. A free democratic society must struggle with maintaining a balance between its exercise of police power and its safeguarding of individual freedom. In this chapter we have examined America's struggles with this problem. We have explored economic, psychological, and sociocultural perspectives on crime. And we have examined the violence that has been a part of most of the important social movements in American history.

Now that you have read Chapter 12, you should be able to

- describe the current status of crime in the United States as evidenced by crime and victimization rates
- describe the basic constitutional protections afforded to persons accused of crime
- describe the various potentially harmful substances—alcohol, tobacco, marijuana, cocaine, and heroin—and current antidrug policies
- describe the theory of deterrence, the requirements for deterrence, and why deterrence does not appear to be working well
- discuss the frustration-aggression theory of violence and compare it with the aggressive-instinct theory
- discuss the subculture theory of street crime
- discuss the constitutional issues arising from capital punishment
- discuss the history of violence in the United States

# DISCUSSION QUESTIONS

1. How did Thomas Hobbes justify the creation of a "Leviathan"? What dilemma is faced by a free society in protecting its citizens?
2. Discuss crime rates. How are they used, how are they determined, and what factors contribute to their inaccuracy? What is their current trend?
3. Suppose you have just been arrested by the police. Describe how the following constitutional rights of defendants would be of use to you: guarantee of the writ of habeas corpus; prohibition of bills of attainder and of ex post facto laws; prohibition of "unreasonable" searches and seizures; freedom from self-incrimination; the right to counsel; guarantee of a fair jury trial; protection against double jeopardy; protection against excessive bail.

4. Choose two of the following cases that were decided by the Warren Court and discuss how each of them strengthened the rights of accused persons in criminal cases: *Mapp* v. *Ohio* (1961); *Gideon* v. *Wainwright* (1963); *Escobedo* v. *Illinois* (1964); *Miranda* v. *Arizona* (1966).

5. What are some of the difficulties that the police may encounter in their law enforcement function? What is the "exclusionary rule"?

6. Describe the major drug threats confronting the United States today. What is the legal status of various potentially harmful substances: alcohol, tobacco, marijuana, cocaine, and heroin?

7. What are the requirements for effective deterrence of crime?

8. Contrast the frustration-aggression theory of violence and the aggressive-instinct theory.

9. Describe the subculture theory of street crime and the problem with the theory.

10. Discuss the arguments for and against capital punishment. Describe the 1972 Supreme Court decision regarding the constitutionality of capital punishment and the changes in state laws that followed it. Discuss the reasoning of the justices in the 1976 Court decision on capital punishment.

11. Discuss the history of violence in the United States. Using at least three specific eras or social movements as examples, describe the type of violence that was used and the kind of social change that was its goal.

Chapter 13

# Power
# and Community

## WHERE DO AMERICANS LIVE?

Three out of four Americans live in population clusters called *metropolitan areas*. Most of the nation's population increase is occurring in the suburbs of these areas. Approximately 44 percent of all Americans live in these suburbs, 32 percent live in central cities, and 24 percent live outside metropolitan areas. (See the Cross-National Perspective, "Worldwide Urbanization.")

What is a metropolitan area? Briefly, it consists of a central city of fifty thousand or more persons and the surrounding suburbs, which are socially and economically tied to the city (see Figure 13-1). The U.S. Census Bureau refers to metropolitan areas as *Metropolitan Statistical Areas (MSAs)* or, in the case of large metropolitan complexes with connecting metropolitan areas, *Consolidated Metropolitan Statistical Areas (CMSAs)*. The nation's largest metropolitan areas are listed in Table 13-1.

**MSA**
metropolitan statistical area, a city of 50,000 or more, plus surrounding urban population

**CMSA**
metropolitan complex of connecting MSAs

**FIGURE 13-1**

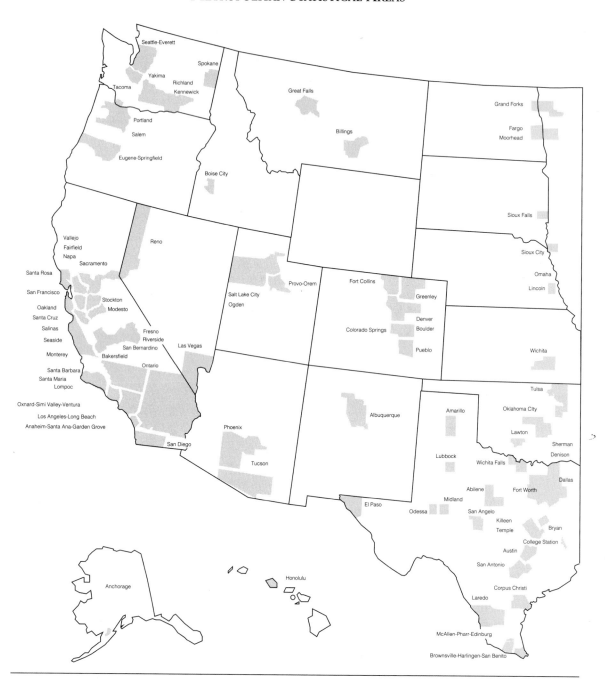

METROPOLITAN STATISTICAL AREAS

Source: U.S. Bureau of the Census.

## CROSS-NATIONAL PERSPECTIVE
### Worldwide Urbanization

Urbanization is occurring worldwide. Cities throughout the world offer greater opportunities than rural areas. It is estimated that the world's urban areas are growing at twice the rate of the world's population generally. Millions of people migrate from the countryside in search of economic opportunity, health care, education, and higher standards of living in the world's largest cities. However poor and unpleasant life may be in many Third World cities, these cities hold the promise of a better life for rural migrants. Mexico City has grown into perhaps the world's largest city. Yet it is estimated that 10 percent of its residents have no running water and that 15 percent lack sewage facilities. Mountains of trash and garbage have become wretched shantytowns where the city's poor pick through waste to survive and build shacks from discarded materials. The problems of Third World cities make those of the largest U.S. cities seem minor by comparison.

Today most of the largest cities in the world are found in less developed societies (see table). Modernization brings urbanization, and as Third World nations moved from agricultural to industrial economies, their cities grew exponentially. Only two of the world's largest cities are in the United States—New York and Los Angeles. In the past fifteen years, Third World cities replaced many Western cities in the list of the world's largest cities.

### THE WORLD'S LARGEST CITIES
#### (IN MILLIONS OF PEOPLE)

| 1985 | | 2000 | |
|---|---|---|---|
| Tokyo | 19.0 | Mexico City | 24.4 |
| Mexico City | 16.7 | São Paulo, Brazil | 23.6 |
| New York | 15.6 | Tokyo | 21.3 |
| São Paulo, Brazil | 15.5 | New York | 16.1 |
| Shanghai | 12.1 | Calcutta | 15.9 |
| Buenos Aires | 10.8 | Greater Bombay, India | 15.4 |
| London | 10.5 | Shanghai | 14.7 |
| Calcutta | 10.3 | Teheran | 13.7 |
| Rio de Janeiro | 10.1 | Jakarta, Indonesia | 13.2 |
| Seoul, S. Korea | 10.1 | Buenos Aires | 13.1 |
| Los Angeles | 10.0 | Rio de Janeiro | 13.0 |
| Osaka, Japan | 9.6 | Seoul, S. Korea | 13.0 |
| Greater Bombay, India | 9.5 | Delhi, India | 12.8 |
| Beijing | 9.3 | Lagos, Nigeria | 12.5 |
| Moscow | 8.9 | Cairo | 11.8 |
| Paris | 8.8 | Karachi, Pakistan | 11.6 |
| Tianjin, China | 8.0 | Beijing | 11.5 |
| Cairo | 7.9 | Manila | 11.5 |
| Jakarta, Indonesia | 7.8 | Dacca, Bangladesh | 11.3 |
| Milan | 7.5 | Osaka, Japan | 11.2 |
| Teheran | 7.2 | Los Angeles | 10.9 |
| Manila | 7.1 | London | 10.8 |
| Delhi, India | 7.0 | Bangkok | 10.3 |
| Chicago | 6.8 | Moscow | 10.1 |
| Karachi, Pakistan | 6.2 | Paris | 8.8 |

SOURCE: U.S. Bureau of the Census, *Statistical Abstract of the United States 1990* (Washington, D.C.: U.S. Government Printing Office, 1990), pp. 836–837.

**TABLE 13-1**

## METRO-AMERICA: METROPOLITAN AREAS WITH ONE MILLION OR MORE RESIDENTS

| | | | | | |
|---|---|---|---|---|---|
| New York | 19.6 | St. Louis | 2.5 | Indianapolis | 1.4 |
| Los Angeles | 14.5 | Minneapolis | 2.5 | New Orleans | 1.3 |
| Chicago | 8.2 | San Diego | 2.5 | San Antonio | 1.3 |
| Washington/Baltimore | 6.7 | Pittsburgh | 2.4 | Orlando | 1.2 |
| San Francisco | 6.3 | Phoenix | 2.3 | Buffalo (NY) | 1.2 |
| Philadelphia | 5.9 | Tampa | 2.1 | Providence (RI) | 1.2 |
| Boston | 5.5 | Denver | 2.0 | Charlotte (NC) | 1.2 |
| Detroit | 5.2 | Cincinnati | 1.8 | Hartford (CT) | 1.2 |
| Dallas/Ft. Worth | 4.0 | Milwaukee | 1.8 | Salt Lake City | 1.1 |
| Houston | 3.7 | Portland (OR) | 1.8 | Rochester | 1.1 |
| Miami/Ft. Lauderdale | 3.2 | Kansas City | 1.6 | Greensboro | 1.0 |
| Seattle/Tacoma | 2.9 | Sacramento | 1.5 | Nashville | 1.0 |
| Atlanta | 2.9 | Norfolk (VA) | 1.4 | | |
| Cleveland | 2.8 | Columbus (OH) | 1.4 | | |

SOURCE: U.S. Bureau of the Census, 1995.

## CENTRAL-CITY VERSUS SUBURBAN GROWTH

Very few large *central cities* are growing. Metropolitan areas are growing because their *suburbs* are growing. In the nineteenth century, industrial workers had to live within walking distance of their places of employment. Hence, the nineteenth-century American city crowded large masses of people into relatively small central areas, often in tenement houses and other high-density neighborhoods. But new modes of transportation—the streetcar, the private automobile, and, finally, the expressway—eliminated the necessity for workers to live close to their jobs. Now an individual can work in a central business district office or industrial plant and spend his or her evening in a residential suburb miles away. The same technology that led to the suburbanization of residences has also influenced commercial and industrial location. Originally industry was tied to waterways or railroads for access to supplies and markets. This dependence was reduced by the development of motor truck transportation, the highway system, and the greater mobility of the labor force. Today many industries locate in the suburbs, particularly light industries, which do not require extremely heavy bulk shipment that can be handled only by rail or water. When industry and people moved to the suburbs, commerce followed. Giant suburban shopping centers sprang up to compete with downtown stores. Thus, metropolitan areas became decentralized as people, business, and industry spread over the suburban landscape.

*Urban life concentrates people with many different economic and occupational characteristics in a few square miles.*

Dion Ogust/The Image Works

# THE SOCIOLOGY OF URBAN LIFE

**sociological theory of urbanism**

urbanism distinguished by numbers, density, and heterogeneity

What is the impact of urbanism on the way people interact? To deal with this question, sociologists first had to formulate a *sociological definition of urbanism*, one that would identify those characteristics most affecting social life. Sociologist Louis Wirth provided the classic definition of urbanism over fifty years ago: "For sociological purposes a city may be defined as a relatively large, dense, and permanent settlement of socially heterogeneous individuals."[1] Thus, according to Wirth, the distinguishing characteristics of urban life were *numbers, density,* and *heterogeneity*—large numbers of people, living closely together, who are different from one another.

## NUMBERS AND HETEROGENEITY

Large numbers of people involve a great range of individual variation. The modern economic system of the metropolis is based on a highly specialized and complex division of labor. We are told that in early farm communities a dozen occupations exhausted the job opportunities available to people. In a simple agricultural society nearly everyone was a farmer or was closely connected to or dependent on farming. But in the modern metropolis there are tens of thousands of different kinds of jobs. An industrial economy means highly specialized jobs; hence the *heterogeneity* of urban populations. Different jobs result in different levels of income, dress, and styles of living. People's jobs shape the way they look at the world and their evaluations of social and political events. To acquire a job, one attains a certain level and type of education that also distinguishes one from those in other jobs with other educational requirements. Differences in educational level in turn produce a wide variety of differences in opinions, attitudes, and styles of living. Urban life concentrates people with all these different economic and occupational characteristics in a very few square miles.

**heterogeneity**
diversity in occupation, income, education

ethnic and racial diversity

## ETHNIC AND RACIAL DIVERSITY

Ethnic and racial diversities are also present. At the beginning of this century, opportunities for human betterment in the cities attracted immigrants from Ireland, Germany, Italy, Poland, and Russia; later the city attracted African Americans, Hispanics, and rural families. Newcomers bring with them different needs, attitudes, and ways of life. The "melting pot" tends to reduce some of the diversity over time, but the pot does not melt people immediately, and there always seem to be new arrivals.

## IMPERSONAL RELATIONSHIPS

Increasing the numbers of people in a community limits the possibility that each member of the community will know everyone else personally. Multiplying the number of persons with whom an individual comes into contact makes it impossible for that individual to know everyone very well. The result is a *segmentalization of human relationships*, in which an individual comes to know *many* people but only in highly *segmental, partial* roles. According to Wirth:

**segmental relationships**
knowing many people, but only in their partial roles

> The contacts of the city may indeed be face-to-face, but they are nevertheless impersonal, superficial, transitory, and segmental. The reserve, the indifference, and the blasé outlook that urbanites manifest in their relationships may thus be regarded as devices for immunizing themselves against the personal claims and expectations of others.[2]

Moreover, urban dwellers frequently interact with others by utilizing them as means to an end, thus giving a *utilitarian* quality to interpersonal relations.

**utilitarian relationships**
interaction with others as a means to an end

## ANOMIE

Large numbers mean a certain degree of freedom for the individual from the control of family groups, neighbors, churches, and other community groups. But urbanism also contributes to a sense of *anomie*—a sense of social isolation

**anomie**
a sense of social isolation and loss of personal recognition and self-worth

and a loss of the personal recognition, self-worth, and feeling of participation that come with living in a small integrated society. The social contacts of urban dwellers are more anonymous than those of rural dwellers; they interact with persons who have little if any knowledge of their life histories.

## SECONDARY GROUP MEMBERSHIPS

**primary groups**
family and neighborhood groups known personally

**secondary groups**
interest or voluntary groups

Rural life emphasized *primary group ties*—interactions within the extended family. Many sociologists believe that urban life emphasizes *secondary group ties*—interactions among members of age and interest groups rather than among families and neighbors. Urban life is said to center around voluntary associations and secondary group memberships—crowds, recreational groups, civic clubs, business groups, and professional and work groups. Sociologists believe that urban dwellers have a greater number of interpersonal contacts than rural dwellers and that urban dwellers are more likely to interact with people as occupants of specific social roles. In contrast, rural dwellers are more likely to interact with individuals as full personalities.

## SOCIAL CONTROL MECHANISMS

**social control**
urban society based more on formal institutions than on social groups

Urban society also presents problems of social control. The anomie of urban life is believed to weaken social mores and social group controls. External controls through a series of formal institutions, such as laws, and organizations, such as the courts and the police, become more essential. Thus, *social control* in the cities depends in large degree on *formal mechanisms*. But laws generally express the minimum behavioral standard, and urban life involves a much wider range of behavior than rural life. Moreover, laws do not always succeed in establishing minimum standards of behavior; crime rates increase with increases in urbanism.

## MOBILITY

**physical mobility**
movement from one location to another

**social mobility**
movement from one social status to another

**both kinds of mobility greater in urban than in rural societies**

Another characteristic of urban life is *mobility*, or ease of movement. Urban mobility is both *physical* (from one geographic area to another) and *social* (from one position of social status to another). Rural communities are more stable than urban communities in both respects. Traditionally rural dwellers were more likely to stay near the place of their birth. In contrast, urbanites frequently move from city to city, or from one section of a city to another. Social mobility is also greater in the city, because of the wider range of economic opportunities there. Moreover, urban dwellers are judged far less by their family backgrounds (which are unknown) than by their own appearances, occupational accomplishments, incomes, and lifestyles. Although mobility creates opportunities for individuals, it weakens the sense of community. City dwellers do not think of their city as a community to which they belong but rather as a place they happen to live—a geographical entity commanding little personal allegiance. Mobility also creates psychological stress (see the Focus, "Urban Stress").

## FOCUS
## Urban Stress

Although no statistics directly measure the psychological health of a city, there are important measures of psycho-social pathology, such as rates of alcoholism, suicide, divorce, and crime. These measures reflect both the causes and effects of psychological stress. By comparing U.S. metropolitan areas on the basis of these measures, it is possible to derive overall rankings that reflect the areas' psychological well-being.[a] The ten highest- and ten lowest-stress metropolitan areas out of the 286 areas ranked are shown in the table.

It is interesting that higher stress ratings are *not* associated with unemployment or poverty levels of cities. On the contrary, higher stress levels were found in cities with milder climates and healthier economic conditions. Psychological well-being is not necessarily related to economic well-being.

However, cities with a large proportion of new residents (migrants from other areas) appear to have higher rates of divorce, suicide, alcoholism, and crime. Thus, southern and western cities with higher rates of new arrivals display higher rates of these pathologies.

Moving to a new area may attract people who are having trouble in life and who think a fresh start will help turn their lives around. For many the move fails, and their residence in new areas drives up the stress ratings. Or the move itself, even for relatively stable individuals and families, may produce stress. New arrivals face new social strains and the pressures of adjustment. They have distanced themselves from their old friends and relations and do not have the psychological support that helped them in the past.

### HIGHEST- AND LOWEST-STRESS METROPOLITAN AREAS

Ranking

| | Lowest stress | Alcoholism | Crime | Suicide | Divorce |
|---|---|---|---|---|---|
| 1 | State College, Penn. | 1 | 33 | 8 | 20 |
| 2 | Grand Forks, N.D. | 38 | 9 | 1 | 52 |
| 3 | Saint Cloud, Minn. | 44 | 3 | 16 | 15 |
| 4 | Rochester, Minn. | 6 | 17 | 19 | 65 |
| 5 | McAllen, Texas | 48 | 102 | 6 | 11 |
| 6 | Altoona, Penn. | 73 | 7 | 77 | 3 |
| 7 | Bloomington, Ind. | 4 | 61 | 3 | 182 |
| 8 | Provo, Utah | 8 | 24 | 40 | 30 |
| 9 | Utica, N.Y. | 29 | 8 | 26 | 34 |
| 10 | Akron, Ohio | 11 | 114 | 53 | 7 |
| | **Highest stress** | | | | |
| 277 | Los Angeles, Calif. | 275 | 284 | 235 | 112 |
| 278 | San Francisco, Calif. | 267 | 276 | 268 | 174 |
| 279 | Jacksonville, Fla. | 262 | 227 | 262 | 274 |
| 280 | Odessa, Texas | 178 | 279 | 217 | 280 |
| 281 | Little Rock, Ark. | 167 | 242 | 264 | 284 |
| 282 | Lakeland, Fla. | 280 | 250 | 219 | 282 |
| 283 | Miami, Fla. | 248 | 285 | 274 | 205 |
| 284 | Las Vegas, Nev. | 285 | 283 | 285 | 285 |
| 285 | Reno, Nev. | 286 | 201 | 286 | 286 |
| 286 | Panama City, Fla. | 260 | 246 | 250 | 278 |

[a]See Robert Levine, "City Stress Index," *Psychology Today*, November 1988, pp. 53–58.

## POLITICAL CONFLICT

Urban life presents a serious problem in *conflict* management. Because a metropolitan area consists of a large number of different kinds of people living closely together, the problem of regulating conflict and maintaining

**political conflict**
heterogeneity of urban life presents greater potential for conflict among diverse peoples

order assumes tremendous proportions. Persons with different occupations, incomes, and educational levels are known to have different views on public issues. The way that persons well equipped to compete for jobs and income in a free market view government housing and welfare programs may differ from the way that others not so well equipped view them. People at the bottom of the social ladder look at police—indeed, governmental authority in general—differently from the way those on higher rungs do. Persons who own their homes and those who do not own their homes regard taxation in a different light. Families with children and those without children have different ideas about school systems. And so it goes. Differences in the way people make their living, in their income and educational levels, in the color of their skin, in the way they worship, in their style of living—all are at the roots of political life in the metropolis.

## Summary of Sociological Theory of Urbanization

Thus, sociological theory provides us with a series of characteristics to look for in urban life:

- large numbers of people
- population density
- social and economic heterogeneity
- ethnic and racial diversity
- numerous but superficial, segmental, utilitarian relationships
- impersonality and anonymity
- greater interaction in secondary groups
- reliance on formal mechanisms of social control
- physical and social mobility
- greater potential for conflict

**weaknesses of theory**

Not all these characteristics of urban life have been documented. Indeed, in a highly industrialized and urbanized society such as the United States, it is sometimes difficult to discern any differences between rural and urban dwellers. Furthermore, urban dwellers display a great range and variation in lifestyle; some reflect the "typical" style described by sociological theory, and others do not. Many retain their commitment to the extended family, and many city neighborhoods are stable and socially cohesive communities. Despite the plausibility of the hypothesis that urban life leads to anonymity, impersonality, and segmentalization in social relationships, it is hard to prove systematically that urban dwellers are becoming more impersonal or anonymous than are rural dwellers. Finally, sociologists can no longer focus on central-city lifestyles in describing urban living. We must now take account of suburban lifestyles because more people live in suburbs than in central cities. And the suburban way of life is in many ways quite different from the way of life described in sociological theory.

# GOVERNING URBAN COMMUNITIES

Local government is not mentioned in the U.S. Constitution. Although we regard the American federal system as a mixture of federal, state, and *local* governments, from a constitutional point of view local governments are really a part of state governments. Communities have no constitutional right to self-government; all their governmental powers legally flow from state governments. Local governments—cities, townships, counties, special districts, and school districts—are *creatures of the states*, subject to the obligations, privileges, powers, and restrictions that state governments impose on them. The state, either through its constitution or its laws, may create or destroy any or all units of local government. To the extent that local governments can collect taxes, regulate their citizens, and provide services, they are actually exercising *state* powers delegated to them by the state in either its constitution or its laws.

> local governments are creatures of state governments; all their powers legally flow from state governments

The fifty states have created over 86,000 local governments (see Table 13-2). What do they all do? Different units of government are assigned different responsibilities by each of the states, so it is difficult to generalize about what each of these types of local government is supposed to do. Indeed, even in the same state there may be overlapping functions and responsibilities assigned to cities, counties, school districts, and special districts.

## TYPES OF LOCAL GOVERNMENTS AND THEIR FUNCTIONS

Nevertheless, let us try to make some generalizations about what each of these types of government does, realizing, of course, that in any specific location the pattern of governmental activity may be slightly different:

■ *Counties: rural*—keep records of deeds, mortgages, births, marriages; assess and levy property taxes; maintain local roads; administer elections and certify election results to state; provide law enforcement through sheriff; maintain criminal court; maintain a local jail; administer state welfare programs.

> functions of
> rural counties
> urban counties
> cities
> school districts
> townships
> special districts

**TABLE 13-2**

### LOCAL GOVERNMENTS IN THE UNITED STATES

| | |
|---|---|
| Counties | 3,043 |
| Municipalities | 19,296 |
| Townships | 16,666 |
| School districts | 14,556 |
| Special districts | 33,131 |
| Total (including states and national government) | 86,743 |

SOURCE: U.S. Bureau of the Census, *Census of Government,* 1992.

- *Counties: urban*—most of the same functions as the rural counties (except police and court systems, which often become city functions), together with planning and control of new subdivisions; mental health; public health maintenance and public hospitals; care of the aged; recreation, including parks, stadiums, and convention centers; and perhaps some city functions.
- *Cities*—provide the "common functions" of police, fire, streets, sewage, sanitation, and parks; over half of the nation's large cities also provide welfare services and public education. (In other cities welfare is handled by county governments or directly by state agencies, and education is handled by separate school districts.)
- *School districts*—organized specifically to provide public elementary and secondary education; community colleges may be operated by county governments or by special districts with or without state support.
- *Townships*—generally subdivisions of counties with the same responsibilities as their county.
- *Special districts*—may be as large as the Port Authority of New York with more than $1 billion in diversified assets. However, special districts are usually established for mass transit, soil conservation, libraries, water and irrigation, mosquito control, sewage disposal, airports, and so on.

## FORMS OF CITY GOVERNMENT

**forms of city government**
mayor-council

commission

council-manager

American city government comes in three structural packages. There are some adaptations and variations from city to city, but generally one can classify the form of city government as *mayor-council, commission,* or *council-manager.* Approximately 51 percent of American cities have the mayor-council form of government; 6 percent have the commission form; and 43 percent have the council-manager form. Figure 13-2 shows the general organization of these three forms of government.

## MAYOR-COUNCIL

The nation's largest cities tend to function under the *mayor-council* plan. This is the oldest form of American city government and is designed in the American tradition of separation of powers between legislature and executive. One may also establish subcategories of strong- or weak-mayor forms of mayor-council government. A strong mayor is the undisputed master of the executive agencies of city government and has substantial legislative powers in the form of budget making, vetoes, and opportunity to propose legislation. Only a few cities make the mayor the sole elected official among

**FIGURE 13-2**

FORMS OF CITY GOVERNMENT

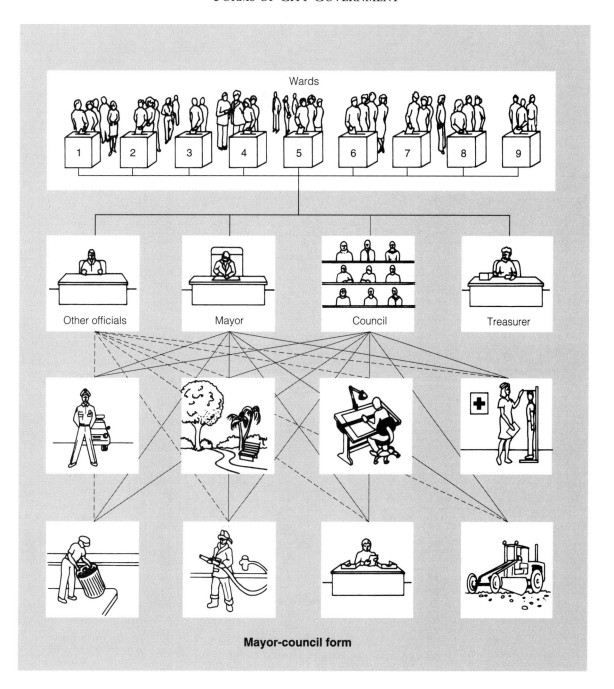

Mayor-council form

*(Continued)*

**FIGURE 13-2**

FORMS OF CITY GOVERNMENT (*Continued*)

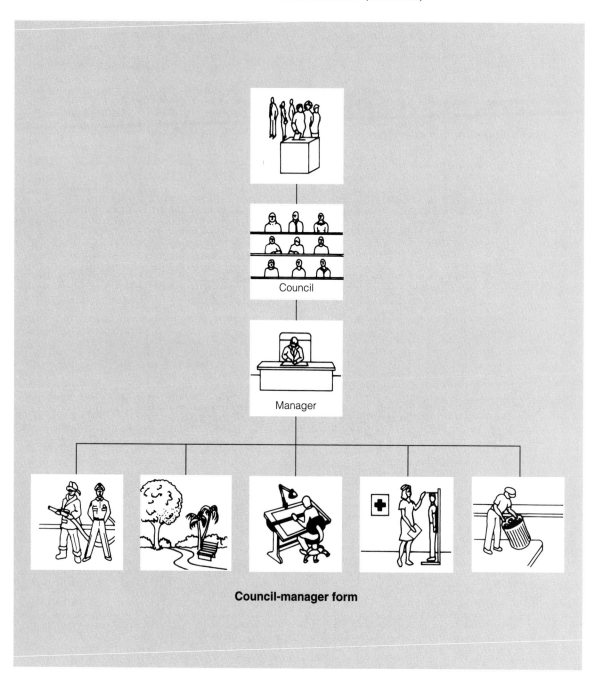

Council-manager form

**FIGURE 13-2**

## Forms of City Government (*Continued*)

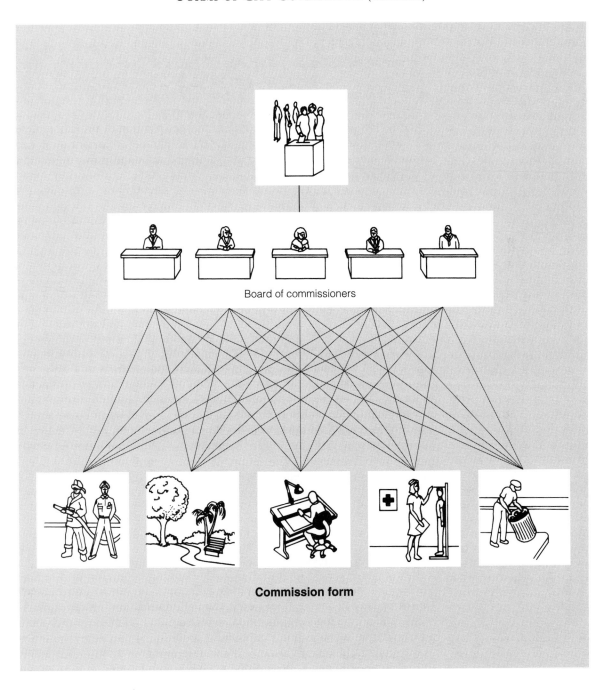

Board of commissioners

**Commission form**

city executive officers; it is common for the mayor to share powers with other elected officials—city attorney, treasurer, tax assessor, auditor, clerk, and so on. Yet many mayors, by virtue of their prestige, persuasive abilities, or role as party leader, have been able to overcome most of the weaknesses of their formal office.

In recent years large cities have been adding to the formal powers of their chief executives. Cities have augmented the mayors' roles by providing them with direction over budgeting, purchasing, and personnel controls. Independent boards, commissions, and individual council members have relinquished administrative control over city departments in many cities. Moreover, many cities have strengthened their mayors' position by providing them with a chief administrative officer (CAO) to handle important staff and administrative duties of supervising city departments and providing central management services.

## COMMISSION

The *commission* form of city government gives both legislative and executive powers to a small body, usually consisting of five members. The commission form originated at the beginning of the century as a reform movement designed to end a system of divided responsibility between mayor and council. One of the commission members is nominally the mayor, but he or she has no more formal powers than the other commissioners. The board of commissioners is directly responsible for the operation of city departments and agencies. In practice, one commission member will become responsible for the management of a specific department, such as finance, public works, or public safety. As long as the council members are in agreement over policy, there are few problems; but when commissioners differ among themselves and develop separate spheres of influence in city government, city government becomes a multiheaded monster, totally lacking in coordination. The results of the commission form of government were generally so disastrous that the reform movement abandoned its early support of this form of government in favor of the council-manager plan.

## COUNCIL-MANAGER

The *council-manager* form of government revived the distinction between legislative "policy making" and executive "administration" in city government. Policy-making responsibility is vested in an elected council, and administration is assigned to an appointed professional administrator known as a manager, chosen by the council and responsible to it. All departments of the city government operate under the direction of the manager, who has the power to hire and fire personnel within the limits set by the merit system. The council's role in administration is limited to selecting and dismissing the city manager. The plan is based on the ideas that policy making and administration are separate functions and that the principal task of city government is to provide the highest level of services at the lowest possible costs—utilities, streets, fire and police protection, health, welfare, recreation, and so on. Hence, a professionally trained, career-oriented administrator is given direct control over city departments. (See the Focus, "Who Really Runs This Town?")

# THE CITY IN HISTORY

The United States developed an anticity bias in its rural beginnings and retained that bias long after it became a nation of city dwellers. When the first census was taken in 1790, a mere 5 percent of the nation's four million people lived in cities; there were only 24 towns with populations of 2,500 or more. A strong anticity bias was already ingrained in the national character. In an age when technological progress was giving rise to the first industrial centers in Europe, the American social and economic outlook was decidedly agrarian. Most politicians and citizens distrusted cities, which Thomas Jefferson believed were not conducive to the exercise of virtue. Jefferson's warning notwithstanding, American cities steadily increased in population. The lure of urban life is reflected in the following Census Bureau figures showing the country's five most populous cities in 1820, 1870, 1950, 1980, 1990, and 1995.

**from a rural to an urban America**

| 1820 | |
| --- | --- |
| New York | 152,000 |
| Philadelphia | 65,000 |
| Baltimore | 63,000 |
| Boston | 43,000 |
| New Orleans | 27,000 |

| 1870 | |
| --- | --- |
| New York | 1,478,000 |
| Philadelphia | 674,000 |
| St. Louis | 311,000 |
| Chicago | 299,000 |
| Baltimore | 267,000 |

| 1950 | |
| --- | --- |
| New York | 7,896,957 |
| Chicago | 3,620,962 |
| Philadelphia | 2,071,605 |
| Los Angeles | 1,970,338 |
| Detroit | 1,849,568 |

| 1980 | |
| --- | --- |
| New York | 7,071,000 |
| Chicago | 3,005,000 |
| Los Angeles | 2,966,800 |
| Philadelphia | 1,688,200 |
| Houston | 1,594,100 |

| 1990 | |
| --- | --- |
| New York | 7,323,000 |
| Los Angeles | 3,485,000 |
| Chicago | 2,784,000 |
| Houston | 1,631,000 |
| Philadelphia | 1,586,000 |

| 1995 | |
| --- | --- |
| New York | 7,333,000 |
| Los Angeles | 3,449,000 |
| Chicago | 2,732,000 |
| Houston | 1,702,000 |
| Philadelphia | 1,524,000 |

# CONTROVERSIES IN SOCIAL SCIENCE

"Who Really Runs This Town?"

Who runs this town? Do the elected public officials actually make the important decisions? Or is there a "power structure" in this community that really runs things? If so, who is in the power structure? Are public officials errand boys who carry out the orders of powerful people who operate behind the scenes? Or are community affairs decided by democratically elected officials acting openly in response to the wishes of many different individuals and groups? Is city government of the people, by the people, and for the people? Or is it a government run by a small elite, with the masses of people largely apathetic and uninfluential in public affairs?

Social scientists have differed in their answers to these questions. Some social scientists (we shall call them *elitists*) believe that power in American communities is concentrated in the hands of relatively few people, usually top business and financial leaders. Elitists believe that this elite is subject to relatively little influence from the masses of people.

Other social scientists (we shall call them *pluralists*) believe that power is widely shared in American communities among many leadership groups who represent segments of the community and who are held responsible by the people through elections and group participation. Interestingly, both elitists and pluralists seem to agree that decisions are made by small minorities in the community. Elitists describe a single structure of power, with a single leadership group making decisions on a variety of issues, whereas pluralists describe multiple structures of power, with different groups active in different issues and a great deal of competition, bargaining, and sharing of power among the elite.

## Early Sociological Studies: "Middletown" and "Regional City"

One of the earliest studies of American communities, the classic study of Middletown (actually Muncie, Indiana), conducted by Robert and Helen Lynd in the mid-1920s and again in the mid-1930s, tended to confirm a great deal of elitist thinking about community power.[a] The Lynds found in Muncie a monolithic power structure dominated by the owners of the town's largest industry. Community power was firmly entrenched in the hands of the business class, centering on but not limited to the "X family."[b] This group's power was based on its control over the economic life in the city, particularly its ability to control the extension of credit. The city was run by a "small top group [of] wealthy local manufacturers, bankers, the local head managers of . . . national corporations with units in Middletown, and . . . one or two outstanding lawyers." Democratic procedures and governmental institutions were so much window dressing for business control. The Lynds described the typical city official as a "man of meager calibre" and as "a man whom the inner business control group ignores economically and socially and use politically." Perhaps the most famous quotation from the Lynds's study was a comment by a Middletown man made in 1935:

*If I'm out of work, I go to the X plant; if I need money I go to the X bank, and if they don't like me I don't get it; my children go to the X college; when I get sick I go to the X hospital; I buy a building lot or house in the X subdivision; my wife goes downtown to buy X milk; I drink X beer, vote for X political parties, and get help from X charities; my boy goes to the X YMCA and my girl to their YWCA; I listen to the word of God in X subsidized churches; if I'm a Mason, I go to the X Masonic temple; I read the news from the X morning paper; and, if I'm rich enough, I travel via the X airport.[c]*

One of the most influential *elitist* studies of community politics was sociologist Floyd Hunter's *Community Power Structure*, a study of Atlanta, Georgia.[d] According to Hunter, no one person or family or business dominated "Regional City" (a pseudonym for Atlanta), as might be true in a smaller town. Instead, Hunter described several tiers of influentials, with the most important community decisions reserved for a top layer of the business community. Admission to the innermost circle was based primarily on one's position in the business world. These top decision makers were not formally organized but conferred informally and passed down decisions to government leaders, professional personnel, civic organizations, and other "front men." Hunter explained that the top power structure concerned itself only with major policy decisions; there were other substructures—economic, governmental, religious, educational, professional, civic, and cultural—that communicated and implemented the policies

at the top levels. According to Hunter, elected public officials are clearly part of the lower-level institutional substructure, which "executes" policy rather than formulates it. Finally, Hunter found that this whole structure is held together by "common interests, mutual obligations, money, habit, delegated responsibilities, and in some cases, by coercion and force."

### Early Political Studies: New Haven

Perhaps the most influential of the *pluralist* community studies was Robert A. Dahl's *Who Governs?*, a detailed analysis of decision making in New Haven, Connecticut.[e] Dahl chose to examine sixteen major decisions on redevelopment and public education in New Haven and on nominations for mayor in both political parties for seven elections. Dahl found a polycentric and dispersed system of community power in New Haven, in contrast to Hunter's highly monolithic and centralized power structure. Influence was wielded from time to time by many individuals, each exercising power over some issues but not over others. When the issue was one of urban renewal, one set of individuals was influential; in public education, a different group of leaders was involved.

The business elite, said by Hunter to control Atlanta, was only one of many different influential groups in New Haven. According to Dahl:

*The economic notables, far from being a ruling group, are simply one of many groups out of which individuals sporadically emerge to influence the politics and acts of city officials. Almost anything one might say about the influence of the economic notables could be said with equal justice about a half a dozen other groups in the New Haven community[f]*

The mayor of New Haven was the only decision maker who was influential in most of the issue areas studied, and his degree of influence varied from issue to issue.

For many years scholars studying community power argued over methods of research and interpretation of findings. Sociologists tended to study whole community social structures and interpret their findings in an elitist fashion. Political scientists tended to focus on local governmental decision making and interpret their findings as confirmation of the pluralist model. Yet even as research continued, American communities were undergoing changes in their power structures.

(*Continued*)

**CONTROVERSIES
IN SOCIAL
SCIENCE**
"Who Really Runs
This Town?
(*Continued*)

### The Old Community Economic Elites

Traditionally, community power structures were composed primarily of economic elites whose goals were to maximize land values, real estate commissions, builders' profits, rent payments, and mortgage interest and to increase revenues to commercial enterprises serving the community. Communities were traditionally dominated by mortgage lending banks, real estate developers, builders, and landowners. They were joined by owners or managers of local utilities, department stores, attorneys and title companies, and others whose wealth was affected by land use. Local bankers who financed the real estate developers and builders were often at the center of the elite structure.

These traditional community elites strove for consensus. They believed that community economic growth—increased capital investment, more jobs, and improved business conditions—benefited the entire community. Local government officials were expected to share in the elite consensus. Economic prosperity was necessary for protecting the tax base of local government. Moreover, economic growth was usually good politics. Growth-oriented candidates for public office usually had larger campaign treasuries than antigrowth candidates. Most local politicians had "a sense of community responsibility." They knew that if the economy of the community declines, "local business will suffer, workers will lose employment opportunities, cultural life will decline, and city land values will fall."[g]

### The New Community Political Elites

Today, in many American communities the old economic elites are being replaced by new political elites. Many of the old economic elites sold their businesses to national corporations and vacated their positions of community leadership. Locally owned stores and factories became manager-directed plants and chain stores. The result was a weakening of community loyalties in the business sector. The new corporate managers could easily decide, in response to national economic conditions, to close the local plant or store with minimal concern for the impact on the community. Local banks were merged into national banking corporations, and local bankers were replaced by banking executives with few community ties. City newspapers that were once independently owned by families who lived in the communities were bought up by giant newspaper and publication chains. Instead of editors and reporters who expected to live their lives in their communities, city newspapers came to be staffed with people who hoped to move up in the cor-

## ECONOMIC GROWTH

**economic needs fuel growth**    First as seaports, then as trading and manufacturing centers, cities in the United States grew in response to economic needs. "Villages expanded into towns; towns became metropolises," historian Lewis Mumford wrote in *The City in History*.

> *Between 1820 and 1900, the destruction and disorder within cities was like that of a battlefield. . . . Industrialism, the main creative*

porate hierarchy—people who strove primarily to advance their own careers, not the interests of the local community.

The nationalization of the American economy and the resulting demise of locally owned enterprises created a vacuum of leadership in community affairs. Professional politicians moved into this vacuum in city after city, largely replacing the local bankers, real estate developers, chambers of commerce, and old-style newspaper editors who had dominated community politics for generations. The new professional political elites work full-time at local politics. They are drawn primarily by personal ambition— not so much for wealth as for the power and celebrity that accompany running for and winning public office.

The political elites are independent entrepreneurs. They win office "by selling themselves to the voters, in person, one at a time, day after day. People who do not like to do this, people who do not like to knock on strangers' doors or who find it tedious to repeat the same thirty-second personal introduction thousands of times, are at a severe disadvantage."[h] Thus, over time these full-time political elites drive out the part-time economic elites.

The new political elites seldom have a large financial stake in the community, aside from their homes. They do not necessarily seek community consensus on behalf of prosperity. On the contrary, it's fashionable among new political elites to complain loudly about the problems created by growth—congestion, pollution, noise, unsightly development, or the replacement of green spaces with concrete slabs. No-growth movements appeal to people who already own their houses as well as to owners of already-developed commercial property. Curtailing growth freezes out competition for new homes, apartment complexes, and commercial centers. It allows owners of existing homes and properties to raise prices and rents to new residents. It is no surprise that "neighborhood associations," led by upper- and upper-middle-class homeowners, are at the forefront of no-growth politics.

[a]Robert S. Lynd and Helen M. Lynd, *Middletown* (New York: Harcourt, Brace & World, 1929), and *Middletown in Transition* (New York: Harcourt, Brace & World, 1937).
[b]The "X family," never identified in the Lynds's books, was actually the Ball family, glass manufacturers. Ball State University in Muncie, Indiana, is named for the family.
[c]Lynd and Lynd, *Middletown in Transition*, p. 74.
[d]Floyd Hunter, *Community Power Structure* (Chapel Hill: University of North Carolina Press, 1953).
[e]Robert Dahl, *Who Governs?* (New Haven, Conn.: Yale University Press, 1961).
[f]Dahl, *Who Governs?*, p. 72.
[g]Paul Peterson, *City Limits* (Chicago: University of Chicago Press, 1981), p. 20.
[h]Alan Ehrenhalt, *The United States of Ambition* (New York: Random House, 1991), p. 22.

*force of the nineteenth century, produced the most degraded urban environment the world had yet seen. . . . Men built in haste, and had hardly time to repent of their mistakes before they tore down their original structures and built again, just as heedlessly. The newcomers, babies, or immigrants, could not wait for new quarters: they crowded into whatever was offered. It was a period of vast urban improvisation: makeshift hastily piled upon makeshift.*[3]

## SOCIAL STRATIFICATION

**social stratification in cities**

By the late nineteenth century most large American cities had become socially and economically stratified. The affluent lived in their posh neighborhoods, comfortably isolated from the poor in their ethnic ghettos, whereas the middle classes tended to move to the less-expensive outlying areas. As populations spread, many central cities simply annexed those areas to which the middle class had gravitated. New York, for example, added more than 250 square miles in 1891, and in 1941 Boston doubled its area. Some states established automatic annexation procedures. By 1920, however, political opposition to the absorption of fringe areas mounted, and large cities, especially in the congested Northeast, found themselves unable to keep pace, through annexation or consolidation, with suburban migration.

## SUBURBANIZATION

**automobiles encourage suburban growth**

During the 1920s general prosperity and the increasing number of automobiles gave new impetus to the growth of the suburbs. In that decade, the suburban populations around the seventeen largest U.S. cities rose by nearly 40 percent, while the rate of growth for most cities fell sharply. But until the 1940s, the central city remained the focal point of business and industry; the surrounding suburbs were primarily commuter villages.

# THE PROBLEMS OF THE INNER CITY

The nation's largest cities have become the principal location of virtually all of the social problems confronting our society—poverty, homelessness, racial tension, family instability, drug abuse, delinquency, and crime. Some of these problems were discussed in previous chapters (especially in Chapter 11, "Poverty & Powerlessness," and in Chapter 12, "Power, Crime, & Violence"), but it is important to note here that these problems are all made worse by their concentration in large cities. The concentration of social ills in the nation's cities is a relatively recent occurrence; as late as 1970 there were higher rates of poverty in rural America than in the cities.

**social problems**
joblessness
poverty
family disintegration
welfare dependency

**economic problems**
fewer high-paying manufacturing jobs
migrating of jobs to suburbs

## SOCIAL AND ECONOMIC PROBLEMS

Why has the inner city become the locus of social problems? It has been argued that changes in the labor market from industrial goods-producing jobs to professional, financial, and technical service-producing jobs are increasingly polarizing the labor market into low-wage and high-wage sectors.[4] The decline in manufacturing jobs, together with a shift in remaining manufacturing jobs and commercial (sales) jobs to the suburbs, has left inner-city residents with fewer job opportunities. The rise in joblessness in the inner cities has in turn increased the concentration of poor people, added to the number of poor single-parent families, and increased welfare dependency.

## Out-Migration

At the same time, inner-city neighborhoods have experienced an out-migration of working-class and middle-class families. The number of inner-city neighborhoods in which the poverty rate exceeds 40 percent has risen sharply.[5] The loss of working- and middle-class families creates further social instability. In earlier decades most inner-city adults were employed, and they invested their income and time in their neighborhoods, patronizing churches, stores, schools, and community organizations. Their presence in the community provided role models for youth. But their out-migration has decreased contact between the classes, leaving the poorest isolated and "truly

**out-migration of working and middle class from inner city**

*Children often are left to play alone in poverty-stricken neighborhoods.*

Michael Weisbrot/Stock Boston

disadvantaged." Inner-city residents now lack not only nearby jobs, but also access to job information, social learning through working role models, and (for some young women) suitable (that is, employed) marriage partners.

## CONCENTRATION EFFECTS

**concentration effects**

absence of working role models

loss of job information

weakened work ethic

street-crime environment

deteriorating business and public services

It is argued that joblessness and poverty are much more demoralizing when concentrated in the inner city. Neighborhoods that have few legitimate employment opportunities, inadequate job information networks, and poor schools not only weaken the work ethic, but also give rise to illegal income-producing activities in the streets—drugs, crime, prostitution. A jobless family living in a neighborhood where these ills are concentrated is influenced by the behaviors, beliefs, and perceptions of the people around them. These *concentration effects* make things worse. Moreover, the deterioration of inner-city neighborhoods saps the vitality of local businesses and public services, leading to fewer and shabbier movie theaters, restaurants, markets, parks, and playgrounds. Inner-city schools are particularly disadvantaged; as educational requirements for good jobs are rising, the quality of education available in the inner city is eroded by the concentration of children from poverty-impacted and disintegrating families. The fiscal burden on city governments increases: the cost of services to the inner city increases at the same time that the tax base is eroded by out-migrating businesses and working residents. In short, the problems of the inner city are the problems of the nation in concentrated form.

## NOTES

1. Louis Wirth, "Urbanism as a Way of Life," *American Journal of Sociology* 44 (July 1938).
2. Ibid., 24.
3. Lewis Mumford, *The City in History* (London: Penguin Books, 1966), p. 11.
4. This thesis derives from sociologist William Julius Wilson, *The Truly Disadvantaged* (Chicago: University of Chicago Press, 1987).
5. See Christopher Jencks and Paul E. Peterson, eds., *The Urban Underclass* (Washington, D.C.: Brookings Institution, 1991).

## ABOUT THIS CHAPTER

It has always been fashionable in the United States to deplore life in big cities. Thomas Jefferson believed cities were the source of human vice and that only a rural and small-town America could maintain democracy. When the first census of the United States was taken in 1790, only 5 percent of the American people lived in cities, whereas today three-quarters of our population live in large urban clusters known as metropolitan areas. We have changed from a rural society to an urban society. We are trying to cope with the social, psychological, economic, and political problems of urban life. We are particularly concerned with the deterioration of older central cities, the creation of African-American ghettos in large cities, "white flight" to the suburbs, and financial and governmental problems posed by growth and decline in metropolitan areas.

In this chapter we have described where Americans live and the impact of urban life on social relations, psychological states of mind, government, and power relations. Now that you have read it, you should be able to

■ describe changes over the past decade in central cities and suburbs of metropolitan areas and in nonmetropolitan areas

■ identify the social characteristics associated with urban life

- discuss suburbanization and increasing separation of African-American central cities from white suburbs in large metropolitan areas
- discuss the social psychology of urban life
- describe various structures of government found in American cities
- describe "community power structures" and how they are changing over time
- describe the "concentration effects" of social problems in the inner city

# DISCUSSION QUESTIONS

1. Describe overall growth and decline in central cities, suburbs, and nonmetropolitan areas of the United States. What is a CMSA?

2. According to sociologist Louis Wirth, what are the distinguishing characteristics of urban life?
3. Why do people choose to live in suburbs? What is meant by the statement "American life is becoming more, not less, segregated"?
4. How can we test the hypothesis that urban life is more impersonal than rural or small-town life?
5. What are the governmental functions of counties (rural and urban), cities, school districts, townships, and special districts?
6. What are the most common forms of city government?
7. What factors might account for the concentration of social problems in the inner city?
8. What is meant by *elitist* and *pluralist* descriptions of community power structures? What differences can be identified between older and newer community elites?

## Chapter 14

# Power among Nations

## INTERNATIONAL POLITICS

The distinguished political scientist Hans Morgenthau wrote:

**international politics**
the worldwide struggle for power

> *International politics, like all politics, is a struggle for power. What-*
> *ever the ultimate aims of international politics, power is always the*
> *immediate aim. Statesmen and peoples may ultimately seek freedom,*
> *security, prosperity, or power itself. They may define their goals in*
> *terms of a religious, philosophic, economic, or social ideal. . . . But*
> *whenever they strive to realize their goal by means of international*
> *politics, they are striving for power.[1]*

In brief, we are reminded that the struggle for power is global—it involves
all the nations and peoples of the world, whatever their goals or ideals.

## NATIONAL SOVEREIGNTY

There are nearly 200 nations in the world today. Of these nations 178 (as of
1992) are members of the United Nations. Yet all the nations of the world—
whatever their size, location, culture, politics, economic system, or level of

technological development—claim *sovereignty.* Sovereignty means formal, legal power over internal affairs; freedom from external intervention; and political and legal recognition by other nations. Sovereignty is a legal fiction, of course: many nations have difficulty controlling their internal affairs; they are constantly meddling in each other's internal affairs and even trampling on each other's political and legal authority. Nonetheless, the *struggle* to achieve sovereignty is an important force in world politics.

**sovereignty**
legal power over internal affairs, freedom from external intervention, and legal recognition by other nations

Although sovereignty is highly valued by all nations, it creates an international system in which no authority—not even the United Nations—is given the power to make or enforce rules binding on all nations. There is *no world government.* Nations cooperate with each other only when it is in their own interests to do so. Nations can make treaties with each other, but there is no court to enforce the treaties, and they can be (and are) disregarded when it becomes advantageous for a nation to do so.

## INTERNATIONAL LAW

There is a series of customs and principles among nations—known as *international law*—that helps to guide relations among nations. But international "law" is also a fiction: there is no international "police force" to enforce the law, and it is frequently broken or ignored. An International Court (at The Hague, the Netherlands) exists to decide conflicts according to international law, but nations do not have to submit to the authority of this court and can, if they wish, ignore its decisions. The United Nations has no real power to enforce its resolutions, unless one or more nations (acting in their own self-interest) decide to try to enforce a UN resolution with their own troops, or contribute troops to a joint "UN force." But UN forces are really the forces of sovereign nations that have voluntarily decided to contribute troops to enforce a particular resolution.

**international law**
a legal fiction that guides relations among nations

The international system can be viewed as a global game of power that is played continuously. All the players pursue different goals against all the other players. Some players are more powerful than others, and occasionally players team up against each other. Periodically fights break out, but there is no referee with enough power to stop the fighting (unless one or more stronger players step in to restrain the fighting nations). The game has been played for centuries. No one really knows all the goals that each player seeks (although we all know that power is the key instrument in achieving any goal). Yet all the players are deadly serious and play to win.

**international politics as a serious game**

## BRINGING ORDER TO INTERNATIONAL RELATIONS

The instability and insecurity of "the global game of power" have led to many attempts over the centuries to bring order to the international system. Indeed, wars among nations have averaged one every two years, and if "civil wars" and "indirect aggressions" are counted, the rate of armed conflict is even greater.

*U.S. Secretary of State Madeleine Albright shakes hands with Yasser Arafat as she arrives in the West Bank town of Ramallah for a meeting with the Palestinian leader.*

5958/Gamma-Liaison

## THE BALANCE-OF-POWER SYSTEM—NINETEENTH CENTURY

**the balance-of-power system, 1815–1914**

One method of trying to bring order to international relations is the *balance-of-power system*. The nineteenth century saw a deliberate attempt to stabilize international relations by creating a system of alliances among nations that was designed to balance the power of one group of nations against the power of another and thus to discourage war. If the balance worked, war would be avoided and peace would be assured. For almost an entire century, from the end of the Napoleonic Wars (1815) to World War I (1914), the balance-of-power system appeared to be at least partially effective in Europe. But an important defect in the balance-of-power system is that a small conflict between two nations that are members of separate alliances can draw all the member nations of each alliance into the conflict.

This defect can result in the rapid expansion of a small conflict into a major war between separate alliances of nations. Essentially this is what happened in World War I, when a minor conflict in the Balkan nations resulted in a very destructive war between the *Allies* (England, France, Russia, and eventually the United States) and the *Central Powers* (Germany, Austria–Hungary, and Turkey).

**World War I**
the Allies versus the Central Powers

Indeed, World War I proved so destructive (ten million men were killed on the battlefield between 1914 and 1918) that there was a worldwide demand to replace the balance-of-power system with a new arrangement— "collective security."

## COLLECTIVE SECURITY—THE UNITED NATIONS

*Collective security* originally meant that *all* nations would join together to guarantee each other's "territorial integrity and existing political independence" against "external aggression" by any nation.[2] This concept resulted in the formation of *the League of Nations* in 1919. However, opposition to international involvement was so great in the United States after World War I that after a lengthy debate in the Senate, the United States refused to join the League of Nations. More important, the League of Nations failed completely to deal with rising militarism in Germany, Japan, and Italy in the 1930s. During that decade, Japan invaded Manchuria, Italy invaded Ethiopia, and Germany invaded Czechoslovakia; and the League of Nations failed to prevent any of these aggressions. Fascism in Germany and Italy and militarism in Japan went unchecked. World War II between the *Allies* (the United States, England, France, China, and the Soviet Union) and the *Axis Powers* (Germany, Italy, and Japan) was even more devastating than World War I: World War II cost more than forty million lives, both civilian and military.

Yet even after World War II the notion of collective security remained an ideal of the victorious Allied powers, especially the United States, Great Britain, the Soviet Union, France, and China. The Charter of *the United Nations* was signed in 1945. The new organization originally included fifty-one members. The UN provided for (1) a Security Council with eleven members, five of them being permanent members (the United States, the USSR, Britain, France, and China) and having the power to veto any action by the

**efforts at collective security**

**the League of Nations**

**World War II**
the Allies versus the Axis Powers

**the United Nations**
General Assembly
Security Council
secretary-general
specialized bodies
veto powers

**USSR**
Union of Soviet Socialist Republics (Soviet Union). Fifteen "republics" including Russia; under communist rule 1917–1991; upon dissolution of USSR in 1991, UN seat assumed by Russia

*The United Nations General Assembly has authority over "any matter affecting the peace of the world."*

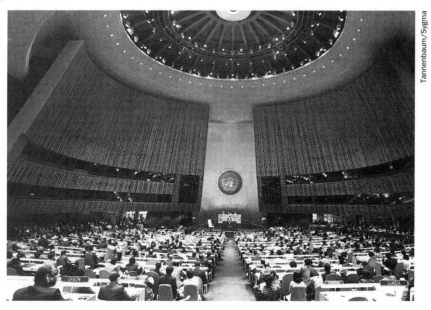

Tannenbaum/Sygma

Security Council; (2) a General Assembly composed of all the member nations, each with a single vote; (3) a secretariat headed by a secretary-general with a staff at UN headquarters in New York; and (4) several special bodies to handle specialized affairs—for example, the Economic and Social Council, the Trusteeship Council, and the International Court at The Hague.

The Security Council has the "primary responsibility" for maintaining "international peace and security." For this reason the world's most powerful nations—the United States, Russia, Great Britain, France, and China—have permanent seats on the council and veto powers over all but procedural matters. (Germany and Japan, originally denied Security Council membership as defeated powers in World War II, are currently leading candidates for permanent Security Council seats.)

The General Assembly has authority over "any matter affecting the peace of the world," although it is supposed to defer to the Security Council if the council has already taken up a particular matter. No nation has a veto in the General Assembly; all UN member nations have one vote, regardless of their size or power. Most resolutions can be passed by a majority vote.

The United Nations proved largely ineffective during the long *Cold War* confrontation between the communist nations, led by the USSR, and the western democracies, led by the United States. Many of the new nations admitted to the UN were headed by authoritarian regimes of one kind or another. The western democracies were outnumbered in the General Assembly, and the USSR frequently used its veto to prevent action by the Security Council. Antiwestern and antidemocratic speeches become common in the General Assembly. The UN was overshadowed by the confrontation of the world's two *superpowers:* the United States and the USSR (the Soviet Union). Indeed, international conflicts throughout the world—in the Middle East, Africa, Latin America, southeast Asia, and elsewhere—were usually influenced by some aspect of the superpower struggle.

## REGIONAL SECURITY—NATO

The general disappointment with the United Nations as a form of collective security gave rise as early as 1949 to a different approach: *regional security.* In response to aggressive Soviet moves in Europe, the United States and the democracies of western Europe created the *North Atlantic Treaty Organization (NATO).* In the NATO treaty, fifteen western nations agreed to collective regional security: they agreed that "an armed attack against one or more NATO nations . . . shall be considered an attack against them all." The United States made a specific commitment to defend western Europe in the event of a Soviet attack. A joint NATO military command was established (with Dwight D. Eisenhower as its first commander) to coordinate the defense of western Europe. After the formation of NATO, the Soviets made no further advances into western Europe. The Soviets themselves, in response to NATO, drew up a comparable treaty among their own eastern European satellite nations: the *Warsaw Pact.* Note that these regional security agreements—

**Cold War**
political, military, and ideological conflict between communist nations, led by the USSR, and the western democracies, led by the United States, from 1945 to 1990

**superpowers**
Cold War term referring to the United States and the Soviet Union as the dominant world powers

**regional security**
an attempt to bring order to international relations during the Cold War by creating regional alliances between a superpower and nations of a particular region

**NATO**
regional alliance of western democracies to protect themselves against Soviet aggression

NATO and the Warsaw Pact—were more like the nineteenth-century balance-of-power alliances than like the true concept of *collective security*. The original notion of collective security envisioned agreement among *all* nations, whereas NATO and the Warsaw Pact were similar to the older systems of separate alliances.

The Warsaw Pact disintegrated following the dramatic collapse of the communist governments of eastern Europe in 1989. Former Warsaw Pact nations— Poland, Hungary, Romania, Bulgaria, and East Germany—threw out their ruling communist regimes and began negotiations leading to the withdrawal of Soviet troops from their territory. The Berlin Wall was smashed in 1989, and Germany was formally reunified in 1990, bringing together sixty-one million prosperous people of West Germany with seventeen million less affluent people of East Germany. United Germany continues as a member of NATO.

**collapse of communist governments and Warsaw Pact**

The reduced threat of attack on western Europe has raised a variety of questions regarding the future of NATO. Is NATO needed at all in view of the collapse of the USSR and the Warsaw Pact? Or should it continue, perhaps with reduced military forces, as insurance against a future renewal of a Russian threat? Should NATO guarantee the security of the emerging democracies of eastern Europe against a possible renewed threat?

**the future of NATO?**

## A Revitalized UN

The end of the Cold War has injected new vitality into the United Nations. Russia inherited the UN Security Council seat of the former USSR, and the government of President Boris Yeltsin has generally cooperated in UN efforts to bring stability to various regional conflicts. No longer are these conflicts "proxy" wars between the superpowers. Cooperation between the permanent members of the Security Council (the United States, Great Britain, France, and Russia, together with the acquiescence of China) has brought "a new world order" to international politics. But the United Nations and its Security Council must rely on "the last remaining superpower," the United States, to take the lead in enforcing its resolutions.

# A Brief History of the Cold War

For forty-five years following the end of World War II, the United States and the Soviet Union confronted each other in a protracted political, military, and ideological struggle known as the Cold War.

## Origins

During World War II, the United States and the Soviet Union joined forces to eliminate the Nazi threat to the world. The United States dismantled its military forces at the end of the war in 1945, but the USSR, under the brutal dictatorship of Joseph Stalin, used the powerful Red Army to install communist governments in the nations of eastern Europe in violation of wartime agreements to allow free elections. Stalin also ignored pledges to cooperate in a unified allied occupation of Germany; Germany was divided, and in 1948 Stalin unsuccessfully tried to oust the United States, Britain, and France from Berlin in a year-long "Berlin Blockade." Former British Prime Minister Winston Churchill warned America in a 1946 speech that the Soviets were dividing Europe with an "Iron Curtain." When Soviet-backed communist guerrilla forces threatened Greece and Turkey in 1948, President Harry S. Truman responded with a pledge to "support free people who are resisting attempted subjugation by armed minorities or by outside pressures," a policy that became known as the Truman Doctrine.

## CONTAINMENT

**containment**
a policy of preventing the enemy from expanding its boundaries and/or influence; describes U.S. foreign policy vis-à-vis the USSR during the Cold War

The threat of Soviet expansionism and communist world revolution caused the American government to assume world leadership on behalf of the preservation of democracy. The U.S. State Department's Russian expert, George F. Kennan, called for a policy of *containment*: "It is clear that the main element of any United States policy toward the Soviet Union must be that of a long-term, vigilant containment of Russian expansive tendencies."[3] To implement the containment policy, the United States first initiated the *Marshall Plan,* named for Secretary of State George C. Marshall, to rebuild the economies of the western European nations. Marshall reasoned that *economically* weak nations were more susceptible to communist subversion and Soviet intimidation. The subsequent formation of NATO provided *military* support to contain the USSR.

**Marshall Plan**
a U.S. program to rebuild the nations of western Europe in the aftermath of World War II in order to render them less susceptible to communist influence and/or takeover

## THE KOREAN WAR

The first military test of the containment policy came in June 1950, when communist North Korean armies invaded South Korea. President Truman believed (correctly) that the North Koreans were acting on behalf of their sponsor, the Soviet Union. The Soviets had already aided Chinese communists under the leadership of Mao Zedong in capturing control of mainland China in 1949. The United States quickly brought the Korean invasion issue to the Security Council. With the USSR boycotting this meeting because the Council had refused to seat the new communist delegation from China, the Council passed a resolution calling on member nations to send troops to repel the invasion.

**the Korean War**
1950–1953

America's conventional (nonnuclear) military forces had been largely dismantled after World War II. Moreover, President Truman insisted on keeping most of the nation's forces in Europe, fearing that the Korean invasion was a diversion to be followed by a Soviet invasion of western Europe. But General Douglas MacArthur, in a brilliant amphibious landing at Inchon behind North Korean lines, destroyed a much larger enemy army, captured the North Korean capital, and moved northward toward the Chinese border. Then in December of 1950, disaster struck American forces as a million-man Chinese army entered the conflict. Chinese troops surprised American forces, inflicting heavy casualties, trapping entire units, and forcing U.S. troops to beat a hasty retreat. General MacArthur urged retaliation against China, but Truman sought to keep the war "limited." When MacArthur publicly protested against political limits to military operations, Truman dismissed the popular general. The Korean War became a bloody stalemate.

Dwight Eisenhower was elected president in 1952 after he had promised to "go to Korea" to end the increasingly unpopular war. He also threatened to use nuclear weapons in the conflict, but eventually agreed to a settlement along the original border between North and South Korea. Communist expansion in Korea was "contained" but at a high price: the United States lost over 38,000 men in the war.

## CUBAN MISSILE CRISIS

The United States initially welcomed Fidel Castro's overthrow of the repressive Batista regime in Cuba in 1959, but when Castro allied his government with Moscow and invited Soviet military intervention into the western hemisphere, Washington sought his ouster. Under President Eisenhower, the CIA had planned a large "covert" operation—an *invasion of Cuba* by a brigade of Cuban exiles. Newly installed president John F. Kennedy approved the Bay of Pigs operation in early 1961, but when Castro's air force destroyed the makeshift invasion fleet offshore, Kennedy refused to provide U.S. Air Force support. The surviving Cubans were forced to surrender.

**thwarted Bay of Pigs Invasion of Cuba**
1961

The young president was tested again in 1961, when the Russians erected the *Berlin Wall,* physically dividing that city. Despite heated rhetoric, Kennedy did nothing. Eventually the Wall would become a symbol of Soviet repression.

**Berlin Wall built**
1961

The most serious threat of nuclear holocaust during the entire Cold War, however, was the Cuban missile crisis. In 1962, Soviet Premier Nikita Khrushchev sought to secretly install medium-range nuclear missiles in Cuba in an effort to give the USSR immediate nuclear capability against U.S. cities. In October 1962, intelligence photos showing Soviet missiles at Cuban bases touched off the thirteen-day *Cuban missile crisis.* President Kennedy publicly announced a naval blockade of Cuba, threatening to halt Soviet vessels at sea by force if necessary. The prospect of war appeared imminent; U.S. nuclear forces went on alert. Secretly, Kennedy proposed to withdraw U.S. nuclear missiles from Turkey in exchange for Soviet withdrawal of nuclear missiles from Cuba. Khrushchev's agreement to the deal appeared to the world as a backing down; Secretary of State Dean Rusk would boast: "We were eyeball to eyeball, and they blinked." Kennedy would be hailed for his statesmanship in the crisis; Khrushchev soon lost his job.

**Cuban missile crisis**
1962

## THE VIETNAM WAR

United States's involvement in Vietnam also grew out of the policy of "containment." President Eisenhower had declined to intervene in the former French colony in 1956 when communist forces led by Ho Chi Minh defeated French forces at the battle of Dien Bien Phou. The resulting Treaty of Paris divided that country into North Vietnam, with a communist government, and South Vietnam, with a U.S.-backed government. When South Vietnamese communist (Vietcong) guerrilla forces threatened the South Vietnamese government in the early 1960s, President Kennedy sent a large force of advisers and counterinsurgency forces to assist in every aspect of training and support for the Army of the Republic of Vietnam (ARVN). By 1964 units of the North Vietnamese Army (NVA) had begun to supplement the Vietcong guerrilla forces in the South. President Lyndon B. Johnson ordered U.S. combat troops into South Vietnam in February 1965 and authorized a gradual increase in air strikes against North Vietnam. Eventually over 500,000 American troops were committed to Vietnam; over 2.8 million served there before the *Paris Peace Agreement* was signed in 1973; 47,366 were killed in action. A short history of the Vietnam War is presented in Chapter 8, "Vietnam: A Political History."

**Paris Peace Agreement**
ending U.S. participation in Vietnam War, 1973

## THE VIETNAM SYNDROME OF THE 1970s

A new isolationism permeated American foreign policy following defeat in Vietnam. The slogan "No more Vietnams" was used to oppose any U.S. military intervention, whether or not U.S. vital interests were at stake. Disillusionment replaced idealism. American leaders had exaggerated the importance of Vietnam; now Americans were unwilling to believe their leaders when they warned of other dangers. The USSR rapidly expanded its political and military presence in Asia, Africa, the Middle East, Central America, and the Caribbean in the late 1970s. The United States did little to respond to this wave of Soviet expansionism until the *Soviet invasion of Afghanistan* in 1979, when President Carter authorized the largest covert action in CIA history—the military support of the Afghan guerrilla forces fighting Soviet occupation. The Soviets suffered a heavy drain of human and economic resources in their nine-year war in Afghanistan, which some dubbed "Russia's Vietnam."

**Afghanistan**
"Russia's Vietnam"

## REBUILDING AMERICA'S DEFENSES IN THE 1980s

A decision to rebuild America's military forces and reassert international leadership on behalf of democratic values gained widespread endorsement. In 1979 President Jimmy Carter presented Congress with the first request for an increase in defense spending in over a decade. The NATO nations jointly pledged to increase their defense efforts. British Prime Minister Margaret Thatcher, French President François Mitterand, and German Chancellor Helmut Kohl all held fast against a "nuclear freeze" movement that would have locked in Soviet superiority in European-based nuclear weapons. When the Reagan administration arrived in Washington in 1981, the defense buildup had already begun.

**U.S. defense buildup**
1979–1985

The Reagan defense buildup extended through 1985—with increases in defense spending, improvements in strategic nuclear weapons, and, perhaps more importantly, the rebuilding and reequipping of U.S. conventional forces. President Reagan also announced a new *strategic defense initiative (SDI),* a research program to develop a defense against a ballistic missile attack, promptly labeled "Star Wars" by the media.

**"Star Wars"**
the strategic defense initiative (SDI) to develop a defense against ballistic missile attack

The American and NATO defense buildup of the 1980s, together with the promise of a new, expensive, and technologically sophisticated race for ballistic missile defense, forecast heavy additional strains on the weak economy of the Soviet Union. Thus in 1985, when new Soviet President Mikhail Gorbachev came to power, the stage was set for an end to the Cold War.

## Gorbachev and Reform

Gorbachev believed that economic progress in the Soviet Union required a reduction in that nation's heavy military expenditures and improved relations with the United States. He announced reductions in the size of the Soviet military and reached agreements with the United States on the reduction of nuclear forces. More importantly, in 1988 he announced that the Soviet Union would no longer use its military forces to keep communist governments in power in eastern European nations. This stunning announcement (for which Gorbachev received the Nobel Peace Prize in 1990) encouraged opposition democratic forces in Poland (the Solidarity movement), Czechoslovakia, Hungary, Bulgaria, Romania, and East Germany to overthrow their communist governments in 1989. Gorbachev refused to intervene to halt the destruction of the Berlin Wall that same year, despite the pleas by the East German hard-line communist leader Eric Honnecker.

But opposition to Gorbachev's reforms by hard-line communists within the Soviet Union forced him into many compromises that led to a rapid deterioration of the Soviet economy and the emergence of disorders and disturbances in various republics seeking independence. Democratic forces, led by Boris Yeltsin, the first elected president of the Russian Republic, were strongly critical of Gorbachev's reluctance to speed reforms. But when hard-liners in the Communist party, the military, and the KGB attempted the forcible removal of Gorbachev in August 1991, democratic forces rallied to his support. Led by Yeltsin, thousands of demonstrators took to the streets, Soviet military forces stood aside, and the coup crumbled. Gorbachev was temporarily restored as president, but Yeltsin emerged as the most influential leader in the nation. The failed coup hastened the demise of the Communist party.

## The Disintegration of the Soviet Union

Strong independence movements in the republics of the USSR emerged as the authority of the centralized Communist party in Moscow waned. Lithuania, Estonia, and Latvia—nations that had been forcibly incorporated into the Soviet Union in 1939—led the way to independence in 1991. Soon all of the fifteen republics of the USSR declared their independence, and the Union of Soviet Socialist Republics officially ceased to exist after December 31, 1991. The red flag with its hammer and sickle was replaced with the flag of the Russian Republic.

# The Control of Nuclear Arms

Nuclear weaponry made the Cold War infinitely more dangerous than any national confrontation in human history. The nuclear arsenals of the United States and the former USSR threatened a human holocaust. Yet, paradoxically, the very destructiveness of nuclear weapons caused leaders on both sides to exercise extreme caution in their relations with each other. Scores of wars, large and small, were fought by different nations during the Cold War years, yet American and Soviet troops never engaged in direct combat against each other.

In 1957 the USSR launched *Sputnik,* the first artificial satellite to orbit the earth. Americans were shocked to know that the Soviets led in the space race. By the early 1960s a new and very dangerous balance of nuclear terror had emerged. Both the United States and the Soviet Union possessed large arsenals of nuclear weapons and intercontinental ballistic missiles (ICBMs), capable of carrying these weapons through space to targets in each other's homeland.

## SALT I

**SALT I: 1972**
the ABM treaty
agreement
limiting numbers
of offensive
missiles

Following the election of Richard Nixon as president in 1968, the United States, largely guided by former Harvard professor Henry Kissinger (national security adviser to the president and later secretary of state), began negotiations with the Soviet Union over nuclear arms. In 1972 the United States and the USSR concluded two and one-half years of Strategic Arms Limitation Talks (SALT) about limiting the nuclear arms race. The agreement, *SALT I,* consists of a treaty limiting antiballistic missiles (ABMs) and an agreement placing a numerical ceiling on offensive missiles. Under the offensive-arms agreement, each side was frozen at the total number of offensive missiles completed or under construction. Both sides could construct new missiles if they dismantled an equal number of older missiles. Each nation agreed not to interfere in the satellite intelligence-gathering activities of the other nation. Both nations pledged to continue efforts at further arms control—the SALT II talks.

## SALT II

**SALT II: 1979**

The United States and the Soviet Union signed the lengthy and complicated *SALT II* treaty in 1979. It set an overall limit on strategic nuclear launchers—ICBMs, SLBMs, bombers, and long-range cruise missiles—for each side. It also limited the number of missiles that could carry multiple nuclear warheads (MIRVs) and banned new types of ICBMs, with the exception of one new type of ICBM for each side. But the Soviets were allowed to keep 314 very heavy SS-18 missiles for which the United States had no equivalent. When the Soviet Union invaded Afghanistan, President Carter withdrew the SALT II treaty from Senate consideration. However, President Carter, and later President Reagan, announced that the United States would abide by the provisions of the unratified SALT II treaty as long as the Soviet Union did so.

## START TALKS

In negotiations with the Soviets, the Reagan administration pushed for *reductions* in missiles and warheads, not merely for limitations on future numbers and types of weapons as in previous SALT talks. To symbolize this new direction, President Reagan renamed the negotiations the *Strategic Arms Reductions Talks,* or *START.* The president emphasized that any new treaty must result in reductions of strategic arms to levels equal for both sides. The Soviets objected strongly to President Reagan's research efforts in the field of ballistic missile defense (SDI). In 1983 the Soviets walked out of the START talks and out of talks seeking to limit European nuclear weapons. But by 1985, after President Reagan's reelection, the Soviets returned to the bargaining table at Geneva, Switzerland.

**START talks**
renamed arms control talks to emphasize reductions

## INF TREATY

The Intermediate-Range Nuclear Forces (INF) Treaty in 1987 was the first agreement between the superpowers that actually resulted in the destruction of nuclear weapons. It eliminated an entire class of nuclear weapons—missiles with an intermediate range, between 300 and 3,800 miles. It was also the first treaty that resulted in equal levels (zero) of arms for the United States and the USSR. To reach an equal level, the Soviets were required to destroy more missiles and warheads than the United States. Finally, INF was the first treaty to provide for on-site inspection for verification. The proportion of each side's nuclear weapons covered by the INF Treaty was small, but this treaty set the pattern for future arms control agreements in its provisions for *reductions, equality,* and *verification.*

**INF Treaty**
eliminated intermediate-range ballistic missiles

## START I AND II

The long-awaited agreement on long-range strategic nuclear weapons was finally signed in Moscow in 1991 by Presidents George Bush and Mikhail Gorbachev. The START I Treaty included a 30-percent reduction in the total number of deployed strategic nuclear delivery systems (ICBMs, SLBMs, and manned bombers); and a reduction of nearly 50 percent in the total number of strategic nuclear warheads to no more than six thousand.

The ink had not yet dried on the new treaty when Russia's first democratically elected president, Boris Yeltsin, agreed to even deeper cuts in

**U.S. principles in arms control**
reductions

equality

verification

**START Treaties**
reduction to three thousand warheads for each side

elimination of all land-based missiles with nuclear warheads

on-site verification

nuclear weapons and, more importantly, to the eventual elimination of all land-based missiles with multiple (MIRVed) warheads. This historic agreement between Presidents Bush and Yeltsin in 1992, when fully implemented in 2003, will virtually eliminate the threat of a massive nuclear attack—a threat that had cast a menacing shadow over the world for decades. The START II Treaty includes a reduction to three thousand nuclear warheads for each side, together with the elimination of all "hard target kill" land-based missiles with multiple warheads, including Russia's huge SS-18 and the United States's MX, and a provision for on-site verification of these reductions by teams of observers from both nations (see Figure 14-1).

## REGIONAL BALANCES OF POWER

**end of Cold War focuses new attention on regional conflicts**

The end of the Cold War does not ensure world peace. Iraq's invasion of Kuwait in 1990 and its threatened military takeover of Saudi Arabia and the Gulf states reminded the world that there are many other international conflicts and threats to peace. (See the Case Study, "American Military Power: 'Desert Storm.'") Regional struggles for power have their own roots. The easing of Cold War tensions focuses new attention on regional conflicts in Asia, Latin America, Africa, and especially the Middle East.

Regional powers can no longer drag the United States or Russia into their disputes by playing one power against the other. The western democracies,

### FIGURE 14-1

#### STRATEGIC NUCLEAR ARMS UNDER START TREATIES

led by the United States, have been victorious in the Cold War, and now it is time to build a "new world order" of stability and peace. Yet questions remain about when, where, and how the United States should use its power to oppose aggression and maintain peace. The United States does not wish to become the world's policeman; yet today only the United States has the capability to project military force worldwide.

**"new world order"**
ending of Cold War provides opportunity for stable world peace

## REGIONAL THREATS

Today the principal threats to U.S. national security arise from regional powers. For nearly a half century, U.S. strategic defenses, force levels, and defense budgets were geared to the worldwide threat posed by the Soviet Union. Now U.S. military power is being redirected toward potential regional aggressors.

- *Iraq*   Saddam Hussein's army was reduced to about one-third of its former size in the Gulf War. The UN-sponsored economic blockade of Iraq has hampered that nation's efforts to rebuild these conventional forces. However, Iraq continues to harbor Scud missiles and continues in its efforts to acquire weapons of mass destruction—nuclear, chemical, and biological.

- *Iran*   Iran has been shopping for both conventional weapons and nuclear components in world arms markets. China and the former Soviet Union have supplied it with surface-to-surface missiles. Iran has also acquired a submarine force for operations in the Persian Gulf and a sizable air force. Iran supports terrorist groups throughout the Middle East and provides a beacon for violent Islamic fundamentalism. The Israelis consider Iran to be the principal threat to peace and stability in the Mideast.

- *Syria*   Syria's military forces are impressive. But with the collapse of the USSR, its key supplier, Syria now must pay for weapons in hard currency—an object in short supply in Syria. Syria's troops occupy most of Lebanon.

- *Libya*   Muammar Khadafy's military forces are not a major threat, yet Libya remains a major base for worldwide terrorist activity.

- *North Korea*   North Korea remains the most authoritarian and militarist regime in the world. It devotes a very large proportion of its economy and population to its military. It supports a one million-man army with four thousand tanks, a large air force, and a large submarine force. North Korea's nuclear weapons program is very advanced. The death of its "Great Leader," Kim Il-Sung, has brought his son, "Dear Leader" Kim Jong Il, to power. Since the Korean War (1950–53), the United States has maintained military forces in South Korea to deter invasion by North Korea. South Korea's army remains only about half as large as that of North Korea; in the event of war, the United States would need to provide immediate air combat support.

## CASE STUDY
American Military Power: "Desert Storm"

The U.S. military leadership had learned its lessons from Vietnam: define clear military objectives, use overwhelming and decisive military force, move swiftly and avoid protracted stalemate, minimize casualties, and be sensitive to the image of the war projected back home.

Saddam Hussein's invasion of Kuwait on August 2, 1990, was apparently designed to restore his military prestige following eight years of indecisive war against Iran, to secure additional oil revenues to finance the continued buildup of Iraqi military power, and to intimidate and perhaps invade Saudi Arabia and the Gulf states and thereby secure control over a major share of the world's oil reserves.

Early on, President George Bush described the U.S. military deployment as "defensive," but he soon became convinced that neither diplomacy nor an economic blockade would dislodge Saddam from Kuwait. The president ordered the military to prepare an "offensive" option.

The top U.S. military commanders—including the chairman of the Joint Chiefs of Staff, General Colin Powell; and the commander in the field, General Norman Schwarzkopf—had been field officers in Vietnam, and they were resolved not to repeat the mistakes of that war. They were reluctant to go into battle without the full support of the American people. If ordered to fight, they wanted to employ overwhelming and decisive military force; they wanted to avoid gradual escalation, protracted conflict, target limitations, and political inference in the conduct of the war. They presented the president with an "offensive" plan that called for a very large military buildup: elements of six Army divisions and two Marine divisions, with 1,900 tanks, 930 artillery pieces, and 500 attack helicopters; and over 1,000 combat aircraft. Coalition forces also included British and French heavy armored units, and Egyptian, Syrian, Saudi, and other Arab forces.

The president announced this buildup of forces on November 8 but immediately faced a barrage of criticism at home for abandoning his earlier defensive posture. Opponents urged the president to continue economic sanctions and avoid the heavy casualties that a land war was expected to produce. But the president was convinced that sanctions would not work, that Saddam would hold out for years, and that Saddam would become increasingly powerful on the world stage. He argued that Saddam would soon acquire nuclear weapons, that if unchecked he would soon dominate the Arab world and Mideast oil reserves. Secretary of State James Baker convinced the UN Security Council members, including the Soviet Union (with China abstaining), to support a resolution authorizing states to "use all necessary means" against Iraq unless it withdrew from Kuwait by January 15. Following an emotional debate in Congress, President Bush won a similar resolution by close margins in the House and Senate.

From Baghdad, CNN reporters Bernard Shaw and Peter Arnett were startled the night of January 16 when *Operation Desert Storm* began with an air attack on key installations in the city. Iraqi forces were also surprised, despite the prompt timing of the attack; Saddam had assured them that the United States lacked the resolve to fight, and that even if war broke out, U.S. public opinion would force a settlement as casualties rose. The air war accomplished three objectives: first, winning air supremacy by destroying radars, air defense control centers, and SAM launchers and airfields, as well as any Iraqi fighters that managed to get into the air; second, destroying strategic targets, including nuclear facilities, chemical warfare plants, command centers, and military communications; third, degrading Iraqi military forces by cutting off supplies, destroying tanks and artillery, and demoralizing troops with 'round-the-clock bombardment. Smart weapons performed superbly, and American TV audiences saw videotapes of laser-guided smart bombs entering the doors and air shafts of enemy bunkers.

General Schwarzkopf's plan for the ground war emphasized deception and maneuver. He wanted to make the Iraqis believe that the main attack would come directly against Kuwait's southern border and would be supported by a Marine landing on the coast. While Iraqi forces prepared for attacks from the south and the east coast, General Schwarzkopf sent heavily armed columns in a "Hail Mary" play—a wide sweep to the west, outflanking and cutting off Iraqi forces in the battle area. The Iraqi forces, blinded by air attacks and obliged to stay in their bunkers, would not be able to know about or respond to the flanking attack. On the night of February 24, the ground attack began with Marines easily breaching berms, ditches, and mine fields and racing directly to the

Kuwait city airport; helicopter air assaults lunged deep into Iraq; armored columns raced northward across the desert to outflank Iraqi forces and then attack them from the west; and a surge in air attacks kept Iraqi forces holed up in their bunkers. Iraqi troops surrendered in droves, highways from Kuwait city were turned into massive junkyards of Iraqi vehicles, and Iraqi forces that tried to fight were quickly destroyed. After one hundred hours of ground fighting, President George Bush declared a cease-fire.

The United States had achieved a decisive military victory quickly and with precious few casualties. Although the war left many political issues unresolved, it was the most decisive military outcome the United States had achieved since the end of World War II. President Bush chose to declare victory and celebrate the return of American troops.

The Gulf War taught the nation a number of lessons about the effective use of military power:

- The rapid employment of overwhelming force is both politically and militarily superior to gradual escalation and employment of minimum force. The use of overwhelming force reduces total casualties and achieves

an earlier and more decisive victory. It reduces the opportunity for diplomatic interventions that may produce compromised, indecisive resolutions.

- The nation's political leadership is vastly more effective when it concentrates on developing and maintaining foreign and domestic political support for the war while leaving the planning and execution of military operations to the military leadership.

- A rapid conclusion of hostilities ensures that public support will not erode over time and that protracted combat and a steady stream of casualties will not fuel antiwar sentiments.

- Military forces can capture territory and destroy enemy forces but they cannot guarantee peace.

- Only total military occupation of a country can ensure the removal of a hostile regime. Saddam continues to rule Iraq and to build chemical and biological weapons of mass destruction. Saddam Hussein remains a threat to stability in the region.

Perhaps the most important lesson is that the end of the Cold War does *not* mean that the United States no longer requires military power.

## CONTROVERSIES IN SOCIAL SCIENCE
When Should the United States Use Military Force?

All modern presidents have acknowledged that the most agonizing decisions they have made were to send U.S. military forces into combat. These decisions cost lives. The American people are willing to send their sons and daughters into danger—and even to see some of them wounded or killed—but *only* if a president convinces them that the outcome "is worth dying for." A president must be able to explain why they lost their lives and to justify their sacrifice.

### Only to Protect Vital Interests?

The U.S. military learned many bitter lessons in its long, bloody experience in Vietnam. Among those lessons:

- The United States should commit its military forces only in support of vital national interests.
- If military forces are committed, they must have clearly defined military objectives—the destruction of enemy forces and/or the capture of enemy-held territory.
- Any commitment of U.S. forces must be of sufficient strength to ensure overwhelming and decisive victory with the fewest possible casualties.
- Before committing U.S. military forces, there must be some reasonable assurances that the effort has the support of the American people and their representatives in Congress.
- The commitment of U.S. military forces should be a last resort, after political, economic, and diplomatic efforts have proven ineffective.

These guidelines for the use of military force are widely supported within the U.S. military itself. Contrary to Hollywood stereotypes, military leaders are extremely reluctant to go to war when no vital interest of the United States is at stake, where there are no clear-cut military objectives, without the support of Congress or the American people, or without sufficient force to achieve speedy and decisive victory with minimum casualties. They are wary of seeing their troops placed in danger merely to advance diplomatic goals, or to engage in "peacekeeping," or to "stabilize governments," or to "show the flag." They are reluctant to undertake humanitarian missions while being shot at. They do not like to risk their soldiers' lives under "rules of engagement" that limit their ability to defend themselves.

### To Support Important Political Objectives?

In contrast to military leaders, political leaders and diplomats often reflect the view that "war is a continuation of politics by other means"—a view commonly attributed to nineteenth-century German theorist of war Karl von Clausewitz. Military force may be used to protect interests that are important but not necessarily vital. Otherwise, the United States would be rendered largely impotent in world affairs. A diplomat's ability to achieve a satisfactory result often depends on the expressed or implied threat of military force. The distinguished international political theorist Hans Morgenthau wrote: "Since military strength is the obvious measure of a nation's power, its demonstration serves to impress others with that nation's power."

Currently American forces must be prepared to carry out

a variety of missions in addition to the conduct of conventional war:

- Demonstrating U.S. resolve in crisis situations.
- Demonstrating U.S. support for democratic governments.
- Protecting U.S. citizens living abroad.
- Striking at terrorist targets to deter or retaliate.
- Peacemaking among warring factions or nations.

- Peacekeeping where hostile factions or nations have accepted a peace agreement.
- Providing humanitarian aid often under warlike conditions.

In pursuit of such objectives, recent U.S. presidents have sent troops to Lebanon in 1982 to stabilize the government (Reagan), to Grenada in 1983 to rescue American medical students and restore democratic government (Reagan), to Panama in 1989 to oust drug-trafficking General Manuel Antonio Noriega from power and to protect U.S. citizens (Bush), to Somalia in 1992–93 to provide emergency humanitarian aid (Bush and Clinton), to Haiti in 1994 to restore constitutional government (Clinton), and to Bosnia in 1995–96 for peacekeeping among warring ethnic factions (see table).

## MAJOR DEPLOYMENT OF U.S. MILITARY FORCES SINCE WORLD WAR II

| Year | Area | President |
|---|---|---|
| 1950–53 | Korea | Truman |
| 1958 | Lebanon | Eisenhower |
| 1961–64 | Vietnam | Kennedy |
| 1962 | Cuban waters | Kennedy |
| 1965–73 | Vietnam | Johnson, Nixon |
| 1965 | Dominican Republic | Johnson |
| 1970 | Laos | Nixon |
| 1970 | Cambodia | Nixon |
| 1975 | Cambodia | Ford |
| 1980 | Iran | Carter |
| 1982–83 | Lebanon | Reagan |
| 1983 | Grenada | Reagan |
| 1989 | Panama | Bush |
| 1990–91 | Persian Gulf | Bush |
| 1992–93 | Somalia | Bush, Clinton |
| 1994–95 | Haiti | Clinton |
| 1995–96 | Bosnia | Clinton |

■ *China*   The People's Republic of China now possesses the world's largest armed forces—over three million soldiers, nearly ten thousand tanks, and over four thousand combat aircraft. China has intercontinental ballistic missiles with multiheaded nuclear warheads capable of reaching the United States. China has always asserted that Taiwan is a province of China (as has the government of the Republic of China in Taiwan); Beijing continues to declare unification a goal. It has stated a preference for peaceful reunification, but the threat of force has always been present. The Beijing government's future policies in Hong Kong, the former British colony incorporated into the People's Republic of China in 1997, may signal China's future approach to Taiwan. Beijing continues to voice support for market reforms of its economy, but it acted with brutal force to suppress the democracy movement in Tiananmen Square in 1989.

## TERRORISM

The threat of terrorism creates two military requirements. The first is the ability to punish nations that sponsor terrorism and to dissuade other nations from continuing their support of terrorism. In 1986, the United States struck at Libya in a limited air attack in response to various Libyan-supported acts of terrorism around the world. In 1993 the United States struck Iraq's intelligence center in Baghdad in response to a foiled plot to assassinate former President George Bush. These types of operation are carried out by conventional military forces. A second requirement is the ability to take direct action against terrorists to capture or kill them or to free their hostages. These operations are carried out by highly trained, specially equipped special operations forces.

## THE SPREAD OF MASS TERROR WEAPONS

The threat of mass terror weapons—nuclear, chemical, or biological weapons, especially those carried by medium- or long-range missiles—is likely to increase dramatically in the next century. Iraq, Iran, Libya, and North Korea, for example, are all likely to acquire mass terror weapons and long-range delivery systems, in the absence of any action by the United States to prevent them from doing so.

## UNANTICIPATED THREATS

The United States anticipated very few of the dozens of crises that required the use of military force over the past decade. Few would have forecast that U.S. troops would be engaged in combat in Grenada in 1983, or Panama in

1990, or even the Persian Gulf in 1991. General Colin Powell has tried to convince the Congress that:

> *The real threat is the unknown, the uncertain. In a very real sense, the primary threat to our security is instability and being unprepared to handle a crisis or war that no one expected or predicted. But it is difficult to convince taxpayers or their elected representatives to prepare for the unknown.*[4]

## Military Force Levels

Overall military force levels in the United States are threat-driven, that is, determined by the size and nature of the perceived threats to national security. The end of the Cold War has brought about major reductions in U.S. military forces (for example, from 2.1 million active duty personnel in 1990 to 1.4 million today), as well as a restructuring of these forces to confront regional threats. Current U.S. defense policy envisions the need to respond simultaneously to two "Iraqi equivalent" threats—the military forces required by the United States to speedily and decisively defeat two opponents equal to Iraq in the Gulf War. (For example, if U.S. forces were involved again in the Persian Gulf region against Iraq or Iran, we would still want to be able to respond in Korea if North Korea decided to take advantage of our commitment in the Gulf and launch an invasion of South Korea.) But it is not clear whether today's forces could confront two such threats simultaneously. The United States benefited from a six-month buildup of forces in the Persian Gulf before "Operation Desert Storm," but it is unlikely that a new crisis would allow such a long lead time (see the Case Study, "American Military Power: 'Desert Storm' "). And the use of U.S. forces for humanitarian and peacekeeping purposes around the world places additional burdens on their war-fighting capabilities.

## Notes

1. Hans Morgenthau, *Politics Among Nations* (New York: Knopf, 1960), p. 27.
2. Terms used in Article X of the Covenant of the League of Nations.
3. George F. Kennan, writing under the pseudonym "X," "Sources of Soviet Conduct," *Foreign Affairs* (July 1947): 25.
4. Testimony of General Colin Powell, Committee on the Budget, U.S. Senate, February 3, 1992.

## About This Chapter

"International politics, like all politics, is a struggle for power." Fighting among peoples and societies has been a common occurrence in the human experience throughout history. From time to time, nations have sought to provide greater order and stability to the international struggle for power. The advent of nuclear weapons made it imperative that nations seek a more stable world order, through direct negotiations as well as collective security arrangements. The collapse of communism in eastern

Europe and the emergence of democracy in Russia reduced the threat of a nuclear holocaust. But regional conflicts continue to threaten world security.

In this chapter we have explored some of the means, past and present, by which people have sought to avoid war. Now that you have read it, you should be able to

- discuss the meaning of *sovereignty* and describe the nature of international law
- discuss the concepts of a *balance of power, collective security,* and *regional security*
- describe the major events of the Cold War and the subsequent collapse of communism
- describe the major efforts to control nuclear weapons
- discuss major regional threats to security

evaluate the relative effectiveness of a balance-of-power system, collective security, and regional activity.

3. Discuss the SALT I ABM treaty. Why was the SALT II Treaty never ratified by the U.S. Senate? What kinds of weapons are eliminated by the INF Treaty?

4. Describe the superpower balance during the Cold War. List the major events of the Cold War.

5. Describe the principal threats to American security today.

6. Discuss the political and military "lessons" of the Gulf War.

7. Compare presidential leadership in the Gulf War with presidential leadership in the Vietnam War (see Chapter 8). How did U.S. military strategy differ in these wars?

# Discussion Questions

1. Define *sovereignty* and discuss the role it plays in international politics. Describe the nature of international law.

2. Describe various systems of international order, giving specific examples of each type of system. Compare and

# INDEX

**370**